HAT IN THE RING

HAT IN THE
RING

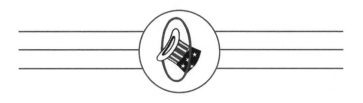

The Birth of American Air
Power in the Great War

Bert Frandsen

Smithsonian Books
Washington and London

Copy editor: Katherine Kimball

Designer: Brian Barth

Library of Congress Cataloging-in-Publication Data

Frandsen, Bert.

    Hat in the ring : the birth of American air power in the Great War / Bert

    Frandsen.

        p. cm.

    Includes bibliographical references and index.

    ISBN 1-58834-150-X (alk. paper)

    1. United States. Army Air Forces. Pursuit Group, 1st—History. 2. World

War, 1914–1918—Aerial operations, American. 3. World War, 1914–1918—

Regimental histories—United States. 4. World War, 1914–1918—Campaigns—

Western Front. I. Title.

D606.F73 2003

940.4'4973—dc21   2003041449

British Library Cataloguing-in-Publication Data available

Manufactured in the United States of America

10 09 08 07 06 05 04 03   5 4 3 2 1

∞ The paper used in this publication meets the minimum requirements of the
American National Standard for Information Sciences-Permanence of Paper
for Printed Library Materials ANSI Z39.48-1984.

To Dad and Gloria

Contents

Acknowledgments

This book is an adaptation of a dissertation completed while I was a doctoral student in the history of technology at Auburn University. Readers who are interested in greater detail, especially on the material covered in Chapters 1 through 3 and the procurement of the Nieuport 28 and SPAD 13, may want to consult the dissertation, which is available at the Ralph B. Draughon Library at Auburn University. I want to thank my colleagues at Auburn, especially W. David Lewis, the chair of my committee, for his inspirational leadership and guidance throughout this project. William Trimble and James Hansen, who also served on my committee, provided helpful suggestions. Thanks are also owed to Guy Beckwith, who acquainted me with the insider-outsider paradigm used in this study.

James J. Cooke, Robert P. White, and Dik Alan Daso reviewed the dissertation and provided helpful recommendations for a more concise presentation and livelier narration, which I have tried to achieve in this book. Walter Boyne reviewed the revised manuscript and also provided several helpful suggestions. I especially want to thank Mark Gatlin, of Smithsonian Books, who has been my guide and mentor throughout the project of revising the dissertation into a book. He knew just when to encourage, when to nudge, and when to hit me with a sledgehammer. I also want to thank Katherine Kimball for her attention to detail in editing the manuscript.

My study of the 1st Pursuit Group led me to the descendants of two of the unit's founders. Bert Atkinson Jr., now deceased, allowed me access to his father's papers and shared memories of his father. Philip J. Roosevelt II and his family were also most gracious hosts and shared the family lore while I consulted their grandfather's letters.

I also want to thank Dr. James J. Parks, now deceased, and his son Andy Parks for allowing me access to the documents in their excellent collection, the Lafayette Foundation, at Wings Over the Rockies Air and Space Museum in Denver, Colorado. Mitchell Yockelson, archivist at the National Archives at College Park Maryland, was especially helpful in finding pertinent records of the American Expeditionary Forces Air Service. Peter Jakab, curator at the National Air and Space Museum (NASM), served as my point of contact there during the early stages of the project and provided valuable assistance with my research on the Nieuport 28, as did Theodore Hamedy, an NASM volunteer research historian. Jeremy Kinney, propulsion curator at NASM, was especially helpful on the relation between motors and propellers. I also want to acknowledge Dan Hagedorn, who heads the NASM archives, and his staff for their assistance.

Dennis Case and Joseph Caver, archivists at the United States Air Force Historical Research Agency, Maxwell Air Force Base, Alabama, were especially helpful in providing me access to official records of the units of the 1st Pursuit Group as well as oral history transcripts from several of its members. I am most grateful for the help of Colonel John Moody, retired, of the United States Army Military History Institute for the assistance provided during my research at that facility. My colleagues at the United States Air Force Air Command and Staff continued to provide encouragement during the final phase of finishing the book.

Alan Towle, a member of the League of World War I Aviation Historians, provided helpful advice and assistance in locating unpublished primary sources that were particularly important to this study. I want to acknowledge the League of World War I Aviation Historians, in general, for their excellent work in documenting World War I aviation in their journals, *Over the Front and Cross and Cockade.*

I want to thank a supportive family, especially my brothers. Richard Frandsen helped me with reproduction of the manuscript. Charles Frandsen and Chad Smith, of Frandsen Architects, developed several drawings for this book. Finally, I could not have completed this project without the support and encouragement of my wife, Gloria.

Introduction

Everyone expected a fight. Lt. Joseph Eastman, a veteran pilot of the 94th Aero Squadron, admitted in his diary that the mission briefing before takeoff had scared him to death.[1] Eastman was probably not the only one struggling with his fear. To a pursuit pilot, attacking an observation balloon was the equivalent of an infantryman deliberately walking into an ambush. The enemy went to great lengths to defend their balloons, surrounding them with carefully sited antiaircraft guns and protecting them with fighters. Because of this, the preferred approach to balloon busting in the 1st Pursuit Group was a stealthy attack by one or two fighters maneuvering through cloudbanks in the twilight of dusk or dawn, when the enemy's senses were dulled and the camouflage paint patterns on the SPAD 13s made the planes difficult to see.[2]

This afternoon's massive attack had no such finesse. It was brute force with all the elegance of kicking down the front door—hey diddle diddle, straight up the middle. It began to unravel even before the raiders crossed no-man's-land. The Germans saw them coming.

The raiders flew with noses down to gather extra speed, gradually descending from thirty-two hundred to two thousand feet for their low-level attack. Antiaircraft shells burst around them as they crossed the lines. Lt. Reed

Chambers, a twenty-four-year-old Kansan, flew ahead of the rest. Uncle Sam's hat in the ring, painted on each side of his airplane's fuselage, identified Chambers as part of the 94th Squadron. Thirteen similarly marked SPADs, single-seat biplane fighters equipped with two machine guns synchronized to fire through the arc of the propeller, followed thirty seconds behind him. Chambers was the balloon buster. The protective formation behind covered his attack.

Two more units from the 1st Pursuit Group flew on either side of the 94th Squadron. The seven SPADs covering the right wing belonged to the 27th Aero Squadron. Lt. William Brotherton, the second balloon buster, led the eight planes on the left from the 147th Aero Squadron. Brotherton anxiously strained his eyes, searching for the raid's objective. The balloon was supposed to be floating tranquilly in the sky near the town of Doulcon, a French village on the left bank of the Meuse River. By now, Brotherton thought, he should have been able to see it.

A lone SPAD, also sporting the hat in the ring, trailed the raiders at an altitude several thousand feet above them. Lt. Eddie Rickenbacker, America's top-scoring ace, checked his watched. It was 3:40 P.M. on the tenth of October, 1918—six minutes before the group's planes were supposed to converge on Doulcon. The sky was clear, though hazy at low altitudes. Glancing down at the formation, Rickenbacker was reminded of a huge crawling beetle—Chambers and Brotherton were the stingers. Rickenbacker commanded the 94th Squadron, but this afternoon he had charge of the entire three-squadron mission to destroy the troublesome observation balloon.[3]

The observers in such balloons, equipped with powerful binoculars and connected by telephone to German artillery batteries, directed devastatingly accurate artillery fire against American doughboys attacking the Hindenberg line. In this fourth year of the Great War, Allied victory finally appeared within reach. An American field army had finally taken the offensive alongside their French and British allies. If American doughboys could penetrate the line of defensive fortifications in this sector, between the Meuse River and the Argonne Forest, the threat to the German lines of communication in northern France and Belgium would require the withdrawal of the enemy or place them at risk of being cut off. Neutralizing the enemy observation balloons was so important that the U.S. 1st Army chief of Air Service, Col.

William Billy Mitchell, ordered the entire 1st Pursuit Group to concentrate on destroying them. Some of the German air force's best fighter units opposed them.[4]

Just after crossing the lines, Rickenbacker noticed a large formation of eleven Fokkers, a mile or two to his left, coming out of the west toward the 147th Squadron. He could not warn his comrades below because fighters were not yet equipped with radios. Rickenbacker began to dive down to dip a signal but returned to altitude when he noticed another formation of eight Fokkers approaching from the opposite direction, from Metz. The first group of enemy airplanes resolved themselves into the red-nosed Fokkers of Baron Manfred von Richthofen's Flying Circus. The Red Baron himself had organized Germany's élite fighter unit in May 1917. Though Richthofen was dead, another high-scoring German ace had assumed command of the war's most famous fighter group. His name was Hermann Göring, and he would be Adolf Hitler's deputy in the next war.[5]

Unaware of the threat, the SPADs continued their low-level attack and closed on the Doulcon area without finding their target—the Germans had winched down the balloon and concealed it. Brotherton headed toward another balloon, whose nest he knew was at Dun, just across the Meuse River. Three SPADs from the 147th Squadron followed him.[6] "True to form," remembered Hamilton Coolidge, who led the protective formation of the 94th Squadron, "the Fokkers came piling down on us a few minutes later. A general 'dog-fight' ensued."[7]

The red-nosed Fokkers headed at the 147th Squadron's formation, now separated by almost a mile from the rest of the SPADs. After the enemy passed beneath him, Rickenbacker "dipped over sharply, and with accumulated speed bore down on the tail of the last man in the Fokker formation." "It was an easy shot and I could not have missed," he later wrote. His first burst set fire to the fuel tank. He was "equally gratified the next second to see the German pilot level off his blazing machine and with a sudden leap overboard" descend to earth under a parachute canopy.[8]

More than anything else, pilots feared being burned alive as their planes went down in flames. Rickenbacker did not wish such a terrible fate on anyone, even his enemy. The Germans had recently begun equipping their pilots with parachutes, but the air forces of the western allies had not yet adopted this safety device. Various excuses for the delay were offered, including a concern that the pilots might jump from a perfectly good airplane to avoid the danger of combat.[9]

After shooting down his nineteenth victim, Rickenbacker climbed to regain the superior position and observed yet another remarkable event. "I turned from this extraordinary spectacle in midair to witness another that in all my life at the front I have never seen equaled in horror and awfulness. The picture of it has haunted my dreams during the many nights since."[10]

A group of three fighters, led by Lt. Wilbert White, had been following Brotherton's attack on the balloon nest at Dun. They lost sight of Brotherton in the haze as he dived amid a hail of machine-gun bullets and antiaircraft fire. At that moment five of the Fokkers attacked. A Fokker with the markings of an ace pilot got on the tail of Lt. Charles Cox, a new pilot, who was unable to shake it. White, the 147th's top ace, saw Cox's predicament and executed a *renversement*—a sharp vertical turn achieved by pulling up the nose, rolling the plane over on its back, and finishing with a half loop. He then "raced to the rescue with throttle wide open and both guns spitting fire at the Fokker. Before he could fly into effective range both guns apparently jammed and ceased firing. The fight seemed all but lost."[11]

The German leader had his prey almost within his grasp. White realized that unless the Fokker were put out of the fight, Cox would be shot down. White never swerved. Lt. Jimmy Meissner, the commander of the 147th Squadron, wrote in his Medal of Honor recommendation for White, "He darted by Lieutenant Cox waving farewell as he passed and rammed the Fokker in mid-air."[12] In the "next instant off came a wing of each plane amid a cloud of splinters and shreds of fabric, and down they went spinning like tops, nose on into the ground, not fifty feet apart."[13] Because of White's sacrifice, Cox survived and escaped. Brotherton was last seen spiraling slowly to the earth, his plane bursting into flames a few yards from the ground.[14] Meissner was sickened at the sight of the collision, but he could not dwell on it; the four remaining Fokkers were coming after him.

Meissner opened his motor wide and retreated toward friendly lines with the Fokkers in hot pursuit, one right on his tail, pouring machine-gun fire at him. "It was poor shooting," he recalled. "As we got back to our lines Rickenbacker and some others saw the chase and dove on the Fokkers, getting three of them, so I was a pretty good decoy as I've been before. But two of our best and oldest men are gone."[15]

On this day, the 1st Pursuit Group won nine confirmed victories, six of them during this mission, while losing two men. Only hours earlier, Brotherton and White had shot down enemy airplanes in this day of intense air-to-air combat.[16] Although the raid failed, the 1st Pursuit Group's sustained attacks on German balloons succeeded in disrupting the enemy's artillery-fire control system and battlefield surveillance. The 1st Army Air Service report of the operation summarized, "No doubt owing to the number of assaults during the last few days by our pursuit patrols, enemy balloons were only in ascension for short periods during the day."[17]

What follows is more than the story of America's first cadre of fighter pilots. It records nothing less than the birth of American air power. The 1st Pursuit Group was America's inaugural multisquadron fighter unit. By the end of the war it was the largest and most successful of the three frontline pursuit groups in the American Expeditionary Forces (AEF). Consisting of a group headquarters, five pursuit squadrons, and a maintenance squadron, the 1st Pursuit Group numbered about sixteen hundred men and a hundred airplanes. It produced the Air Service's first aces. Most of the famous American fighter pilots of World War I, including Medal of Honor winners Eddie Rickenbacker and Frank Luke, belonged to this unit. It was the only pursuit group that fought in all of the AEF's campaigns during the war—including America's first air-land battle. It also fought, together with units of the British Royal Air Force and the French Air Service, the combined air campaign that helped defeat the Germans at the Second Battle of the Marne and changed the course of the war.

The 1st Pursuit Group blazed the path for American combat aviation. The leaders of America's first large fighter unit confronted a difficult task. Although the American brothers Wilbur and Orville Wright had invented the airplane, a complacent United States fell far behind the warring European nations in military aviation. When Congress declared war on 6 April 1917, the American air force consisted of only a handful of aviators in the Aviation Section of the Army Signal Corps, equipped with a meager number of unarmed and, by European standards, obsolete planes. An American combat aviation arm did not exist.

In contrast, the belligerents in Europe had achieved tremendous advances in military aviation, including the development of specialized aircraft for the missions of observation, bombardment, and pursuit. Each side quickly realized the importance of gaining command of the air because air power provided the means by which to observe the enemy and direct accurate artillery deep behind the lines. During World War I, commanders expected pursuit aviation to win air superiority through air-to-air combat. The modern reader can substitute "fighter" for "pursuit." The competition for air superiority spurred the warring nations to develop increasingly advanced aircraft. By the time the United States declared war, the Europeans had fielded a third generation of fighters. These airplanes flew at speeds in excess of 100 miles an hour and mounted two machine guns synchronized to fire through the arc of the propeller.[18]

Officially organized on 5 May 1918, the 1st Pursuit Group soon met the élite veteran fighter units of the German air force in the skies over France. Many of those who fought as members of the 1st Pursuit Group during the summer of 1918 became leaders of the AEF's new pursuit formations that took to the air for the subsequent American offensives at St. Mihiel and Meuse-Argonne. These veterans carried with them the tactics and techniques of aerial warfare they had learned in the 1st Pursuit. This fighter group thus performed an important progenitor role in American combat aviation. It provided the model that the rest of the AEF's pursuit aviation would emulate.

The 1st Pursuit Group's experience in the Great War is thus an epic tale about the birth of American air power. Its story helps explain how the United States mastered the new technology of aerial warfare. It is a story about combat leadership, the culture of the pursuit units, and their machines. Most of all, however, it is a story about the courageous young men who served as America's pathfinders in a new and unfamiliar dimension of war.

1

The Insiders

On 16 January 1918, a small convoy departed Paris and headed toward the front. Maj. Bert M. Atkinson, of the U.S. Army, rode in the first vehicle, a seven-passenger Hudson touring car. Three Fiat trucks loaded with supplies followed. His outfit included two officers, six sergeants, and an interpreter. Atkinson's orders directed him to proceed to the French aerodrome at Villeneuve-les-Vertus, in the heart of the Champagne region of France, and to establish the 1st Pursuit Organization and Training Center. His mission: to organize and train America's first pursuit squadrons.[1]

Atkinson was one of the fifty-six qualified aviators on duty with the Aviation Section of the U.S. Army Signal Corps when the United States entered the war. These men moved into key positions throughout the expanding aviation arm to direct the creation of what newspapers boldly proclaimed would be a great aerial armada capable of trouncing the Germans. This zeal for airpower was more than a mere reflection of American technological enthusiasm. It was fueled by a $640 million appropriation, the largest single appropriation by Congress in its history, to build a mighty air force. Unfortunately, the Army's small cadre of aviators was as unprepared as American industry for the task that lay ahead. Atkinson may have been the

Lt. Bert M. Atkinson, March 1916, at the Signal Corps Aviation School
Atkinson's facial expression suggests a sense of
  determination, his strongest asset.
Atkinson Papers, Auburn University Archives

best man available for the job of organizing and training America's first
fighter squadrons, but like the rest of the officers in the Aviation Section of
the Signal Corps, he knew practically nothing about aerial warfare.[2]

Bert Atkinson hailed from a politically powerful family in Newnan,
Georgia. His father had been governor of the Peach State in the 1890s. After
graduating from the University of Georgia in 1911, the younger Atkinson
joined the Army and became an infantry officer. His career turned toward aviation during a two-year tour in the Philippines, where he led a three-man top-

ographical survey team that mapped, among other places, the Bataan Peninsula.[3] While Atkinson was leading his men and mules through the jungle, Congress enacted legislation creating the Aviation Section of the Army Signal Corps and additional authorizations for the pilots. Perhaps the sight of the Army's pontoon-equipped Wright C-model Flyers taking off and landing in Manila Bay sparked his interest in flying, or maybe he was just fed up with the infantry.[4] Whatever his motivation, Atkinson applied for pilot training and left the Philippines in 1915 to attend the United States Army Signal Corps Aviation School at North Island, San Diego. Upon graduation, he joined the 1st Aero Squadron at Columbus, New Mexico.

The 1st Aero Squadron was commanded by Maj. Benjamin Foulois, the Army's most experienced aviator-he had flown with Orville Wright on the acceptance tests for the Army's first airplane. The unit's eight unarmed Curtiss JN-3 airplanes had been part of Brig. Gen. John J. Pershing's Mexican punitive expedition to capture Pancho Villa and restore order along the southwestern U.S. border. It was an odd expedition, with one foot in the past-the U.S. Cavalry chasing Mexican revolutionaries-and the other in the future-in the form of Foulois's airplanes and their healthy complement of motor vehicles.

The squadron's underpowered aircraft proved practically useless for their observation mission and wound up serving instead as a courier service for Pershing. Nevertheless, this experience formed the basis for the Army's meager knowledge about air power.[5] Even more important, though, were the informal bonds that developed among Foulois's aviators. These veterans of the Mexican campaign represented an informal network of such influence that they saw themselves as the "insiders" of America's nascent air force.

On 5 April 1917, Atkinson led a flight of four Curtiss JN-4 "Jennies" to a landing field "amid a boundless stretch of waste covered by prickly pear cactus and mesquite" outside San Antonio, Texas, at Kelly Field. His best friend, Carl Spatz (later changed to Spaatz), landed right behind him. Theirs were the first aircraft to arrive at Kelly Field, the primary mobilization base for American airpower. The next day the United States entered the Great War. During Atkinson's tour at Kelly Field, trainloads of men arrived almost daily and were counted off by noncommissioned officers and organized into standard-service aero squadrons. After commanding two squadrons at Kelly Field, Atkinson left in late September to lead seven squadrons in their movement to Europe.[6] Pilots had not yet been assigned to these units, but by January 1918 the American Expeditionary Forces (AEF) had graduated its first pursuit pilots, and they were anxiously awaiting assignment to a pursuit squadron. The first of these was to arrive at Atkinson's 1st Pursuit Organization and Training Center in France in a matter of weeks.

After five and a half hours on the road from Paris, Atkinson's convoy arrived at Vertus, a colorless, forlorn town, like many of the towns in the so-called Zone of Advance. The front lines lay about eighteen miles distant-close enough that one regularly heard the booming of the guns, and in clear weather one could see the line of observation balloons stretched across the rear of the battlefield.[7]

The aerodrome on the outskirts of Villeneuve-les-Vertus served as the headquarters for Escadre [Wing] 1, the world's first multigroup fighter wing. Escadre 1 was made up of three *groupes de combat,* each consisting of four squadrons of twelve to fifteen fighters. This massing of fighter aviation reflected French general Henri Pétain's plan to use combat aircraft in a role similar to that of heavy cavalry, now obsolete because of the machine gun, in the critical battles anticipated with the arrival of spring.

The preceding November the Bolshevik revolution had knocked Russia out of the war. As a result, German troop trains were steadily transferring troops from the eastern to the western front in a race against time. The Germans hoped to achieve numerical superiority and launch a war-winning offensive before the arrival of the Americans tipped the balance in favor of the Allies. Pétain's strategy called for large combat aviation units, made up of separate fighter and bomber wings, to serve as a strategic reserve that he would commit en masse to help win the decisive battles expected to begin in the coming weeks.

By establishing the 1st Pursuit Organization and Training Center alongside Escadre 1, the Americans hoped to learn how to conduct squadron- and group-level pursuit operations from France's best combat aviation units. Locating the unit here, however, put Atkinson and company at a distance of one hundred miles from Air Service headquarters at Chaumont and far from the sector where the bulk of the American Army was being assembled. Consequently, they found themselves on their own while embarking on a historic mission the like of which had never before been attempted by the United States Army.[8]

Atkinson was accompanied to Vertus by two officers, Capts. Philip J. Roosevelt and Gordon Rankin. Rankin, who had a son in the AEF's Marine

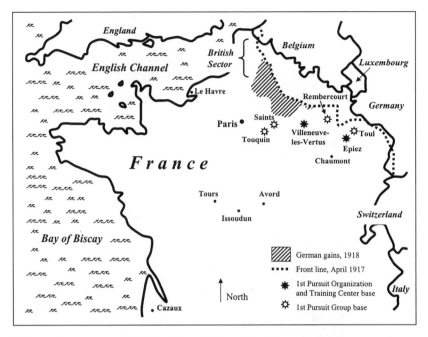

Western front, 1917–1918, with 1st Pursuit Group locations during the war and major training bases

Created by the author, based on data from "Situation général du front et des arrières des armées Allemandes le 18 Juillet 1918," Map 6 in État Major de l'Armée, Service Historique, *Les Armées françaises dans la Grande Guerre,* vol. 1, *Cartes* (Paris: Imprimerie nationale, 1938); "France 1918," Map 1 in *The United States Army in the World War, 1917–1919,* vol. 1, *Organization of the American Expeditionary Forces* (Washington, D.C.: Center of Military History, 1988), xiv.

Brigade, was the older of Atkinson's two assistants and was in charge of supply. One officer remembered him as "an old soldier who couldn't possibly sleep after five o'clock in the morning under any circumstances."[9] Atkinson's right-hand man was his adjutant, Philip J. Roosevelt. Standing six foot five, this twenty-five-year-old journalist appeared even taller because of his thin frame. Roosevelt was the son of a wealthy New York investment banker and quite close to his cousin, President Theodore Roosevelt. Upon graduation from Harvard in 1912, Philip devoted himself "with all the earnestness in the world" to the Progressive party and his cousin's third-party campaign for

Maj. Philip J. Roosevelt, 1919

*A man of giant stature and intellect, with a wry sense
of humor, Roosevelt was Atkinson's confidante
throughout the war.*

Courtesy of Family of Philip
J. Roosevelt

president.[10] After the sinking of the *Lusitania* in 1915 he similarly threw himself into Theodore's "preparedness movement" by founding and editing
American Defense, a mouthpiece of the movement, and helping to organize
the first Plattsburg camp, the famous "Business Men's Camp," where like-
minded businessmen took military training in hopes of qualifying for commissions in the event that America entered the war.

While at Plattsburg, a small group of these "businessmen in uniform,"
under the leadership of Raynal Bolling, another Harvard graduate, hatched the
plan of organizing a National Guard aviation unit. Shortly after the camp

ended, Philip joined them in organizing the 1st Aero Company of the New York National Guard in 1915. About a year later, he became the military editor of *Aviation and Aeronautic Engineering* (later known as *Aviation Week*). Roosevelt's poor eyesight disqualified him from a career as a military aviator, but through his editorial experience he had become about as well versed on the subject of aerial warfare as anyone in the United States, because a strict policy of neutrality had restricted military-to-military contacts with the Allies. This expertise, together with his military involvement in the preparedness movement, brought him in touch with the Army's aviation leadership.[11]

Just two days after Congress declared war, Philip Roosevelt received a cable from the chief signal officer that stated simply, "Your services are desired." The next morning, after an overnight train ride to Washington, he joined five other officers in beginning to map out the aviation mobilization program. He served as a member of the Organization and Training Section, which was concerned with the organization of aviation school squadrons and standard aero squadrons, under Foulois's Airplane Division of the Signal Corps's Aviation Section.[12] When Foulois sailed to France in October to take charge of the AEF's Air Service, he took Roosevelt with him.

Shortly after arriving in France, Roosevelt helped solve an urgent problem by helping to establish the Air Service Concentration Camp at St. Maxient. This barracks facility served as a temporary holding area for the oversupply of aviation cadets waiting to begin basic flight training. Most of them were honor graduates who had been sent directly to France as a reward for their superior performance at ground school in the United States. Unfortunately, because of a foul-up in coordination, more cadets had arrived than could be accommodated. Roosevelt considered the situation "one of the most pathetic sights" he had ever seen.[13] Morale plummeted because many of the honor cadets ended up waiting, some of them for months, while their classmates who had not done so well completed flight school in the United States and arrived as officers.

Roosevelt had played such a significant role that a local newspaper incorrectly named him as the camp commander, though he was actually the adjutant. The experience left him sour about the state of organization in the AEF. He had proved himself capable of starting up a camp, though, which is probably why he now found himself with Atkinson. His assessment of the southerner's future was none too positive. Roosevelt wrote his father, "As I had three [commanding officers] in five weeks at my last post, I don't put any faith in [Atkinson's] being at all permanent."[14]

Upon arriving at Vertus, Atkinson reviewed the purpose of the expedition with his two officers. Atkinson's organization and training center was to be one of several in the Zone of Advance used for the organizing, equipping, and training of specific types of units-observation, bombardment, pursuit, and balloon. At their 1st Pursuit Organization and Training Center, converging streams of personnel and equipment would be transformed into combat-ready pursuit squadrons. The first stream consisted of pilots from the Third Aviation Instruction Center at Issoudun, the Army's advanced flight-training school in France. Second were the mechanics, supply technicians, cooks, and other support personnel from the Kelly Field aero squadrons. Then came the equipment, from a variety of locations in the United States and Europe: French fighter aircraft, American and European motor vehicles, airplane hangars, machine guns, tools, kitchen units, and so forth. In addition, standard operating procedures would be established, aircraft issued and tested, aerial formations and tactics practiced, teamwork developed, and myriad other final preparations completed before the unit was ready for combat.[15]

Atkinson impressed Roosevelt and Rankin with the urgency of their mission. He explained that a false impression existed in the United States that the Air Service was already operating extensively on the front, and it was therefore imperative that they get started as quickly as possible.[16] According to the instructions of his superiors, the 1st Pursuit Organization and Training Center was to be part of the French 4th Army, and French pursuit units would assist with training. The large airfield at Villeneuve-les-Vertus was supposed to have ample hangars and barracks, enough to accommodate the three squadrons that were almost ready to be sent forward from the American pursuit pilot training center at Issoudun. French SPAD airplanes were to be ready in a week or ten days.[17] The plan sounded perfect. The Americans would be equipped with the latest French fighters and learn how to fight the Germans under the tutelage of France's most experienced combat aviation units. In the event, it did not happen this way.

"As was usual in the A.E.F.," groused Roosevelt, "everything we were told by 'higher authority' was wrong. To be sure, the airdrome . . . was peach. But it was entirely occupied to overflowing by Escadre 1. . . . There were no hangars and no barracks ready for us." The French did not have the "slightest idea we were going to arrive or what to do with us." The nearest rations were at Mailly, a heavy-artillery base and supply depot, some thirty-seven miles away. "Moreover, no squadrons were ready at Issoudun and no planes were ready at Paris. There wasn't a chance of getting any SPAD planes out of the French for 6 months, but what the hell did Paris care. . . . The whole performance was typical of the AEF in January 1918."[18]

Roosevelt did not hold the generals responsible. "The whole blame, or nearly the whole blame," he wrote his mother, "lies in the fact that nobody did anything from 1914 to April 1917."[19] His grumpiness may have been exacerbated by the state of his quarters: A decade later Rankin remarked that he "could still see Roosevelt trying to fit into that enclosed bed with frost a half inch thick on the wall" on their first night in Vertus.[20]

For the most part the weather was "loathsome fog and intense cold." On Roosevelt's daily visits to the airfield he passed champagne vineyards "with every twig looking as though it were made of silver lace, and one much bedraggled chicken-wire fence, outlined in white frost so that it looked like a white cotton tennis net."[21]

Atkinson and company set about the task of building the 1st Pursuit Organization and Training Center. By orchestrating the necessary leverage from AEF headquarters, and through some artful champagne-lubricated negotiation with French officials at Villeneuve, they began to see results. Near the end of January construction material began to arrive at the Vertus train station. Atkinson's trucks delivered the supplies to French and Italian laborers, who built hangars, buildings, and roads. As Roosevelt summed up, "From January 16 to February 15 Atkinson, Rankin, and I worked like hell." By 16 February their efforts had produced barracks for one squadron and hangars for thirty-six planes.[22]

On the afternoon of 9 February, Commandant [Maj.] Paul Armengaud, aviation chief of the French Military Mission to the AEF, arrived with troubling news: plans called for supplying them with thirty-six Nieuport 27 aircraft, an airplane that was considered out of date but was still in use by some French units. Besides causing them to worry that they would be receiving second-class fighters, Armengaud's visit illustrated the extent to which French advisers were influencing activities in the Air Service. A few days later Atkinson "learned that orders had been requested for one squadron to report to this station, because Commandant Armengaud reported (as a result of his inspection) that this post would be ready for one squadron by February 15th."[23] A French adviser, not an American officer, conducted the initial inspection of the 1st Pursuit Organization and Training Center and set events in motion for the arrival of the first squadron.

At nine in the morning on 16 February the Third Aviation Instruction Center at Issoudun sent a telegram to Atkinson stating that the 95th Aero Squadron had left Issoudun by train. Unfortunately, the message did not arrive at Atkinson's headquarters until a day later, and men and vehicles were rushed to the train station to greet their first squadron. Only two days earlier, eighteen pilots had awakened in their barracks at Issoudun to learn that they would become members of the first American-trained pursuit squadron to be sent to the front. "We gaped with amazement, the chosen few, incredulous that our prayers were finally answered," observed Harold Buckley. "We were the lucky dogs, the first Americans to go."[24]

The officers and men of the 95th Aero Squadron lined up together in formation for the first time on a muddy street in Issoudun on the morning of their departure for Villeneuve. This squadron was one of the units that had left Kelly Field under Atkinson's command the previous fall. After arriving in France it had proceeded to the Third Aviation Instruction Center at Issoudun, where it pitched in with the construction effort and provided maintenance support for pilot training.[25]

Why did the first American pursuit squadron to be sent to the Zone of Advance have a number as high as 95? Aero squadrons received their numerical designation in the sequence of their activation. Initially, planners in Washington attempted to program squadrons for specific missions, but because it was impossible to forecast requirements accurately they abandoned this approach. Consequently, "standard aero squadrons of the Army" were organized at its mobilization bases.[26] Each of these units consisted of 150 enlisted men, based on Foulois's recommendation after the Mexican punitive expedition. The number of officers assigned to the standard aero squadron varied according to the size of the flying crew needed for an airplane. An observation aircraft needed a pilot and an observer, whereas a pursuit plane needed only a pilot.[27]

This system of standardization simplified mobilization planning. After squadrons had completed basic training, they could be sent wherever they were needed and modified as necessary for their assigned mission. Many of the first squadrons to be organized were school, construction, or other support units that were needed to develop the infrastructure of the mobilization system, first in the United States and later in Europe. Others remained in the United States waiting for pilots to complete their training at such places as Kelly Field. Some, like the 95th Aero Squadron, were sent to France without pilots. Once pilots had completed their training and were available for assignment in France, the aero squadrons arriving in France were designated pursuit, reconnaissance, or bombardment based on the immediate requirements of the AEF. It simply was not possible to make a reliable prediction in the United States about what sort of unit would be needed in Europe. Such planning would have required a degree of perfection in transatlantic coordination and communication that was beyond the capabilities of the day. Reliance on the European Allies for shipping, advanced pilot training, and frontline aircraft further complicated the problem.

Once the standard-service aero squadrons arrived in France they were modified to conform to the aviation structure developed by the AEF. Lt. Col. Billy Mitchell, the first American aviation officer to arrive in France after the United States declared war, developed the tables of organization for pursuit, observation, and bombardment squadrons using the standard 150-man aero squadron as his basic building block. Mitchell toured the front after his arrival and was especially impressed with the tactical organization of the British Royal Flying Corps (RFC). Although some in the RFC argued that six airplanes constituted too large a formation for one man to control, the British adopted an eighteen-airplane squadron composed of three six-plane flights under the leadership of a flight commander. Following the British example, Mitchell made the eighteen-plane, three-flight squadron standard for the AEF. In contrast, French pursuit squadrons were increasing in size during the winter of 1917-18 from ten or twelve aircraft to fifteen per squadron.[28]

Thus Foulois's standard-service aero squadron became Mitchell's pursuit, observation, or bombardment squadrons. The mobilization and training that spanned two continents reflected the same technological ethos of efficiency, interchangeability, and system that culminated in Henry Ford's program of mass production, which was revolutionizing American industry at the time. Table 1.1 illustrates the organization of the American pursuit squadron.

Table 1.1

Table of Organization for Pursuit Squadron of Eighteen Planes, Personnel and Vehicles

Personnel Duty	Number	Grade
Officers		
Squadron commanders	1	Captain (1 major in three squadrons)
Flight commanders	3	1st lieutenant
Pilots	15	2d lieutenant
Adjutants	1	1st lieutenant
Supply officers	1	2d lieutenant
Engineer officers	1	2d lieutenant
Information officers	1	1st lieutenant
Total officers	23	
Enlisted men		
Headquarters		
Sergeants major	1	Sergeant 1st class
Mess sergeants	1	Sergeant
Clerks	4	Private, private 1st class
Supply section		
Supply sergeants	1	Sergeant 1st class
Clerks	2	Private 1st class
Supply	1	Corporal
Mechanics	1	Corporal
Cooks	6	Cook
Transportation section		
Truckmasters	1	Sergeant 1st class
Assistant truckmasters	1	Sergeant
Chauffeurs	13	Chauffeur, chauffeur 1st class
Motorcyclists	5	Private 1st class
Engineering section		
Master signal electricians	4	M.S.E.
Radio and telegraph electricians	3	Sergeant

Air section

Chiefs of section	18	Sergeant 1st class
Mechanics	36	Private 1st class through sergeant
Riggers	18	Private through sergeant
Armorers	18	Private through sergeant
Privates	11	Private
Chauffeurs	5	Chauffeur
Total enlisted men	150	

Vehicles

Touring cars	2
Motorcycle sidecars	5
Trucks	16
Trailers	12
Total vehicles	35

Source: Pursuit Squadron, Tables of Organization for Units of the AEF Air Service, 15 January 1918, Table 12, in Gorrell's *History of the American Expeditionary Forces Air Service* (Microfilm Publication M990), 1917–19, RG120, National Archives at College Park, series A, vol. 12.

Whereas the AEF adopted the Royal Flying Corps squadron as its model for the American aero squadron, the French Air Service provided the model for the force structure above the squadron-the group and wing-because the Americans would be fighting alongside the French.

By the time Atkinson arrived in France, Mitchell's proposed force of 260 squadrons, consisting of 120 pursuit, 80 observation, and 60 bomber squadrons, had become the official program for the AEF. The preeminence of pursuit aviation reflected the importance placed on gaining air superiority and the belief that "a decision in the air must be sought and obtained before a decision on the ground can be reached."[29] More to the point, the large number of planned pursuit squadrons demanded an efficient organization and training program-one that would not congest the transatlantic pursuit-squadron production system that began at Kelly Field and ended at Villeneuve.

A case in point is the 95th Aero Squadron, organized on 20 August 1917 at Kelly Field; the 91st, 94th, and 96th Squadrons were organized the same day. According to the account of an observer at Kelly Field, as trainloads of recruits disembarked "men would be lined up and after 150 were counted off, they would be designated a certain squadron, [then] the next 150 in line would be designated the next numbered squadron."[30] Each of these squadrons underwent about five weeks of training, which consisted mostly of "drilling, digging ditches, making roads, and putting up tents for newcomers," before leaving Kelly Field for France at the end of September.

The 95th Aero Squadron departed Kelly Field on September 30 as part of a contingent of ten aero squadrons, the 88th through 97th, deploying to Europe. (Three additional squadrons joined the original seven that Atkinson had led from Kelly Field). Major Atkinson took charge of these units, designated the 1st Provisional Wing, at the Aviation Concentration Center at Garden City, Long Island, New York. They sailed on 27 October in a convoy that also carried Foulois and Roosevelt.[31] Once they arrived in France, AEF Air Service requirements dictated their destiny. The 91st and 96th Aero Squadrons became, respectively, observation and bombardment squadrons, the 94th and 95th Aero Squadrons became pursuit squadrons. While the 95th Aero Squadron went directly to Issoudun, where it pitched in with the construction effort and later provided maintenance support for flight training, the 94th Aero Squadron underwent a program of training at French airplane factories. That several of these factories did not produce pursuit airplanes indicates that the 94th Aero Squadron's destiny had not yet been determined when it arrived in France, even though it was the second squadron sent to Atkinson. Thus the 95th Aero Squadron became America's first pursuit squadron in the Zone of Advance. It was simply a matter of luck.[32]

The 95th Squadron's departure from Issoudun represented a significant milestone for the AEF's Air Service. Enthusiasm gripped the flight school, and the entire post turned out to cheer the unit on its way. Red Cross girls fluttered their handkerchiefs as the formation, with pilots leading and enlisted men behind, marched to the music of the aviation band leading them to their train. Lt. Harold Buckley recalled the favorable omens that seemed to accompany their parade:

> Above us the sun split the low-hanging clouds and for a fleeting moment
> shone on our heads. . . . It gave new strength to the colors of the flag, snapping

in the February gusts from the top of the pole high over the headquarters hut. It cheered us [and] seemed to prophesy the favor of the gods.[33]

Two squadrons left Issoudun that day. The 103d Aero Squadron departed two hours earlier than the 95th. Each was mistakenly sent to the other's destination. While Atkinson waited at Vertus for the 95th Squadron, Maj. William Thaw watched for the 103d at Chalons. Thaw commanded the Lafayette Escadrille, based at La Noblette Farm about ten miles northeast of Chalons. The French Air Service was about to transfer this famous squadron to the United States Army. Because the Lafayette Escadrille consisted of American volunteer pilots and French soldiers as nonflying support personnel, the French troops would have to be replaced before the unit was transferred to the AEF. Accordingly, the 103d Squadron that departed Issoudun had no pilots assigned. But instead of the 103d Squadron, Thaw was surprised to meet the 95th Squadron, which arrived at Chalons at eleven o'clock that night.[34]

Thaw drove to the Vertus railroad station, where he found Atkinson and explained the mix-up. Roosevelt made the one-hour drive to Chalons to meet the 95th Squadron. While the squadron waited, German airplanes bombed the city, providing the airmen a harsh welcome to the Zone of Advance. None of the Americans were injured, though some of their equipment was damaged. The 95th did not arrive at Vertus until 2:30 P.M. on the rerouted train.[35] All of the officers of the 1st Pursuit Organization and Training Center met the squadron at the Vertus station that cold February afternoon. At the end of their three-day train journey, the men were "practically in a state of doddering imbecility from lack of sleep and food . . . hollow-eyed and gaunt, with empty stomachs and full beards."[36]

The 95th Squadron marched down a narrow, muddy road behind the convoy that carried its baggage and equipment. As the men approached the entrance to the airfield, a noncommissioned officer began calling cadence, and the squadron stiffened into a quick step. Atkinson got out of his car and stopped the formation in front of the base headquarters, where Victor Menard, the commander of Escadre 1, stood with his staff, awaiting the arrival of the first all-American pursuit squadron to arrive in the Zone of Advance. Roosevelt translated Commandant (Major) Menard's welcoming remarks to the squadron. After dinner the men settled down in their new barracks, located across the field perpendicular to the hangars and buildings of Menard's Escadre 1.

The officers' barracks measured ninety by twenty feet and housed twenty-seven officers in fourteen rooms-two to a room, Atkinson having his own quarters. Three small stoves provided heat. Electric lights and telephones had not yet been installed. The hangars were still empty when the men moved in, but Roosevelt felt confident that things were on the right track. Some of the best outfits in the French Air Service were at Villeneuve. "In one of the French squadrons here there are 5 aces and in their squadron mess they can count 51 Boches [pejorative term for Germans] around the table among them on their string."[37] Finding leaders with this sort of experience had been one of the major problems confronting the AEF.

The AEF attempted to make up for its lack of combat experience by commissioning American volunteers who had flown with the Allies, including the pilots of the Lafayette Escadrille. In 1916 the French Air Service organized this squadron of American volunteer pilots as a pursuit squadron because fighters represented the most glamorous and publicized type of military aviation, and they hoped such publicity would help draw a neutral United States closer to the Allied side. [38]

The exploits of the Lafayette Escadrille quickly attracted more American volunteers into the French Air Service, many more than the limited number of slots in the original squadron. As a result, the majority of Americans who joined the French Air Service were scattered among other French squadrons along the front, and like the pilots of the Lafayette Escadrille, most of these men also served in pursuit squadrons. This larger group became known as the Lafayette Flying Corps.[39] Together, the Lafayette Escadrille and Flying Corps represented a convenient pool of combat experience upon which the AEF's Air Service could draw. Ninety-three of them eventually joined the Air Service. One of the first was Raoul Lufbery.

Lufbery was an obvious candidate for command. He was a hero; newspapers both in France and America had been full of his exploits. In the words of his comrades, "Children were named after him [and] scores of silly girls wrote letters to him. . . . How we unheroic and unknown airmen envied him."[40] Credited with sixteen confirmed victories, he was by far the most successful American pilot at the front. In January 1918 Lufbery joined the AEF. He wore the gold leaves of a major because a committee of officers had decided that he should command a squadron.[41]

Lufbery arrived at Villeneuve on 22 January with orders to take command

Raoul Lufbery, January 1918

*At the time this picture was taken, Lufbery was the top
American ace with seventeen confirmed victories. He
was held in awe by fellow pursuit pilots but was
deemed unsuitable for command.*

RALPH ROYCE PAPERS, U.S AIR FORCE
HISTORICAL RESEARCH AGENCY

of the first squadron to be sent to the 1st Pursuit Organization and Training
Center. At this time, Atkinson and his staff had been at Villeneuve less than a
week and were still trying to solve the problem of billets and hangars. Lufbery
told them that there was sufficient room for a squadron at the Lafayette
Escadrille's airfield at La Noblette Farm, about thirty-five miles from Villeneuve.
Atkinson and Roosevelt accompanied him there the next day to inspect the
accommodations but decided the plan was not feasible. There was little room
at La Noblette Farm, and by this time Atkinson and Roosevelt were committed

to building their own facilities at Villeneuve. More important, however, the trip provided an opportunity for Atkinson to size up Lufbery, and his impression was not favorable.[42]

The following day Lufbery left Villeneuve and traveled to Issoudun, took command of the 95th Aero Squadron, and prepared to bring it forward as soon as the barracks were completed. Before Lufbery's departure from Villeneuve, Atkinson had given him a detailed list of instructions: select men according to qualification and divide them into flights and sections; ensure that the pilots learned all they could about machine guns; make few promotions until the squadron was issued airplanes and an appropriate assessment could be made of each man's abilities; get nine armorers, if at all possible, and at least three good rotary-engine mechanics-more, if they were available, "as there will be nothing but Nieuports here." Also included was procurement of mundane but necessary items, such as sufficient clothing for the men, "as very little can be obtained from here," and at least two pairs of field shoes for each man. Lufbery was to check the kitchen equipment, as well, and if it were found to be old, to get a "new outfit." Finally, he was told to make sure to bring a three months' supply of blank forms, if they were obtainable.[43] Atkinson's list reflected an experienced officer's appreciation for the administrative and logistical details of command. This was his forte. His impulse to spell out instructions in such detail for the famous fighter pilot provides a clue about his assessment of Lufbery's fitness to command.

As soon as Lufbery was on his way to Issoudun, Atkinson wrote his immediate superior, Col. Robert O. Van Horn, the chief of the Advance Section, Zone of Advance, recommending that Lufbery be relieved of command: "I strongly recommend that he be not placed in command of a squadron at present. He will be much more useful to our service in some other capacity than squadron command." Atkinson suggested that Lufbery be made an instructor pilot instead. "He would be of great value here to take small patrols over the lines for the first time and as a general instructor in combat work. I am sure he would be of much more value in this capacity than any other at present." For the time being, Atkinson concluded, Lufbery should remain at Issoudun.[44]

Atkinson's recommendations were approved. Lufbery was relieved of command of the 95th Aero Squadron and remained at Issoudun, in a state of shock, until March.[45] It was a drastic step for Atkinson to take, and it exhibited his decisive, some might say hard-line, style of command. Lufbery himself held the rank of major, and his hero status strengthened his position. Moreover, Atkinson's recommendation challenged the collective judgment of those who had been involved in the decision to place Lufbery in command. Atkinson, in effect, told his superiors that had they had made a poor decision in selecting Lufbery-no small matter for Atkinson, who was himself a newly appointed commander in the AEF. His superiors' immediate acquiescence to his recommendation reflected the power of his insider status as well as his stock among the insiders.

What motivated Atkinson's recommendation? Unfortunately, his letter to Van Horn did not elaborate on his recommendation. According to fellow Lafayette flyers James Norman Hall and Charles Bernard Nordhoff, however, "Any average judge of character could have known after a five-minute talk with Lufbery that he would never make a paper-work squadron commander. He knew nothing, and wanted to know nothing, about the routine of making reports and of keeping lists and records and [requisitions]."[46] Were the administrative requirements of command so important to Atkinson that he would disqualify Lufbery because of the ace's failure to manage them? Perhaps there were other reasons as well.

Lufbery's social background was at odds with the mainstream of the officers' corps in the Air Service. Unlike almost all of the officers in the Air Service, Lufbery had never been to college. He had grown up in France and seemed to his fellow officers to be more French than American. He was far more comfortable speaking French, his native language, and expressed himself poorly in English.[47] He had first come to the United States at the age of twenty-one, in 1906, in a fruitless attempt to find his father, after several years of wandering about North Africa and Europe. He remained in America for only a few years, but long enough to enlist in the Army, which sent him to the Philippines. When his enlistment ended, he wandered about Asia until meeting Marc Pourpe in Calcutta in 1912.

Pourpe was a French aviator conducting exhibition flights in Blériot monoplanes. Lufbery became his mechanic, and the two traveled throughout the Orient giving flight demonstrations. By the time the war broke out, they had returned to France. Pourpe joined the French Air Service, and Lufbery, an American citizen because of the father he hardly knew, joined the French Foreign Legion. Pourpe managed to get Lufbery assigned as his mechanic. When Pourpe was killed attempting a night landing in fog, Lufbery, for some unexplained reason, blamed the Germans for his closest friend's death and swore eternal vengeance. He became a *chasse* pilot himself and one of the original members of the Lafayette Escadrille.[48] Lufbery had a quiet, sphinx-like character but could become violent on the ground as well in the air. As recently as December 1917 he had engaged in a fistfight with an American sergeant from the 1st Division in the Escadrille's bar. Simply put, Lufbery was an adventurer who had become an ace.[49]

The insiders also had an adventurous streak in their character-that tolerance for risk needed to fly the unreliable aircraft used by the Army at San Diego and in Mexico. But the insiders were first and foremost Regular Army officers. Prewar aviators were selected from officers of the line, and these professionals had begun their careers as infantry or cavalry officers. They had paid their dues in the various mundane assignments of a peacetime army. Together, they had endured the rites of passage into the Aviation Section at North Island and had bonded while campaigning in the desert Southwest.

This band of prewar Army aviators had also agitated for independence from the Signal Corps, and in the AEF they had achieved their dream of a separate Air Service, which General Pershing approved shortly after his arrival in France in June 1917.[50] The precedent having been set in the AEF, it was only a matter of time before aviation would achieve a similar status back in the United States. Having finally won their independence, the insiders were suspicious of outsiders such as Lufbery, who threatened to take over some of the most prestigious positions in the AEF's Air Service. They knew that there was opportunity in war. Reputations and promotions were at stake. They took the long view, which extended to the Air Service after the war.

The desire to prevent outsiders from taking over the most prestigious positions in their caste reflected a larger trend in American society. As the historian Louis Galambos has observed, the progressivism that dominated the American political and social scene between 1900 and 1918 also manifested itself in the development of new professional organizations. In this respect, the insiders were no different from the doctors, lawyers, and engineers who were erecting gates, defined with specific education and experience requirements, to keep out those deemed unqualified while establishing for themselves a private monopoly.[51]

At the same time, the quest for efficiency in the Army also reflected a broader social trend. The captains of American industry were revolutionizing production technology with the principles of scientific management and the efficiency movement. The Army also adapted the mantra of efficiency, and it should come as no surprise that the efficiency movement gained particular favor in the Aviation Section of the Signal Corps, the Army's most technologically oriented organization.[52] "Efficiency boards" selected officers for promotions. The term "good officer" was synonymous with "efficient officer." Atkinson placed a high value on efficiency, conflating it, perhaps, with effectiveness. The insiders' desire to protect their turf and the high value they placed on efficiency help explain why Atkinson had Lufbery removed without so much as a trial period in command.

Most of the Lafayette Escadrille pilots entered active duty with the United States Army on orders issued at the 1st Pursuit Organization and Training Center during the first part of February. Atkinson administered the oath of service and presented them with official orders sending them back to their base at La Noblette Farm as officers in the United States Army. Atkinson thus had the opportunity to "look over" each of these experienced pursuit pilots.[53] Once Lufbery had been removed from command, Atkinson had to find a replacement, and he did not seek one of these experienced Lafayette pilots. When the 95th Squadron arrived at Villeneuve, a nonflying officer commanded it, but this situation was soon remedied when Atkinson appointed Capt. James E. Miller to command the squadron.[54]

Miller was not an insider, but he was well connected. After graduating with high honors from Yale in 1904, he joined a prominent Wall Street financial firm and became a senior officer. Like Roosevelt, he was one of the wealthy New York aviation enthusiasts who attended the 1915 Plattsburg camp and had helped Bolling organize the 1st Aero Company of the New York National Guard located at the Wright Company airfield at Mineola, on Long Island.[55] Their unit had been briefly mustered into federal service during the Mexican punitive expedition, though it had not been deployed. It had, however, undergone intensive training under two insiders from Foulois's 1st Aero Squadron in Mexico, Lts. Joseph E. Carberry and W. G. Kilner.[56]

After the United States entered the war, the 1st Aero Company became the nucleus of a larger unit designated the 1st (Reserve) Aero Squadron, which was activated into federal service in May 1917. Raynal Bolling commanded the squadron for only a few weeks before being selected to lead a contingent of experts, remembered as the Bolling mission, to Europe to determine what sort of airplanes American industry should produce. Miller sailed for France in July with a contingent of 1st (Reserve) Aero Squadron officers to help organize training activities in France. By the time they arrived, Bolling had become responsible for AEF Air Service logistics and training. He appointed Miller as the commanding officer at Issoudun–a logical assignment, given that the 1st (Reserve) Aero Squadron's personnel and equipment formed the core of the training center.[57]

Pershing visited Issoudun in early November 1917 and was dissatisfied with its state of discipline and progress. These were difficult times at Issoudun for many reasons, but Pershing decided the training center needed a Regular Army officer to instill the appropriate level of discipline. As a result, Maj. Carl Spatz replaced Miller in command of Issoudun.[58] Miller remained at Issoudun, where he was in charge of flying at Advance Field 5. The insiders he had known at Mineola were now lieutenant colonels holding key positions in the AEF's Air Service. Carberry was chief of the Instruction Department and therefore Miller's immediate supervisor while he was in charge at Issoudun. Kilner replaced Spatz, who remained at Issoudun as chief of training, as the commanding officer at Issoudun on 25 November.[59]

Events unfolded quickly in the chaotic environment that characterized the AEF's Air Service. Lufbery was relieved on 10 February, a matter of days before the 95th Squadron departed for Villeneuve. Miller was available, was well known to the insiders, and had completed all of the required instruction. He exuded enthusiasm, self-confidence, and courage. Physically, he was as "near perfect as a man can be."[60] He arrived at the 1st Pursuit Organization and Training Center several days before the 95th Aero Squadron. His old friend from Mineola, Philip Roosevelt, was Atkinson's right-hand man.

On February 20, two days after the unit arrived, Atkinson assigned Miller command of the 95th Aero Squadron. Miller led a group of pilots to Paris to pick up their combat aircraft and returned to Villeneuve on 6 March with the first fifteen Nieuport 28s. The airplanes were unarmed because machine guns had not yet been procured. The pilots conducted test flights over the next few days, and on one of these flights Miller experienced engine trouble and had to make a forced landing at Coligny, a French aerodrome northeast of Villeneuve. He returned to Villeneuve by motor vehicle.[61]

On the same day, Majs. Davenport Johnson and Millard Harmon, who

Captain James Ely Miller
A charismatic commander, Miller was the AEF's first
pilot killed in action.
NATIONAL AIR AND SPACE MUSEUM,
CM-414000-01

were temporarily attached to Escadre 2, flew over to Villeneuve. Miller knew
them both, so he asked them to come into his room for a talk:

> "Can't you fix it up for me to come over and visit you?" he asked them. "I am
> in an awfully difficult position here," he went on, "In command of the first
> American Pursuit Squadron on the front [but] I have never seen the lines from
> the air." [He] fought to go. "I need the experience for myself but I need it more
> to give me some prestige with these pilots." So after quite a talk they said they

would see what they could do. That night they telephoned over that if Jim [Miller] would come over the next day the French commander, Commandant Féquant, would lend him a plane.[62]

Roosevelt, who bunked with Miller, witnessed how pleased Miller was that night: "Jim's dream was realized. After we had blown out the candles, he said to me, 'Good Lord, I have waited for tomorrow. This makes me feel as though I had received a new lease on life.'"[63] It turned out instead to be his death warrant.

Miller retrieved his repaired Nieuport and flew it to Coincy. There he borrowed a SPAD, because his Nieuport was not armed, and joined Johnson and Harmon on a patrol. Harmon returned to the airfield shortly after takeoff because of engine trouble. Johnson and Miller continued and near Reims engaged in combat with two German aircraft. Johnson's gun jammed and he left Miller, last seen going down in a tailspin inside German lines with the two Germans spiraling down in pursuit.[64]

Everyone was shocked. One of the enlisted men, Master Signal Electrician Vanderwater, who had been with Atkinson since Kelly Field, broke down and cried for an hour when he heard what had happened. Roosevelt felt lost. "I cannot imagine what we shall do without him. . . . Everything is in the air and Jim was the only man who seemed to have definite ideas about what a squadron ought to be, to have and to do." He later wrote that he considered Miller's death "the greatest single loss to the group."[65] Only a little more than a month earlier, Atkinson had written home that "my education for the last seven years has been war, and I hear the guns at the front every night, yet I just can't realize that men are actually trying to kill one another."[66] Now he found himself writing to Miller's wife back in New York explaining that her husband was missing in action.[67]

Atkinson immediately placed 1st Lt. Seth Low, another of the former officers of the 1st (Reserve) Aero Squadron who had recently arrived, in command of the squadron. A week later Major Johnson took command of the squadron on a permanent basis. Those who questioned his conduct on the patrol with Miller began referring to him as "Jam" Johnson in reference to his excuse that his machine guns had jammed.

Johnson was a graduate of West Point, class of 1912. After receiving his commission to the infantry he had spent most of his first four years of active duty on the troubled Mexican border. He completed his training at the Army

Signal Corps Aviation School in San Diego in August 1916 and was assigned to the 1st Aero Squadron on the southwestern border. In February 1917 the Army ordered him to France as an observer with the French army. After Pershing arrived, Johnson joined the headquarters of the AEF's Air Service in Paris, where he served as assistant chief of the Instruction Department.[68]

Johnson was one of the first Americans to attend the aerial gunnery course at Cazaux, the capstone school for pursuit pilots. After completing this course, he arrived at Atkinson's headquarters on 24 January with orders attaching him to the French Air Service to gain experience flying with the élite French 12th Pursuit Group, the Cigognes [Storks].[69] He was obviously being groomed for pursuit squadron command. Johnson was not a pilot of the same caliber as Lufbery, but he fit the profile for command, and he was an insider who was available.

Although Johnson was the only one to provide an immediate account of the aerial engagement in which Miller lost his life, another account surfaced shortly after the war. Lt. Zenos "Red" Miller, a pilot in the 1st Pursuit Group's 27th Aero Squadron, was shot down during the summer and became a prisoner of war. After repatriation he visited the 94th Aero Squadron, which was stationed near Koblenz, Germany, as the lone pursuit squadron in the Army of Occupation in Germany. Red gave his comrades a different account of Jim Miller's death, one that included his dying words. Lt. Joseph Eastman, a veteran pilot of the 94th Squadron in Koblenz, recorded Red's account of Miller's death in his diary.

> Pertaining to Col. "Jam" Johnson, Red says, Dusty Rhodes, also a prisoner, is bringing back an official paper signed by the German pilot who brought down Jim Miller and the paper is a report on Jim's descent and his dying statement. It is remembered that when we first were organized at Villeneuve, "Jam" J. returned with the story that he and Jim [were] on a wildcat patrol wherein his gun had jammed causing him to retire-while Jim was shot down. The paper quotes Jim as saying (and the Hun also) that Johnson alone seeing the distant Hun formation had immediately left without warning Jim. And Jim's last words read: "— — Johnson, he's a yellow son of a —! You can tell them that, and I hope he's stuck up against a brick wall and shot!" We, who know Johnson, his vindictiveness and unscrupulous career can't help but derive satisfaction in hearing further proof of our convictions.[70]

Majs. Bert Atkinson, left, and Davenport Johnson, right, France 1918

The insiders were pilots who, like Atkinson and Johnson, had served in the prewar Aviation Section of the Signal Corps along the American southwestern border.

2

Jimmy Meissner
and the First Team

The 1917 Harley-Davidson motorcycle was equipped with a three-speed transmission, step-starter, grip controls, and electric lights. According to the official history of the Harley-Davidson Motor Company, it was capable of speeds in excess of sixty miles an hour. Jimmy Meissner, a third-year student at Cornell University in the spring of 1917, hit seventy on his way back to college. He had just submitted his application to join the Aviation Section of the Army Signal Corps.

Meissner was the sort of young man the Army wanted in aviation. A student-athlete majoring in mechanical engineering, he was active in wrestling, rowing, tennis, and cross-country. He played in the orchestra and was a member of Sigma Phi Epsilon fraternity. He had connections, too. His father was chairman of the principal operating committees of the United States Steel Corporation, the largest corporation in the world and an enterprise of great importance for a nation at war.[1]

A week earlier, on 12 May 1917, Meissner had met Maj. Raynal Bolling at his father's office at the U.S. Steel headquarters in New York, and the two men accompanied him to the Signal Corps Aviation School at Mineola, where he submitted his application. Despite his connections—his father knew Bolling, one of the top lawyers for U.S. Steel—Meissner was not accepted. Jimmy Meissner was only twenty years old at the time, and one of the requirements, as his father had warned him, was that he be at least twenty-one.[2] But his youth was probably not the sole reason for the denial of his application: Harvard student Quentin Roosevelt, a son of President Theodore Roosevelt, at only nineteen years of age, had managed to enlist in the 1st (Reserve) Aero Squadron a month earlier.[3]

Fortunately for Meissner, a new training system was about to get under way to fill the expanded need for pilots as the country mobilized for war. Under the new system, aviator training would take place in three stages: ground school at selected universities, basic flight training at an airfield in the United States (such as Kelly Field), and advanced training in Europe. Army officials decided to model the ground school after the University of Toronto's School of Military Aeronautics, which provided initial training for aviation cadets of the Royal Flying Corps.

The Army's chief signal officer, Brig. Gen. George O. Squier, selected the Yale historian and noted explorer Hiram Bingham to take charge of the first phase of the American training program. Bingham attended a conference at Toronto's School of Military Aeronautics with representatives from the universities that had been chosen for the locations of the American ground schools. He and the other representatives agreed that they were looking for "fellows of quick, clear intelligence, mentally acute and physically fit. . . . The next thing was to make soldiers of them and teach them the value of military discipline." They also agreed that they should eliminate the unfit as quickly as possible. They did not want men who would be undisciplined or who followed "individualistic tendencies." Such men "would soon come to grief over the lines where team play was so essential."[4]

The ideal candidate, Bingham concluded, would be a college student from one of America's leading universities, thereby sure to possess the appropriate mental capacity, and also an athlete, versed in the concept and practice of teamwork. The inclusion of major engineering universities would help attract those with the appropriate technical orientation, as well. After the meetings concluded the men hastened back to their respective universities to initiate their selection and training programs. Ground schools opened in May at the University of California at Berkeley, the Georgia School of Technology, the University of Illinois, Ohio State University, Massachusetts of Institute of Technology, Princeton, the University of Texas at Austin, and Cornell.[5]

Meissner learned about the new program from an article in the *Cornell*

Brothers Harold G. Meissner, left, and James A.
Meissner, right, in front of the Meissner home in
Brooklyn, May 1917
*At the time this picture was taken, Harold Meissner had
enlisted in the American Ambulance Unit, and Pfc.
James A. Meissner was an aviation cadet.*
Southern Museum of Flight

Sun.[6] He applied the next day and underwent two days of physical and mental evaluations. This time he succeeded, on his own merits, and was accepted into the Cornell Government Ground School for Aviation. The vetting had been a highly selective process: By the end of the war, at least 50,000 young Americans applied to become pilots; only 1,402 (2.8 percent) graduated from advanced training schools and served at the front.[7]

Immediately after passing his examinations, Meissner packed up his belongings and moved out of the fraternity house and into Cornell's Schoellkopf Field House, where cots had been set up in the locker room. The first two weeks of training consisted of drill, rifle marksmanship, five-mile road marches, and some basic infantry tactics. The routine began with reveille at a quarter to six in the morning, calisthenics at six, breakfast at seven, drill and lectures for the rest of the morning, more drill and lectures in the afternoon, followed by supper and taps at a quarter to ten. In Meissner's third week he attended classes on the theory of flight, photography, map drawing, and meteorology. The cadets also began assembly of a Curtiss JN-4 airplane, the ubiquitous "Jenny" used in the war for primary flight training. In week four they took classes on engines, wireless radio, and the Lewis machine gun; work also continued on their Curtiss airplane, adjusting alignment and installing cables, rigging, and landing gear. Week five concentrated on motors, and the next week included more work on motors and machine guns. During the seventh week, Meissner was made sergeant of his squadron. About 30 percent of those who attended ground school at Cornell never completed the course.[8]

Meissner's scores were excellent. He was one of the top graduates in his class. As a reward, he was selected to go directly to France for flight training rather than attend basic flight school in the United States. To expedite pilot training, Capt. Joseph E. Carberry, one of the first aviation officers to arrive in France, arranged in late April 1917 for the French to train 100 American cadets a month in French flight schools. Bolling also argued for such a program before departing for Europe and was assured that suitable candidates would be sent immediately to France. Unfortunately, the first contingent of ground-school graduates did not arrive until mid-August, and as a result of the delay space that had been made available in French flight schools went unused by the United States Army. Some slots were filled by American volunteers making their own way to France to join the Lafayette Flying Corps.[9]

The top graduates of the ground schools won the privilege of being immediately sent to France through competitive selection. As Bingham noted, this opportunity served as a powerful incentive "because every young man wanted to get to France as soon as possible."[10] Yet by the time the program was in full swing, the available training slots had disappeared because the French Air Service needed them to accommodate their own expansion. Finally, on 14 July, the first class of cadets graduated from the first six ground schools around the United States. Those selected for immediate deployment to France reported to Fort Wood, adjacent to the Statue of Liberty in New York harbor, to receive their instructions for overseas movement.[11]

Meissner sailed on 23 July aboard the *Orduna*. The aviation contingent aboard this ship consisted of forty-seven ground-school graduates and eleven aviation officers of the 1st (Reserve) Aero Squadron. Many of the 1st Pursuit Group's earliest pilots were aboard. Capt. James E. Miller of the 1st (Reserve) Aero Squadron commanded the entire contingent.[12] First Lt. Quentin Roosevelt was one of Miller's assistants. Since joining the 1st (Reserve) Aero Squadron in April, Roosevelt had completed his basic flight training at Mineola, passed the Reserve Military Aviator test, and received his commission. Before America declared war, he had been a second-year student at Harvard, where he was studying mathematics and mechanics. Like many of the aviators, Roosevelt was mechanically inclined and prone to tinkering with motorcycles and automobiles. He attended the Plattsburg camp during the summer of 1916 and initially planned to join the Royal Flying Corps, which was aggressively recruiting Americans and training them in Canada, but when he learned of the opportunity to train at Mineola he instead volunteered to join the Signal Corps.[13]

One of Roosevelt's boyhood friends, Hamilton Coolidge, was one of the ground-school graduates aboard the *Orduna*. Also a student at Harvard, Coolidge had been president of his freshman class and in 1916 had played varsity football. He had been a member of the Harvard Flying Club, which provided him the opportunity to attend the Curtiss School of Aviation at Buffalo and Miami, from which he graduated in June 1917. Hiram Bingham, who attended the Curtiss School at the same time, remembered Coolidge as the "most conscientious of all and most uniformly cheerful in performance of his duty." Capt. James Miller apparently had the same impression of the lad, as Coolidge was appointed "top," or 1st, sergeant in charge of all the cadets aboard the *Orduna*.[14]

First Lt. Hobart "Hobey" Baker, one of the 1st (Reserve) Aero Squadron officers aboard the *Orduna*, was one of the most famous college athletes of his generation. He gained fame as an All-American football player at Princeton, during the era when football's Big Three were Princeton, Harvard, and Yale and helmets were not required. He was also the best hockey player in America. In 1916 Baker joined the Governor's Island Training Corps. Like Bolling's 1st Aero Company of the New York National Guard, this group was an outgrowth of the Military Training Camp for Business Men at Plattsburg. A few wealthy businessmen had bought airplanes and seaplanes and received permission to use Governor's Island in New York harbor for their flying school. Baker took early morning flight lessons before catching the train to his job with J. P. Morgan on Wall Street. In April 1917 the Governor's Island Training Corps moved to Mineola, Long Island, and merged with Bolling's 1st Aero Company to form the 1st (Reserve) Aero Squadron. Bolling sent Maj. Billy Mitchell at Signal Corps headquarters a list of officers whom he recommended for this unit. Both Baker and Philip J. Roosevelt were on this list. Baker made the cut, but Philip Roosevelt did not.[15] James Miller, Quentin Roosevelt, Hamilton Coolidge, and Hobey Baker all became fighter pilots in the 1st Pursuit Group. None of them would survive.

Also aboard the *Orduna* were Waldo Heinrichs and Douglas Campbell, graduates of the ground school at Massachusetts Institute of Technology (MIT). Heinrichs noted in his diary that he thought Campbell was the strongest man in the MIT squadron, and this opinion would prove to be quite accurate, as Campbell became one of the informal leaders of the first contingent. He had been a senior at Harvard when America entered the war. Eager to get into the "flying game," as he called it, he and some friends hurried to the Aviation Section's headquarters in Washington to find out how to join. In one of the letters he wrote aboard the *Orduna,* he expressed his awareness of the significance of his company: "This bunch is in on the ground floor of the Aviation Service, and if we can make good the sky's the limit. It's a great opportunity."[16] And for Campbell, it was.

The trip to England took three weeks. The first stop was Halifax, Nova Scotia, where the *Orduna* waited six days for a convoy to assemble before the North Atlantic crossing. During the passage, the men occupied themselves by writing, reading, studying French, standing submarine watch, and, in an almost laughable reflection of the Signal Corp's control of aviation, practicing their flag signals. On the ninth day out of Halifax, a flotilla of six friendly destroyers met the convoy and escorted them to Liverpool.[17] The company left Liverpool at two o'clock the same day on a special train that hurried them across England. After spending the night at a boarding house on the coast of the English Channel, they crossed the channel, again with destroyer escort.

When they arrived at Boulogne, France, the men saw for the first time the signs of war. Soldiers and military equipment were everywhere. British ambulances filled with wounded lined the wharf. They boarded a train and arrived in Paris that night, 13 August. They stayed near the Bastille, at the Casserne de Rouilly, which had been lent to the American military. The barracks were so infested with lice that many slept outside in the courtyard or at a nearby hotel. Heinrichs saw a soldier murder a civilian in an alley. In the morning, the cadets lined up in the barracks square. Ten of them learned to their dismay that they would remain in Paris to work on the Air Service staff. Campbell and Coolidge became members of Miller's staff and helped establish the Third Aviation Instruction Center at Issoudun. The remaining thirty-seven continued to flight school at Tours.[18]

First Lt. Seth Low, who had been captain of the Yale rowing crew in 1915 and was an officer of 1st (Reserve) Aero Squadron, took command of the thirty-seven and accompanied them through training. The French Aviation School at Tours, located about 125 miles southeast of Paris, conducted basic flight training. This aviation training facility was to be turned over to the AEF in November and renamed the Second Aviation Instruction Center. Already, most of the 100 students at Tours were Americans, from the Army, Navy, and a few American volunteers for the Lafayette Flying Corps. Seven or eight students were assigned to each instructor. Meissner reported about two hundred airplanes at the Tours school, mostly two-seat Caudron G-3s.[19]

Already in production when war broke out, the Caudron G-3 was obsolete by 1917, but it was still used as a basic trainer at many of the French schools. A single engine propelled this biplane at a cruising speed of about sixty miles an hour. Instead of a traditional fuselage it had twin fins at the end of each of four booms. Its stability and slow speed made it remarkably easy to fly and therefore perfectly suited to the first phase of flying training in the French system.[20] Because the Caudron had no ailerons, the pilot controlled the airplane through wing warping, a technique invented by the Wright Brothers. This control system required "a considerable amount of exertion and a very heavy hand" because the control cables were fixed to the wings in such a way that manipulation of the control stick caused the wings to twist, or warp. Yet maneuvering the plane must not have been all that difficult. After his first flights, Waldo Heinrichs noted, "It was easy, simple and exciting, the greatest sport in the world."[21]

The training program on the G-3 took about fifty days and produced a licensed pilot ready to progress to advanced training. Dual flight controls made it possible for the student first to accustom himself to the movements of the controls and then gradually to assume responsibility for various maneuvers and phases of flight.[22] Training started at 4:30 A.M., so that pilots could take advantage of the calm morning winds. Students did not eat break-

Caudron G-3 biplane with 100-horsepower Anzani engine
The G-3 served as an observation plane early in the war. Its stability and ease of piloting
made it an ideal beginning trainer.
National Air and Space Museum, CD-ROM 7B-01001

fast until after the morning flights and then usually took a nap in the early afternoon until training resumed again at three o'clock. The afternoon sessions usually began with one-hour lectures on various subjects, including map reading, airplane design, and engines. Evening flying commenced after a small snack of coffee and bread and ended by nine o'clock, when supper was eaten.[23] On good days, Meissner took two flights in the morning and two in the afternoon. Initial training flights consisted of practice in taking off, climbing to 250 or 325 feet, circling the field, and landing.

French instructors sat behind their English-speaking students and communicated with them by using various signals. A slap on the right shoulder signaled "turn right." A knock on the helmet meant "Let go all controls and turn around so as to look at the instructor." In spite of this "signing," the language barrier could be troublesome for those who spoke no French. The American students often had to guess at what their instructors wanted them to do. When they guessed wrong, they got "the devil." The G-3 was such a safe airplane that even when it crash-landed, the crew usually walked away. Unfortunately, one of the Americans died in a midair collision in the heavy traffic around the airfields.

Meissner made his first complete flight under his own control, though still accompanied by an instructor, about a week into flight school. By the end of the second week, he had advanced to the hardest part of the course, landing school, which took place at a three-mile-long field. A typical day at landing school might involve fourteen landings in the space of one morning. During the third week, Meissner made his first solo flights. The following week he was making thirty-minute flights at altitudes as high as 11,500 feet on cross-country courses that tested his map-reading ability.

The *brevet* (military flying license) given by the Aero Club of France required fifty solo landings, twenty-five hours in the air, and an hour and a quarter of flying at an altitude above 6,500 feet. It also required two triangular cross-country flights of about 150 to 200 miles and two *petits voyages* (in which the pilot made a trip of about twenty-five miles one way, landed, reported, and returned). Additionally, pilots had to pass spiral tests from 650 and 2,000 feet, in which they cut their engines and spiraled down so as to land near a designated point.[24] The requirements for the French *brevet* exceeded the American requirements for Reserve Military Aviator (RMA) rating. For example, the RMA test's cross-country triangular flight was only thirty miles, and its altitude test required pilots to fly for forty-five minutes at an altitude of only 4,000 feet.[25] By the last week of September, Meissner and other members of the first contingent had received their *brevets* but not the officer's commission, which the United States Army normally awarded for the equivalent RMA certification.[26]

After several days' leave in Paris, Meissner proceeded to the French aviation school at Avord for the next phase of his training. Located 160 miles south of Paris, Avord was the largest single flying field in France, with several busy subsidiary fields—one of the Americans counted twenty-six airplanes of various types in the air at one time, mostly Nieuports, Caudrons, and Blériots. Those who successfully completed this course became *chasse* (hunt) pilots. Those who failed went to bombardment or observation training.

The Americans had heard a number of bad stories about the living conditions at Avord, which some called "the Cess-Pool of all creation," but according to Meissner, it turned out to be "not half so bad as everyone had painted it." Still, the women's quarters were known as "Syphilis City," and 45 percent of the men were supposedly infected with the disease. Lice and fleas were rampant in the straw mattresses used for bedding, but toilets, food, and drinking water were better than at Tours.[27]

The training process at Avord involved mastery of basic flight maneuvers

The Penguin, a Blériot modified for instruction in rudder control
The Penguin's shortened wings, clearly visible in this front view, kept it from taking off.
NATIONAL AIR AND SPACE MUSEUM, CD-ROM 1A-10545

on increasingly powerful and maneuverable aircraft. First in the series was a modified single-seat Blériot monoplane, little changed since Louis Blériot completed the first crossing of the English Channel in such a machine in 1909. The modified Blériot had shortened wings. The students called it a Penguin— a bird that could not fly and tended to spin around in circles.

The Penguins provided pilots the opportunity to learn rudder control in a plane whose aerodynamics kept it from taking off. One of the difficult things in piloting the Nieuport, the next airplane in the training series, was its tendency to pull left and even spin on takeoff, owing to the torque supplied by its rotary engine. If this action was not corrected the machine could tip over and crash as it tried to leave the ground. To prevent this type of emergency, the pilot had to anticipate the tail swing with rudder movements.[28]

Meissner was amused to see these machines suddenly veer off course, spin in a circle, and tip over. The cadets would run their Penguins a little faster each time until they reached a top speed of about fifty miles an hour. The machines would "go bouncing and flopping around like . . . [chickens] with [their heads] off."[29] After gaining experience on the three-cylinder powered airplanes, Meissner moved up to the six-cylinder version for higher-speed "rolling" and short hops into the air. When bad weather curtailed training, he spent his days reading, writing, hiking, or visiting the YMCA hut. Students also attended machine-gun classes and practiced rifle marksmanship.

Midway through the course Maj. Davenport Johnson, at this time serving as assistant chief of instruction for Air Service training, visited the class and informed them that they would not receive their commissions until they were ready for the front. Such news was disturbing to the trainees because their contemporaries back in the United States, who were not honor graduates, were receiving their commissions upon completion of basic flight training—a qualification that the first contingent had already completed at Tours. The good news was that they would be become *chasse* pilots. Upon successful completion of the course at Avord, they would go to Pau or Issoudun for aerobatic work, then to gunnery school, and on to the front by Christmas. They also learned that they had been ranked as cadets and their pay would be backdated from the time they entered flying school at Tours. All were jubilant.[30]

By 15 October, Meissner had advanced to the 28-meter, two-seat Nieuports (28 meters—about 92 feet—refers to surface area of the wing). He felt like a rookie on the Nieuport because of its greater speed and need for delicate handling. Subsequently, he worked on progressively smaller versions of the Nieuport, the 23-meter and 18-meter, each faster and more difficult to handle because of the smaller wing surface. The 18-meter Nieuport had been a popular airplane for use on the front during 1915 and 1916 and was capable of attaining speeds of 87 miles an hour.[31]

Although Meissner had no difficulty at Avord, his friend Waldo Heinrichs was unable to master takeoff and landing on the 23-meter Nieuport. Heinrichs blamed his instructor, who had not informed him of the need to compensate for the Nieuport's powerful rotary motor: "Found out in talking to the boys that my failure to take-off was due to my failure to realize that the torque of the propeller on a Nieuport is strongly to the left," he wrote. Heinrich's subsequent attempts to control this tricky machine were still unsatisfactory, however. Consequently, he was classified as a poor pilot and designated for bombardment or observation training. Bitterly disappointed, he wrote, "I have failed—the only one of 37."[32]

Meissner, the fifteenth cadet to finish the Nieuport training, received orders to proceed to the Third Aviation Instruction Center at Issoudun. On his departure from Avord, he penned in his diary, "Never happier at leaving a place in my life."[33]

Issoudun was located about seventy-five miles southeast of Tours. This region of France consisted of many large open spaces because the soil was so poor that farmhouses were relatively few and far between. In general, students arrived at Issoudun from two main sources. First were those cadets, like Meissner, who had proceeded directly to Europe after ground school and taken their preliminary flight instruction in France. Successive graduating classes from the ground schools continued to send their honor graduates directly to France throughout the summer and fall of 1917. Second, in what would become standard as training in the United States gathered momentum, were those who completed preliminary flight training at such places as Kelly Field and came to France for advanced training.[34]

The first part of the training program at Issoudun essentially repeated the program Meissner had already completed at Avord—flying Penguins, dual-control Nieuports, and 23- and 18-meter Nieuports. Had Meissner stayed in the French training system he would have gone to the school at Pau for more advanced training in aerobatics and combat flying. The American base at Issoudun combined the functions of Avord and Pau into one huge training center, reflecting the American preference for economies of scale. By the end of the war, it would be the largest aviation-training facility in the world.[35]

Capt. James E. Miller had the task of organizing the AEF's Third Aviation Instruction Center. Shortly after arriving in Paris the previous August, he proceeded to Issoudun with Hamilton Coolidge and Douglas Campbell. At that time the camp at Issoudun consisted of twelve tents and a company of engineers, who were constructing a few buildings among the large flat fields of the countryside. The group soon returned to Paris and during the next weeks worked on procuring airplanes, supplies, and equipment for the new base. In early October, Miller and his assistants returned to take charge of the camp. When Miller took command of activities at Issoudun, his staff included Coolidge, Campbell, Quentin Roosevelt, and a famous race-car driver and expert mechanic, Eddie Rickenbacker. The 1st (Reserve) Aero Squadron, whose main body arrived at Issoudun in late September, provided other support personnel, vehicles, and equipment.[36]

When Meissner arrived at Issoudun on 27 October, the facilities were still in the early stages of construction, though training had begun three days earlier. During October winter rain, snow, and winds reduced the average number of flying days from twenty-five to fifteen.[37] The wet weather and construction activity combined with the poor drainage characteristics of the topography to create a sea of mud—one of the dominating images in the memories of those who were there at this miserable time. Reed Chambers, an officer student and future pilot with the 94th Aero Squadron, remembered, "Issoudun was a mess. Construction wasn't finished. No duck boards. You waded around in mud up over your ankles. It was probably the lowest morale of any point in my entire experience."[38] There were still no baths and only a few barracks because priority had been given to construction of equipment and training facilities. All the while men were pouring in. Shortly after Meissner arrived, fourteen hundred mechanics and sixty-five cadets arrived in a single day.[39]

Another serious morale problem involved rank. Meissner and the other "honor graduates" who had proceeded directly to France after ground school were still cadets, but their classmates from the ground schools who had attended basic flight training in the United States were now arriving in France as lieutenants—with less than half the flying time behind them of Meissner and the others who had learned to fly with the French. To make matters worse, fellow members of the *Orduna* contingent who had been detached from the group at Paris, such as Douglas Campbell and Hamilton Coolidge, now had their commissions, too.

Campbell, for example, was Meissner's commanding officer for a time at Issoudun. In addition to drawing higher pay, Campbell lived in comfortable officer quarters, while Meissner lived in the barracks.[40] Officers also enjoyed the privilege of "bucking the line" in the training program at Issoudun, allowing Campbell to advance rapidly through Issoudun's system, even though he had not attended the training programs at Tours and Avord. As a result, Meissner complained, "the chief indoor sport is crabbing about withholding of commissions." He continued, "We are now told to expect them when ready for the front!"[41]

When Carl Spatz relieved Miller in the command of Issoudun, he cancelled training for a week and put everyone to work building barracks for all the newly arriving men. Meissner and other students jokingly referred to themselves as the RFC—Regular Flying Carpenters. Meissner eventually got a job putting new wings on crippled planes and making targets for the machine-gun range. He practiced firing the Lewis machine gun at stationary and moving targets until he became an excellent shot. He also learned how to correct jams and misfires. Trapshooting was another activity the cadets practiced to develop their marksmanship skills. When not otherwise occupied, Meissner took long walks, sometimes up to ten miles, to view the French countryside and its medieval castles. Some evenings he watched movies at the camp's YMCA, where there was also "always something to eat if you did not get enough supper."[42] Morale began to improve when flight training resumed and the men learned that they would soon receive their commissions. They also received "wonderful flying clothes" consisting of fur-lined coats, gloves, socks, and hood all wired for electricity. Warm clothing was essential for open-cockpit flying. A small propeller attached to a strut or the fuselage of the airplane drove an electrical generator that provided the electricity for the heated clothing.[43]

Because of his previous training at Tours and Avord, Meissner skipped the initial phases of training at Issoudun and started where he had left off, with the 18-meter Nieuport. He completed thirty-six flights on the aircraft, claiming in his diary that this number was far more than anyone else, before he was allowed to graduate to the 15-meter model. The smaller Nieuport was used extensively as a frontline fighter during 1916. Because of its small wingspan and short body, it landed very fast and was difficult to handle on the ground. Its control was so delicate that a student who mastered it was considered ready for any type of airplane that might be assigned to him on the front.[44] The 15-meter Nieuport marked the first stage of advanced training specifically for pursuit pilots. Only the best went on to pursuit training. Seventeen of Meissner's fellow students who did not make the cut received their orders to proceed to Clermont for bombardment school. Meissner was delighted not to be among them, for his goal was to become a *chasse* pilot.[45]

On 3 December there were only five planes in Meissner's 15-meter Nieuport class for thirty-one men. By the end of the day only one of these airplanes was still flyable. Moreover, because of the wet and windy winter weather, maintenance of training aircraft was a significant problem that curtailed training. In addition to the normal wear and tear, especially severe in a training environment where accidents were common, the muddy flying fields contributed to this problem. As the airplanes taxied over the field, their wheels threw rocks embedded in the mud into the propellers, causing them to break. To solve this problem, officials at Issoudun regularly formed the students into lines and had them sweep the field picking up rocks. Lt. Eddie Rickenbacker was one of the officials in charge of this unpleasant but necessary activity. Rickenbacker also contributed a more permanent solution to this problem by developing "fenders" for aircraft landing gear. His maintenance crews constructed and attached them to the aircraft at the engineering hangars on the main field.[46]

Rickenbacker, the future American "Ace of Aces," was not of the same lofty socioeconomic background of the citizen-soldier aviators like Campbell, Coolidge, Roosevelt, Meissner, and most of the others of the first contingent. The son a Columbus, Ohio, construction worker, Rickenbacker had dropped out of school in seventh grade. He eventually began working as an automobile mechanic, a field in which he seemed to have an instinctive skill. This along with his desire for thrills eventually led to automobile racing. By 1916 he was a racing superstar, having placed third among all money winners on the American Automobile Association tour. He managed the Prest-o-Lite Racing Team that belonged to the owner of the Indianapolis Speedway.

The prospect of being a fighter pilot appears to have first caught his imagination while visiting Britain in the winter of 1916–17. Before the United States declared war, Rickenbacker went to Washington to persuade Signal Corps officials to authorize a volunteer squadron, similar to the Lafayette Escadrille, but they were not interested in him or his ideas. As Rickenbacker's biographer, W. David Lewis, has observed, "Having passed his twenty-fifth birthday, he was already too old for aerial service. Even more important, however, he did not have a college degree. . . . He lacked polish, his speech was laced with slang, his grammar was faulty, and his manners were unrefined."[47]

Nevertheless, Rickenbacker remained determined to achieve his goal of becoming a fighter pilot. After enlisting he managed to become one of Pershing's chauffeurs and sailed with the general's party across the Atlantic. He used his reputation as a famous race-car driver and excellent mechanic to maneuver his way steadily toward aviation. He eventually became Billy Mitchell's chauffeur. When Capt. James Miller was in Paris planning the construction of Issoudun, he ran into Rickenbacker on the Champs Elysées one day, and said, "You're just the fellow I'm looking for." "Why?," Rickenbacker asked. Miller relied, "I've been assigned the duty of developing Issoudun training center for fighter pilots. . . . I need an engineering officer, and you're it." Rickenbacker agreed to take the position, but only if he would also be allowed to learn how to fly. Miller convinced Mitchell to release Rickenbacker in September to take charge as his engineering officer.[48]

As chief engineering officer at Issoudun, Rickenbacker was responsible for maintenance, which became a constant struggle to keep the training fields sup-

Eddie Rickenbacker behind the wheel of Maxwell racing car, 1915
The famous race-car driver was determined to be America's leading ace.
AUBURN UNIVERSITY ARCHIVES

plied with operational aircraft. This never-ending and frustrating battle created a great degree of hostility between Rickenbacker and the students, who routinely broke his airplanes. Similarly, Meissner and other students blamed Rickenbacker when they were unable to make a training flight for lack of flyable planes. "Lt. Rickenbacker won't give us more planes if we bust any, so we waste good flying weather cussing him out," Meissner again complained.[49]

Reed Chambers, who had also advanced to pursuit training, had his first encounter with Rickenbacker about this time. Chambers flew a Nieuport in need of an engine overhaul from one of the training fields over to Rickenbacker's maintenance hangars at the main field. Feeling his oats, Chambers decided to land right next to the engineering hangars, amid the airplanes awaiting maintenance, rather than out on the main airfield and then taxiing to the maintenance hangars. He flew toward the hangars and "landed on a dime" right where he had planned—among the parked airplanes.

Chambers recalled, "About this time a motorcycle with a sidecar attached to it came up, and this fellow started screaming at me, and called me about everything under the sun—blankety-blank fool, and 'Don't you realize that all we do is spend our lives here trying to keep these things working, and you come in and land right among a gob of them, with a chance of cracking them all up?'" Rickenbacker tolerated no such foolishness from the students.

But Chambers was Regular Army. He knew Army regulations, and he knew that he outranked Rickenbacker, who had only recently been commissioned. Chambers called Rickenbacker to attention, threatened to press charges against him for insubordination, and "gave him a good dressing down." Rickenbacker was apparently unaware of the old Army saying that rank among lieutenants is like virginity among whores. "When it was over," Chambers remembered, Rickenbacker "grinned, as only Rick can grin," and apologetically offered, "I wish I could make that kind of a landing." Rickenbacker offered Chambers a ride to the officers' mess in his motorcycle's sidecar, and the two had dinner together, marking the beginning of a close friendship.

Chambers later recalled, "I found that he was one of the most sincere fellows that I'd ever seen. . . . He was really working at this job, and he was—despite his German name . . . a patriotic American." That night when Chambers returned to Field 7 he told his classmates, "We've been wrong about this fellow. . . . He's really a swell guy, when you get to know him." But most remained hostile to Rickenbacker, and they were not happy about Chambers's new attitude. Chambers remembered, "They accused me of being a backslider, and I'd been sold out, I was a sucker for a left punch, and that I was . . . all wrong." A few weeks later Rickenbacker was excused from his maintenance duties and joined Chambers and the others at Field 7 for training. He remained ostracized by everybody except Chambers, who was also given the cold shoulder for befriending the unpopular maintenance officer.[50]

To get their commissions, Meissner and the others who had trained with the French still needed to pass the Junior Military Aviator test with its requisite spirals, altitude, and cross-country flights. Because of the experience Meissner had been accumulating, he easily passed. By the end of the first week in December he was on the waiting list for aerobatics.[51] Meissner passed this phase of training in a single day, after making a series of flights in which he demonstrated his ability to execute specific maneuvers. First was the *vrille*, also known as the tailspin or spinning nosedive. Pilots learned this maneuver first for safety reasons: In the event they inadvertently went into a spin while executing some other maneuver, they had to know how to get out of it. Next came the *virage,* or vertical bank, in which the airplane was banked over to ninety degrees. When the plane was in this position, the aileron and rudder controls' effects reversed. Next was the *renversement,* in which the pilot reversed direction by rolling the aircraft over on its back and executing a half loop. Finally there was the wing slip, similar to a vertical bank but with less airspeed, so that the airplane fell off rapidly sideways. Pilots used all these maneuvers in combat.[52]

Pilots learned these maneuvers in single-seat machines. There was no instructor to take over and rescue them if they failed, as was the case in the dual-control machines used in the British system of training. One pilot later recalled,

> Field 9 was the cemetery. I'll never forget the first time I learned to spin or do any acrobatics. They used to send you up in the air and they'd say, "Pull the joystick back on your belly and kill your motor and kick your right rudder and see what happens." That's how you learned acrobatic flying. "Then, when you come out of whatever you're in and you're nose down, then ease the throttle up and try to pick up, to swing your prop—" This was my first introduction into actual acrobatic flying.[53]

One of the Lafayette Escadrille flyers has suggested that the French system produced a better flyer. "Except verbally, no one had shown us the way. We taught ourselves, and it made a splendid solid foundation, with loads of self-confidence to back it up."[54] Bingham criticized the more dangerous French method but agreed that "the pilot who was able to master these various evolutions, quickly and safely, had nothing to fear from the air." A considerable amount of weeding out occurred in this stage of training. It seems remarkable that Meissner completed the requirements with such apparent ease in a single day. He moved his gear to a new barracks between Fields 7 and 8, where he would live with twelve other students during the next phase of training, which focused on formations and aerial tactics. He closed his diary entry on this happy day with, "Cold but I'm glad to be with [the] 'first bunch.'"[55]

Meissner began flying a more advanced version the 15-meter Nieuport that featured a powerful 120-horsepower engine. Students practiced flying in formations with a thirty-yard interval between planes—a difficult task, according to Meissner. They also practiced strafing trenches, flying from just above the ground to an altitude of three hundred feet over the countryside, "zooming over trees and having great fun." The usual formation was the V, with a single leader followed by the second men at slightly higher altitude, the third men higher yet, and so on.[56]

Each pilot was assigned to his own airplane. Meissner began to think of his as more than a machine: For him, it was alive, like a large bird or flying horse. "My own plane is [number] 19 now, a silver boid but oily—Oh Lord! . . . . We clean and water [our] own animals after flights." Having his own airplane assigned allowed him to accumulate flying time whenever the weather permitted, which was not often. There were only seven flying days during the last half of the month.

On 19 December commissioning orders finally arrived for Meissner and the others who had learned to fly at Tours. That night, they sewed on their lieutenant's bars and polished their Sam Browne belts, one of the distin-

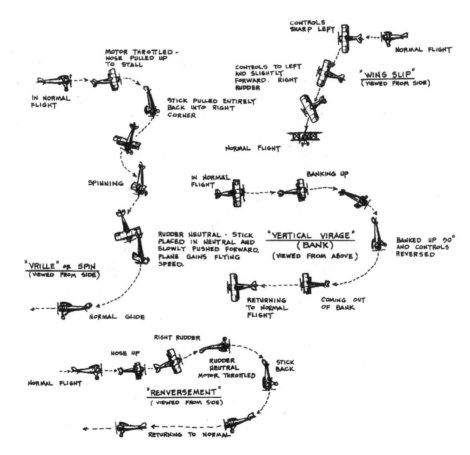

Aerobatic maneuvers taught at Issoudun and used in combat

guishing accouterments worn by officers. Unfortunately, the next day a cloud of sorrow replaced the good feelings engendered by this happy occasion: One of the pilot trainees died on his first flight in the 15-meter Nieuport after an inadvertent spin. The accident must have had a depressing effect on Meissner. Usually his diary included at least a few sentences of entries for each day. For the next two days, he wrote simply, "No flying." That Sunday he read his Bible, an activity recorded in his diary for the first time.

Meissner took advantage of free time by going on walks to farms in the area. Because the camp was quarantined for measles at this time, he often used the pretext of going hunting. On these walks, he would buy honey and nuts, sometimes a "good omelet," from local farmers before returning to the camp. The aviators ate a Christmas feast of wild game, including duck, pheasant, goose, and turkey, with eggnog punch and champagne. By New Year's Eve, Meissner's class was practicing large-formation flying—fifteen aircraft, in three groups of five.

On New Year's Day, Meissner's brother, who was stationed in Paris with the Ambulance Corps, visited him. Meissner took up one of the Nieuports and flew some stunts to show what he had learned. "Great feeling as he shook hands when I landed!," he wrote in his diary after his brother left. Later, rumors circulated, as they had before, that a number of them would be going to the front any day; but instead Meissner received orders to attend yet another school, for gunnery training. He packed his gear and boarded a train for Cazaux the next day.[57]

Meissner was a member of the first full class of seventeen Americans sent to the French aerial gunnery school located on the north shore of Lake Cazaux, about forty-four miles southwest of Bordeaux. This three-week course gave the pilots the opportunity to conduct live-fire training with their machine guns. The commander of the American contingent during this period was Maj. Davenport Johnson. Johnson had been at Cazaux since late December, when Meissner and two other students arrived, becoming the first American officers to take the course while at the same time making arrangements for those who would follow.[58]

First they learned about deflection shooting (aiming ahead of the target so that it moves into the gun's cone of fire) by shooting carbines from a motorboat to familiarize themselves with the problem of engaging a moving target from a moving platform. Subsequent instruction emphasized marksmanship while flying the 15-meter Nieuport with 120-horsepower engine. Airborne training techniques included first ascending several thousand feet, dropping a paper parachute, and chasing it. Instruction progressed to shooting at stationary and free-floating balloons. They also practiced firing at a sleeve towed behind a Caudron G-4 flying at about sixty miles an hour. The course entailed more formation flying in both offensive and defensive situations, including mock combat in which gun cameras assessed "kills." Other training conducted on the ground emphasized how to correct machine-gun stoppages, the mechanics of the synchronizing mechanism that allowed pilots to fire their guns through the arc of the propeller, and carbine, trap, and machine-gun firing. Meissner also fawned over one of the girls on the staff. At the end of the course on 29 January, he wrote that it was the "*best school* possible."[59]

Meissner spent an extra few days at Cazaux being fitted for a new uniform. The cadets were highly conscious of their clothes. Campbell indicated this most clearly in a letter home asking for money. "We are ordering rather expensive uniforms, for dress counts a good deal over here, and we don't mean to be held back for that reason. That's why I'm asking for some money."[60] After ordering his uniform, Meissner traveled to Paris and reported to Air Service headquarters to await subsequent orders.

By the time Meissner and the other members of the first contingent completed their training at Cazaux, they had been preparing to become fighter pilots since the end of May 1917—eight months. In addition to the Cornell Ground School, which was modeled after the British system, Meissner had attended the French Air Service's basic and advanced flight training courses at Tours and Avord. He repeated some of this training at Issoudun, where he also completed advanced flight training to become a pursuit pilot. Finally, he completed the combat gunnery course at Cazaux. According to a recent study, the Americans developed what was "arguably the finest program in the world" by incorporating some of the best elements of the British and French system of training. American pilots averaged more than 100 hours of training, nearly triple the number of hours logged by Royal Air Force (RAF) pilots when reporting to their combat units two years earlier.[61] The Americans had proved in the Lafayette Flying Corps that they could become excellent pursuit pilots under Allied command. The question remained whether the United States Army could be as successful in fielding combat aviation units under American command.

Meissner was one of a number of pilots who had completed their training and were awaiting orders in Paris while Atkinson was busy building the 1st Pursuit Organization and Training Center. The young pilots took advantage of

Parisian nightlife. They went to the theaters and casinos, ate dinner at fancy restaurants, and spent late nights at Parisian nightclubs with names like Club Femina Revue and the Follies. Meissner contributed wholeheartedly to the infamous reputation those off-duty aviators earned as they caroused and cavorted about Paris. He met Yvonne, who became a regular companion over the next three weeks: "A fresh young beauty and fun—oh boy." After a week of nights on the town, Meissner was out of money, but that did not deter him: "No money, but we can borrow!" he exclaimed in his diary. He also reported daily at Air Service headquarters in Paris, seeing everyone who could possibly "help us in our exit from Paris to the front." He was not about to wait for the "system" to decide his fate. "It's a case of working out our own solution," he penned.[62]

The nights of partying were sometimes so late that he slept until afternoon. Finally, on 19 February, orders came for Meissner and three others to report to the 1st Pursuit Organization and Training Center at Villeneuve. He bade farewell to Yvonne, picked up a few souvenirs from the local shops and a supply of cigarettes from the commissary, and was off to the front.[63] Jimmy Meissner was finally going to war.

3

Organizational Training

Meissner arrived at Villeneuve on 21 February, about the same time as Eddie Rickenbacker and several other pilots who had recently finished the Cazaux course. These gunnery-school graduates remained in an unattached status because the 95th Squadron already had its full complement of pilots. Airplanes for them had yet to be procured, and so they joined the others in such diversions as playing football or reading, when they were not longingly watching the flight operations of Menard's Escadre 1. Menard's SPADs were constantly taking off and landing and could be seen practicing combats, formations, and aerobatics over the aerodrome. He and Rickenbacker returned to Paris a week later with a detachment of nine officers under Maj. Jean Huffer to augment the nine pilots under Maj. James E. Miller, who had departed the day before to begin bringing the Nieuport 28 pursuit planes to Villeneuve.[1]

The Nieuport 28 was the latest in a series of increasingly sophisticated French pursuit aircraft from one of France's premier aircraft manufacturers. Édouard de Nieuport (originally Nieport) established the Société Anonyme des Établissements Nieuport in 1909 to manufacture airplanes. In 1911 a Nieuport airplane took first place among forty-three other manufacturers in a competition held by the French army and thereby established itself as an important maker of military airplanes.[2] The arms race created by tensions in Europe in

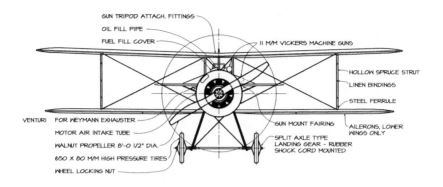

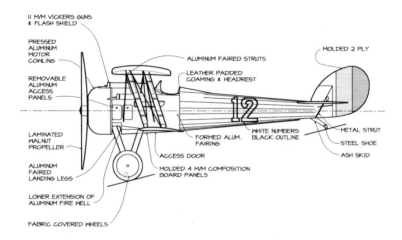

The Nieuport 28

The Nieuport 28's aerodynamic design and clean lines made it one of the most beautiful
*   fighters of the war.*

COURTESY OF CHARLES FRANDSEN ARCHITECTS, P.C.

the years before World War I stimulated the aircraft industry, and this trend
accelerated with the outbreak of war in 1914. By 1915 the warring powers recognized that observation, bombardment, and pursuit had become specialized
roles. By the end of that year an effective fighting machine required speed and
maneuverability as well as a fixed forward-firing machine gun. Nieuport
exploited the requirement for a specialized pursuit airplane and established
itself as one of France's premier manufacturers of fighter aircraft.

The Nieuport 28, a biplane constructed of wood and fabric, continued the "light and maneuverable" theme that characterized the earlier Nieuport fighters. A larger wing area and a more powerful engine improved speed and climbing ability. Depending on the desired trade-offs of speed, altitude, and firepower, the Nieuport 28 carried one or two Vickers machine guns synchronized to fire through the propeller. Moreover, the Nieuport 28's aerodynamic design and clean lines made it one of the most beautiful fighter planes of the war.[3]

The heart of an airplane is its engine. The Nieuport 28 was designed to take advantage of the 160-horsepower, 9-cylinder Gnome Monosoupape (single-valve) rotary engine. In a rotary engine the cylinders and propeller whirl around a stationary crankshaft. Rotary engines were widely used in early aircraft and were a consistent theme of Nieuport designs because of their small weight per horsepower. This resulted from two principal causes. First, the engine was cooled by the spinning of the cylinders in the ambient air. The air-cooled engine eliminated the need for a water pump, water jackets, water pipes, radiator, and the water itself, all of which were necessary in the heavier water-cooled engines such as the SPAD's Hispano-Suiza. Second, the crankcase and crankshaft were much shorter, resulting in a shorter overall engine length, thereby saving additional weight. Because a rotary engine needed no warm-up, the airplane could quickly respond to alerts. Its light weight also made for an extremely short takeoff roll and a rapid rate of climb.[4]

The rotation of the cylinders in the rotary engine also created a gyroscopic effect, which made the airplane more difficult to fly. It had to be flown with hands on the controls at all times, and it tended to climb when turned to the left and dive when turned to the right.[5] Yet a pilot could exploit this tendency in ways that made the Nieuport 28 extremely maneuverable. The simplicity of the engine also made it easy to service and overhaul. All a mechanic had to do was remove the cowling to access the cylinder heads and the rest of the engine. Engine replacement was simplified because of its small size and easy mounting and detaching from a vertical plate at the end of the fuselage. It also had fewer parts than a conventional engine. Because European manufacturers were not generally fabricating engines with interchangeable parts, this provided a significant advantage in maintainability.

The Nieuport 28 and its Gnome rotary engine, however, had several disadvantages. The cylinders had to be machined to exact dimensions to avoid

The 160-horsepower, 9-cylinder Gnome Monosoupape (single-valve) rotary
  engine

The Gnome engine is shown here mounted on a Nieuport 28 under restoration by the
  Smithsonian National Air and Space Museum. The cylinders whirled around a sta-
  tionary crankshaft.

National Air and Space Museum, Nieuport 28 curatorial file

unbalanced centrifugal forces. The heat produced by the rotary engine was of
such intensity that the only lubricant it could use was castor oil. Because it
was impossible to attach an exhaust manifold to the rotary engine, the pilot
ingested a constant vapor spray of castor oil that induced nausea and diar-
rhea. Consumption of fuel and, especially, oil was high. Airspeed could be
controlled only by using a "blip" switch that varied the number of cylinders
firing at a particular time. This feature could cause an engine fire: If the pilot
did not cut off the fuel flow when switching off cylinders, fuel could accumulate inside the cowling and ignite when the engine was switched back on.
The large diameter of the engine impeded forward visibility during takeoff
and landing, requiring the pilot to fishtail while taxiing and sideslip while
descending toward the ground.

Col. Raynal Bolling, portrait painting
The agreements Bolling negotiated largely determined
which airplanes the Americans used in World War I.
National Air and Space Museum,
CD-ROM 2B-02680

Why did the first aviation arm of the American military use French war-planes? When the Bolling mission arrived in France during the summer of 1917 to determine what sort of aircraft the United States should build, they realized that American aviation technology was so far behind that it would be necessary, at least initially, to rely upon their European allies for airplanes. As it turned out, American industry had so much difficulty producing accept-able warplanes that practically all of the AEF's planes came from foreign sources. Expectations for the new fighter, powered by the latest Gnome rotary engine, were high. Bolling believed that the Air Service needed two different types of pursuit planes, one with fixed engines and another with rotary engines. "Both types appear to be essential," he explained in the Report of the Aeronautical Commission he sent to Washington in mid-August. "We hold the opinion that the rotary engine is much less reliable and has much less length of service than the stationary engine; but for certain purposes it appears to be indispensable."[6]

A cable sent to Washington at about the same time provides further clarification of Bolling's reasoning. "One type [of plane has a] fixed engine with great horizontal speed and great diving speed. This is [the] fixed engine SPAD[. The] second type must have high ceiling and ability [to] maneuver [at] great altitudes without losing altitude." The latter, Bolling explained, was the fighter that would be equipped with the new Gnome rotary engine.[7] Bolling apparently envisioned the rotary pursuit plane as a high-altitude fighter. The airplane's design and lightweight would provide superior maneuverability at high altitudes, while heavier airplanes would lose altitude when turning.

Bolling negotiated an agreement with the French, known as the 30 August Agreement, to supply the AEF with airplanes. In the category of pursuit aircraft, the agreement called for supplying the AEF with two thousand fixed- and fifteen hundred rotary-engine fighters. The fixed-engine fighter would be the SPAD 13 with the 200-horsepower (later upgraded to 220) Hispano-Suiza engine. Early production models of the SPAD 13 were already in the field with the French army, but the new rotary-engine fighter was still under development by three of France's leading manufacturers of fighter planes. Bolling's agreement called for delivery of either the new SPAD or the Nieuport rotary-engine fighter, depending on which one would be available.[8]

Air Service plans called for equipping the AEF's first pursuit units with rotary-engine fighters, as indicated by the delivery schedule in Table 3.1. It is also apparent that delivery expectations—both in quantity and speed of delivery—were significantly greater for Nieuports than for SPADs. In other words, the table suggests a high probability that America's first pursuit squadrons would be equipped with the Nieuport. The SPAD rotary-engine fighter never progressed beyond the development stages, and Nieuport's new rotary, designated the Nieuport 28, became the AEF's first fighter, in accordance

Table 3.1

Pursuit Airplane Delivery Schedule

Month	New SPAD (200-hp Hispano-Suiza)	New SPAD (150-hp Gnome)	Nieuport (150-hp Gnome)
November	0	0	0
December	0	0	0
January	0	50	300
February	135	100	400
March	300	200	400
April	400	300	400
May	550	350	0
June	615	500	0
Total	2,000	1,500	1,500

Source: Schedule B, "Agreement of French Government Dated Aug. 20, 1917 to Furnish to the United States Government Certain-Specified Airplanes and Engines," Gorrell's *History of the American Expeditionary Forces Air Service* (Microfilm Publication M990), 1917–19, RG120, National Archives at College Park, series I, vol. 28.

Note: The SPAD with 200-horsepower Hispano-Suiza engine would later become the SPAD 13, the SPAD with 150-horsepower Gnome engine would be designated the SPAD 15, and the Nieuport with 150-horsepower engine would become known as the Nieuport 28. In the event, the Nieuport was chosen over the rotary-engine SPAD.

with the 30 August Agreement. But that was not so clear to AEF officials in January and February 1917.

Initially Atkinson and his staff had been told that they would be equipped with SPADs. Next it was the Nieuport 27. On 9 February the influential French adviser Commandant Paul Armengaud informed Atkinson that he would be issued thirty-six Nieuport 27s-enough for two squadrons. Back in November, Armengaud had proposed equipping the first two pursuit squadrons with Nieuport 27s as part of a larger plan for organizing the AEF's first pursuit, observation, and bombardment squadrons-eleven in all. The French undersecretary for military aeronautics approved the plan and sent it to the AEF. This plan did not consider the Nieuport 28, which was still undergoing testing, because its intent was to speed the organization of American aero squadrons, reflecting the French government's sense of urgency to have at least some American units ready to meet the spring's German offensive.[9]

The Nieuport 27 was a less capable fighter, powered by a 120-horsepower rotary engine, and was still being used on the front by some French units. It was also used as a training aircraft at Issoudun. A few days after hearing that he would receive Nieuport 27s, Atkinson was told that the status of airplanes for his organization was being discussed in Paris. He and Philip Roosevelt traveled to Paris and met with Foulois. Upon arriving they learned that the French had "commandeered" the Nieuport 27s "to fill pressing need elsewhere."[10]

Why was Foulois about to equip his first pursuit squadrons with Nieuport 27s just as the first the Nieuport 28s were coming out of production? In a memo to General Pershing on 14 February he complained about the "Nieuport (Chasse)" planes that the French were about to provide. Foulois objected to equipping his units with such "second class and inferior" aircraft. He noted, as if to soften the blow, that "great numbers are being used by the French, at the present time, for front line service" but cited "military necessity" as his reason for taking them.[11] These "Nieuport (Chasse)" planes must have been Nieuport 27s, because the French Air Service was indeed using substantial numbers of them. Foulois's failure to identify the Nieuports by their appropriate model number also suggests that he simply did not grasp the details on this highly technical issue.

Foulois faced many difficult issues in February, and he did so without the benefit of the person most knowledgeable about airplane procurement, Raynal Bolling. When Foulois sailed for France he brought his own staff. He placed them in the top positions and cast Bolling and Mitchell out of the headquarters to lesser positions. In addition to creating hard feelings, the decapitation of the AEF's Air Service caused a great deal of confusion. At the same time, the Airplane Division, the organization responsible for overseeing procurement, was hampered by personnel shortages and the departure of several key personnel in January and February.[12] Consequently, staff coordination throughout the AEF Air Service was in a miserable state of affairs during this period. Harry Toumlin, who occupied a key position in the logistics organization, later commented that "the Air Force was like a man suffering from that disease where control is lost over members of the body, but the body in its independent parts is perfectly healthy."[13]

Meanwhile, at the 1st Pursuit Organization and Training Center, Atkinson continued to prod Paris for information. On 21 February he learned for the first time that Nieuport 28s might be available. Four days later Captain Du Doré, Commandant Armengaud's assistant on the French Aviation mission and the liaison officer responsible for pursuit aviation, visited Villeneuve and informed Atkinson that five Nieuport 28s were available and "that others would become available at the rate of about four a day until thirty-six are at this station."[14] Things had happened so quickly that Atkinson's immediate superior, Col. Robert O. Van Horn, who had replaced Mitchell as the officer in charge of the Zone of Advance, was also under the mistaken impression that Atkinson's pilots were taking delivery of Nieuport 27s rather than Nieuport 28s when they arrived in Paris at the end of February to begin ferrying aircraft back to Villeneuve.[15]

Capt. Gordon Rankin later recalled,

> Of course all this time the important question of obtaining ships was not forgotten[.] Many trips back to Paris [were made] resulting in locating the only possible ship we could secure, Nieuport 28s, which had been rejected by the British and French. After much discussion, consultation and almost in desperation we took them for our use.[16]

Philip Roosevelt observed that the Nieuport 28s seemed to appear out of nowhere and were accepted only reluctantly. "By this time we had located some type 28 Nieuport planes which all hands figured would be O.K. for work at the front. Anyway, they were better than nothing and we sent some pilots to Paris to get them."[17]

Cold, snowy weather delayed the departure of the Nieuports from Paris until 6 March. Of the fifteen Nieuports that left Paris that day for Villeneuve only six arrived, including planes flown by Meissner and Rickenbacker. The rest had to make forced landings along the way. Three of these were crash landings that "smashed" the aircraft but did not injure the pilots. Astoundingly, many had run out of fuel on this sixty-mile flight. It was "rather bad results for the first time," noted Rickenbacker.[18]

Uncertainty and suspicion surrounded the new rotary-engine fighter, which, like the new American pursuit squadrons, had yet to be tested in combat. When the planes arrived at Villeneuve, the logistics needed to support them, including provision of gas, oil, and special tools, were not yet in place.[19] "It was a fine thing to feel we had some planes," wrote Roosevelt, "but there were still a number of drawbacks. Nineteen of the pilots who had been sent to us had never fired a machine gun in the air." He was referring to the pilots of the 95th Aero Squadron, who had not progressed to the Cazaux course, as had Rickenbacker, Meissner, and the other pilots now arriving at Villeneuve. "This, I suppose made the less difference," Roosevelt continued, "as we had no machineguns on the model 28 Nieuports. No French Vickers guns were available."[20]

Lack of munitions did not prevent Atkinson from beginning training. Joint training with the French began a week later with the receipt of an agreement between Foulois and the French under secretary of aeronautics that established guidelines for the training of the two American pursuit squadrons now at Villeneuve. The plan called for joint patrols, with Menard's Escadre 1, along the Marne River. Because the French were equipped with SPADs and the Americans with Nieuports, the leaders decided to conduct a test patrol to ensure the compatibility of the different aircraft in a single patrol. On 14 March two Nieuport 28s flew with one of Menard's SPAD 7s. The Nieuports not only kept up with the SPAD, they outclimbed it, proving the feasibility of joint patrols.[21]

The next day Maj. Davenport Johnson assumed command of the 95th Aero Squadron, and the unit began its training patrols. Each patrol consisted of three unarmed Nieuports and one or two SPADs. Atkinson and Roosevelt considered these the AEF's first *chasse* patrols, and in a letter home, Richard Blodgett wrote his mother that he had been "the leader of the first American patrol ever to patrol the lines."[22] These joint patrols were under French command, and because the Americans did not yet have machine guns mounted, Atkinson gave strict orders for them not to fly beyond the line of friendly observation balloons. The 95th Squadron flew a total of eight unarmed patrols, two a day beginning on 15 March.[23]

Rickenbacker, for one, was not enthusiastic about the 95th Squadron's unarmed patrols. He wrote in his diary,

The much talked of suicide fleet used by [the] English to fool Germans in [the] North Sea has nothing on the suicide chase squadron which is going over the lines every day, three Americans in Nieuports without machine guns and two Frenchmen with SPADs, this will be good reading matter in years to come.[24]

Rankin later noted that the French pilots accompanying these patrols were initially unaware that the Americans were unarmed and "almost collapsed when finding out this condition."[25] One of the pilots in the 95th Squadron wrote, "Our French comrades threw up their hands in horror at the mere suggestion" of patrolling the lines without guns.

> They waved their arms and rolled their eyes and called upon the "Bon Dieu" to give us wisdom. We pointed out that the strength of the plan lay in its very absurdity. The Germans would never expect such informal tactics, such irreverence for the rules of war. And finally we won their reluctant consent.

"Everything was most irregular," noted Philip Roosevelt.[26]

Such bravado also made a dubious impression on Quentin Roosevelt, the officer in charge of training at Issoudun's finishing field. He described the 95th Squadron's mission as

> decoy work—a most profitless occupation to my mind. They are sent out over the lines escorted by two French planes with machine guns. The object is to get the German to attack them. Then they leave for home in a hurry and let the Frenchmen look after the Boche.

Evidently because of these missions, the 95th Aero Squadron's Nieuports initially sported a duck as their squadron insignia. "The poor souls who have to go across without machine guns have adopted a decoy duck," Roosevelt continued, "with one leg stuck out stiffly in front as if it were doing a goose step. They have got it painted on all their planes."[27]

In spite of the bravado in the fraternity-like atmosphere of the 95th Aero Squadron, not all of its pilots were thrilled with the idea of conducting unarmed patrols. Waldo Heinrichs, who had made his way back into pursuit aviation at Issoudun, had recently been "elected to be flight commander." It was as if the squadron were choosing fraternity officers or picking teams for the daily football game. The election occurred on 12 March, while Lt. Seth Low was still in temporary command of the squadron. Afterward, the new flight commanders took turns choosing the officers and men who would make up their flights. Then they adjourned for a game of football. "We are all men first and then soldiers and officers," wrote Heinrichs.[28]

Heinrichs's flight was tasked with providing three Nieuports for the second of the unarmed missions on 15 March. Heinrichs himself did not fly because he had an earache, "which the doctor said would disturb my sense of balance." After medically disqualifying himself, he accused one of his pilots of cowardice, writing in his diary, "Quick, who was forced on my flight as last choice and whom I always knew was yellow, turned and refused to fly."[29] Blodgett wrote, to his mother,

> We have what we call "kiwi's" here, or the boys who have lost nerve. It comes from the Australian bird of that name that spends it time sitting on the ground, flapping its wings and making a lot of noise. Another name for these hot-air heroes is "barracks flyer."[30]

Atkinson and his staff had their hands full as activity accelerated. The arrival of the squadrons and airplanes also brought an increasing number of visiting officials from higher headquarters. Official correspondence began to appear from higher headquarters demanding information about activities at the newly operational pursuit center. Henri Pétain, chief of the French army, also visited the center and looked over the American fliers, indicating the high level of French army interest in the development of American combat aviation.

The increasing level of official activity was punctuated by the unpredictable incidents that always seem to be magnified when bringing people and equipment together in new organizations. Murphy's Law was alive and well at Villeneuve. An observation plane landing at the field at dusk on 14 March crashed into the roof of the 94th Aero Squadron barracks. Fortunately, the pilot merely suffered some cuts on his face and was the only person injured. Mud was also a problem at the American cantonment area because the streets had not yet been paved with stone. Heavy vehicular traffic churned up the street to such a degree that four trucks had to be stationed at strategic positions in the barracks area to act as recovery vehicles. There were also frictions between the squadrons and the staff at Atkinson's headquarters. Flight commanders of the 95th Squadron refused to authorize flights one day because of a dispute between the squadron and training-center supply chief Rankin over parts requisitions. And then there was the enemy. German planes periodically bombed the nearby town of Epernay at night, causing air raids in which the men at Villeneuve scrambled for nearby trenches that had been dug to provide cover. The base was on a high level of alert because papers found on a captured German aviator indicated that just before the great German offensive was launched, the Villeneuve aerodrome would be bombed completely.[31]

Once the Nieuports began to arrive, finding machine guns was Atkinson's top priority. This problem was complicated by the discovery that American ammunition, which was three millimeters (about a tenth of an inch) longer than that of the French or British, was too large to fit in the factory-supplied ammunition boxes. Roosevelt described their efforts to acquire machine guns and supplies:

Either Atkinson or one of his staff used to go to G.H.Q., or Paris about once a week to try to make life disagreeable for our superiors. But we got very little out of it. We certainly did not get any guns, though Lufbery had blarneyed the French who were on the field with us into letting him have a couple personally for his own ship. One morning we got a telegram from the Chief of Air Service because on one of these roving trips to Paris trying to get machine guns and failing someone had found a hidden cache of 18 wristwatches & 25 fountain pens and had promptly requisitioned them and gone off with them in his car. In a fifty word telegram the Chief of Air Service wanted to know why we had seen fit to put in an emergency requisition and why we hadn't sent it through channels.[32]

Roosevelt continued that they had done it that way because, "We did not know what [the appropriate] 'channels' were ... because we had no idea who or where our next superior officer was located." The confusing channels of authority in the AEF's Air Service, exacerbated by constant reorganizations and the jealousies among its senior commanders, continued to have a negative effect on the 1st Pursuit Organization and Training Center. According to Roosevelt, the pursuit center was receiving orders from four different general headquarters: at Chaumont, Tours, Colombey-les-Belles, and Paris.[33]

One of the senior Air Service officials tasking Atkinson for information was Col. Joseph E. Carberry, the AEF Air Service chief of training. Carberry, an insider, was now in charge of all aviation training centers in the AEF, including those at Issoudun and Tours. Atkinson's letter to Carberry, written the day after 1st Pursuit Organization and Training Center initiated regular joint patrols with the French, provides an appraisal of the situation from Atkinson's perspective.

Atkinson first explained his mission.

The purpose of this Center, as I interpret it, is to form pursuit squadrons from completely trained personnel, both commissioned and enlisted, and to coordinate and adjust them to their equipment. At the same time, with the aid of the French here, to break the pilots in over the front.

He also informed Carberry of the joint patrols with the French but did not include the fact that his Nieuports were unarmed. "I am at present maintaining barrage patrols between Epernay and Chalons, with the object of keeping out Photo. Machines [reconnaissance planes]. One or two French machines and three American constitute the patrols." Atkinson explained that his intent was "to gradually work the pilots up to and over" the enemy lines. He added that he had seventeen Nieuport 28s and expected to have a total of thirty-six at the center in the next ten days. He briefly mentioned the performance of the Nieuport 28, observing that "they keep up with the 180 SPAD [SPAD 7] as high up as we have tried them (5,000 M)."[34]

Atkinson stated that he thought he could complete the organization and break-in period faster than the six weeks that had originally been planned. Once "the system gets to working they can get out of here in three weeks," he said, but he was not sure how long it would be before he achieved that degree of efficiency.

> The greatest troubles I have are due to a lack of knowledge on the part of both officers and men of the handling of property, paper work and administration in general. If they were going to stay here the rest of their lives where I could nurse them it wouldn't be so vital, but they have got to be made independent.

Another concern was the development of future leaders. Atkinson noted that nonflying officers were being assigned to aero squadron administrative and logistical staff positions. This practice would prevent flying officers from getting the necessary staff experience they would need to become effective squadron commanders in the future. "Where are our squadron commanders coming from? I do not think there should be a non-flying officer in the Z. of A., except at depots," he declared.

Atkinson's most emphatic message concerned requirements for the training of pursuit pilots before they were sent forward to his center. "No pilot should be ordered into the Z. of A. until he has had as complete an aerial gunnery course as possible. I am wrecking a squadron now to send them to

Cazaux (19 pilots). . . . They have no business here until they have had aerial gunnery." He addressed other training as well. "Your course in advance flying cannot be overdone. A pilot cannot have too much of it if he is intelligently criticized." Finally, he informed Carberry that he had instituted the same training program that Menard had adopted for his Escadre.

As this correspondence indicates, the 95th Aero Squadron with its unarmed Nieuports did indeed have an operational mission: to maintain a "barrage" along the front between Chalons and Epernay. The American reader is usually familiar with term "artillery barrage," but a barrage in the air may require some explanation. In French, the term *barrage* means a cordon or barricade. A barrage conducted in the air was essentially a defensive patrol to prevent enemy aircraft from penetrating friendly airspace. The official history, written shortly after the war, stated that these patrols flew against enemy long-distance photographic airplanes and that the moral effect of their presence "was in all probability sufficient to insure the retreat of an isolated enemy photographic airplane."[35] Thus the risk involved in the unarmed patrols was not too great and provided valuable experience, Atkinson must have reasoned, as long as his patrols did not cross over the lines. Some of the most audacious of the 95th Aero Squadron's pilots apparently disregarded this restriction. Heinrichs complained in his diary about having to gather detailed information about each patrol because headquarters was trying to determine "the man or men who were reported to have been seen beyond lines in German territory."[36]

Atkinson was intent on continuing with the 95th Squadron's training program even though he had decided as early as 6 March (three days before Miller's death) to send its pilots to the aerial gunnery school Cazuax. Why, then, did Atkinson persist with these unarmed patrols if he knew the 95th Aero would soon be departing for Cazaux? The sense of urgency that he had announced to his staff when they first arrived in Villeneuve probably continued to press him forward. In addition to heralding the overdue arrival of American air power at the front, the squadron's training operation also helped Atkinson validate his concept of organizational training. Lessons learned could be applied to the 94th Aero Squadron, which would soon begin its own training program. It was hoped that the organization and center could be turning out combat-ready pursuit squadrons every three weeks, avoiding a bottleneck at the end of the pursuit-squadron production system.

"A very heavy gloom" began to settle across the 95th Squadron as they heard rumors that they were to be sent to Cazaux, and when it became certain, the news came as a "terrible blow." "Boneheaded U.S. Army as usual," penned Heinrichs, "Blunders, blunders, blunders. It means that we will never rejoin the first Chasse group and lose all chance of being flight [commanders] or the first ones over the lines. It has so affected us that we not only hate but despise our commanding & superior officers."[37] Harold Buckley wrote,

> Our hearts were broken. Assurances and promises that soon we would be back left us unmoved and cold as ice. There was no comfort anywhere and there was never a sadder or more disheartened crowd than we when the day of parting came. We climbed into the old Fiat truck, gazed forlornly for the last time on the scene of our lost happiness, and rumbled mournfully down the road.[38]

The departure of the 95th Squadron's pilots for Cazaux on 25 March provided Meissner, Rickenbacker, and the men of the 94th Aero Squadron the opportunity to seize primacy in the history of American combat aviation.

Fortune had indeed smiled on the 94th Squadron. Douglas Campbell and four other recent graduates of the Cazaux course joined the squadron shortly before it departed Issoudun for the front. Beside these Cazaux graduates were six pilots who had been members of the Lafayette Flying Corps and were gunnery-course graduates. Although four of them had no frontline experience, two of these Lafayette flyers had served at the front with French pursuit squadrons. William Loomis had flown with a French fighter squadron from 23 November 1917 to 19 February 1918, and Alan F. Winslow had been with one from 24 December 1917 to 12 February 1918.[39]

Like the 95th Squadron, the 94th Aero arrived with a nonflyer in command. Atkinson transferred Capt. Henry L. Lyster to the 1st Pursuit Organization and Training Center headquarters, where he eventually replaced Roosevelt as adjutant, and Maj. Jean Huffer assumed command of the 94th Aero Squadron on 7 March. Huffer was an experienced veteran of the Lafayette Flying Corps, having been a frontline pilot since April 1916. He had served in three different escadrilles, including both combat and reconnaissance units on the western front and in Italy. He had been credited with three victories. Because of his distinguished service, he had risen to the rank of *sous-lieutenant* (second lieutenant)—a significant accomplishment in the French Air Service, most of whose pilots were not officers.[40]

Huffer was one of the few Lafayette flyers who had attained the rank of major in the AEF Air Service. The son of a tobacco merchant from Virginia and a French woman, he had been born and raised in Paris. He was widely traveled and well educated, and he spoke French fluently. He would become a well-respected and popular commander in the 94th Aero Squadron, and though he ran afoul of the insiders, he ultimately became one of the Air Service's pursuit group commanders.[41] According to the unit's official history, "The early successes of the 94th Squadron were largely due to his leadership."[42]

Atkinson rounded out the squadron's complement of officers by assigning six unattached officers, including Jimmy Meissner and Eddie Rickenbacker. By 22 March the 94th Aero Squadron had eight of its Nieuports on hand. Lufbery had returned by this time and had become the 1st Pursuit Organization and Training Center's chief of training. Testing the unit's pilots on 27 March on their aerobatics, the ace was especially impressed with Rickenbacker and Campbell. After dinner that night, he told them that they would accompany him in a patrol over the lines in the morning. The next day, 28 March, Lufbery led a patrol consisting of himself, Rickenbacker, and Campbell-the first official American-led armed patrol over enemy lines.[43]

The Nieuport 28 was supposed to carry two machine guns, but because of the armaments shortage Campbell and Rickenbacker each mounted only one. Lufbery had scrounged two from his sources. An antiaircraft shell explosion slightly damaged Rickenbacker's airplane during the patrol, providing physical evidence that the patrol had crossed into enemy airspace.[44] Campbell's letter home that day gives a concise summary of the patrol, including the technique of combat flying in which pilots made continual S-turns so that they could observe in all directions. He also noted the difficulty inexperienced pilots initially had seeing other planes in the air:

> Major Lufbery led, with Rick and myself above and behind him on the right and left respectively. With these fast and powerful little machines it didn't take us long to reach the lines at an altitude of 4,000 meters. Then we turned to the left and patrolled up and down two times on a front of about 30 kilometers. Our planes were scarcely ever flying in a straight line; we were continually banking and turning from one side to the other, in order to see at all angles and to make it harder for the anti-aircraft battery which shot at us occasionally. The sector was so calm

it was almost dead. I could see no artillery activity at all; merely two intricate systems of trenches with a pockmarked area of variable width between them. I didn't spend much time looking at the ground, but now and then I would glance at a spot where a few marks on the ground indicated the site of a village blown to atoms. The Major saw one Boche flying very low, but my untrained eyes didn't even observe that. Once I saw two black specks out of the corner of my eye, and glanced back quickly, thinking they were planes; but they widened out into large clouds of black smoke, and I knew that they were only two A.A. shells which had exploded about 600 meters away from me. I'm sorry we didn't see any Boches, but I guess we will next time, and anyway it is something to have been one of the first two American-trained chasse pilots over the lines.[45]

Lufbery led only one additional 94th Squadron patrol from Villeneuve. The long-anticipated German offensive began on 21 March, and the initial German success caused the French army to rush all available forces to the north. Atkinson received orders on 30 March to move the 1st Pursuit Organization and Training Center to a new base at Epiez because plans called for bombers to be stationed at Villeneuve, leaving no room for the Americans. The move brought Atkinson into closer communication with his immediate superior, Colonel Van Horn, whose staff was in the process of formulating a training doctrine to govern the organization and training centers.

As the assistant chief of Air Service, Zone of Advance, Van Horn was responsible for all of the various organization and training centers. Whereas Atkinson oversaw pursuit units at Villeneuve, a center at Amanty was responsible for observation squadrons and one at Chermisey for bombardment squadrons. Van Horn's responsibilities included equipping, coordinating supply, allocating flying personnel, supervising the training of units, and deciding when the units were ready for frontline duty.[46] He established the Advanced Section headquarters at Colombey-les-Belles on 21 February. By March he had three aero squadrons in the final phases of receiving equipment and preparing for operations on the front: the veteran 1st Aero Squadron of the Mexican punitive expedition, one of three observation squadrons located at the observation training and organization center at Amanty; and the 94th and 95th Aero Squadrons at the 1st Pursuit Organization and Training Center at Villeneuve.[47]

Van Horn directed his headquarters to formulate detailed plans for pursuit, observation, and bombardment organization and training in the Zone of Advance. Additional squadrons would be added to each training center as rapidly as the Services of Supply could furnish trained personnel and material. As squadrons became available they would be organized into groups whose location would be determined by the Airdrome Site Board, which was in the process of selecting them. Van Horn explained that the number of squadrons that would go to the front as a group might vary. The goal was "to get the first groups to the line as soon as possible, even if they contain fewer squadrons." He directed Capt. Walter Lovell to develop plans for "Pursuit Organizational Training" and to do so "in conference with Major Atkinson and the French (liaison) Mission."[48]

The AEF Air Service staff suffered greatly from its lack of combat experience, but Captain Lovell was an exception to the rule. A former member of the Lafayette Escadrille, he had often flown as part of a special patrol under Raoul Lufbery. He advanced to flight leader with the rank of adjutant (warrant officer) in the unit. The French Air Service attached him to the AEF Air Service headquarters at Chaumont in October 1917, where he conducted a study of various allied squadrons on the western front. Lovell was overage for flight duty, by American standards, and had poor color vision, but this was probably not the reason he was kept on the staff. Physical standards were being routinely waived for Americans with combat experience. Lovell had graduated from Harvard in 1907 and had been in the brokerage business before sailing for France in 1914. The combination of his combat experience, education, and maturity made him indispensable. He was commissioned as a captain in January 1918 and assigned to Van Horn's staff as the pursuit expert.[49]

Lovell traveled from Colombey-les-Belles to Villeneuve on 26 March to collaborate with Atkinson on the formulation of a concept for pursuit organization training.[50] This planning effort forced Atkinson to analyze his mission and articulate in writing the essential tasks, recommendations, and concept of operations of the 1st Pursuit Organization and Training Center. He submitted his plan to Van Horn in a memorandum entitled "Organizational Training for Pursuit Units."

Atkinson's letter began with the statement, "Organizational training of pursuit units is the coordination of both commissioned and enlisted personnel with their equipment." The training included "the institution of administrative systems" required for normal unit functioning. For pilots, organizational training provided "the bridge between instruction flying and actual operations in liaison with other branches of aviation and with line troops." Atkinson stated that he expected to receive fully trained pursuit pilots, adding for emphasis, "Training that can be done elsewhere should not be done in the Zone of Advance." He specifically noted that pilots who reported to an organization center should have completed basic and advanced flight courses, including aerial gunnery. He obviously had in mind the pilots of the 95th Squadron, whom he had recently sent back to school.[51]

Based on the assumption that pilots should be assigned to the center only after they had completed the full panoply of training courses, Atkinson thought the length of organizational training should be determined mainly by logistical and administrative requirements. "The time required for organizational training is fixed by coordination with equipment and the institution of administrative systems rather than by the work of the pilots." In Atkinson's view, "A properly trained pilot should be qualified for work over the lines in two weeks of average weather" after reporting to an organization center.

In contrast, he did not think the logistic and administrative tasks could be concluded as quickly. "The personnel cannot become properly organized ... in that time." Several times in the body of the text Atkinson used the term "organization center" instead of "organization and training center"-further indicating his emphasis on logistical and administrative tasks. "A pursuit organization center should be the receiving station for initial equipment, viz; planes, tools, spares, armament, transportation, etc., and of commissioned and enlisted personnel; and its function should be the forming of these into squadrons." Atkinson thought flight training was "a secondary consideration from a standpoint of time." Pilots "should be assigned the machines they are to use in actual service and should be given practically a free hand in their care, equipment and use." He thought they should be encouraged to practice combat, aerobatics, and formation flying under the tutelage of their squadron commanders.

Atkinson made an important recommendation that could only occur through the offices of the Zone of Advance, which was responsible for assigning pilots to the squadrons: "Two or three experienced officers, drawn from squadrons already at the front should be assigned to each new squadron ... as instructors for the new pilots in work over the lines." The obvious implication here, because there were no American squadrons operational along the front, was that these would be Americans who had been flying with Allied pursuit units such as the Lafayette Escadrille and Flying Corps.

These experienced pilots, Atkinson recommended, should lead the new-comers on their first patrols. "The most satisfactory method is to send two new pilots with an experienced one, the experienced one in the lead, the new pilots being instructed not to engage in combat unless attacked." Once the patrol had returned, its members would compare their observations. A typical outcome, Atkinson predicted, would be that the experienced pilot might report seeing four SPADs and one enemy airplane while the new pilots had seen nothing. Atkinson concluded that all pursuit squadrons, whether at an organization center or at the front, should have access to an air range properly equipped with towing machines and air targets to use in practicing their gunnery skills.

Aviation staff officers at the Zone of Advance headquarters scrutinized Atkinson's memorandum. Van Horn was a nonflying officer, but to his credit, he had a highly qualified group review Atkinson's analysis of his mission. They were Maj. Millard F. Harmon and Capts. Walter Lovell and Du Doré. Harmon, a 1912 graduate of West Point, had been an aviator on the Mexican punitive expedition. He had recently been on temporary duty with French pursuit squadrons to gain flying experience and had been part of the ill-fated patrol on which Capt. James Miller had lost his life.[52] Because of the recent tragedy involving Miller, Harmon would have been especially sensitive about the final stages of pilot preparation. Du Doré, of the French Air Service, was an experienced pursuit squadron commander, having commanded Escadrille de Chasse 95 until October 1917. Since then he had been Armengaud's fighter expert on the French mission to the AEF Air Service.[53]

These staff officers, focusing on Atkinson's relative neglect of the flying part of the mission, modified his mission analysis with marginal notes. They deleted entirely Atkinson's statement that flying was a secondary considera-tion from the standpoint of time. They also qualified Atkinson's notion that pilots assigned to his center would already be fully trained by adding, "Sufficient practice should be given all pilots to verify the completeness of training in all respects. Should a lack of training appear, advantage should be taken of the organizational training period to complete all the required instruction to fit pilots for service at the front." Significantly, they also increased the scope of the mission beyond the formation of squadrons, which was the largest organization that Atkinson had considered. They added that the center's function included organization of an entire pursuit group con-sisting of multiple squadrons.[54]

They also added additional details to Atkinson's concept of introducing pilots to flights over the front. "It is desirable to have the pursuit organizational training center at a distance of 40 to 60 kilometers from the front lines," they wrote. This distance suggests they thought it important to provide plenty of relatively safe airspace well behind the front lines for training flights. The guidelines also suggest that they believed a "pursuit organization and training center" would be a permanent feature of the Air Service in France, one whose location would be adjusted according to the location of the front lines and the sector assigned to the American Army.

The staff officers approved of Atkinson's concept of training using the three-plane patrol led by an experienced pilot but also qualified it, noting that "patrols of two new pilots with one experienced pilot" should be sent "to the vicinity of the line, gradually working closer and closer." Where Atkinson had stated that pilots should practice group (formation) flying, the reviewers added, "Enough group flying should be done to get the pilots accustomed to one another." Such a qualification would have the effect of establishing a flight-training criterion that could determine whether a unit was ready for operations on the front, instead of simply identifying required administrative and logistical tasks.

Finally, they added an organizational task: "Permanent flights should be formed with their flight commanders and deputy commanders." This had been implied in Atkinson's mission analysis as part of the process of forming the men and equipment into squadrons because flight sections and commanders were specified in the tables of organization for a pursuit squadron. Nonetheless, the inclusion of this "flight" organizational task again reflects the staff officers' emphasis on the aviation mission.

Atkinson tended to see warfare in terms of administrative discipline, organization, and logistics. He was primarily a system builder. In contrast, Van Horn's reviewers were more sensitive to the complexities of aerial combat. They had a better understanding of the difficulties that had to be overcome in the task of transforming a group of student aviators into a fighting unit.

Another important point concerns the nature of Atkinson's organization itself. The letterhead of Atkinson's memorandum boldly proclaimed "1st Pursuit Group," not "1st Pursuit Organization and Training Center." According to Philip Roosevelt, "From the beginning Jan. 16, we regarded ourselves as the 1st Pursuit Group. We ran two files of orders. One dealt with camp restrictions, etc., the other with personnel. The 1st Pursuit Organization & Training Center

Orders covered orders applicable only to Villeneuve-les-Vertus, the 1st Pursuit Group orders covered regulations which we expected to continue in force in case and when we moved." In Roosevelt's and Atkinson's minds, the facilities at Villeneuve were the training center, not Atkinson and his staff. Van Horn's reviewers disagreed, glaringly scratching out the heading, "1st Pursuit Group."[55]

This disagreement about the fundamental nature of Atkinson's organization helps explain why the 95th Squadron arrived at Villeneuve with pilots who had not completed gunnery training. Quentin Roosevelt had pleaded to be allowed to join the 95th Aero before it left Issoudun. His boss, Lt. Col. W. G. Kilner, refused, and Roosevelt put up a tremendous fuss. Kilner then told Roosevelt,

> That squadron that is going out is merely a political move,-sent so we can say we have a squadron at the front. They haven't even got machines for them yet,—or any sort of an organization to allow for breakage and spare parts. . . . They will probably form not the first squadron, but the finishing school staff of the zone of advance.

He ended by telling Roosevelt that he would send him out later "in a real squadron."[56]

Thus the commander of Issoudun, who was responsible for all pursuit-pilot training, considered the 1st Pursuit Organization and Training Center as a sort of finishing school in the Zone of Advance. In his mind, the 95th Aero Squadron was destined to provide the personnel and equipment to support that center, just as various other aero squadrons had been used to form all of the training centers in the AEF. It was the 1st (Reserve) Aero Squadron all over again. Kilner's words are the clearest evidence that confusion reigned in the upper echelons of the AEF's Air Service about the mission of the Pursuit Organization and Training Center and the creation of American pursuit forces.

Carl von Clausewitz has written that war provides "the play of chance and probability within which the creative spirit is free to roam."[57] The chaotic organizational environment of the AEF's Air Service provided such dedicated opportunists as Atkinson and Philip Roosevelt the ideal setting in which to achieve their goals. The 1st Pursuit Organization and Training Center would be no finishing school if they had anything to say about it.

4

First Victories

The long-anticipated German offensive began on 21 March and gained ground at a rate that had not been seen on the western front since 1914. Within a week, the Germans penetrated forty miles to the outskirts of Amiens. The western Allies suddenly found themselves "fighting with their backs to the wall." As the historian B. H. Liddell Hart has observed, "These weeks ranked with those of the Marne in 1914 as the two gravest military crises of the World War."[1] The offensive's main effort exploited the boundary between the British and French armies, and German infantry used new "storm" or infiltration tactics in which small units equipped with automatic weapons bypassed strong points and attacked rear areas. As the defense disintegrated, British staff officers lost track of the location of the front lines. Col. Raynal Bolling, who was inspecting American air units training with the British, unwittingly entered one of these zones and was killed in a gun battle with German soldiers.[2]

By concentrating their air forces, the Germans were able to achieve initial air superiority over the battle area. German air battle units, or *Schlachstaffeln*, which were specially organized and equipped for ground attack, used machine guns and grenades to attack Allied troops. Some of these units were equipped with all-metal Junkers battle planes specifically designed for engaging ground troops. German fighters, such as Manfred von Richthofen's Jagdgeschwader (Fighter Wing) 1, provided air cover. The Red Baron himself, flying a highly maneuverable red Fokker triplane, scored eight kills between 24 and 28 March, increasing his victory count to seventy-four. Most of the German air victories were against the Royal Flying Corps, which received the brunt of the German attack. Air battles of unprecedented size took place, such as the dogfight over Rosieres, where thirty German and twenty-seven British fighters engaged in a swirling melee for more than an hour.

Menard's Escadre 1 departed Villeneuve to join the battle on 27 March. They received their orders at five o'clock in the afternoon. The Americans assisted the French, for a change, as Atkinson dedicated his trucks to helping Menard move equipment to the railway. At three o'clock the next afternoon Menard led a single formation of sixty-one SPADs in an attack against the German infantry. Such attacks helped to slow the impetus of the German offensive enough to allow for the arrival of reinforcements, causing Gen. Erich von Ludendorff to suspend the first phase of the offensive on 4 April. Philip Roosevelt, who monitored these events, wrote to his father, "We can do it from the air, I know." Allied deployments to counter the offensive called for the stationing of night bombardment units at Villeneuve, and so the 1st Pursuit Organization and Training Center had to leave.[3]

At 11:30 A.M. on 30 March 1918 Atkinson received a telegram from Van Horn's headquarters, directing him to move his operation to Epiez. This move brought Atkinson's unit into the Toul sector, where Pershing was assembling an American field army. The orders called for immediate movement and triggered a flurry of excited activity as men loaded equipment, tools, spare parts, and personal gear onto trucks. Truck convoys of both squadrons and the headquarters departed Villeneuve at 11:00 A.M. on 31 March—less than twenty-four hours after receiving the order to move. Pilots were supposed to take off that afternoon, but during the rushed decampment an unfortunate incident postponed their departure.[4]

While the straw used for the men's bedding was being burned, a spark ignited one of the canvas hangars, which contained twelve of the 94th Aero Squadron's airplanes. Cries of "Fire!" alerted everyone. Douglas Campbell was one of those who rushed into the burning hangar to save the planes. Pieces of flaming canvas from the roof fell about them as they pushed their precious Nieuports out of the burning hangar. Two of the Nieuports were completely destroyed. Seven more were damaged, with holes burned in the wings. Fortunately, only one man was injured. Departure was delayed until repairs could be made to the damaged aircraft.[5]

The morning of 2 April was cloudy and windy, but by late afternoon conditions had improved enough for the American aviators to make the eighty-mile flight to Epiez. The new aerodrome was "a tiny field that had been scraped out of some woods" on a hill in the rainy and foggy valley of the Meuse.[6] Of the twenty airplanes that took off from Villeneuve, nineteen arrived in good condition. One of the Nieuports somersaulted after landing in the airfield's soft ground. Rickenbacker described how he and the pilots "walked out to the wreck to secure the remains of the raw pilot who hadn't learned yet how to land a machine." Some made "rather caustic comments" about the skill level of the new aviators who had arrived. "Imagine our stupefaction," Rickenbacker continued,

> when we discovered the grinning face of Captain Hall himself looking at us upside down! Fortunately he wasn't hurt in the slightest, and I think he would be glad if he could know how much good it did all of us young pilots to discover that even the best airmen can sometimes come a cropper.[7]

Capt. James Norman Hall was one of the three veteran pilots of the Lafayette Escadrille transferred from the 103d Aero Squadron to the 1st Pursuit Organization and Training Center immediately before departure from Villeneuve. The reassignment resulted from the collaboration between Atkinson and Captain Lovell during their analysis of organizational training. As Lovell also served as Van Horn's chief of pilot assignments, the reassignment was a simple matter for him to arrange. Atkinson traded three of his green pilots (Lts. Seth Low, Hobey Baker, and Edgar Tobin) to the 103d Aero at nearby La Noblette Farm in exchange for three combat veterans. Accompanying Hall to Atkinson's unit were Capts. Kenneth Marr and David McKelvey Peterson.[8]

Captain Hall had scored his second and third victories just days before the transfer.[9] James Norman Hall is best remembered for such literary classics as *Mutiny on the Bounty* (1936) and *Botany Bay* (1941), which he wrote in Tahiti after the war had ended. Indeed, it was the publication of his first book,

Kitchener's Mob (1916), based on his experiences with the British army in 1915, that brought him to the attention of the Lafayette Escadrille. Its organizers realized the propaganda potential of having an author like him in the unit. After joining the French Foreign Legion and attending flight school, Hall became a member of the famous squadron in June 1917. Within two weeks he was wounded. During his convalescence, he wrote *High Adventure,* an exciting tale of his experiences in the French Air Service that inspired others to become fighter pilots. By October 1917 he was back in the air with the Lafayette Escadrille.[10]

Capt. David McK. Peterson joined the Lafayette Escadrille the same day as Hall. The son of a medical doctor, he had earned his degree in chemical engineering in 1915 from Lehigh University and had briefly worked at the Curtiss aviation plant in Buffalo, New York, before embarking for France in 1916. Peterson was known among his Lafayette companions for his excellent air vision—he was often the first to spot enemy aircraft. By the time he left the unit, he had led more patrols than any other pilot in the squadron and had one victory to his credit.[11]

Capt. Kenneth Marr, who was living in Nome, Alaska, when the war broke out, had contracted with the French government to deliver malamute dogs to assist in evacuating casualties from the snow-covered Vosges Mountains. After delivering the dogs, Marr enlisted in the American Ambulance Service and, like many others who had first volunteered in this capacity, eventually made his way into the Foreign Legion and aviation. Of the three flyers, Marr had been with the Lafayette Escadrille the longest, since March 1917, and had credit for one victory.[12] On being commissioned into the United States Army these three pilots were awarded the rank of captain, indicating the Army's assessment of them as potential flight commanders. "We had all heard of these boys and idolized them before we had seen them," wrote Rickenbacker. "I cannot adequately describe the inspiration we all received from the coming of these two veteran air fighters to our camp."[13]

The arrival of the Lafayette veterans inspired Rickenbacker to transfer out of the 94th Aero and into the 103d Squadron as a fourth green pilot offered in the trade. After arriving at Epiez he returned to Villeneuve to pick up one of the Nieuports that had been left behind; the 95th Squadron's pilots having gone to Cazaux, there were not enough pilots left to fly all the planes. Accompanying Rickenbacker were the three lieutenants being transferred to

Capts. James Norman Hall, left, and Kenneth Marr, right

Hall and Marr were two of the Lafayette Escadrille veterans who became flight commanders in the 94th Aero Squadron.

the 103d Squadron. Rickenbacker first delivered them to Noblette Farm, where he learned that the unit would still be short a pilot because one of its officers had recently been killed in action. Once he had landed back at Epiez, he had "a long talk" with Lovell, who was still collaborating with Atkinson on the organizational training program. Rickenbacker thought he had succeeded in getting Lovell's approval for transfer "at once."[14]

The next day the commander of the 103d Squadron, Maj. William Thaw, visited Epiez, probably intent on making up his pilot shortage. Thaw tantalized Rickenbacker by letting him know that he still had a SPAD without a pilot. Rickenbacker hoped it would be his, but Huffer nixed the transfer because he did not want to lose him. Shortly after taking command of the squadron he had put Rickenbacker in charge of Flight 1 while also appointing him adjutant and second in command of the squadron.[15]

Rickenbacker could have had several possible motives for wanting to join the 103d Aero Squadron. The squadron was already active on the front with Groupe de Combat 21, and the Americans in it were already winning victories. The prospect of flying the 103d Aero Squadron's rugged SPADs instead of the Nieuport 28 also appealed to him.[16] Rickenbacker's scheming to leave the 94th Aero Squadron also suggests a lack of unit cohesion in the 94th Squadron and his feeling about his own place in its social hierarchy.

As the aviation historian Lee Kennett has observed, the number of victories won by a pilot determined the social hierarchy among the pilots in fighter squadrons.[17] Owing to their lack of combat experience, however, the men of the 94th Aero Squadron had not yet adopted such norms. There was a social hierarchy in the unit, but it had less to do with a pilot's contribution to the mission than with his class and educational background. Rickenbacker, with a seventh-grade education and working-class origins, was at the bottom of this hierarchy. It was a difficult situation for him to accept, especially given his highly competitive nature and his previous status as a famous race-car driver.

Reed Chambers, recalling the atmosphere of the 94th Squadron in those days, noted that "Rickenbacker and I were still ostracized" during the spring of 1918. In fact, anybody who associated with Rickenbacker was considered a lowlife. As a result, "Rick wasn't—I would say—fully accepted by the gang in our own squadron, until after he got about his 5th victory."[18] Chambers's socioeconomic background was similar to Rickenbacker's. This commonality supported their pairing.

Reed Chambers had grown up on a farm in Kansas. He was thrown out of high school in his junior year for getting into a fight with a teacher. For the next several years he made a living trapping, working on farms, and finally, because of his mechanical inclination, as a chauffeur for a real estate company, where he also proved to be an adept salesman. His sales and chauffeuring experience helped him land a job in Memphis, Tennessee, as a salesman for the Willys Overland Company (later renowned as the maker of the World War II Jeep). As a member of the Tennessee National Guard, he was called to active duty during 1916 and served on the Mexican border in Texas, where he quickly worked his way up to the rank of regimental sergeant major. Attempting to become a pilot, he passed the screening test at Fort Sam Houston but was refused because Congress had not appropriated any money for the National Guard pilot program. He returned to Memphis and used his connections to land a spot as an aviator in the Signal Corps, eventually becoming a flight instructor at Rantoul, Illinois. He was ordered to France and arrived at Issoudun for pursuit training in time to become one of the original pilots of the 94th Aero Squadron.[19]

Leroy Prinz, another officer who joined the 94th Aero Squadron in June, suffered the same discrimination. Prinz was also a high school dropout who had run away from home. He made his way to France before the war as a cabin boy, jumped ship, and entered the country without a visa. He was a talented dancer and harmonica player and used these skills to help parlay his way into a position at a Paris nightclub, where he taught nude dance routines to young women. He later fled Paris with the police on his heels and joined the Foreign Legion but remained in it for only a short time, making his way back to the United States after war broke out in Europe. When the United States declared war he finagled his way into aviation. He became a popular member of the squadron because of his ability to find women and organize a good party. Yet, as he remembered, "If it would be a nice [social] event I would be left out. . . . I didn't realize until suddenly I found these guys were all college men. They were all fraternity men. They were all clubmen. They had grip handshakes, you know what I mean?"[20]

Since ancient times, military organizations have adopted symbols to help forge a common identity, and squadron insignia had become customary among aviation units during the war. For the 94th Squadron, Huffer, before leaving for Villeneuve, suggested his personal insignia during his time in the Lafayette Flying Corps: Uncle Sam's stovepipe hat with a Stars-and-Stripes hatband. When the unit was ordered to the front, the squadron's surgeon, Capt. Paul H. Walters, commented, "Well I guess our hat is in the ring now." The symbolism of throwing a hat into the ring as a willingness to fight seemed a perfect herald for America's entry into the war in the air.

Lt. John Wentworth, an apprentice architect in Pittsburgh before the war, drew the design. The squadron's Nieuport 28s began to display this insignia on their fuselage while they were at Epiez. It became the most famous unit

Lt. Douglas Campbell, April 1918

Campbell, who became the Air Service's first ace, stands next to a recently painted hat-in-the-ring insignia on Lt. John Wentworth's Nieuport 28.

National Air and Space Museum, CD-ROM 2A-46986

insignia in U.S. aviation history, and the 94th became known as the Hat-in-the-Ring Squadron. As the historian James J. Cooke has observed, ground forces were not permitted to have insignia until after the Armistice because of operational security considerations. The Air Service squadron insignia were the only unit insignia allowed by Pershing because he recognized the critical need to identify friendly aircraft in the air.[21]

Each of the 94th's pilots also applied distinctive paint schemes on the engine cowlings of their airplanes. Meissner's cowling, for example, sported a red-and-silver zigzag design resembling lightning bolts.[22] Meissner and Rickenbacker also adorned their wings with a war-bond poster that featured a young girl unfurling the American flag and the slogan "Fight or Buy Bonds." Rickenbacker later joked that since he could not buy bonds while he was flying he had no choice but to fight. Because of the 94th Squadron's high profile in the press, the posters might have been part of a concerted publicity command by higher headquarters in support of the Liberty Bond drive. Some of the pilots also decorated their airplanes with personal insignia. An Elks medallion was attached immediately below the cockpit of Rickenbacker's Nieuport. Alan Winslow's Nieuport bore the name Priscilla underneath his cockpit. John Wentworth's personal insignia was a dragon painted on the forward part of the fuselage.[23]

Many of the pilots also carried good-luck charms. According to one member of the squadron, at least a third of the pilots carried "lucky ivory pigs on their wrists."[24] Winslow remembered that some of the most popular good luck charms were women's clothing items liberated during adventures in Paris: "The most popular mascot of this type was a woman's silk stocking. The pilots who acquired these would knot them at the knee and wear them as a skullcap under the air helmet." Winslow's talisman was an old sock that had come back from the laundry without its mate. He threw it away several times but it kept reappearing, so he decided to keep it as his good-luck charm.[25]

The buildings at Epiez were "scattered all over a forest," which helped make it "remarkably well camouflaged." It rained almost every day throughout April, and along the paths that connected the barracks and hangars the mud was ankle deep.[26] The weather, mud, and inactivity made Epiez "a loathsome memory to all of us," recalled Philip Roosevelt.[27] Like Rickenbacker, Atkinson's number two man was also experiencing an inclusion crisis. Roosevelt was an exceptionally capable man who wanted more than anything else to command. He knew the Air Service needed capable commanders. The Issoudun graduates were extraordinary pilots, he thought, but not good officers. "They have little or no idea of how to look after the men, they are irresponsible and very few realize that an order is something to be obeyed. They are still college undergraduates," he wrote his father. He was probably the senior captain in the Air Service, he continued, but felt like an *embusqué* (behind the lines slacker) because his work was behind a desk instead of flying—only flying officers commanded. He asked for his father's advice about his idea to transfer to bombardment, where he thought his chances might be better, and added, "If I fail, I contemplate requesting transfer to the infantry." His father responded, "My advice is to make no effort to change but stick to your work and take whatever orders come."[28] In other words, Buck up.

The pilots were anxious to begin operations, though Campbell admitted in a letter home that "men who haven't yet learned how to see planes before they are visible to the untrained eye wouldn't be much use."[29] The only patrol flown from Epiez by the 94th Aero Squadron was manned by Hall and Peterson, who flew unarmed Nieuports to familiarize themselves with the sector.[30] As Atkinson squished around in the mud at Epiez, he must have wondered whether he would ever get his squadron into combat. It had now been a full year since the Americans had entered the war. The boast of darkening the sky with American airplanes was far from reality. He had but one squadron, and many of his airplanes still lacked guns.[31] On the other hand, the 94th Aero Squadron had been under his command for more than four weeks. The coordination of people with their equipment was substantially completed. He was as eager as his young pilots to get an American pursuit squadron into operations on the front. So was the brass at headquarters.

American units were moving onto the front lines to relieve French army units in the relatively quiet sector around Toul. By replacing French units the Americans made it possible for the French to concentrate additional combat power against the Germans in the battle area near Amiens. The front lines directly north of Toul formed the southern portion of the St. Mihiel salient, which had existed since September 1914. The salient was a German bulge in the front line that measured twenty-four miles across the base and fourteen miles deep. The trench lines on the southern portion of this salient extended from the small city of St. Mihiel in the west to Pont-à-Mousson in the east.

Pershing was assembling the American Army in this sector and hoped to launch an offensive toward Metz. A deep penetration in that direction would threaten the German army's lines of communications in northern France. It would also result in the capture of the Briey iron region and nearby coalfields, causing significant problems for German war production. Finally, it would position the American Army for an invasion of Germany territory through the Moselle River Valley and Saar industrial area. As Pershing's chief of staff wrote, "In our minds the tentative American theater of operations lay between St. Mihiel and Pont-à-Mousson in the region of the Woëvre."[32]

The U.S. 1st Division had early occupied a portion of the front in this sector, but Pershing sent it in toward Amiens to help with the battle against the Germans. The 26th Division, which had recently completely its battle training, replaced the 1st Division in early April. The 42d Division also moved onto the line at this time, relieving two French divisions farther to the south (an American division was twice the size of a French division). Other units that would form the nucleus of the American Army were also in the area.

Gen. Hunter Liggett commanded the U.S. 1st Corps, the senior American headquarters in the region. With its headquarters at Neufchâteau, the 1st Corps exercised administrative command of the American units in the Toul area. Liggett's corps headquarters had been established in January and was itself undergoing organizational training while also supervising the training of American units in its area of responsibility. "It was our purpose to make the First Corps a satisfactory model of the organization of all other Corps," wrote Liggett.[33] Because many of the units in the area, including the 1st Corps headquarters itself, were in various stages of organizational training, the American units that assumed operational missions were placed under the operational command of the French army. This meant they received their tactical missions from the French, but administrative and logistical matters remained an American responsibility.

The Army emphasized the combined use of all arms to win the ground battle, and as American divisions took up positions on the front lines aviation units were expected to support them. Lt. Col. Frank Lahm, who was temporarily in charge of the Zone of Advance headquarters while Van Horn was away, received orders from general headquarters on 1 April to move the 1st Aero Squadron (Observation), undergoing organizational training at Amanty, to the airfield at Ourches to support the 26th Division. Lahm had flown with Orville Wright on 9 September 1908 during the Army tests of the Wright Flyer, thereby becoming the first person in the American military to fly in an airplane. Since February 1918 he had been serving as the balloon chief at Van Horn's Advance Section headquarters. He ordered the squadron to Ourches on 4 April, and it began operations on 11 April.[34]

The decision to commit the 94th Aero Squadron to an active combat mission thus fit the larger pattern of events occurring within the AEF. Atkinson and Roosevelt met with Van Horn at his headquarters on 7 April and "received verbal orders to move the 94th Aero Squadron to Gengoult,

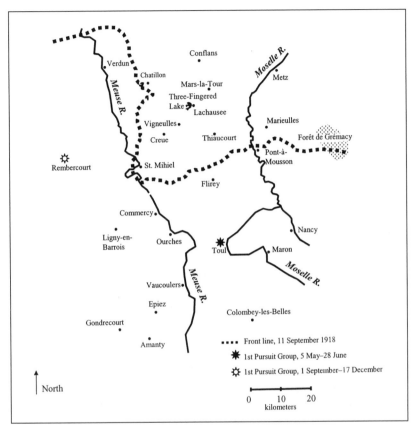

Conflans

Verdun

Chatillon

Mars-la-Tour

Three-Fingered
Lake · Lachausee

Metz

Moselle R.

Meuse R.

Vigneulles ·

Creüe

Thiaucourt

Marieulles

Forêt de Grémacy

Pont-à-
Mousson

☼
Rembercourt

· St. Mihiel

Flirey

Commercy ·

Ligny-en-
Barrois

Ourches

Toul

Maron

Nancy

Vaucouleurs ·

Meuse R.

Epiez

Gondrecourt

Colombey-les-Belles

Moselle R.

Amanty

▪▪▪▪ Front line, 11 September 1918
✹ 1st Pursuit Group, 5 May–28 June
☼ 1st Pursuit Group, 1 September–17 December

North

0   10   20
kilometers

St. Mihiel salient

The first Pursuit Group patrolled the southern side of the salient from Toul during the
spring of 1918. In September the group covered the western side of the salient from
Rembercourt for the St. Mihiel offensive.

Created by the author, based on data from "Bataille de Saint Mihiel," Map 30 in
État Major de l'Armée, Service Historique, *Les Armées françaises dans la*
Grande Guerre, vol. 1, *Cartes* (Paris: Imprimerie nationale, 1938); "Combined
Order of Battle, St. Mihiel Operation," Map 110 in *The United States Army in*
the World War, 1917–1919, vol. 8, *Military Operations of the American*
Expeditionary Forces (Washington, D.C.: Center of Military History, U.S. Army,
1990), 279.

an airfield just three kilometers northeast of Toul, to operate with [the] 32nd division of the French Army." Immediately after the meeting with Van Horn, Atkinson and Roosevelt visited Gengoult airfield and coordinated with the French 32d Corps aeronautical officer for the arrival of the 94th Aero. On the following day Atkinson returned to Gengoult with Huffer and Peterson to arrange for billeting and to complete plans for its occupation. The facilities were a big improvement—concrete buildings with two men per room, a separate shower facility with quick heating apparatus, good roads, and no mud.[35]

While Atkinson led the unit's leaders on a reconnaissance of Gengoult, Roosevelt supervised final preparation for the commitment of the first American-trained squadron into combat. Every possible measure was taken to ensure that the 94th Aero would succeed. Lufbery was assigned to the squadron as Huffer's assistant, and Captains Marr, Peterson, and Hall became the unit's three flight commanders. Six Nieuport 28s were transferred from the 95th to the 94th Squadron so that it would have its full complement of eighteen fighters. Additional machine guns were obtained from a French airpark at Nancy. Truck convoys with equipment left Epiez for Gengoult on 9 April; poor weather prevented the airplanes from leaving until two days later.[36]

The movement of the Hat-in-the-Ring Squadron from Epiez to Gengoult marked the end of the unit's organizational training and the beginning of combat operations. It was therefore removed from the authority of Atkinson's 1st Pursuit Organization and Training Center and Van Horn's Zone of the Advance. The 94th Aero now came under the operational command of the French 8th Army, which controlled the front lines and airspace in the sector. Placing units on the front line under French tactical control allowed American units to gain experience before the AEF's larger units, such as the corps and field army, were prepared to take over a sector. Like other American units in the Toul sector, the 94th Aero Squadron came under the administrative jurisdiction of Liggett's 1st Corps, which provided both administrative oversight and logistical support for all of the American units in the area.[37]

Billy Mitchell was the chief of Air Service for the 1st Corps. Like the other members of the corps staff, Mitchell had been conducting a study of his area of responsibility during the past months as part of Liggett's organizational training for the corps headquarters. Mitchell was an outsider. He had never served in the field with the Aviation Section of the Signal Corps until the war. Nevertheless, he had become unquestionably the most knowledgeable

Brig. Gen. Billy Mitchell, 1919

Originally a Signal Corps officer, Mitchell became

the Air Service's senior tactical commander in 1918

and America's most famous advocate of air power

thereafter.

ATKINSON PAPERS, AUBURN UNIVERSITY

ARCHIVES

American officer about the employment of air power. He was also its most flamboyant executive. Since his arrival in Paris on 19 March 1917, he had conducted a thorough study of British and French air operations and used the knowledge gained to play a leading role in designing the AEF's Air Service. During a period referred to as the dual monarchy, he and Bolling ran the AEF Air Service jointly. Though Pershing later appointed Brig. Gen. William Kenly to coordinate the efforts of Bolling and Mitchell, each continued to have a great deal of autonomy and prestige. As the air commander of the Zone of Advance, Mitchell had no aviation units to command, because none had yet arrived, and therefore continued to function mainly as a planner, anticipating, studying, and laying the groundwork for the future employment of American air power. Since arriving in France, he had regularly spent his evenings recording his detailed observations of the day on his portable typewriter. By registering, reviewing, and processing his daily observations he developed the insights that would help him become the AEF's senior tactical air commander.[38]

Mitchell bitterly resented the arrival of Benjamin Foulois and his entourage. His memoir, published a decade later, still exuded his contempt for the new regime: "A more incompetent lot of air warriors had never arrived in the zone of active military operations since the war began. . . . As rapidly as possible, the competent men, who had learned their duties in the face of the enemy, were displaced and their positions taken by these carpetbaggers."[39] The deep feelings of antagonism were mutual. Many decades later, Foulois wrote that he "could find no evidence of solid accomplishment" that he could attribute to Mitchell's efforts and that he was "furious with Mitchell's gross incompetence" in handling the Zone of Advance.[40] Ironically, by relieving Mitchell in January from his position as chief of the Zone of Advance and assigning him to Liggett's 1st Corps, Foulois shielded Mitchell from the mounting administrative and logistical burdens that occupied Van Horn's days. Mitchell thus continued to improve his flying skills (he had arrived in France without wings, though he had taken some private flying lessons in Virginia) and embarked on a study of the organization, operations, and equipment of his enemy, the German air force—undistracted by the daily grind of command.[41]

Liggett intended to make the 1st Corps a "model organization" that could be emulated by the subsequent corps that would be organized in the AEF. Mitchell embraced Liggett's concept and did his best to make his first aviation units model organizations as well. He was merciless when the first aviation units arrived, and he did not hesitate to relieve the commander of the first balloon company because it did not meet his exacting standards.[42] He also took a keen interest in the pursuit units moving into the 1st Corps area. Mitchell had envisioned the organization of both strategic and tactical components of the Air Service, but logistical constraints and the war's end in November 1918 prevented the organization of any sort of independent force along the lines of Hugh Trenchard's Independent Force in the Royal Air Force.

More significantly, the corps aviation organization that Mitchell had designed the previous summer was finally beginning to take shape. He envisioned aviation squadrons being attached to Army organizations much like artillery. An observation squadron and a balloon company would be attached to each forward division of the corps. Divisions that were not on the front lines would not have observation units attached—observation squadrons would never be held in reserve. An observation squadron and a balloon squadron would also be attached to the division's heavy artillery regiment to help adjust indirect fire. Besides providing for the adjustment of artillery fire, observation airplanes and balloons provided division and corps intelligence officers information on enemy activities through observation reports and photographs. In Mitchell's earliest plans, two pursuit squadrons were attached to each corps; in later plans they were instead formed into groups and attached to the army.[43]

Mitchell now had the 94th Squadron at Gengoult and the 1st Aero Squadron (Observation) at Ourches in addition to his balloon units. He knew that additional observation and pursuit squadrons were in their final stages of organizational training. Although the 94th Aero Squadron was officially under the operational command of the French, in Mitchell's mind this was only a formality. As he explained in his memoir, "All of these squadrons were now definitely assigned to my command. . . . We of course were still under French command but I arranged with the Commander of French Aviation of the Eighth French Army to give us a definite sector to defend." Mitchell wanted pursuit aviation "to stop all the German photographic machines from taking pictures of our back areas where the troops were being assembled."[44]

Although the 94th Squadron had not yet received a formal mission, it began operations the day after its arrival at Gengoult. While the "hat-in-the-ring" insignia was being painted on Meissner's and Rickenbacker's Nieuports, Lufbery made the first combat flight from Epiez on 12 April. "He's in his element again, crazy to add to his score of 17," Meissner noted.[45] Lufbery attacked a group of three Albatros planes and reported that he had brought one of them down, but he did not receive credit because the action had taken place too far behind enemy lines to be confirmed.[46] The French army had strict rules for awarding a victory credit: A ground or balloon observer had to witness the event.

On the evening of 13 April the French 8th Army issued orders making the 94th Squadron responsible for a sector from St. Mihiel on the west to Pont-à-Mousson on the east. Enemy pursuit-aviation forays were neither aggressive, numerous, nor equipped with the latest aircraft, because the Germans had concentrated their air forces in the Amiens region to support their offensive. Nevertheless, they were active. On the previous day, a German airplane had almost downed one of the 1st Aero Squadron's observation planes, now operating out of Ourches.[47]

The liaison between aviation units and the front in the Toul sector was extraordinarily good because the trench line had scarcely moved for three and a half years. This stability allowed for the development of an integrated air-defense system consisting of pursuit aviation, antiaircraft artillery, machine guns, and observation posts linked by a mature network of telephonic communications. Observers trained in the use of antiaircraft artillery and observation balloons were connected by telephone to three centers of control; from west to east they were Commercy, Lironville, and Disulouard. Each of these in turn was connected by telephone to the observation post at Mont St. Michel, outside Toul, and from there a direct line continued to the American operations center. It took less than four minutes for a report of enemy aerial activity, which included number, type, altitude, and direction of flight, to be received by the American pursuit operations center.[48]

After receiving his mission from the 8th Army's aviation headquarters, Huffer notified them that he would start regular patrols and alerts the next day.[49] The squadron's initial concept of operations focused on preventing enemy air incursions over its sector through a combination of patrols and alerts. The squadron would normally launch two or three patrols a day. These patrols flew along the front line from Pont-à-Mousson to St. Mihiel, a distance of about twenty-five miles. Meanwhile, two or three pilots at a time rotated through alert duty at the airfield. Their job was to respond immediately to any reports from the observation network of enemy aircraft incursions into the sector. The squadron operations officer posted pilot mission assignments on the operations board each evening. Rickenbacker was thrilled when he learned that he would be a member of the squadron's first combat patrol:

> On the evening of 13 April 1918 we were indeed a happy lot of pilots, for we were reading on our new Operations board the first war-flight order ever given by an all-American squadron commander to all-American pilots. It stated in simple terms that Captain Peterson, Lieutenant Reed Chambers and

Lieutenant E. V. Rickenbacker would start on a patrol of the lines tomorrow morning at six o'clock. Our altitude was to be 16,000 feet; our patrol was to extend from Pont-à-Mousson to St. Mihiel.[50]

The anticipation reminded Rickenbacker of the night before Christmas. He lay in bed for several hours trying to get to sleep, all the while remembering everything he had learned about aerial combat. He was just about to open fire on a German airplane when the orderly woke him from his nightmare, reassuring him that "everything was alright" and telling it was time to get up.[51]

The dominating topic at breakfast was just how they would act in the event they met the enemy. Upon leaving the mess hall for the hangar, Chambers yelled back to Campbell and Winslow that they "were going to stir up the Huns, and for them to be sure and knock and them down."[52] At six o'clock sharp the patrol took off as planned, but Peterson, the patrol leader, decided shortly after take-off to scrub the mission because of the poor weather and returned to the airfield. Defying Peterson's orders that his inexperienced pilots were to follow him if he turned back, "Rick [Rickenbacker] decided that he was going to go out and have a look at the lines," and Chambers, not be outdone, followed.[53]

The two green pilots climbed, following the Moselle River until they reached their assigned altitude, and were not aware that they had entered German airspace until an antiaircraft shell burst under Chambers's tail. His first time under fire, Chambers flew from Rickenbacker's left to the right and came in so close that Rickenbacker was unable to maneuver for fear of a collision. But after a half dozen rounds, remembered Rickenbacker, "we felt comparatively at home and permitted them to burst quite near without any fear." After two hours and four round-trips of the sector, Rickenbacker turned toward home. To his horror, he found that a thick blanket of clouds now covered the entire sector to his south.

Rickenbacker lost Chambers as he cautiously descended through the clouds. When he finally got below them, with fuel running low, Rickenbacker had difficulty getting oriented because he was still unfamiliar with the new sector and unable to see the major landmarks from an altitude of a few hundred feet. Fortunately, he found Toul and located the field. As soon as he had landed and taxied up to the hangar, Peterson stepped up and admonished him as "a bloody fool for flying off in a fog." To make matters worse, Chambers was missing. It was not a good performance from the two blue-collar members of the squadron, but, unbeknownst to them, their patrol had apparently triggered the dispatch of two German fighters of the Jagdstaffel 64 squadron based at Mars la Tour to intercept them. As Rickenbacker was making his report to the operations officer, the phone rang with news that two enemy airplanes were approaching Toul.[54]

The 94th's alert flight, consisting of Campbell, Winslow, and Meissner, were playing cards in the small alert tent at the edge of Gengoult airfield. At 8:45 A.M. their telephone also rang, interrupting their game. The operations officer told Winslow that two German planes were reported at three thousand feet above Toul. In moments Winslow and Campbell were in their Nieuports. Winslow was the mission leader. He was twenty-three years of age, a little older than most of the pilots, and had been an undergraduate at Yale when the United States declared war.[55] Initially he joined the New York State Naval Militia with some Yale classmates, but he had become discouraged with the prospects for its aviation program and resigned. He sailed for France in June 1917 to join the Lafayette Flying Corps. Winslow was one of the Lafayette flyers with a few months of frontline experience assigned to the squadron.[56]

Winslow shouted to Campbell to meet him at fifteen hundred feet above the northeast corner of the field. They would then climb together to the spot where the German planes had been reported. Meissner, unable to start his airplane, was left on the ground. It was raining; a blanket of gray clouds shut out the sky at about two thousand feet, and the early-morning mist was still hanging over the airfield. Rickenbacker, chastened after Peterson's scolding, heard the distinctive roar of the rotary engines as the alert mission scrambled off the field.

Campbell took off first. Winslow followed forty-five seconds later. Winslow had scarcely cleared the treetops at the edge of the field when he saw, slightly above him and not more than a few hundred feet away, a German fighter rushing directly at him. It seemed incredible to him that a German fighter could appear like this on his first mission with the American squadron. He felt angered and surprised at the same time. Winslow had missed downing an enemy aircraft in one of his previous combats with the Lafayette Flying Corps because of a second's hesitation.

This time he reacted immediately.

> I swore, clenched my fingers about the machine-gun triggers, and veered
> toward the speeding enemy plane until I could see my line of tracer bullets

entering its fuselage. The German slipped off on one wing to avoid my fire and then came roaring down on me, his guns barking with a volley of lead that screamed by, dangerously near.

Winslow later remembered he had his opponent "at a rare advantage, which was due to the greater speed and maneuverability of our wonderful machines." His next maneuver instantly gained him the advantage. "I pulled up my Nieuport sharply in a vertical climb, kicked over my right rudder, and went plunging down on his tail, spraying his wings and fuselage with a long rattling burst of fire. In another instant he dashed toward earth in an uncontrolled dive." Winslow had shot away the rudder controls of the Albatros D-5, a fairly new German fighter that had been introduced the previous summer. He saw the plane crash, somersaulting over on its back in a field about three hundred feet from the edge of Gengoult airfield. The undergraduate from Yale had scored the 94th Aero Squadron's first victory. He then "zoomed up" to assist Campbell.[57]

His companion from Harvard did not need his help, however. Because Campbell had taken off first, he had circled the small airfield to rendezvous with his companion and was above and behind Winslow when he suddenly saw Winslow engage the oncoming Albatros. In a matter of seconds Campbell passed over the engagement and his wings obstructed his view. He turned, banking his airplane ninety degrees so he could see the engagement and position himself to come to Winslow's assistance. As Campbell was turning, he came under attack from the second German fighter, a Pfalz D-3a, which he had not seen but which was bearing down on him from a higher altitude. Campbell pulled up to fire, and his airplane stalled. It fell to within a hundred feet of the ground before he recovered control.

He found himself flying below and behind the German. He maneuvered into position directly underneath his opponent. "I finally found myself right under him. Then I pulled my nose straight up into the air and let him have the bullets, and I think he got some in his motor, for I saw some tracers hitting his nose." When Campbell nosed his airplane up it carried him to a higher altitude. "The next thing I knew, he was diving at about 45 degrees, and I was behind and above him." At this moment Winslow, who had finished his opponent, "zoomed up" to assist Campbell, arriving within firing distance of the Pfalz, and saw a burst of tracers from Campbell's guns enter the German's fuselage. The German machine burst into flames and crashed behind the 94th

Lt. Alan Winslow

Winslow, smoking a cigarette, leans on his first victory.

RICKENBACKER COLLECTION, AUBURN UNIVERSITY ARCHIVES

Aero Squadron's hangars, just off the opposite side of the airfield from where the first enemy aircraft had crashed. All of this took place in less than four and half minutes from the alert call.[58]

It was miraculous. On its first day of operations, the squadron had brought down two enemy fighters right next to their airfield and in plain view for all to see—every fighter pilot's dream. Winslow and Campbell landed and congratulated each other. Meanwhile, French citizens and American soldiers hurried on foot, bicycles, motorcycles, and in automobiles to the crash sites. Winslow pushed his way through the crowd and had the "curious sensation" of coming "face-to-face with the man with whom I had been having a machinegun duel in the air but a few minutes before." Winslow asked his enemy in German if he was wounded. The German replied in French that he had only been bruised. Winslow, offering him a cigarette, noticed that the German was a noncommissioned officer. Normally, all German pursuit pilots were officers. Winslow asked why he was not an officer. The pilot responded that he had been a pursuit pilot for more than two years but his commission had been withheld because he was a Pole.

By the time Campbell got to the plane he had downed, the pilot had already been sent to the hospital in "ghastly agony," where he died shortly afterward. Winslow and Campbell joined the French and American soldiers scavenging for souvenirs from their victories. The stripping of the downed aircraft for souvenirs caused Van Horn to issue General Order 17, which required a guard to be placed on future enemy aircraft to ensure that technical experts could examine them for intelligence purposes.[59]

The citizens of Toul were delighted. "They wrung our hands, kissed us, toasted us in their best Moselle wine and yelled: 'Vive la France! Vivent les américains!'" Subsequently the planes were exhibited in the main square of Toul. Billy Mitchell and Alan Winslow suspected the pair of German fighters had actually intended to conduct an air raid against the 94th Aero Squadron at Gengoult, attacking its Nieuports on the ground and setting fire to its hangars. As evidence, Winslow noted that the cartridge belts of the German machine guns contained only tracer and incendiary bullets. "It would have been a decidedly discouraging baptism for the American Air Service," he added.[60] Regardless of the German intent, the outcome was a huge moral victory for the Americans. How the American Air Service would perform, according to Mitchell, had been an open question. Mitchell believed these victories "had a more important effect on American fighting aviation than any other single occurrence. It gave our men a confidence that could have been obtained in no other way."[61]

Chastened and upstaged by the Ivy League fraternity men, Rickenbacker was determined to get the next victory. Fortunately, Chambers showed up later on the day of the spectacular victories, after making a forced landing nearby. As the 94th Aero continued operations its pilots familiarized themselves with the sector and worked to acquire "the vision of the air." Rickenbacker continued to have difficulty.

On 23 April he mistakenly stalked a SPAD. The French pilot reacted to the aggressive maneuverings of Rickenbacker's Nieuport 28 (an airplane unfamiliar to most French pilots), almost resulting in an engagement between friendly aircraft. The next day Rickenbacker narrowly avoided being shot down by enemy fighters while responding to an alert against an enemy reconnaissance plane. On another alert on 29 April, with Capt. James Hall, Rickenbacker thought he had spotted the enemy. He dipped his wings to signal his leader, but according to Rickenbacker, Hall "stupidly continued on straight north." Rickenbacker left the formation and began an attack on the airplane, only to break it off at the last moment when he realized it was a French craft—another case of mistaken identity. Once he had linked up with Hall, they attacked a Pfalz D-3, a streamlined single-seater meant to replace the Albatros D-3. As Rickenbacker held back, Hall initiated the attack and caused the Pfalz to fly right in front of Rickenbacker, who shot it down. Hall had delivered Rickenbacker his first victory on a silver platter; both pilots received credit for the squadron's third enemy airplane shot down.[62]

Back at Epiez, the 95th Aero Squadron's pilots returned to the 1st Pursuit Organization and Training Center after graduating from Cazaux and began flight-testing their Nieuports during the last week of April. Davenport Johnson took the first patrol to the lines on 27 April. On 2 May the squadron engaged in combat for the first time. Johnson was leading a four-plane flight that encountered two enemy two-seaters. Everyone but Johnson attacked. "The major who was with me had a jam, and so [he] could only watch the fight," Richard Blodgett wrote his mother. He continued, "I followed [the enemy] nearly to his own aerodrome shooting all the time." Blodgett expended 350 rounds while clearing three jams before breaking off the attack deep behind enemy lines, with the enemy machine gunner either dead or wounded and the plane trailing smoke. He wrote home that he had downed the German, but the victory was not confirmed. Johnson led another combat patrol that afternoon.[63]

Atkinson had cleared these "training" patrols with the French 8th Army but not with Mitchell—a big mistake, as it turned out. When the Hat-in-the-Ring Squadron learned that their sister squadron was flying patrols in their sector, they "raised hell," remembered Philip Roosevelt, "and we got a balling out" from Mitchell for flying through their airspace. Atkinson and Roosevelt were confused. They had cleared the missions with the 8th Army. Who was in charge? Mitchell wired Van Horn, complaining that patrols were appearing over the lines without specific missions—he had issued none to the 95th Squadron. Van Horn replied that corrective action had been taken but also gloated, "During its unauthorized flight over the lines, the training patrol of the 95th Squadron brought down one enemy plane."[64] Mitchell was also upset with Atkinson and company "for having the nerve to call [themselves] the 1st Pursuit Group Headquarters." He probably had little regard for Atkinson and Roosevelt at this time. They were Foulois men—carpetbaggers. In turn, Atkinson and Roosevelt were not sure about Mitchell. "God knows what" his authority was, wrote Roosevelt, noting that 1st Corps had not become operational. "But as usual we decided that if it came to a question of getting along . . . we would do all the getting along."[65]

Atkinson and Roosevelt were not entirely without guilt. They had been lob-
bying hard for movement of their headquarters and the 95th Aero to Gengoult
to join the 94th Squadron and had pressed for the assignment of additional personnel so they could reorganize as a tactical command instead of as training
headquarters. Determined to transform themselves into the 1st Pursuit Group,
they quietly visited Gengoult and made preparations for the move.

Van Horn directed Atkinson to discontinue all flights from Epiez except
test flights and to keep the number and duration of those to a minimum. It
seemed ridiculous to the 95th Squadron because they had already spent more
than a month in the organizational training mode back at Villeneuve. The
obvious solution was to order the 95th Aero to Gengoult to operate with its
sister squadron. A controlling headquarters, though, would be needed to
coordinate the daily activities of the two squadrons. Atkinson met with Van
Horn and argued that it was time to activate the 1st Pursuit Group. The goal
shared by Atkinson, Roosevelt, and Rankin since first arriving at Villeneuve
was now within reach. Van Horn approved and beefed up their headquarters with another fifty men from the 1st Air Depot. Atkinson reorganized his
staff with Henry Lyster as adjutant and Roosevelt taking charge of the new
operations section. Atkinson and the 95th Aero Squadron flew their
Nieuports to Gengoult on 4 May. The 1st Pursuit Group was in the war.[66]

5

Wings

The Nieuport 28's initial performance won enthusiastic endorsements. When Meissner took his first short test flight in a Nieuport 28 before ferrying it back to Villeneuve, he noted in his diary that the "machine runs beautifully, easy and delicate as can be." On a more rigorous flight back at Villeneuve, however, he seemed a bit unnerved by its range of performance after practicing aerobatics and combat maneuvers.[1] Waldo Heinrichs, of the 95th Squadron, noted that the airplane had outclimbed and easily kept up with the 180-horsepower SPAD 7 during the tests at Villeneuve. Rickenbacker observed the same superior performance in his near case of fratricide with a French SPAD during the first days of patrolling the Toul sector, writing, "To my delight I found that I could not only out climb my adversary, but I could outmaneuver him while doing so."[2] Most impressive, though, were the spectacular victories by Winslow and Campbell on the 94th Aero's first day of operations. Although they had just taken off, were at lower altitude, and had less experience than their opponents, the American pilots quickly turned the tables on their enemy and won the day because, as Winslow put it, "of our wonderful machines."[3]

Billy Mitchell was also impressed with the Nieuport 28. He cabled his praise of the airplane to Foulois, stating that

the Nieuport 28 with Gnome motor has proved very satisfactory as a pursuit airplane. . . . I believe that this airplane will not be obsolescent as a single seater next year. I therefore recommend that its construction and that of the Gnome Monosoupape be continued with all speed for the use of the American Air Service in France.[4]

It was indeed a strong endorsement for the new rotary-engine fighter. His prediction that the Nieuport 28 would still be operative in 1919 was quite remarkable, given the pace of technological advance among fighters. The historian Richard Hallion, in his study of World War I fighters, identifies the development of five separate generations of aircraft between 1915 and 1918 and concludes that "even successful designs were forced into an early obsolescence by the pace of technological development: the average fighter design retired from operational service in a little over a year following its introduction to combat."[5]

Mitchell, the Air Service's most astute observer of aerial warfare, would have been aware of this phenomenon, as were others in the Air Service. An Air Service memo during the summer of 1918 observed that "the life of a pursuit machine as a first class type actually on the front is between three and six months."[6] Mitchell thus shared the same degree of enthusiasm as his young pilots for the Nieuport 28. He also liked its rotary engine because of its superior reliability in freezing weather. During the previous winter he had noticed that airplanes with water-cooled engines could become inoperative owing to freezing up during cold weather. "One of my airplanes had a rotary motor which was air-cooled and I did not have these troubles with it," he wrote.[7]

Mitchell's positive assessment was also based on his own experience piloting both the Nieuport 28 and the SPAD. He had been provided with a single-seat SPAD for his personal use the previous February.[8] With his office at Toul, it was easy for Mitchell to visit the 94th Aero Squadron on the outskirts of the city at the Gengoult aerodrome. He made at least four flights in the Nieuport 28 before sending the cable to Foulois. He made another seven in May, including an exhibition flight after an awards ceremony on 15 May that was observed by several senior officers, including the commanding general of the 8th Army and General Liggett of the U.S. 1st Corps. The purpose of the ceremony was to present the croix de guerre to Hall (who was missing in action), Peterson, Rickenbacker, Meissner, and Lt. Charles Chapman. Mitchell led a six-plane flight in the demonstration immediately after the ceremony.[9] His piloting skill had improved greatly—he could barely fly when he left the United States.[10]

Atkinson's supply officer remembered that the Nieuport 28s "had many good features. I have heard a very competent pilot describe the Nieuport 28 as a highbred racehorse, minding the slightest touch of the rider. . . . In a German report I saw after the Armistice, they said the Nieuport 28 was the best pursuit plane the Allies had."[11] Lt. Lucien Thayer, the official historian of the AEF in 1918, remarked similarly, "The Nieuport was an excellent machine and was regarded by many, including a large number of Germans, it is said, as the best chase plane the Allies had."[12] Confidence in the nimble fighter plunged, however, as the first American fighter squadrons gained increasing combat experience in the Toul sector. Jimmy Meissner was the first to experience one of the airplane's most serious shortcomings.

In addition to running patrols and alerts, the 1st Pursuit Group provided protection patrols for friendly observation aircraft. On 2 May Lts. Jimmy Meissner and Philip Davis of the 94th Aero Squadron had orders to protect a French reconnaissance airplane photographing enemy positions near Thiaucourt. As the French airplane gained altitude over their field, Meissner and Davis nodded to their mechanics, who swung over the propellers. "The motors spat, choked, then caught with a roaring song of power." After the pilots had checked to make sure that all nine cylinders were firing, they nodded again and the mechanics jerked the blocks from the wheels. The two Nieuports rolled across the aerodrome and took off together, raising their noses in a climbing spiral and setting out for Pont-à-Mousson.[13]

From his cockpit, Meissner looked out on a clear spring day in which Toul looked especially beautiful and peaceful, surrounded by its shining rivers and canals. As the Nieuports climbed higher they did a series of S turns so that by the time they crossed the lines at Pont-à-Mousson they would be at an altitude of eighteen thousand feet. The S turns also enabled the pilots to check their rear, the most vulnerable point of attack. They planned to protect the French observation aircraft by flying eight thousand feet above it—an ideal position from which to identify any airborne threats. The flight plan was to continue over Thiaucourt, as the observation plane photographed the hub of

German communication lines for the entire sector, and "then sweep in a wide arc back to Fleiry and home."

Meissner and Davis flew along side by side, "searching constantly in all directions for anything with a hostile appearance in all that empty looking sky." As Meissner looked for the French observation plane below them he noticed two other planes headed toward them. They looked like Germans, but he was not sure—in his three weeks of combat flying he had not yet seen a German plane in the air. These seemed darker in color than any French planes he had seen. "This, coupled with an instinctive distrust acquired by all war fliers," made Meissner "dive and zoom quickly several times" to signal Davis "to come close and be ready." They tightened their formation and watched as the unidentified aircraft approached.

Just as the first of these aircraft passed underneath him, Meissner "made a vertical bank, swinging into the sun" over the leader. A glance at his dashboard clock indicated it was five minutes to twelve and his altitude was fifty-three hundred meters (about seventeen thousand feet)—essential information that would be needed for a combat report. As Meissner straightened out he looked to see the markings on the wings of the plane below him. The vibration of Meissner's plane made it difficult to see, so he dived closer until he saw big black crosses and the birdlike wingtips of a German Albatros, a single-engine fighter comparable to the Nieuport. Meissner instantly forgot about Davis and the second German as he concentrated on attacking the German leader, who was so intent on stalking the observation plane far below that he was still unaware that he was himself being stalked by Meissner.

A quick dive placed Meissner directly behind the German. He slowly pulled the nose of his Nieuport up until "the sights were in perfect line with the Albatros fuselage only two hundred yards away." "Very much excited," Meissner "pulled the trigger and held it" while watching the tracers from his machine gun scatter all around the German without seeming to hit him. The German dived a thousand feet and turned north, with Meissner in hot pursuit. A trail of black smoke poured from the German airplane, but Meissner was still not sure he had hit him. Just a few days earlier, Douglas Campbell had reported that a German had tricked him by pretending to be on fire. Meissner "fired again till the gun jammed," but luckily it was only a misfire, "which two jerks of the charging handle fixed."

"The Albatros was going into a spiral when two tracer bullets went straight into its fuselage" behind the motor. "Flames burst out from the cockpit instantly." Meissner had struck the gasoline tank, "but to be sure the pilot was not still alive and suffering, I kept up the shooting," he wrote.

> Diving with full motor in the excitement of the moment, I got so close that a lurch of the blazing enemy made me plunge almost vertically to avoid a crash. The strain was too great, with a crack my top wing seemed to break loose and whip back overhead at the instant I shot under the Boche, so near that I thought we had met.

Meissner thought they had collided. With the top wing gone, he "wondered how soon the bottom wing would fold up," leaving him in a "wingless fuselage pointed straight down at Mother Earth 15,000 feet below." "What beastly luck to die just as my first victory had been won, and myself alone to blame!" he exclaimed in recollection.

Suddenly Meissner realized that "the top wing wasn't all gone, and the bottom wing hadn't folded up yet." The plane "was still diving with motor cut off" and "still answering to the controls" as he "gently rocked the stick and pushed on the rudder." "Surprised at still being alive," he looked up to check the top wing. The front edge of the wing back to the main spar had been torn off, taking with it all of the fabric covering the upper surface of the wing. About two-thirds of the linen covering the lower surface of the wing was still present, but it was being held in place by wind pressure alone. Meissner "couldn't figure how such a thing could occur in colliding, but being down to less than 12,000 feet, and heading deeper into enemy territory," he let that thought go for the time being. He restarted his motor by opening the fuel valve and switched on three, six, and finally nine cylinders. He leveled out as the motor picked up speed and gently turned the plane until its compass indicated he was heading south, back toward friendly lines.

Just as Meissner started to relax, an explosion went off to the side of his airplane—German antiaircraft fire. He swerved instinctively, and "the next two or three bursts were a few hundred yards away, mere harmless 'woofs' sounding above the motor." The black puffs in the sky, however, advertised his presence to any German fighters that might be in the vicinity. Meissner "watched all around," hoping that none were about, for in this crippled condition he was an easy kill. With his Nieuport losing altitude fast, he knew he

Lt. Jimmy Meissner

Meissner's somber expression reflects the near-fatal consequences of his first victory. The fabric covering the upper surface of the top wing was stripped away with the leading edge.

would never make it back to the aerodrome. Fortunately, he managed to stay aloft long enough to cross no-man's-land at an altitude of six thousand feet before safely landing at Martincourt.

When Meissner arrived by automobile at Gengoult an hour or two later, photographers and newspapermen were already on hand.[14] Meissner's first victory was the squadron's fourth. A piece of Meissner's wing was found in the vicinity of the crashed German two-seater. Later research would show that Meissner had mistaken a two-seat reconnaissance plane on a photographic mission for a single-seat Albatros, but errors of this kind were not uncommon. The excitement of first combat, the fast movements of the planes, and the fact that Meissner's own machine had been damaged probably contributed to this case of mistaken identity.[15] Meissner had been lucky. As he made his way back to friendly territory he was in no condition for combat. Alone and nursing his crippled plane back to friendly lines, he made an easy target for enemy fighters. His first combat reflected skill and luck, both important qualities in combat. He was certainly luckier than his squadron mate, Lt. Charles Chapman, who went down in flames the following day. Chapman's was the squadron's first combat death. No form of death was more dreaded by pilots than being burned alive.[16]

At first Meissner thought a collision had caused the damage to his upper wings. Immediately after the flight, he wrote in his diary, "Collision on way down ripped top surface off upper wings."[17] Meissner later wrote an essay about his first victory, on which the foregoing account is based. By the time he wrote this account, he had come to a different conclusion on the cause of the wing failure: It was the air pressure associated with his vertical dive, he now believed. "The strain was too great. . . . I couldn't figure how such a thing could occur in colliding."[18] Thus it seems that at some future date Meissner had learned additional information that led him to decide that his wing damage was caused not by a collision but by the increased air pressure associated with a vertical dive.

Other pilots soon experienced the same terrifying phenomenon that Meissner had encountered. Only five days after Meissner's victory, Capt. James Hall was making a steep dive and preparing to fire when he heard the ominous sounds of wood cracking and fabric tearing. He pulled up and off the enemy plane he had been pursuing and immediately saw that "his upper right wing had broken and was torn, and in the prop wash the fabric was tearing further and further back along the width of the wing." Hall tried to nurse his aircraft back home, but a German antiaircraft gun scored a direct hit on his motor. Crash-landing behind enemy lines, he was captured and taken prisoner. American pilots did not learn about his wing-stripping problem until after the Armistice. They did hear about a similar problem experienced by Rickenbacker, however, which occurred little more than a week later.[19]

On 17 May Rickenbacker scored his second official victory, but the leading edge of his top right wing failed like the others, sending him into a tailspin from which he just barely recovered. After this harrowing ordeal, Rickenbacker noted in his diary—just as Meissner had done—that he had lost his upper right wing in a collision: "I met 3 Albatross planes which I attacked. In so doing I lost my upper right wing in a collision with the enemy plane."[20] Again like Meissner, however, he later changed his explanation and attributed the incident to wind pressure. In his memoir, *Fighting the Flying Circus*, Rickenbacker wrote, "I pulled my stick back close into my lap and began a sharp climb. A frightening crash that sounded like the crack of doom told me that the sudden strain had collapsed my right wing. The entire spread of canvas over the top wing was torn off by the wind and disappeared behind me."[21] The contradiction between Rickenbacker's diary and his later reminiscence followed the same pattern of change as Meissner's account. At first, Rickenbacker believed he had been in a collision; only later did he learn the true cause.

Two days later the 1st Pursuit Group experienced one of its most devastating losses, and the Nieuport 28 shared in the blame. At about nine o'clock in the morning on 19 May the Toul antiaircraft batteries opened fire at an enemy intruder. It seemed to Atkinson as if everyone in the 1st Pursuit Group suddenly rushed outside, looked up, and saw a German observation plane, so low its black crosses were plainly visible. According to Atkinson, the plane had actually landed south of Toul because of engine trouble and after making repairs had taken off again. "The alert pilots were already in their planes even before the order to go could be phoned down to the hangars, but the excitement was so great that two of the planes ran together in taking off and another was unable to start the motor."[22] Two planes, piloted by Maj. Jean Huffer and Lt. Oscar Gude, finally took off. Huffer returned to the airfield with engine trouble. Gude attacked, expending 350 to 400 rounds of machine-gun ammunition, but did got get close enough to be effective.[23]

Raoul Lufbery, who had been watching from the barracks, jumped on a motorcycle and rushed to the hangars. His own plane was not ready, so he climbed into another Nieuport and took off. Lufbery had a mighty desire to bring down a German airplane on the friendly side of the lines. He had told his friends that he had shot down more than fifty German planes but had received credit for only seventeen because the rest had occurred so deep behind enemy lines that they had not been observed. Perhaps he was stirred by the thought of recreating a spectacular victory like Winslow and Campbell's; perhaps it was simply the frustration of seeing the Germans, whom he blamed for the death of his friend, Marc Pourpe, over his aerodrome.[24]

By the time Lufbery caught up with the German, Atkinson notes, "They were two specks almost at the limit of vision. We saw him attack twice, when eyes could stand no more and both planes went out of sight."[25] A few minutes later Atkinson received a telephone call that an American pilot was down at the village of Maron, about twelve miles away. Atkinson immediately left for the village. When he arrived he found Lufbery's body in the town hall covered with flowers. Mitchell received a phone call from 1st Pursuit Group notifying him of Lufbery's death and joined Atkinson in the village to find out what he could.

After interviewing several eyewitnesses, Mitchell learned that the small American fighter, approaching from Toul "with unbelievable speed," had overtaken the German airplane. The Nieuport maneuvered so close to the German airplane's tail that it appeared they had touched each other. Lufbery fired a short burst and pulled away, while the two-seater evasively turned one way and then the other. Lufbery made another attack, again getting so close that it appeared that they were touching, and fired another short burst. The German gunner returned fire with four or five rounds. According to Mitchell, the Nieuport 28 gradually drew off and rolled, and Lufbery fell out, landing about one hundred yards from the Moselle River behind a shoemaker's house. The Nieuport caught fire, glided several hundred yards, and crashed.[26]

The proximity of the body's landing to the river resulted in two versions of what caused Lufbery's death. One posits that when the Nieuport 28 caught fire, Lufbery jumped in desperation from his burning airplane in hopes of landing in the Moselle. Practically everyone in the 1st Pursuit Group believed this account to be true. Mitchell did not. He doubted that Lufbery jumped because all of the eyewitnesses he interviewed told him that "Lufbery fell out before the plane caught fire."[27] Mitchell speculated that Lufbery, in his haste to take off, had failed to buckle himself into the plane and that his controls were shot away during engagement, causing the Nieuport to roll over and Lufbery to fall out. Rickenbacker noted that only a few days earlier Lufbery had said that he would never jump out of a burning airplane because there was "always a chance of side slipping your aeroplane down in such a way that you fan the flames away from yourself and the wings" and that in doing so it might even be possible to put out the fire.[28] The historian Royal D. Frey visited the village in 1961 and obtained signed affidavits from several eyewitnesses, corroborating Mitchell's version of the story. According to Frey, "The witnesses stated that the Nieuport suddenly flipped over and two things came out. One was Lufbery and the other was a cushion." The airplane then rolled upright and crashed about a half mile beyond where the body had landed.[29]

Nevertheless, most of the members of the 1st Pursuit Group firmly believed that Lufbery had jumped to save himself. Even Rickenbacker, in spite of what Lufbery had told him, wrote, "Lufbery had preferred to leap to certain death rather than endure the slow torture of burning to a crisp."[30] The official history of the 94th Aero Squadron, compiled by Reed Chambers shortly after the war, states that Lufbery had jumped.[31] Atkinson, who was among the first on the scene, wrote, "At 1500 meters, his plane in flames, he jumped." He also stated that Lufbery's airplane "was undoubtedly set on fire by an incendiary bullet, as there was a hole in his reserve tank."[32]

Alan Winslow was also convinced that Lufbery had tried to save himself by jumping from the burning plane. Winslow explained that he had almost done the same thing: "I, too, later had occasion to experience, that to leap under such conditions is instinctive." Winslow was referring to his last aerial combat flight, in July 1918, when he was hit multiple times by enemy machine-gun fire. Stunned with pain, he tried to regain control of his plunging airplane, which he thought was on fire because everything looked red. "Instinctively, thinking I was in flames, I put my remaining hand on the release button of my safety strap, intending to jump. Just in time, however, I realized that with a stunned brain what I had first thought to be flames was in reality blood."[33] Winslow managed a forced landing next to the German trenches and became a prisoner of war.

We may never know for sure whether Lufbery fell or jumped. The significance of Lufbery's death, however, is in the way it affected the 1st Pursuit Group. In addition to the accounts of Rickenbacker, Chambers, Atkinson, and Winslow, there are others. Meissner's diary entry for that day reads, "Luf down in flames & jumped."[34] Pilots in the 95th Aero Squadron shared a similar view. Waldo Heinrichs recorded in his diary, "An incendiary bullet having passed thru gas tank, set him on fire, dropped from 4000 m. to 700 m. & jumped from his plane in effort to land in river."[35] Harold Buckley's memoir records, "Unable to bear the terrible heat from the blazing gasoline he had taken a long chance, as we all agreed, on jumping into a river which flowed by near the spot where he fell."[36] Perception creates its own reality. As far as the 1st Pursuit Group was concerned, the invincible Lufbery had died because the Nieuport 28 was unsafe—a firetrap. Its reserve fuel tank, located to the right and forward of the pilot's seat, was of special concern to them. Meissner was probably not the only pilot in the 1st Pursuit Group who began to fly without fuel in his reserve tank during the weeks after Lufbery's death.[37]

Lufbery had never liked the Nieuport 28. As Philip Roosevelt observed, "Lufbery was not only quiet but cautious. He told his friends he had no confidence in the type of plane assigned him, after his transfer to the American army. He was through, he said, with war flying."[38] His death wounded the group's confidence in its airplane and began the slow, painful demise of the Nieuport 28.

Meissner won his second victory on 30 May. His victory was a narrow one, though, because he experienced wing failure yet again. This time he lost the leading edge and upper surface of his top right wing. Again, the reports recorded on the day of the combat attributed the wing damage to a collision. Meissner noted in his diary that a German plane "rammed me, top wings ripped as before, landed O.K. at camp."[39] Rickenbacker's combat report also stated that Meissner and the German had collided, causing Meissner to lose most of his upper wings. Yet Rickenbacker, in *Fighting the Flying Circus,* states that Meissner's wing was damaged because "the strain was too great." The pattern of changing accounts is repeated yet again. In each case, the reports filed immediately after the event stated that the wing damage was caused by collision, while later accounts attributed the damage to the stress of maneuvers.[40]

On the same day that Meissner lost wing fabric while scoring his second victory, another American pilot, Lt. Wilfred V. Casgrain, also experienced wing failure. Unlike Meissner, who returned, Casgrain made a forced landing in no-man's-land and mistakenly walked in the wrong direction, into the German trench. He became a prisoner of war and was therefore unable to relate his experiences, but the Germans retrieved his Nieuport and stood the top wing upright in front of their trenches—a witty gesture, according to Rickenbacker, in which the American cockade, with its red and blue circles around a big white center, was presented as a bull's-eye.[41]

Meissner's ignorance of the upper wing's weakness explains why he repeatedly conducted violent maneuvers that his aircraft was incapable of withstanding. Had he been aware of the problem, he would have avoided inflicting such potentially fatal damage on his aircraft for a second time in less than a month. Within days of Meissner's second experience of wing damage, pilots of the 1st Pursuit Group came to realize that there was indeed a problem with the Nieuport's upper wing. Perhaps Meissner himself finally discovered the true cause.

By the beginning of the second week of June, written reports began to make their way to Air Service headquarters calling attention to the weak upper wing as well as a number of other technical problems with the aircraft. The first report was from Captain Du Doré. His 8 June memorandum was meant to alert French authorities that urgent modifications to the Nieuport 28 were needed. "The front of the wing is too weak; it gives way, the ribs between the front of the wing and the central beam break, the cloth tears off and the wing loses its covering completely (always the upper wing, particularly the right one)." He also noted that this had occurred "on several different occasions, and always under the same circumstances during a combat," indicating that the wing could not stand up to the stress associated with particularly violent maneuvers.[42]

Du Doré reported that structural failure was occurring in the ribs forward of the main spar. Two spars ran the length of the Nieuport's top wing, providing it structural support. Ribs, affixed to the spars, provided the framework for the wing's aerodynamic shape. A total of fourteen ribs, including four extra-strong compression ribs, extended from the leading to the trailing edge of the wing. Additional support was provided by short nose ribs, which were interspersed between the compression and standard ribs and extended from the leading edge to the main spar. Most of the ribs consisted of poplar "webs," hollowed-out pieces that gave the wing its aerodynamic shape. Poplar is a soft, light wood ideally suited for being shaped to the required camber, or curvature, called for in the wing's design. When the poplar had been shaped according to design specifications, the interior was hollowed out, making it lighter still. Once in place between the leading and trailing edges, and separated by the spars, these hollow structures resembled a web, hence the name.

The poplar webs were held in place by cap strips, thin strips of ash (a

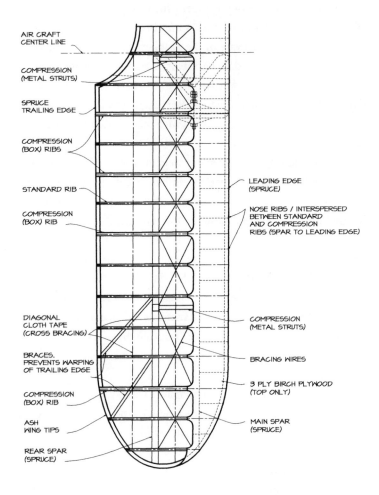

AIR CRAFT
CENTER LINE

COMPRESSION
(METAL STRUTS)

SPRUCE
TRAILING EDGE

COMPRESSION
(BOX) RIBS

STANDARD RIB

COMPRESSION
(BOX) RIB

LEADING EDGE
(SPRUCE)

NOSE RIBS / INTERSPERSED
BETWEEN STANDARD
AND COMPRESSION
RIBS (SPAR TO LEADING EDGE)

DIAGONAL
CLOTH TAPE
(CROSS BRACING)

BRACES,
PREVENTS WARPING
OF TRAILING EDGE

COMPRESSION
(BOX) RIB

ASH
WING TIPS

REAR SPAR
(SPRUCE)

COMPRESSION
(METAL STRUTS)

BRACING WIRES

3 PLY BIRCH PLYWOOD
(TOP ONLY)

MAIN SPAR
(SPRUCE)

Nieuport 28 upper right wing, top view, illustrating wing without fabric
The ribs, rear spar, and leading edge are clearly visible in the drawing.
COURTESY OF CHARLES FRANDSEN ARCHITECTS, P.C.

strong, elastic wood) nailed and glued onto the top and bottom surfaces of
the web. Besides holding the webs in place, the tough cap strips protected the
soft poplar webs while also providing the wing with structural support. It is
important to note that the cap strips on the upper surface of the wing did not
extend forward of the main spar. Instead, a thin piece of plywood sheathing,

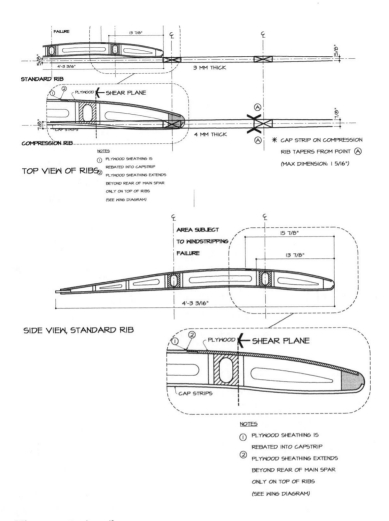

Nieuport 28 wing ribs

The enlarged view at bottom shows "shear plane," where aerodynamic stress caused the leading edge to separate from the main spar.

COURTESY OF CHARLES FRANDSEN ARCHITECTS, P.C.

consisting of three-ply birch, extended from the main spar to the leading edge. Thus the part of the wing that extended forward of the main spar lacked a supporting upper cap strip. The Nieuport designers must have thought the three-ply veneer birch would be sufficient. It was not.

As the historian Theodore Hamady has shown, when the wing failed the line of shear was located where the ribs that formed the leading edge were joined to the main spar.[43] Once the ribs had broken, the entire leading edge forward of the spar was swept back, taking the fabric covering the upper surface of the wing with it. The photographic evidence of the damage to Meissner's Nieuport 28 clearly shows that the leading edge forward of the main spar is missing.

In his report, Du Doré also listed the airplane identification numbers of four Nieuports that had experienced wing failure, along with a brief note of circumstance: 6152 (Casgrain's?), 6144 (Meissner's) "on two different occasions," 6169 (Huffer's Nieuport 28, flown by Rickenbacker), and 6160 (Heinrichs's). The report did not identify at least two apparent other occurrences. Capt. James Norman Hall had been shot down behind enemy lines, and the Americans still had "no clear idea how he was brought down."[44] Lt. William H. Plyler of the 27th Aero Squadron experienced failure of the upper left wing of his Nieuport 28 on 13 June. Plyler crash-landed and was also taken prisoner.[45] Counting Hall and Plyler, then, it appears that 1st Pursuit Group pilots had survived at least seven incidents of wing failure between Meissner's first incident on 2 May and Plyler's on 13 June. Perhaps there were more occurrences of wing failure. In each of the recorded incidents, the pilots survived to relate their narrow escapes. Nothing is known about those who did not survive.

Du Doré's report also advised of a number of other problems with the airplane. The landing carriage was too weak; numerous breaks occurred in the outer tubes of the landing carriage on hard landings. The oil tank tended to break because it was attached to the landing carriage. The cowling covering the rotary engine was of poor quality and broke easily. The gasoline tanks were too weak because of poor soldering and could not hold up under engine vibration. Larger pipes were needed for conveying fuel and oil. The location of the gasoline tank was also a problem. "Pilots complain of the fact that the gasoline tanks are too exposed to bullets. Five American pilots have been brought down in flames." Du Doré also noted that the Gnome rotary engine "in general overheats" and had an average life of only twenty-one hours. He concluded that reinforcement of the leading edge of the upper wing was "urgent." Although he also recommended strengthening the landing gear and gasoline tanks, it is clear that the weak upper wing was foremost in his mind.[46]

Atkinson also reported to Foulois about the Nieuport 28, addressing its wing failure in particular. In Atkinson's opinion, the source of the problem

Meissner's Nieuport 28 after wing failure

The top wing's main spar is clearly visible at center. The wing's leading edge (missing in this photo) extended about twelve inches forward of the spar.

was that the wing spars were too close together in the middle of the wing, and thus the leading edge of the wing extended too far forward for the ribs to hold up during violent combat maneuvers.[47] Atkinson included a detailed assessment of the airplane. In his view, the Nieuport 28 had only two favorable characteristics: its maneuverability and the rotary engine's ability to start quickly when responding to alerts. On the other hand, the airplane had a number of significant flaws. The rotary engine vibrated so much that it caused oil and gas leaks. The fuel leaks, Atkinson noted, were especially dangerous because the gas could come into contact with the "rather exposed" distributor plate in the fuselage, causing the airplane to catch fire. He also noted that the gasoline tanks were "very badly placed," especially the reserve tank. To improve a pilot's chances of surviving a fire, Atkinson stated, the fuel tanks needed to be low and farther back, with a pressure-feed system to move the gasoline forward. Moving the reserve tank, he suggested, would also provide room for another ammunition box.

Atkinson also noted other concerns about the design and ruggedness of the airplane. He reiterated Du Doré's concern that the landing chassis was too delicate. Furthermore, the airframe's delicacy often made complete realignment necessary after rough landings or even after a few days in the hangar. Machine guns were badly placed and should be positioned on top of the fuselage. The cockpit was too cramped, and the rudder bar needed to be moved about two inches farther forward to accommodate the longer legs of American pilots. The cowling was made of too light a material, easily cracked owing to vibration, and showered the pilot with castor oil from the motor.

Atkinson's final points were particularly scathing. He declared that at altitudes above thirteen thousand feet, the Nieuport was inferior to the SPAD as well as many of the German aircraft it encountered. More to the point, the Nieuport lacked "sufficient speed in a dive for a pursuit plane." He closed by stating that the fragile aircraft lost about 25 percent efficiency after fifteen to thirty-six hours of flying. Whereas Du Doré's report requested emergency modifications to make the Nieuport more combat effective, Atkinson's made the case that this fragile, fire-prone airplane simply did not measure up as a frontline fighter.

Yet a third letter, this one by the 94th Aero Squadron's commander, detailed the Nieuport's problems. Maj. Jean Huffer's report to Foulois also highlighted the wing problem, among other weaknesses. Huffer would have been in the best position of all to assess the cause of wing failure because most instances had occurred in the 94th Aero Squadron, and Huffer's own airplane (serial number 6169) had experienced wing failure while being piloted by Rickenbacker.[48]

Whereas Atkinson thought that the ribs could not bear the air-pressure load because of the distance from the front spar to the leading edge, Huffer suggested that the wing's wooden components were warping at different rates in response to weather exposure. Specifically, the three-ply birch-veneer covering warped at a rate different from that of the spar, causing a weakening of the joint between these two parts of the wing. Huffer listed a number of other faults and recommendations similar to Atkinson's.[49]

Thus three letters emerged from the 1st Pursuit Group, within days of one another, alerting headquarters to problems with the Nieuport 28. Although the weak upper wing appears to have been of utmost concern, the letters described all manner of problems with the new rotary-engine fighter. What accounts for this sudden outpouring of information about the Nieuport 28's weaknesses? More to the point, how did the men become aware that the wing failures were not caused by collision but rather by an overly fragile design of the wing?

Pilots in the 95th Squadron became aware that a problem with the Nieuport 28 had been discovered in their sister squadron, but as Lt. Harold Buckley recorded, "this had been immediately hushed up by the authorities as much as possible. No doubt they were afraid we would all get the 'wind up.' All inquiries were met by mysterious smiles. We knew something was wrong but exactly what we couldn't find out."[50] Lt. Joseph Eastman, of the 94th Aero Squadron, also thought that information was being withheld. He noted in his diary, "The story of colliding with a Hun was given out and believed in three instances (Jimmy twice and [Rickenbacker] once)—but in fact the frail Nieuport leading edges of the upper wings had collapsed thru too sudden pulling out of dives. The [commanding officer] or Col. Mitchell forbade the truth to be told the pilots."[51]

Discovery of the Nieuport 28's wing problem and corrective action came about as a result of the twisted politics that continued to plague the upper ranks of the Air Service. The relationship between Mitchell and Foulois had continued to deteriorate during the preceding months as Mitchell openly criticized the effectiveness of the Foulois administration. Many shared Mitchell's conclusion that the Air Service was a "practical failure" and that Foulois, as its commander, should accept responsibility.[52] As Philip Roosevelt observed, "General Foulois decided, just about the time that it was decided for him, that he would do better at the front." Pershing tapped his West Point classmate, Brig. Gen. Mason Patrick, an engineer officer, to replace Foulois. It was a sudden change to everyone in the Air Service, striking Lt. Col. Frank Lahm "like a thunderbolt."[53]

Foulois's new position was chief of aviation of the 1st Army. Unfortunately, Mitchell had expected to be given that assignment and had already established his office at Toul as its provisional headquarters. Foulois arrived at Mitchell's office on 3 June and notified him that he was taking over. Foulois recalled, "The expression on Mitchell's face was pathetic. He turned gray and his jaw sagged open in shock as if I had kicked him in the groin. . . . He began a loud monologue about how I had been out to get him ever since I had been promoted to brigadier general." Mitchell "babbled on almost incoherently and burst into tears like an immature child." Foulois asked him to stay on for a few days to help with the transition. Mitchell responded, "Not on your life, *General.* . . . You couldn't possibly acquire the knowledge to run this office in a few days and I'll be damned if I'm going to make it easy for you."[54]

The news of yet another "demotion" by his nemesis came at a particularly bad time for Mitchell. His brother, John, had died in a crash-landing at the 1st Air Depot at Colombey less than a week earlier.[55] After a strained luncheon, Mitchell accompanied Foulois on an inspection of the 1st Pursuit Group, never missing an opportunity to criticize Air Service Supply.[56] Foulois learned about the Nieuport 28 wing failures at this time.

The previous evening Lt. Waldo Heinrichs, of the 95th Aero Squadron, had experienced wing failure and managed to return to Gengoult airfield. The pilots of the 95th Squadron realized collision was not the cause of the repeated wing failure. "All the boys seem well agreed that my wing collapsed last night in the fight and that I did not hit the Boche," Heinrichs penned in his diary. Ironically, the squadron placed Heinrichs's wing on display in the mess hall, an exhibit that surely caught Foulois's attention. He met with Heinrichs that afternoon. They must have discussed Heinrichs's wing failure.[57]

Foulois acted quickly, tasking his subordinates to write letters detailing the Nieuport 28's faults and forwarding them along with his own recommendation to Brigadier General Patrick on 12 June: "The defects in this type of aeroplane are of such a serious nature that in my opinion they cannot be corrected. . . . I therefore urgently request that immediate steps be taken to replace all aeroplanes of this type, by one place [single-seat] Spads, or by [an] equally efficient and reliable British type."[58] He concluded by recommending that the Nieuport 28s be turned over to the training section. Foulois had never liked the Nieuports, and he considered Mitchell's failure to take similar action further proof of his technical incompetence.

Foulois had so much difficulty with Mitchell in completing the transfer of command that he sought Gen. Hunter Liggett's help at 1st Corps headquarters. News of Mitchell's tantrum had already reached headquarters, and one of its staff officers had been dispatched to Toul to ensure Mitchell's cooperation. Foulois also sent a letter to Pershing requesting that Mitchell be sent back to the United States.[59] Getting rid of Mitchell required the approval of Pershing, but this was not the case with the 94th Aero Squadron's commanding officer. Rickenbacker's diary for 4 June recorded tersely, "Huffer left today." According to the 1st Pursuit Group's diary the orders for his relief were not published until the next day. Huffer was ordered out of the squadron area even before the orders were published.[60] Foulois was again cleaning house—of Mitchell, Huffer, and the Nieuport 28.

Lt. Waldo Heinrichs's Nieuport 28 with damaged wing

Note the 95th Aero Squadron "kicking mule" insignia on the fuselage.

NATIONAL AIR AND SPACE MUSEUM, 98-15191

By this time Huffer had acquired a great deal of prestige. In addition to being one of the few Lafayette flyers awarded the rank of major, he had successfully guided the debut of America's first fighter squadron into combat. The 94th Squadron could boast seventeen confirmed victories with only five casualties. It had been cited and congratulated by the French and American military authorities and was the most famous and prominent American squadron on the front. Ironically, on the day that Huffer was ordered out of his unit, a committee representing the citizens of Toul presented a case of champagne to the squadron to show their appreciation for being kept safe from German aerial attack.[61]

Collectively, these first engagements with the Germans in the Toul sector might be considered America's first air battle. If so, the 94th Aero Squadron under Jean Huffer had won it. Admittedly, these engagements had no significant operational effect on the war, but they did constitute, as Mitchell noted, an important moral victory, one that was especially important because the United States had been so far behind the Europeans when it entered the war. As Mitchell observed, failure "would have had a dampening effect on our morale and would have greatly improved that of the German aviators." Instead, he continued, "we were inflicting a loss of at least three to one on the enemy, which is remarkable for a new outfit. Our men were full of dash and exceptionally cool in combat."[62] Stories about the 94th Aero Squadron had become a regular feature in the press. "Each evening the *New York Herald* has something to say of our squadron's work," noted Eastman in his diary.[63]

Huffer also demonstrated sound organizational leadership. He easily reorganized the squadron to integrate Captains Hall, Marr, and Peterson as flight commanders and wisely refused to release Rickenbacker to join the 103d Aero Squadron. The 94th Squadron had developed a high level of esprit de corps, reflected in the jaunty hat-in-the-ring insignia that Huffer had helped design. A visiting American pilot described Huffer as an old French pilot (he was twenty-three years old) "who knows how a gentleman's escadrille should be run. As he is commander we are treated in real French style. . . . You can see that this crowd would not suffer long from an American Army idea of what is good for a soldier." This included a "damn good" bar and an officer's mess with food that was so good that American pilots serving with French squadrons managed to find excuses to land at the Toul airfield.[64]

The assembly of such talent and their organization into an effective fighting team helped ensure that the American Air Service's introduction to combat would be successful. As military historians have shown, the American first-battle experience has often been a disaster.[65] To be sure, there were other important contributors to this American success, but the 94th Aero Squadron's first commander deserves a share of the credit. Partly because of him, the 1st Pursuit Group's early history and that of the American Air Service would be one of building on success instead of failure.

All of this had occurred while the squadron was under Huffer's command, so his swift removal without explanation or fanfare was quite remarkable. Compare, for example, Huffer's departure with that of fellow squadron commander, Maj. Davenport Johnson, who left the 95th Aero Squadron later in June to begin forming the 2d Pursuit Group. The officers of the 95th Aero Squadron organized a party for Johnson complete with multicourse dinner accompanied by the appropriate wine for each course, toasts, and speeches.[66] Unlike Johnson, Huffer did not move onto a prestigious command. He became assistant operations officer of the 1st Air Depot, an obvious demotion.[67] It may well have been that the 94th Aero Squadron's high profile in the press persuaded Foulois to keep the circumstances of Huffer's dismissal confidential, in the best interests of the service.

It seems reasonable, therefore, to conclude that Foulois relieved Huffer of command because of some sort of inappropriate conduct that came to Foulois's attention immediately after arriving at Toul, something requiring drastic action. The coincidence of Huffer's relief with Foulois's discovery of the Nieuport 28 wing problem, Eastman's diary entry, "The CO or Col. Mitchell forbade the truth to be told the pilots," and suspicions of a cover-up by members of the 95th Aero Squadron suggests that Huffer may have been involved in masking the Nieuport 28 wing problem. But one must ask, why would Huffer do such a thing? What could his motive have been?

Based on the evidence, Mitchell is the only one whose actions might indicate a motive for controlling damaging information about the Nieuport 28. He sent the telegram extolling the Nieuport 28's virtues at the beginning of May, though he was aware at the time of several problems with the SPAD 13. Moreover, Mitchell, not Huffer, was in a high enough position to be a significant actor in Air Service pursuit airplane procurement. Mitchell, not Huffer, sent the telegram to Foulois recommending continued procurement of the Nieuport 28 into the year 1919. At the very least, Mitchell should have ordered the reports on the Nieuport 28's failures and sent them to Air Service headquarters, but it took the arrival of Foulois for this to happen.

If a cover-up was taking place, it is difficult to believe that Mitchell was not party to it, given his close involvement with the 94th Squadron since its arrival at Gengoult. Indeed, the Nieuport 28 that Mitchell regularly flew (Huffer's) was one of those that experienced wing failure. The speed with which the letters by Du Doré, Atkinson, and Huffer detailing the Nieuport 28 wing failures were composed also suggests that knowledge about the problems already existed among certain leaders in the 1st Pursuit Group. It was not necessary to conduct an investigation to determine the findings that appeared in their letters; and there is no record of an investigation having been performed.

How long the information about the wings was kept from the pilots is uncertain, though the members of the 95th Aero Squadron still seemed to have been uncertain at the time of Heinrichs's accident. By 1 June, however, a few Air Service Supply officials knew. Capt. John Satterfield, of the Airplane and Motor Division, sent Atkinson a memorandum that day to let him know that corrective action had been initiated. The memo began, "Sergeant Vandewater [*sic*] called on me today and stated that you wanted me to be informed as to trouble with the leading edge of the wings on the Nieuport type 28." Vanderwater was Atkinson's most trusted noncommissioned officer, someone he could depend on to personally deliver information too sensitive to be placed in a cable. Satterfield added, "Lieut. Faunt Le Roy [*sic*], who was at Toul two or three days ago, has just reported back to me and has described the difficulty."[68] Cedric Fauntleroy was in charge of the American aircraft acceptance group in Paris. He had been Rickenbacker's roommate during basic flight training at Tours.[69] If he had been at Toul two days earlier, his visit would have coincided with Meissner's second case of wing failure. Perhaps Meissner and Rickenbacker finally discovered the true cause of their broken wings after Meissner's second failure, and they passed the information to Fauntleroy.

The memo continued, "We have taken this [wing problem] up with manufacturers in order to make necessary changes in the new series." Satterfield warned that it would take time to correct the problem. "There are still about 70 Nieuports coming through on the first series. These planes are so far advanced in construction that it will probably be difficult to make radical changes in the wing construction such as are necessary to correct this defect."[70]

Was the truth about the Nieuport's weak wings deliberately kept from the pilots to keep them flying a defective airplane while the problem was being fixed? Much of the evidence is circumstantial, and more is obviously needed for an airtight case. But like Lufbery's jumping to his death, what is significant for the 1st Pursuit Group is what was believed at the time, and it is certain that at least some of the pilots in the 94th and 95th Squadrons thought that a cover-up of the Nieuport 28's wing weakness had been orchestrated and that Mitchell, Atkinson, and Huffer, or some combination of the three, had kept the truth from them about the broken wing. It follows that once the pilots learned they had been deceived, the credibility of their leaders declined along with their confidence in their airplanes.

Foulois's discovery of the Nieuport 28's problems and the decisive action he took to remove the aircraft from frontline service, however, did not end the controversy over the rotary-engine pursuit plane. The rifts in the 1st Pursuit Group widened with the arrival of two new squadrons. The newcomers challenged the veteran squadrons for primacy in the 1st Pursuit Group, held little respect for the old-guard commanders, and waged a campaign to save the nimble rotary-engine fighter.

6

The Clash of Cultures

The 94th and 95th Squadrons were sister squadrons of the French tradition; they were led by officers who had flown with the French Air Service and staffed by pilots who had learned to fly under French instructors in France. The 27th and 147th Aero Squadrons arrived at the Gengoult aerodrome on 31 May to join the 1st Pursuit Group. The new squadrons had been trained in Canada and were commanded by officers who had been members of Britain's Royal Flying Corps. The 27th and 147th Squadrons were also sister squadrons, though having been trained by the British they were infused with values from the RFC. These squadrons were products of the Reciprocal Training Program, an agreement between Britain and the United States under which the RFC agreed to train ten American squadrons; in return, the RFC was provided the use of airfields around Fort Worth, Texas, which would enable it to continue its Canadian-based flight-training program without interruption during the harsh northern winter. Thus two traditions, one derived from the French, the other from the British, came together in the 1st Pursuit Group. The two new squadrons also originated at Kelly Field.[1]

The troop train carrying Cpl. Walter S. Williams arrived in San Antonio on 5 June 1917. The men unloaded, slung their haversacks and blanket rolls onto their backs, clipped their canteens to their belts, shouldered their duffel bags, and marched to Kelly Field. After they arrived, Williams and a score of men were organized into Company K of the 3d Provisional Aero Squadron. A little more than two weeks later, Company K became the 27th Aero Squadron, the oldest of the aero squadrons to join the 1st Pursuit Group. Before the war Williams had been an automobile mechanic and a journeyman machinist with the Midvale Steel Company of Philadelphia. His experience helped him win acceptance into the Aviation Section of the Signal Corps when he enlisted in April 1917. After a month at the Signal Corps Training School at Fort Wood on Bedloe's Island, New York, he proceeded to Camp Kelly, where he was put to work clearing the area of cactus, mesquite, scrub oak, rattlesnakes, and "all kinds of varmints." Williams later remembered, "We enlisted for the Aviation, but I believe we were the founders of the Engineer Corps for all we did was make roads, build barracks, lay pipe lines, dig gravel quarries, work out camps, drill, then a pleasant little twenty mile full pack (blanket roll type) hike for exercise."[2]

As a private, Williams earned thirteen dollars a month, which he used for gambling—one of his favorite pastimes—on free evenings in San Antonio. "Here is where we learned to fight, only our enemies were the Artillery and the Mexicans," he quipped. One of the chief complaints in the new squadron was the quality of the food. The day after the men were officially designated the 27th Aero Squadron, Williams recorded that the squadron mutinied "for better grub." The army responded by having an artillery unit take them out onto the plains to work under guard. "We agree to the Grub we get. Mutiny over," he stated. During this period Williams ran afoul of authorities and was confined in the guardhouse. "A full fledged soldier now," he boasted.[3]

The 27th Squadron left Kelly Field and arrived at Leaside, Ontario, on 18 August, joining two other American squadrons already there. Leaside was one of the fields in the aviation training complex that the RFC had established around Toronto during the spring of 1917. Williams lived in a twelve-man tent with wooden floors. On the first day of training the squadron marched to the center of the parade field and received a hearty "Welcome, 27th Squadron!" from the Canadian soldiers and the troops of two American squadrons already formed on the field. The sergeants of the RFC considered their new charges "loud mouths, rude, ill-mannered, discourteous"—in short, untrained. Williams complained that "they do not understand us as their army methods are greatly different from ours. They still have the old 'Dog Beat Method' not the Free Lance Method as ours."[4]

The American troops first had to relearn drill according to British regulations, using the distinctive quickstep and the palm-out salute. They carried swagger sticks, to keep their hands out of their pockets, and sewed strips of red ribbon on their shoulder straps to reflect their status as "attached" to the British army. Shortly after arriving in Canada, Williams spent his second tour of duty "in the clink" for insubordination and was again busted from corporal to private. In September RFC officials divided the 27th Aero Squadron into several detachments that were sent to the various flying fields around Toronto for on-the-job training. "We received instructions from the best trained men in Canada," wrote Williams, who found himself assigned to the Camp Borden motor shop, working on Curtiss OX-5 engines.[5]

While the enlisted men of the 27th Aero were drilling and learning their trades, the squadron's future pilots were also undergoing training. The American cadets first attended the Preliminary School of Military Instruction at Long Branch, also near Toronto, where British noncommissioned officers (NCOs) put them through a basic training course. Frederick Ordway, a third-year student at the University of New Hampshire, and his fellow cadets followed their NCOs on daily early-morning runs down to the shores of Lake Ontario for mandatory swims in the frigid waters. Cadets also learned to drill according to the British manual of arms. After successfully completing three weeks of basic training, Ordway attended the RFC ground school at the University of Toronto. The course was similar to the one Jimmy Meissner had attended, as the Cornell program copied the Toronto curriculum.

Next, Ordway proceeded to Camp Mohawk near the town of Deseronto, about 130 miles east of Toronto. Here he received primary flight training—takeoffs, landings, circuits around the field, solos, and cross-country flights. The life of the cadets at Camp Mohawk was better, as they ate with the officers and shared their lounge rooms. Before leaving Canada, Ordway was among the first American cadets assigned to the 27th Aero Squadron. On 22 October the 27th Aero Squadron was reunited at Leaside, Ordway and other cadets were assigned to the unit, and Maj. Harold E. Hartney took command.[6]

Hartney was a Canadian captain in the RFC who had volunteered to become an American citizen and train American pilots. After graduating from the University of Toronto in the arts "with a two-year dash of engineering," he studied law at the University of Saskatchewan. He also became an officer in the local militia and was an infantry platoon leader headed for the front when he joined the RFC in 1915. After completing flight training, he arrived in France in June 1916 and joined the 20th Squadron with only nineteen hours flying time. His unit flew the FE-2B, a second-generation two-seat biplane with a pusher propeller. Along with the Nieuport 11 Bébé, the FE-2B helped win Allied air superiority over the Fokker Eindecker, the first fighter to mount a synchronized machine gun that fired through the propeller.[7]

Hartney's unit pioneered formation flying in the RFC. By February 1917, when he was shot down, he was an ace with six victories and the senior flight commander in his squadron. Hartney claimed he was downed by the Red Baron, but historians later learned that a member of Richthofen's squadron, not Richthofen himself, had brought him down. It was not uncommon for pilots to attribute their ill fortune to the enemy's most notorious pilot. Nevertheless, the belief that Hartney had fought the famous German ace contributed to his reputation. Fortunately, Hartney crash-landed after this combat in friendly territory.

After recuperating he attended the Gosport School of Special Flying, where he received advanced training in piloting single-seat scouts. He also learned that he had been accepted by the U.S. Army and would be appointed to the rank of major and slated for squadron command.[8] When Hartney took charge of the 27th Aero, it was preparing to leave for Texas along with four other American squadrons and ten RFC squadrons. The 27th Squadron arrived at Hicks Field, near Fort Worth, on 29 October.[9]

Hartney served as both squadron commander and flight instructor for pilots of the 27th Aero Squadron. He trained his men according to the system he had learned at Gosport: the instructor occupied the front seat and communicated with the student through a rubber hose with a small funnel on each end. The British system involved using a single type of airplane equipped with dual controls rather than the series of different airplanes, beginning with the Penguins, of the French system. Under the British system, the instructor normally remained with his students through the entire course of instruction.

Instruction at Hicks Field focused on advanced flying techniques, including forced landings, aerial combat, and aerobatics. Training also included artillery spotting, aerial gunnery, machine-gun marksmanship, and bombing. The cadets flew the Canadian version of the Curtiss JN-4, usually referred to as the

Maj. Harold Hartney, France 1918

*Hartney, a Canadian lawyer, flew a two-seat pusher in
the RFC and won six victories with his gunner before
transferring to the U.S. Army.*

National Air and Space Museum,
CD-ROM 2B-11719

Canuck. It was of lighter construction that the American Jenny, and its "stick" control system differed significantly from the steering-wheel system used at Kelly Field and other American training bases. (Aviators who learned on the American JN-4 had to relearn control techniques with the stick control when they arrived in Europe.) Hartney's 27th Aero Squadron trained more than 100 cadets, including many of the officers of 147th Aero Squadron.[10]

The 147th Aero Squadron was organized at Kelly Field on 11 November and immediately sent to the Fort Worth complex and posted at Taliaferro Field 2 (Everman Field). Because it was the first squadron to arrive at the new airfield, its troops were put to work preparing facilities for the five RFC squadrons that arrived on 18 November. Ten days later, the 147th Squadron began instruction on repair, construction, and maintenance of airplanes and their engines. On 22 December the squadron joined the 27th Squadron at Hicks Field. Flight training began on 4 January with the assignment of forty-two cadets to the unit. Though most of its personnel had already been assigned, it was not until after 23 January, when twenty-seven-year-old Maj. Geoffrey H. Bonnell took command, that the squadron found its spirit.[11]

Bonnell, like Hartney, had been a captain in the RFC. An American of Canadian ancestry, Bonnell hailed from Staten Island, New York. He enlisted in the Canadian army as a private in the field artillery almost immediately after the war began in August 1914 and served for eleven months at the front, advancing to sergeant first class, as chief of a gun crew. He joined the RFC in November 1915. After only eleven hours of solo flying, he was assigned to the front. He served with the 32d Squadron (Scout), flying the DH-2, from July to December 1916.

Like the FE-2B flown by Hartney, the DH-2 was a second-generation fighter with a pusher propeller mounted behind the cockpit. This engine configuration was one of the solutions that allowed the mounting of a forward-firing machine gun in the days before the Allies had learned the importance of the Fokker synchronizing mechanism. Unlike Hartney's FE-2B, the DH-2 was a single-seater powered by a rotary engine—of which both Bonnell and Hartney were strong proponents. By the time Bonnell left his squadron he had advanced to acting flight commander and the rank of captain. Though he and Hartney were not in the same unit, Hartney had heard of Bonnell "because many people gave him credit for bring down Boelcke." This story was as false as the one that cast Hartney as a victim of the Red Baron, but it elevated Bonnell's stature because Oswald Boelcke was one of Germany's most famous fighter pilots, the father of organized fighter tactics, and the Red Baron's tutor.[12]

Bonnell was part of the initial cadre assigned to the RFC training complex at Toronto. He established a solid reputation, according to his superior, as one of "the few excellent officers" in Canada.[13] His record and American citizenship made him an ideal candidate for transfer to the U.S. Air Service. He became a major in the U.S. Army Signal Corps on 3 October 1917, making him junior to Hartney's date of rank of 21 September. Still, he initially served as the commanding officer of all the American squadrons sent to Canada and then as commander of the flying school at Hicks Field in Texas, where he was the officer in charge of training. Bonnell was a forceful commander with an aura that commanded respect and perhaps even awe.[14]

Geoffrey Bonnell in the cockpit of a Royal Flying Corps DH-2, 1916

A pusher propeller (not visible here) located behind the cockpit allowed the pilot to operate a forward-firing machine gun.

COURTESY OF T. C. MILLAR/REESE VIA ALEX REVELL

Bonnell's assumption of command had an immediate and positive impact on the 27th Aero Squadron. "Immediately, it seemed, a new spirit was born in the entire organization, morale, before rather indifferent, became a thing to fight for and maintain and the number of hours in the air increased by leaps and bounds." Like Hartney, Bonnell reorganized his squadron into three flights. He increased the pace of training by instituting a feverish regimen designed to get the squadron combat ready before its departure for Europe, setting a record on 13 February for the number of hours flown in a single day.[15]

Hartney's 27th Aero Squadron departed first, leaving Hicks Field by train on 22 January. When it arrived at Mineola Field, New York, six days later, the squadron was immediately placed in quarantine because of an outbreak of scarlet fever that forced the transfer of sixty enlisted men and two officers. The quarantine also caused the squadron to miss its scheduled 9 February departure on the *Tuscania*. Although Hartney complained, it turned out to have been a fortunate setback, as a German submarine sank the ship near Ireland. Evidently, the men still wore the red stripes of the RFC on their shoulders while at Mineola Field: Williams noted that when they began to circulate through the city and compete for the attention of the opposite sex, other soldiers started a rumor "that all guys with red shoulder bars are V.D. cases." The squadron embarked on the *Olympia* on 25 February and arrived on March 20 at Tours, France, where it spent nine days before being sent to Issoudun.[16]

The 147th Aero Squadron departed Hicks Field on 15 February, three weeks after the 27th Aero, and arrived at Mineola four days later. The 147th Squadron sailed on the *Cedric* on 6 March. The squadron's morale was almost shattered when it learned that it was to be treated the same as several other Reciprocal Training Program squadrons (the 17th, 22d, 28th, and 148th Squadrons) before them: officers would be sent to train and fly with British squadrons, while the enlisted men were assigned to other British squadrons for on-the-job training. Bonnell disappeared for a few days and, "wise to the ways of army red tape and how to overcome it," returned triumphantly with news that the squadron would be sent intact to France.[17] The unit arrived at Tours on 24 March. The enlisted men of the 147th Squadron remained at Tours and worked in the hangars while the officers continued to Issoudun for flight training, arriving at midnight on 30 March. The next day Hartney briefed Bonnell and his pilots on the situation at Issoudun.[18]

Although Hartney was senior to Bonnell according to date of rank, the latter was always in charge when the two were together. Bonnell commanded all of the American squadrons during the movement to Texas as well as the training program at Hicks Field, probably because he was well grounded in the RFC's Canadian training program. His domineering personality and physical size contributed to the continuation of his ascendancy once they arrived in France. Bonnell called Hartney "Petit," in reference to his small stature, while Hartney's nickname for Bonnell was the more masculine "Bo." After arriving at Issoudun, Hartney, the idea man, came up with a plan to accelerate the pace of training by using his squadron's mechanics to repair a hangar-full of condemned Nieuport trainers. When he meekly brought his plan to Bonnell for approval, Bonnell retorted, "It's five hundred francs for you if we win. And if the reverse happens, I'll beat you to a pulp and go home

Walter Williams, left, and his fellow enlisted men of the 27th Aero Squadron
enjoying some free time at Toul

*Williams carried his mandolin with him throughout the war, entertaining comrades with
songs like "Mademoiselle from Armentieres."*

National Air and Space Museum, CD-ROM 7B-39187

voluntarily in disgrace. I could never face my men again." Hartney reflected
that Bonnell "was—and is—like that."[19]

Hartney's scheme worked; their officers were rushed ahead of the others.
They began at Field 1, flying the Penguins, and advanced through the complete Issoudun training program. The 147th Aero Squadron's Lt. Kenneth
Porter, among the first to finish, had completed the course by 30 April. Two
of the 27th Aero Squadron pilots died in flying accidents at Issoudun, but all
of the 147th Aero Squadron's pilots survived the course.[20] While the pilots
continued their training, the two squadrons received orders to move to the
1st Pursuit Organization and Training Center at Epiez. The 147th Squadron,
minus pilots, arrived at Epiez on 22 April. The 27th Squadron, also without
its aviators, arrived two days later. The level of activity around Epiez further
intensified with the concurrent return of the pilots of the 95th Aero Squadron
from the Cazaux gunnery school.

"Battle front all around us," wrote Corporal Williams shortly after arriving at Epiez. "We hear the guns of Hell. We can even feel the ground tremble. How far from the lines we are we don't know but it must be near. . . . Me scared? SURE and so [is] every other soldier in the lines for the first time too." The soldiers were immediately put to work making the camp more habitable. "Good gosh," complained Williams, "it's one day at instruction, then four days at labor . . . laying duck boards to walk on in the mud, and cutting fire wood." Williams got so disgusted to find himself again working as a common laborer that he wrote critical remarks in a letter home. The unit mail censor saw the comments and preferred charges against Williams. After a summary court-martial by Hartney, Williams was busted to private for the third time since joining the Army and sentenced to thirty days hard labor, including the odious duty of servicing the base's latrines. Another irritant was the presence of old mustard-gas contaminants in the woods at Epiez. The persistent agent dripped down from the trees with the rain and made Williams's skin blister. The 147th suffered its first fatality in Europe at this time when one of its soldiers was struck by lightning while on guard duty.[21]

When Atkinson left to activate the 1st Pursuit Group at Gengoult, Bonnell took charge of activities at Epiez and placed Lieutenant Porter in temporary command of the 147th Squadron. Bonnell organized numerous ball games and barbecues to keep up morale, while the two new squadrons steadily received their vehicles and equipment and waited for their Nieuport 28s.[22]

The first Nieuport 28s began to arrive during the second week of May. Hartney gleefully exclaimed, "Our men were in a gloom over the expected arrival of inferior planes, when there landed on our funny little field the first of the ships we really were to use. And what a superb machine—a Nieuport 28!" He continued,

> She climbed even better than the [Sopwith] Camels at Gosport. For the first time in all my flying I felt that the plane and I were really one. She maneuvered like a bird in flight, almost in response to my thoughts. . . . The little ship could zoom, dive, and about-face much better than any of our modern fighting planes and I stayed up in it so long that I was accused of being afraid to land.[23]

Hartney's enthusiasm for rotary-engine fighters stemmed from his days at Gosport, where he "qualified as an expert on the Gosport Camels" and learned the peculiarities of the rotary engine. While the 27th Aero waited in England before crossing the Channel, he took some of his officers on a visit to Gosport. "The eyes of our men popped and they stood in wonderment at the Camels," he wrote, describing how instead of "circling in wide paths consuming a minute or two," the Camel "turned the full 360 degrees instantly, almost 'on a dime.'"[24] The Sopwith Camel was the most famous British fighter of World War I and is often remembered as the war's premier dogfighter. A fourth-generation fighter, the Camel made its debut in the summer of 1917 and continued to be used until the end of the war. Its extended life in this era of rapid technological change is indicative of its successful design and ability to be upgraded with more powerful engines. It was so popular that production by Britain's leading manufacturer of this airplane did not peak until March 1918.[25]

As a rotary-engine fighter, the Camel was in many respects similar to the Nieuport 28. It was unstable, and even more difficult to fly than the Nieuport 28. Like the Nieuport, its rotary engine created a gyroscopic effect that made it necessary for the pilot to use the rudder to counteract the engine torque during takeoff. The gyroscopic effect could also be exploited, however, to provide superior maneuverability in combat. As Richard Hallion has observed, "The Camel demanded excellent piloting and constant vigilance. The reward for competence was a highly agile aircraft capable of outturning virtually all German fighters; the penalty for inexperience or clumsy handling, however, could be fatal."[26] Opinions were divided within the RFC about what attributes made for the best fighter. Some pilots insisted on supreme maneuverability, exemplified in the Camel. Others preferred the SE-5, with its stronger airframe and more powerful water-cooled Hispano-Suiza engine. The technological relation between these two British fighters paralleled that between the French Nieuport 28 and the SPAD.

Hartney's trip to Gosport involved more than a demonstration of British aircraft technology. He also wanted his men to meet the British officers "who had gone there to train under my successor in E Flight." He wanted them to "get the feel of that team work, fair play, and gentlemanliness which are so vital to an honest-to-goodness war pilot." The British, Hartney believed, were the best in aerial warfare—superior to the Germans, who were, in turn, superior to the French. He credited the English public schools with building "character and moral fiber," in contrast with the French and German schools that he thought excelled more in technical training. "But when it comes to [the]

The Sopwith Camel, trailing a castor-oil cloud of exhaust from its rotary engine
as it climbs

*One of the most famous fighters of the war, the Sopwith Camel was noted for its maneu-
verability.*

National Air and Space Museum, CD-ROM 1B 39735

culture of the intangible (and most important) phases of the inner self, these
unique English schools lead the world," he wrote.[27]

Hartney next defined the specific values taught in the schools that he
wanted to develop in his squadron. "They breed patriotism, devotion, [and]
self-sacrifice," attributes which he believed were a prerequisite for a fighter
pilot. He further elaborated, "Doggedness, determination, loyalty, fearless-
ness, gallantry, and good sportsmanship—many of those things which count
for practically nothing in business, but are priceless when men's souls are in
stress—are bred in the bone of the English schoolboy." As the chief instructor pilot for his squadron, Hartney was concerned with their technical education, but he demonstrated other dimensions of leadership as well; he sought
to build an organizational culture based on the values that he believed would
provide the basis for success. "You cannot beat character even with the most
modern of war inventions," he concluded.[28]

His beliefs also reflected his Anglo-Saxon nationalism. "The British are one race," he wrote, "and their aviator-type youths are bred in one tradition with a peculiar singleness of loyalty, sportsmanship, courage, independence, and doggedness." In contrast,

> The French, like the Italians, are more brilliant in spots, but after ten centuries of almost constant warfare and economic struggle, their blood has been stabilized and it is only the exceptional individual who . . . can rise above a mass mind perplexed by politics, labor disputes, political confusion and the inevitable social and mental hodgepodge which has been the aftermath of the French Revolution.[29]

Hartney's belief in British cultural and racial superiority reflected a widespread conviction among many English-speaking people that the British, the North Americans, and the Germans were the "success races" of the nineteenth and twentieth centuries.[30] In addition to what he saw as the cultural superiority of the British over the French, he articulated other advantages held by his and Bonnell's squadrons:

> These were the first two squadrons to arrive at the front in which most of the officers including leaders had trained together from the beginning, with fundamentals taught by two men of actual front-line experience. The enlisted men were just as intensely interested in the coming sky battles as the pilots.[31]

Enlisted men and pilots did indeed come together earlier in the Reciprocal Training Program squadrons—in November 1917, in the case of the 27th Aero Squadron, for example, in comparison with the 95th Aero Squadron's unification in February 1918. Hartney and Bonnell remained in command of their units longer than the other squadrons' leaders. By June the 94th Squadron had experienced its second change of command and the 95th Squadron its fourth. Moreover, because Hartney and Bonnell had both trained and commissioned their pilots, they had a more intimate knowledge of their men and took interest in them on a deeper level. Bonnell matched Hartney's pilgrimage to Gosport after the 147th Aero arrived in France by taking some of his officers to meet Gen. Hugh Trenchard, Britain's most famous air commander of the war, who made the RFC the most offensively oriented air force of the war.[32]

Trained by the RFC in Canada, drilled by British NCOs, instructed and commanded by experienced RFC officers with celebrated, though not impeccable, credentials who felt a sense of cultural superiority and embraced the doctrine of the offensive, the squadrons of the British tradition exuded a confidence that seemed quite arrogant to the rest of the 1st Pursuit Group. Events on the battlefield hastened their arrival to Atkinson's command.

On 27 May the third blow of the German offensive fell along the Chemins-des-Dames between Reims and Soissons. In the face of the surprise attack and the intensity of the artillery fire, the Allied lines collapsed. Three days later, German troops reached the Marne River near Château-Thierry, only forty miles from Paris. In panic, parts of the French government and civilian population began to evacuate the city. In response to the emergency, Pétain called on Pershing to send American troops to that area,[33] thereby increasing the urgency to complete the formation of the 1st Pursuit Group. On the day the Germans reached the Marne, Bonnell received orders to bring both squadrons to Toul. On 31 May the two squadrons joined the 1st Pursuit Group at the Gengoult aerodrome, where they shared a large steel hangar with the French 122d Escadrille (Observation).[34]

Flight operations began on 2 June, with each squadron mounting three patrols. To orient the newcomers, pilots from the 95th led the patrols of the 27th Squadron, while pilots of the 94th led those of the 147th Squadron. The new squadrons became known as the Canadian Circus because they had been trained in Canada.[35] The veterans, however, had other names in mind—such as the "thirty-day wonders" because of the short time the newcomers had spent at Issoudun.[36] Lt. Joseph Eastman of the 94th Aero Squadron noted, "Now that two more green squadrons, 'the Canadian Circus,' are on our field, a fellow's no longer safe flying over the lines." Eastman was referring to the near cases of fratricide that he, Eddie Rickenbacker, and others had experienced while gaining their "vision of the air." Eastman also scoffed at their boasts that they would regularly fly patrols fifteen miles behind enemy lines.[37]

Atkinson required the new squadrons to stay well behind the front lines during their break-in period while maintaining a barrage against enemy photographic airplanes. He later modified these orders, permitting them to approach as far as the trenches, but at no time while they were based at Gengoult were the two squadrons ever allowed to penetrate German airspace unless explicitly authorized. He urged the commanders to take full advantage of the opportunity to familiarize themselves with the sector and allowed them to determine the size of the patrols—following the same rules used at Villeneuve in training the 94th and 95th Squadrons.[38]

Waldo Heinrichs considered it a "rank injustice" that the pilots of the Canadian Circus had advanced ahead of other pilots, some of them friends of his, at Issoudun. He also doubted their competence, having heard about all the Nieuports that had been "cracked up" at Epiez. He thought no better of the enlisted men: "Their mechanics are the undesirables who were left at home after the first overseas squadrons had left." Heinrichs also resented their arrogance: "They tell us they will soon be able to handle this sector alone without 94 or 95." Heinrichs's opinion softened after he led an orientation patrol of C Flight of the 27th Aero Squadron. "I glided, dove, zoomed, right and left turns, reverse turns, *renversement* and finally a barrel role, but they still stayed with it. Very good work," he wrote.[39]

Hartney and Bonnell cherished the Nieuport 28's maneuverability in spite of its other weaknesses. They considered the wing failures that had occurred in the 94th and 95th Squadrons to be a training problem, not a technical problem. Hartney explained that "we loved them and they performed perfectly for us. This was because both Bonnell and I had learned, from similar machines in England, the frailty of the Nieuport wing structure and the likelihood of the fabric ripping off in a too-sharp dive, and pull out." "Being unwarned about this weakness," he further noted, "both the 94th and 95th had some mean experiences with it before they discovered it and moderated the steepness of their dives."[40] To Hartney, safely piloting the Nieuport 28 simply required a healthy respect for its limits.

The united front offered by the Canadian Circus in defense of the Nieuport 28 reflected the underlying value they placed on maneuverability. Their preference conflicted with the equally strong feelings against the Nieuport 28 shared by the veteran squadrons of the French tradition, who were partial to the SPAD, which had become the primary fighter of the French Air Service. The SPAD was rugged and fast but not especially maneuverable—great for slashing attacks and diving away from trouble but a poor dogfighter. The surprise slashing attack was the ideal type of aerial combat, but as aerial warfare evolved to engagements between larger and larger formations, surprise became more difficult to achieve. Consequently, a good dogfighter like the Sopwith Camel or the Nieuport 28 suited Hartney's and Bonnell's preference for the offensive. Unfortunately, for the Canadian Circus, the position taken by the 94th and 95th Squadrons had the support of Brig. Gen. Benjamin Foulois.

Bonnell's squadron, in particular, agitated for retention of the Nieuport 28—reflecting the bombastic qualities of its leader. When they learned that

Foulois intended to eliminate the Nieuport 28 from frontline service, the squadron's officers bypassed army channels, a severe breach of military procedure, and went straight to Col. Halsey Dunwoody, chief of Air Service Supply in Paris, to press their case. They convinced Dunwoody that the Nieuport 28 was worth keeping. The supply chief sent a telegram to Foulois on 18 June requesting that he "get in touch with the pilots of the 147th Aero Squadron, all of whom state they prefer Nieuport 28 planes to SPADs." Dunwoody further recommended that the planned cancellation of a contract for six hundred more Nieuport 28s be withheld, because Air Service technicians had amassed a list of twenty-three changes that would correct the problems that had been reported with the airplane. In the meantime, Dunwoody stated, he was making every effort to obtain as many SPADs as possible.[41]

Foulois quickly countered the insurgency, cabling Dunwoody that he was "familiar with the view of the pilots of the 147th squadron [and] also familiar with the view of the pilots of other squadrons who have had much more experience with [the] Nieuport 28 plane." Regardless of the modifications contemplated, he argued, the airplane had limited value as a front-line fighter. "It is a very delicate machine and does not stand rough service. Urgently insist you continue to substitute SPAD monoplace. . . . The time has now arrived when our pilots at the front must be supplied with the finest equipment that can be obtained either from France or England."[42] Dunwoody responded that he would procure SPADs to replace the Nieuports as soon as possible.[43] By 20 June replacing the Nieuport 28 with the SPAD 13 was top priority for Air Service logisticians.

Pilots in the 94th and 95th Squadrons were delighted with the position that Foulois had taken, but some despaired at the lack of immediate action. On 15 June, when Capt. Kenneth Marr, the new commander of the 94th Aero Squadron, informed his men that the 1st Pursuit Group would soon leave to join the battle raging near Château-Thierry, pilots in the 94th Squadron wondered whether they would receive SPADs or be required to fight with the Nieuport 28s. Lieutenant Eastman thought it would "be highly desirable to dispense with the make-shift planes now on hand."[44] Rickenbacker later wrote in *Fighting the Flying Circus* that the principal fear that hampered him in the midst of combat was the knowledge that the Nieuport's wings might give way under the stress of a necessary maneuver.[45]

By mid-June the 1st Pursuit Group's focus had shifted to the upcoming battle. As a result of an agreement between Pétain and Pershing made earlier in the month, the 1st Corps headquarters was preparing to move from Neufchâteau to the Château-Thierry region.[46] As usual, the first inkling that something important was about to happen came by way of the French liaison officers. On 13 June Lt. Col. Frank Lahm, now acting as Foulois's deputy, met with the French mission. Commandant Paul Armengaud, who had just returned from French army headquarters, told Lahm that the 1st Pursuit Group was needed in the battle near Château-Thierry.[47] Lahm notified the 1st Pursuit Group and warned them to prepare for battle. Atkinson ordered his squadrons to practice squadron-size formations. At the same time, the units began packing equipment and preparing for the move.[48]

As the 1st Pursuit Group continued its preparations, several days of bad weather prevented flying. During this period a series of parties were held—final celebrations before leaving for the big battle near Paris. The first was given by the officers of 95th Aero Squadron to bid farewell to Maj. Davenport Johnson. Lt. Quentin Roosevelt, who had finally been released from his training responsibilities at Issoudun and had recently joined the squadron, was one of the principal organizers of Johnson's farewell bash. The dinner took place at a restaurant in the nearby city of Nancy. Toasts, speeches, and libations continued into the wee hours of the morning.[49] Not all of the 95th Squadron's officers attended, however. Heinrichs, who boycotted the affair along with two other squadron officers, stated in his diary that they "refused to give honor to a man whom we despise and never can respect." Having little respect for Johnson because of his failure of leadership in the air, he continued, "He is a joke! A Major because a West Pointer and commanding a squadron because of rank!"[50]

Inspired, perhaps, by the soiree given by their sister squadron, the 94th Aero organized an even grander one the following day. The arrival of photographers who took "moving pictures" of the squadrons added to the festive atmosphere of the day. After the photographers left, preparations for the "ball" began in earnest—included picking up their dates from the nearby hospital, Red Cross stations, and other places where women could be found.[51] Atkinson had left earlier that day with Philip Roosevelt and an interpreter to conduct a reconnaissance of the group's next base in the Château-Thierry area, leaving Major Johnson in charge of the group. The festivities were centered in the 94th Aero Squadron's mess hall, lasting, as one of the officers remembered, "until 3 A.M. when a great struggle began among us aviators to find places in automobiles that were driving our girl-friends back to their headquarters!"[52]

The next day Johnson brought court-martial charges against Maj. Jean Huffer, one of the guests, for "conduct unbecoming an officer and a gentleman." Specifically, Johnson charged that Huffer had brought a "notorious prostitute" as his date. Although Huffer's court-martial did not take place until December 1918, it again illustrates the conflict between insiders and outsiders that beset the group. Huffer's court-martial must have been quite a spectacle, as everyone who was anyone in pursuit aviation was in attendance. Harold Hartney, a lawyer by training and by then commander of the 1st Pursuit Group, served as Huffer's military defense counsel. Davenport Johnson, the prosecution's key witness, had become commander of the 2d Pursuit Group. With Mitchell's help, Huffer had redeemed himself from his June relief and risen to command of the 3d Pursuit Group, even though he was facing a court-martial. Atkinson, who had advanced to command of the 1st Pursuit Wing, was one of the jurors. Rickenbacker, Meissner, and Reed Chambers were among the witnesses.[53]

Laurence La Tourette Driggs, a prestigious lawyer from New York City and a famous aviation writer, served as Huffer's civilian attorney. At the time Driggs was also collaborating with Rickenbacker on *Fighting the Flying Circus*.[54] The defense argued that though Huffer may have been an American, his culture was French, and he should be exonerated because the French army's attitudes toward prostitution were more liberal. The defense also argued that the charge was nothing more than a pretext by Johnson to destroy Huffer. Normally, the defense rests after its closing statement, but Billy Mitchell, by this time a brigadier general, made a late and dramatic entrance into the court and spoke in Huffer's defense. The jury decided that Huffer had, indeed, attended the 1st Pursuit Group ball with a notorious prostitute but that he was not guilty of conduct unbecoming to an officer—an impossible verdict given the Army's system, in which just such behavior defined the charge. The court was ordered to meet again, and this time it exonerated Huffer.

Johnson's charge against Huffer reflected the continuing prejudice that insiders felt toward outsiders. Mitchell was less inclined to hold prejudice against the outsiders because he himself was an outsider. In considering the charges Johnson brought against Huffer, one should also keep in mind the general view about prostitution in the army at this time. In addition to its concern for military efficiency, progressivism had created a concern for morality. Anxiety over the ravages that venereal disease could have on army manpower strengthened the linkage between efficiency, morality, and patriotism. In the days before antibiotics, venereal disease (VD) could put the equivalent of several divisions out of service.[55]

Progressive reformers used the anti-VD campaign as an opportunity to inculcate their values in the U.S. Army, which they hoped would transform the larger society. One way to control VD might have been to regulate prostitution, as the French did; the prostitute Huffer brought to the party was registered with the Nancy police. Progressive reformers of the United States Army, however, wanted to eradicate prostitution, not regulate it.[56] Pershing himself staunchly opposed prostitution and observed that "this question was destined to give us considerable concern because of the difference between the French attitude and our own regarding the suppression of the sources of infection."[57]

A directive published by AEF headquarters in October 1917 stated that "all officers and soldiers should realize that at no time in our history has discipline been so important; therefore, discipline of the highest order must be exacted at all times. The standards for the American Army will be those of West Point."[58] Johnson understood this guidance. His loyalty to his alma matter was reflected in the adoption of the West Point mascot as his squadron's insignia: A kicking mule adorned the fuselage of the 95th Squadron's aircraft, and a mule was even hitched to a post outside their barracks.[59] From the insiders' point of view, Huffer had failed to meet the standards for morality, just as Lufbery had failed to meet the standards of administrative efficiency. In sum, both the conflict over the Nieuport 28 and the bringing of charges against Huffer reflected the continuing struggle taking the place within the 1st Pursuit Group. The values of the insiders and the French and British traditions collided with one another as the unit attempted to merge into a cohesive team. Each faction sought to make its values dominant in the group's organizational culture.

Operationally, the arrival of the 27th and 147th Aero Squadrons doubled the number of aircraft the 1st Pursuit Group was capable of putting into the air, making it all the more dangerous for the outnumbered and less well equipped Germans who opposed them. Consequently, American observation aircraft were able to accomplish their missions with relatively little threat from German fighters. A few years after the war's end an officer assigned to an observation squadron recalled,

> The early days in the Toul Sector are remembered by the aviators in the obser-
> vation end of the game as quiet ones. All the time I was there with the
> Americans I had never even seen a Boche plane. I understand they were

around all right, but all of your pursuit pilots of the 94th and 95th Squadrons were so determined, individually, to become the first American Ace that they scoured the sky from daylight to dusk, and to such a degree of success that the Boche thought it rather risky to even leave their own airdrome.[60]

Philip Roosevelt observed the same audacity: "At present they all want to go out and commit suicide by taking on half a dozen Boches at a time, 10 kilometers across the lines while all by their little lonesomes and under orders to stay behind the line of friendly balloons," he wrote shortly after the arrival of the Canadian Circus.

> Then when they do get back all shot up one is so glad to see them at all that it is impossible to treat them as men who have deserted their posts, and to prefer General Court martial charges against them. And apparently all the men we have had killed produce no effect of caution at all. The lure of the Croix de Guerre is too strong.

Thinking of the future, he added,

> If we can only get through another two months without their losing their nerve and without too many losses we can stack this group up against anything in the world. . . . I think we have the makings of a lot of good squadron commanders here all right, if they'll let us have two months to get 'em in.[61]

The Air Service produced its first aces, Douglas Campbell and Eddie Rickenbacker, in the Toul sector. Capt. David McKelvey Peterson, who already had credit for one victory while flying with the Lafayette Escadrille, also became an ace. All of these men were in the 94th Aero Squadron, and most of their victories occurred in May. Campbell scored his fifth victory on 31 May while flying alone on a voluntary patrol. His lone battle with a German two-seater was more representative of the aerial warfare of the past than of what was to come. He shared his sixth victory with Meissner (Meissner's third) when they both responded to an alert call for an enemy observation airplane. This was Campbell's last combat. He was wounded during the engagement and subsequently ordered back to the United States to assist with training, leaving Rickenbacker as the leading ace.[62]

The blue-collar pilot who had been shunned by the collegiate élite saw his stock rise as the social structure in the squadrons continued to be transformed by the life and death struggle of aerial combat. Rickenbacker scored his fifth victory on 30 May; technically, that made him the first ace, but confirmation was delayed until almost two weeks later.[63] The 30 May combat occurred in a large dogfight, which was unusual in the Toul sector but representative of what was to come in Château-Thierry. In the Toul sector, most of the missions were of small size, consisting of one to three airplanes, because of the relatively weak threat posed by German fighters.

German fighter forces opposing the Americans initially consisted of a single understrength fighter squadron, Jagdstaffel (Jasta) 64, based at Mars la Tour airfield, about forty miles north of Toul and centered on the St. Mihiel salient.[64] Jasta 64 was equipped with Albatros and Pfalz single-seat fighters. Initially, the German unit had to contend with the 94th Squadron as well as at least two French pursuit squadrons, Escadrille SPA.23 (a SPAD unit) of the French 2d Army and Escadrille N.90 (a Nieuport unit) of the French 8th Army. During May another understrength pursuit squadron, Jagdstaffel 65, reinforced Jasta 64 at Mars la Tour, but the added support was more than offset by the arrival of the 1st Pursuit Group headquarters with the 95th Aero Squadron; the Allies retained a large numerical superiority.[65]

At the end of May, in response to the departure of French squadrons east of the 1st Pursuit Group's sector, the French 8th Army extended the 1st Pursuit Group's sector farther eastward—as far as the forests of Gremacey and Champenoux, an additional distance of approximately twenty-two miles, while the westward limit remained along the Meuse River. This extended sector, almost double in size, included two additional German fighter squadrons against the 1st Pursuit Group, but the arrival of the 27th and 147th Aero Squadrons insured that the Americans still had a superiority of better than two to one. At the same time, the German fighters had to defend against British DH-9 bombers of the RAF's 42d and 43d Wings, which were flying to targets around Metz and Trier.[66]

A German air commander's report to higher headquarters illustrates the extent to which the 1st Pursuit Group was able to control the air: "The enemy Arbeitsflieger [literally, worker or observation aircraft] and especially the Jagdflieger [fighters] were often over the German lines. At high altitudes the German Arbeitsflieger were attacked on all sides by aggressive

American single-seaters." A comparative view of the air war from 17 May through 23 May illustrates how badly things were going for the Germans. During that week, the Germans launched a total of 23 observation sorties and 125 pursuit sorties resulting in 17 aerial engagements—only one of which was successful from the German point of view. "In contrast, the American pursuit squadrons reported no fewer than 293 flights and 22 air combats of which five were successful."[67]

The Toul sector was just challenging enough to enable the pilots of the 1st Pursuit Group to gain combat experience and develop tactics and techniques while having a high probability of survival. On the mission on which Rickenbacker became an ace, the 1st Pursuit Group was escorting the egress phase of a bombardment mission by the RAF. A combined patrol consisting of six fighters each from the 94th and 95th Squadrons provided the protection. Meissner led the flight from the 94th Aero Squadron; Rickenbacker did not take off until after the two flights had already departed. Flying separately, above and behind the combined protection patrol, he positioned himself to take advantage of any opportunity that might present itself. From this vantage point Rickenbacker could stay above the fray, in relative safety, and wait for the perfect moment to strike—when his quarry was engaged and distracted in combat with the patrol of Nieuport 28s. The Nieuports served as Rickenbacker's bait.

Rickenbacker saw the American fighters racing forward to meet the British bombers, with a formation of enemy fighters in hot pursuit. Suddenly a second formation of enemy fighters came out of the west and intercepted the Nieuports of the 1st Pursuit Group. In the melee that followed, Meissner suddenly found himself with two Germans on his tail. He ripped the leading edge off his top wing (the second such occurrence for Meissner) as he attempted to maneuver away. At this moment Rickenbacker launched his attack, downing one of the German Albatros fighters and scaring off the other. Rickenbacker did not realize at the time that it was Meissner at the controls of the beleaguered plane. But Meissner found out that Rickenbacker had saved his life, and this strengthened the bonds that had already been developing between the two. Meissner was popular because of his good nature and cheery grin. His friendship helped redeem Rickenbacker from the social isolation he had experienced in the early part of his career in the 94th Aero Squadron.[68]

Although the 1st Pursuit Group managed to keep its sector clear of enemy fighters while protecting French and American observation aircraft, it was not able to prevent completely the penetration of German observation aircraft. This was especially true of high-flying German observation aircraft with ceilings greater than that of the Nieuport 28. German Rumpler reconnaissance aircraft were capable of reaching altitudes above twenty thousand feet. When flying this high they were virtually immune to interception. Rumplers came equipped with small bottles of oxygen for the crew to use above altitudes of 11,500 feet, though high-altitude flight sometimes caused their crews to die of the bends after landing.[69]

Mitchell claimed that the Nieuport 28 could go as high as the German Rumpler; but though the Nieuports may have been capable of reaching high altitudes because of their light construction, this statement does not appear to be entirely correct.[70] "I remember chasing one up to—well, I got up almost twenty-one thousand feet in a Nieuport one day," Douglas Campbell recalled. "The Rumpler was a thousand to two thousand feet higher than I was . . . and I would get under him and pull straight up and take a pot shot but too far away to hit him. And then I'd drop two or three thousand feet before I'd catch myself."[71] At these high altitudes the Rumplers were barely visible from the ground, but Hartney saw one flying over Epiez shortly after his arrival there. A couple of days later a German airplane "came scudding over" the airfield and dropped a photograph of the Gengoult aerodrome with the message, "Welcome 27th and 147th. Prepare to meet thy doom."[72] German fighter forces in the Toul sector, however, simply lacked the capability to make good on this threat.

The Toul sector provided an ideal opportunity for pilots to fly their missions, reflect, and experiment with new techniques. Alan Winslow described a plan, hatched by a trio of 94th Aero Squadron pilots over a period of several days, to down one such high flyer. He, Meissner, and Thorne Taylor had encountered a large two-seat Hannover photographic plane almost daily during the first part of June. The German plane "annoyed us by the nonchalant manner in which it completely ignored our attacks. . . . Every morning, as punctual as though it were a prearranged meeting, we could count on finding the Hannover not far from St. Mihiel lumbering along at about 18,000 feet." The three pilots studied the problem and came up with a plan to sucker their quarry to a lower altitude.

First, Thorne was to climb to his maximum ceiling at the right of the Hannover, dive with full motor, zoom up vertically, and give it a short burst from directly below. A moment later, Jimmie, flying at the German's left, was to dive several hundred feet from his ceiling, pull up sharply and rattle out another volley of bullets at the big plane's belly.

Subsequently, Winslow would use the same maneuver to attack the German from the rear with a third burst. They would continue these attacks in succession. They were aware that because of the range, their bursts had practically no chance of bringing the German plane down, but they hoped their repeated and persistent attacks might "tempt the pilot to tip his plane first to the right and then to the left in order to give his gunner a free shot at each of us as we climbed up from beneath in quick succession."[73]

On the morning of 13 June, Winslow, Meissner, and Taylor found the Hannover photographing American and French positions, and they put their plan into action. At first the plane ignored them, but after fifteen minutes of successive attacks the enemy pilot took the bait and began to tip his plane slightly to the left and then to the right so his observer could fire down at the Americans. Winslow had second thoughts about the plan as he heard the "tac-tac-tac and whiz of machine gun bullets" from the observer's gun spray at the wings of his Nieuport. Finally, after three quarters of an hour of successive attacks, the pilot leaned the Hannover just a fraction of an inch too far to one side, causing the airplane to sideslip and lose altitude. In a moment the plane was below the Americans, and they were diving after him with machine guns roaring. The German observation plane burst into flames.[74] The shared victory was Meissner's fourth and Winslow's second.

When the tempo at the aerodrome slackened, Atkinson ordered his squadrons to practice gunnery. Shortly after arriving at Gengoult, he coordinated with the French Air Service for use of an aerial target range located northeast of Toul and for aircraft of the 122d Escadrille to tow the targets. He directed his squadron commanders to make full use of the range time allocated to each squadron. Near the aerial target range was a small lake that was also used for practice surface attacks. Finally, the range on Gengoult field itself was extensively used to test-fire machine guns and align sights. During June enough machine guns arrived that each Nieuport 28 could be equipped with two guns. Campbell had just received his second machine gun the night before his last flight, on 6 June, though he had not yet mounted it before leaving on his unfortunate mission.[75]

The official history of the 1st Pursuit Group states that "its pilots had brought down 58 Hun planes, 27 of which were confirmed." Several official accountings of victories have been conducted since World War I. The most recent, published in 1965, credits the 94th Squadron with bringing down nineteen enemy aircraft, which was the preponderance of the 1st Pursuit Group's victories—as might be expected, as it was the first to commence operations. But it was not the veterans of the Lafayette Flying Corps who scored most of the victories. It was the neophytes: Campbell had six, Rickenbacker five, Meissner four, Winslow two, and Taylor one (some of these were shared victories). Of the Lafayette veterans, Peterson had credit for three (and one more after being transferred to the 95th Squadron), while James Norman Hall had credit for one. The 95th Aero received credit for seven. The 27th Squadron scored three victories during the last two weeks in the Toul sector, more than any other squadron during the last days of June. The 147th Aero Squadron won none.[76]

Philip Roosevelt had been thriving since taking over as group operations officer. He worked from half past four in the morning until ten o'clock at night "under a tension and necessity for speed that makes the newspaper business seem like a rest cure."[77] He was responsible for the daily group operations that directed the squadron-level patrols and alerts, and he decided how many aircraft should respond to alerts. He was also in charge of securing victory confirmations. An unconfirmed victory counted for nothing. The award of medals and citations, and the prestige of being designated an ace, depended upon *confirmed* victories, the most important indicator of success and determinant of prestige for fighter pilots and their units. Consequently, the confirmation process could be a controversial topic among pilots, especially when they felt they had been cheated.

In the wake of the French army's refusal to confirm two victories that pilots were certain they had won, Roosevelt sent his squadrons a memorandum explaining the French army's rules for confirmation. "The French will not confirm the result of an aerial combat unless there is not the slightest room for doubt that the German plane hit the ground, and fell as a result of a combat with the pilot in question. Thus a machine seen to descend in a vrille will not be confirmed unless somebody actually sees it crash on the ground."[78]

Roosevelt illustrated the strictness of these rules with two recent examples. Capt. David McK. Peterson, who had just transferred from the 94th to the 95th Squadron, claimed a victory on 17 May. "Although a French officer reported that observation posts saw the machine descending vertically at the height of the tree tops," Roosevelt noted, the French 8th Army head-quarters had refused to confirm Peterson's victory because no one had seen it crash into the ground.[79] Peterson eventually received credit for this victory, but he had to wait until 18 September, when a captured airman reported that the airplane in question had made a forced landing with its engine on fire.[80]

Lt. Thorne Taylor of the 94th Squadron, who reported having sent an Albatros down in flames on 18 May, was less fortunate. At approximately the same time, but nine miles distant from the location of the combat Taylor reported, observers confirmed having seen a German airplane crash. Nevertheless, French Army officials refused to award Taylor the victory. In a letter written home at about this time, Roosevelt discussed the same incident:

> An infantry or artillery observer has to see the plane hit the ground and his report must coincide as to time and place with the pilot's report. . . . 15 kilometers is not a long distance seen from a plane traveling over 100 miles an hour at 15,000 feet yet one of our pilots brought down a machine at "A" at 9:30 A.M. according to his report. The infantry observer saw a machine fall at "B," fifteen kilometers distant, at 9:25 A.M. the same date, but the pilot does not get credit for it so you see how strict they are. . . . This may give you an idea of how hard it is to get full credit. Nevertheless this system is better than the British one, which credits a man with anything he claims. All a man has to do to get a Bosche (British style) is to get separated from his patrol and then come back and say he got one. The only defect of the French system is that it discourages attacking enemy planes more than two or three kilometers in Germany (up here we speak of everything "over there" as "in Germany") as a man knows it will never be confirmed, and to the Frenchman the citation which goes with it means at least as much as the successful fight.[81]

To be fair, the difference between French and British confirmation rules reflected different incentive systems for different air strategies. The offensive strategy of the Royal Air Force required its pilots to take the fight deep into enemy territory—far too deep for victories to be confirmed by frontline observers. In such situations, confirmations could only come from fellow airmen. It should not be surprising, therefore, that when the AEF began offensive operations in September it adopted a more lenient system of confirmation, similar to that of the British.[82] But this change would not take place until after the Château-Thierry campaign.

Because he assembled the squadron operations reports at the end of the day, Roosevelt had the most comprehensive picture of the air war. His intellect directed the air battle. "It is largely guesswork for me for it requires a lot of study of the tricks and habits of the Bosche. For they are good. This is no game to them and they are methodical in all their activities." He was the battle captain, totally immersed in a job that had never before existed in the American Army.[83]

In the late afternoon of 25 June, Philip Roosevelt ordered the alert commander to destroy two enemy aircraft that had been spotted near Metz. Hartney's 27th Squadron had alert duty, and as fate would have it, Hartney himself had decided to stand the alert.

Hartney had drilled each of his men in mock combat. He constantly studied their patrol reports and quizzed them in teaching sessions during which he used the Socratic method to make his points. "By this time I really believe I knew every flight commander, every leader and every officer in the 27th better than he knew himself," Hartney remembered. With Roosevelt's order in hand, it was now Hartney's chance to set the standard for the fighting-squadron commander. After taking off with his two wingmen, Hartney spotted two enemy aircraft, an observation airplane with a fighter escort about two thousand feet above it. The experienced pilot kept his eagerness in check. He took his time to lead his flight of three Nieuports into an advantageous position. When they had the advantage of the sun and altitude he led the attack on the observation aircraft and killed the rear gunner. He then withdrew, as he had taught his men the leader should do, and turned the attack over to Lt. John MacArthur, who finished it off. Meanwhile, the enemy escort fighter had attacked Lt. Robert Hill, and both planes were plunging toward earth with the German hot on Hill's tail, spewing tracer bullets into the Nieuport 28.[84]

Hartney's experience and sharp sense of situational awareness came to the fore in the next moments. He broke off from the engagement against the observation plane, which was now well in the hands of MacArthur, and dived after the German fighter as it pursued Hill. The German pilot had not anticipated Hartney's action, and because of this mistake he became Hartney's second victim that evening. Hill survived but made a forced landing. Hartney remembered, "From that moment on, not one word that I uttered not any wish that I expressed was doubted or debated by my men, officers or enlisted. So far as discipline or confidence were concerned, it was the luckiest break I ever had in my life."[85]

Casualties in the 27th and 147th Aero Squadrons were light in the Toul sector because of the restrictions Atkinson had placed on the squadrons and the decreasing level of activity during June. Only one pilot of the Canadian Circus died while flying from Gengoult—Lt. Edgar H. Lawrence, a civil engineer from the University of Illinois in the 147th Aero Squadron—and his death was probably not a result of enemy action.[86] On 4 June his Nieuport suddenly dived from his patrol, eventually striking the ground and bursting into flames. The plane burned completely, so no investigation could determine whether mechanical failure had been the cause of the crash. The 1st Pursuit Group carried the death as accidental. One of the members of the 147th Aero thought Lawrence had "undoubtedly" succumbed to hypoxia from the high altitude at which his patrol had been flying.[87]

The 147th Squadron lost another pilot to Swiss neutrality: Lt. James Ashenden, an engineering graduate from Loyola Academy, crash-landed near Solerno, Switzerland, where his plane was seized and he was interred for the rest of the war. His Nieuport 28 is on display in the Swiss Air Force Museum at Dubendorf and is the only known 147th Aero Squadron aircraft still in existence. The fate of this patrol is a good example of the difficulty the new squadrons had because of their lack of experience. The five Nieuports took off from Gengoult on 25 June to protect a French Salmson reconnaissance airplane. German antiaircraft fire broke up the patrol, and the inexperienced pilots lost their bearings in a fog bank. The scattered members of the patrol eventually made forced landings throughout the countryside—none landed at Gengoult, and one, Lt. William E. Brotherton, mistakenly attempted to land in Germany but was driven off by machine-gun fire.[88]

In the 27th Squadron, Lt. William H. Plyler was missing, but the group would later learn that he was a prisoner of war. Contrary to Hartney's claim that it had never occurred in his squadron, Plyler experienced wing failure while in combat and was forced down behind enemy lines.[89] Apparently, Plyler was a new man who was unaware of the wing problem and had not yet learned Hartney's precautions for safe operation of the Nieuport 28.

The 95th Squadron's losses included Lt. Richard Blodgett, who had gone on a "hunting expedition" by himself after flying a protection mission for the

1st Aero Squadron. Two hours later his badly burned body was found in the wreckage of his plane less than a mile from the Gengoult airfield. He was taken to Evacuation Hospital 1, where he died within an hour. Wilfred Casgrain was initially listed as missing on 30 May, but before leaving Gengoult the group learned he was a prisoner of war. The 95th Aero's only other casualty in the Toul sector was the temporary loss of Lt. William H. Taylor, whose wheels caught a rut during takeoff on 25 June, causing his Nieuport to nose over and crash. Taylor was injured but would return to his squadron in September after a period of recuperation.[90]

The 94th Aero Squadron suffered the most casualties. Lt. Charles W. Chapman, one of the officers who had served a short time with the Lafayette Flying Corps but had no previous frontline experience, went down in flames on 3 May in the course of an aerial combat in the Luneville sector in which a patrol of five Nieuports met five enemy aircraft.

Lt. Paul B. Kurtz was on his first day of duty with the squadron on 22 May. Kurtz had accompanied Rickenbacker and Chambers on a patrol at an altitude of fifteen thousand feet. After a combat he returned to the field separately and prepared to land but had to put on power as another airplane was just taking off. Shortly afterward Rickenbacker saw Kurtz's airplane circling to land and then suddenly plunging to the ground, burning. Rickenbacker thought that Kurtz had also succumbed to hypoxia. In his report of the incident, Atkinson seemed to suggest that the crash might have been caused by a fire, but he could not tell for sure.[91] One possible explanation is that because of his unfamiliarity with the Nieuport 28's Gnome rotary engine, Kurtz might have failed to decrease the fuel flow as he turned off the engine's cylinders to land—it was common to glide to landings. If so, when he "blipped" the cylinders back on for increased power, the accumulated fuel in the engine might have caught fire.

Five days earlier, Lt. Joseph Eastman had had a similar experience, one that could have brought him down, too, with horrible burns. Eastman had not been warned about the Gnome's peculiarities or about the weak fuel lines. His diary entry stated,

> Just over the field I smell a strong odor of gasoline, and find a steady stream pouring from the motor by my feet. "Fire!" thinks I, and I cut off my magnetos—which shows that I am precautious if not nervous. Deprived of power, I

"S" into the field immediately sans taking the extra tour to refocus my eyes—
so land a little heavily—bending my axles.[92]

Lt. Philip W. Davis went down in flames in combat on 2 June. Davis was on
a protection patrol with four other Nieuports that engaged six Pfalz of Jasta
64. Douglas Campbell, the flight leader, reported the airplanes engaged in a
melee that lasted about five minutes. Davis's plane burst into flames from the
side gasoline tank. Willard Hill, though not killed, was also a permanent loss
after being severely injured by a bullet wound to his leg.[93]

The 94th Aero also lost most of its experienced Lafayette flyers through a
combination of casualties and reassignments. The most shocking loss was that
of Raoul Lufbery. Capt. James Norman Hall, who had commanded A Flight, had
been taken as a prisoner of war after suffering wing failure. Capt. Kenneth Marr,
the commander of B Flight, replaced Maj. Jean Huffer when he was relieved as
squadron commander. Captain Peterson, commander of C Flight, was transferred to the 95th Aero Squadron in mid-May, probably in anticipation of replacing Maj. Davenport Johnson as squadron commander. Douglas Campbell initially replaced Peterson as commander of C Flight in the 94th Aero.

Thus by the time the 94th Squadron left Toul, Capt. Kenneth Marr was in
command and the only experienced Lafayette pilot in the squadron. Marr was
assisted, however, by a new group of leaders who had gained their experience
in recent months. This was an advantage that the 94th had over the other
squadrons, especially the Canadian Circus, which lacked any experienced flight
commanders. Rickenbacker, an ace, had been moved up to assistant squadron
commander. Reed Chambers commanded A Flight. Jimmy Meissner, with four
victories to his credit, commanded B Flight. William Loomis, who had flown
with Escadrille SPA.153 from 23 November 1917 to 19 February 1918, commanded C Flight.[94]

An advance party convoy led by Capt. Gordon Rankin departed Gengoult
early in the morning of 26 June to make initial preparations at the new base for
the reception of the main body the next day. For everyone else the day was spent
packing baggage on the group's vehicles. The next morning the baggage, personnel, and equipment of the squadrons departed by truck convoys for the new
station near Château-Thierry. The commanding generals of both the French
32d Corps and the U.S. 26th Division were present to see them off. Pilots and
mechanics remained behind an additional day to give the main body time to

arrive at the new base and prepare for their arrival. After the convoys left, the remainder of the group "decamped en masse, in Fiats and in side-cars to 'Historic Nancy,'" where they "gorged heavily both noon and evening."[95]

That night the Germans conducted their first and only air raid on the Gengoult airfield while the 1st Pursuit Group was there. "As we watched the archies spitting from the hill and mapping above, a smashing jolt sent us all running," Eastman reported. "There were four more to follow, all of which seemed to have grazed the walls of our barracks—yet were at least a half mile away." The bomber returned for a second pass "and spat down a vindictive little stream of glowing incendiary bullets from his machine gun."[96] Cpl. Walter Williams, who had already left, remarked in his diary, "We just missed a raid by the Huns at Toul. They knocked [the] Hell out of our old field after we left. . . . Fooled you that time, Heinie, Eh???" The next morning the Nieuport 28s of the 1st Pursuit Group took off, squadron by squadron, and flew to their new base and their first battle.[97]

7

America's First
Air-Land Battle

The fourth of the series of blows that compromised the German offensive was unleashed on 27 May. The attack achieved startling success against the French 6th Army, creating a deep wedge in the French line with its nose at Château-Thierry. The arrival of German troops only forty miles from Paris caused a general panic, and the government prepared to evacuate to Bordeaux. Gen. John Pershing had intended to collect his army in the quiet Toul sector, but in response to the emergency and Gen. Henri Pétain's urgent request for aid, he began dispatching American units to reinforce the French 6th Army. After visiting the 6th Army headquarters in June to coordinate aerial reinforcements, Billy Mitchell reported that he had "never seen a more stunned group of people. . . . They had lost miles of territory, thousands of men and hundreds of airplanes."[1] The 1st Pursuit Group replaced the 6th Army's *groupe de combat* because "hostile aviation had shot the Allied defense right out of the air."[2]

On 28 June fifty-two of Bert Atkinson's Nieuport 28s landed at an airfield near the villages of Touquin, Ormeaux, and Pezarches. Small canvas hangars, each capable of holding three Nieuports, lined the aerodrome that, over the past two weeks, had been carved out of the crop fields, which were still partly covered by standing wheat. Because of the precarious enemy situation, the

Château de la Fortelle

The chateau served as the officers' quarters for the 27th Aero Squadron during July and August 1918.

Jerry C. Vasconcells Collection, U.S. Air Force Academy Library

airfield was set about twenty-five miles from the front lines—twice the distance of the 1st Pursuit Group's previous base at Gengoult. Even at this distance, the tremendous amount of artillery fire along the front illuminated the night sky. The new field was also only twenty-five miles from Paris, thereby facilitating logistical support. The officers of three of the squadrons and the group headquarters moved into nearby chateaus; the pilots of the 147th Aero Squadron were quartered in local homes. Enlisted men of the 1st Pursuit Group found less comfortable billets—Cpl. Walter Williams and his comrades took up residence in a barn near the airfield.[3]

Part of the 27th Aero Squadron became hopelessly lost during the flight to the new base, flying south, instead of north, and landing in southern France at Lyons before regaining their bearings and arriving at Touquin late that evening.[4] As Atkinson waited for the lost flight of the 27th Squadron he must have wondered how his pilots would survive the coming battle if they could not even make their way through the friendly skies at the rear of the French army. He had just received an intelligence report informing him that German pursuit was "extremely active and aggressive." Enemy fighter patrols usually flew in groups of ten to twelve planes at an altitude of about sixteen thousand feet. Their standard tactic was for one or two planes to descend from the group to attack while the rest remained above to cover them. These high patrols were considered the most dangerous, but fighters also flew low patrols, usually consisting of three or four planes at about sixty-five hundred feet that attacked Allied observation aircraft and balloons and occasionally strafed friendly ground troops. Enemy reconnaissance flights were increasing and "unusually numerous." The report also included the locations of eight enemy observation balloons along the front. Atkinson forwarded the report to his squadrons.[5]

Mitchell, who had established his 1st Air Brigade headquarters nearby, calculated that the Americans were "outnumbered in the air almost five to one."[6] Lt. Joseph Eastman of the 94th Squadron noted similar odds: "Reconnaissance reports show 97 German flights (5 planes equal 1 flight) observed over this portion of our lines. That many flights—while we haven't a maximum of more than 75 individual planes!"[7] The enemy arrayed against the 1st Pursuit Group included two élite units, Jagdgeschwader (JGs) 1 and 3, which occupied bases directly opposite Atkinson's unit on the other side of the lines. The four squadrons of Jagdgeschwader 3 were based at Coincy, about nine miles north of Château-Thierry, while Jagdgeschwader 1 occupied fields at Beugeaux, another three miles farther north.[8]

Manfred von Richthofen organized JG 1 in May 1917 using his own Jasta 11 as the base unit and three additional squadrons, Jastas 4, 6, and 10, all specially selected because of their outstanding records. As Germany's first fighter wing, JG 1 was the enemy's counterpart to the 1st Pursuit Group, though clearly different in origin. Richthofen's Flying Circus was an élite organization commanded by Germany's top aces and staffed with pilots specially selected from a large pool of those with wartime experience. The Red Baron taught his pilots the tactics that he had learned from Oswald Boelcke and infused them with his aggressive spirit. Aerobatic displays did not impress him, nor did he encourage such practices. He carefully selected his pilots and replaced those who would not aggressively pursue and shoot down enemy aircraft. As the historian Peter Kilduff has observed, "Numerous combat successes within a short time were key to remaining in JG 1." Richthofen amassed

Château-Thierry sector

The 1st Pursuit Group served as the French 6th Army's groupe de combat and fought against Germany's most élite fighter wings.

Created by author based on data from "Récapitulation schématique des opérations du 18 juillet au 25 septembre 1918," Map 32 in État Major de l'Armée, Service Historique, *Les Armées françaises dans la Grande Guerre*, vol. 1, *Cartes* (Paris: Imprimerie nationale, 1938); "Initial Plan of Attack in the Aisne-Marne," Map 71 in *The United States Army in the World War, 1917–1919*, vol. 5, *Military Operations of the American Expeditionary Forces* (Washington, D.C.: Center of Military History, U.S. Army, 1989), 231.

eighty victories before he was brought down in April 1918, but his successor, Capt. Wilhelm Reinhard, continued the policy of transferring out "nonproducers." Shortly before the 1st Pursuit Group arrived in the Château-Thierry sector, Reinhard sent a report to his superiors indicating that the Germans had established air superiority: "Since the beginning of the planned assault the Frenchman has been very cautious completely on the defensive and only seldom crosses the lines. The individual French airman is very skilled technically, but avoids serious fighting."[9]

The number of airplanes in German squadrons had been increased to eighteen airplanes, and qualitative improvements were also being made. On 29 June, Jasta 4 commander Ernst Udet, who was Germany's leading ace at the time, saved himself by parachuting out of his airplane after being shot down. Although balloon observers on both sides were equipped with parachutes, the Allies never adopted parachutes for their pilots. The Germans had recently done so, however, allowing pilots to bail out and, if over friendly territory, return to fight another day. Udet returned with another technological advantage, a new Bavarian Motor Works (BMW) 185-horsepower Fokker D-7, which many historians argue was the best fighter of the war.[10]

In May, Fokker D-7s were sent to Jagdgeschwader 1 to replace its Fokker triplanes, but these first production models had a 160-horsepower Mercedes engine that provided mediocre performance. On 22 June, less than a week before the 1st Pursuit Group arrived at Touquin, JG 1 began receiving a new version of the Fokker D-7 equipped with a 185-horsepower "fixed" BMW engine. The new engine vastly improved the Fokker's performance, halving its climbing time to five thousand meters (16,400 feet) to sixteen minutes while also increasing its maneuverability at high altitude. Coincidentally, the early Fokker D-7 models also experienced wing-rib failures, akin to those of the Nieuport 28, as late as June 1918, but this did not cause the Fokker to be cancelled. Instead, Fokker fixed the problem, and the D-7 became the mainstay fighter of the German air force. The first 185-horsepower BMW Fokkers went to Jasta 11, whose fighters bore the red noses and tails symbolizing their élite status as Richthofen's original squadron. The Americans in the 1st Pursuit Group referred to them as the "Scarlet Scouts."[11]

The 6th Army front extended from the village of Faverolles on the left to Dormans on the right, tracing a salient about twenty miles across and twenty miles deep, with Château-Thierry at the apex. The bowed shape made the distance from Touquin to the front near Faverolles about thirty-four miles. These distances significantly decreased a patrol's flying time, and because the prevailing winds usually blew toward the enemy, 1st Pursuit Group pilots had to be careful not to run out of fuel.

Ernst Udet in front of his Fokker D-7

Udet's personal markings are partially visible on the fuselage.

National Air and Space Museum, CD-ROM 2B-27823

The 1st Pursuit Group's top-priority mission was "to allow our Corps Observation Aviation to work freely and so help the artillery and the infantry;" its second, "to interfere with enemy observation by airplane and balloon;" and its third, "to cause such other casualties and inflict such other material damage on the enemy as possible."[12] Mitchell informed Major Foulois more succinctly, "This Group operates for the main purpose of preventing hostile pursuit incursions into our territory."[13]

The 1st Corps Observation Group, commanded by Maj. Lewis H. Brereton, had charge of the American observation squadrons. Familiarity between the two commands had already been established in the Toul sector and was further enhanced by the relationship between Philip Roosevelt and Brereton that had begun while the two worked in Foulois's Airplane Division in Washington during the summer of 1917. The 1st Corps Observation Group's 1st and 12th Aero Squadrons were stationed at Saints, about four and a half miles north of Touquin. The group's third squadron, the 88th Aero, would not arrive until 6 July, so a French observation squadron temporarily rounded out the group.[14]

Atkinson again found himself subject to the confusing command relationships resulting from the army's inexperience with coalition warfare. His orders required him to operate under the French 6th Army, but two different American officers also wanted to tell him what to do. The 1st Corps chief of Air Service, Maj. Ralph Royce, came to the group headquarters "and said that as far as American orders were concerned we would take them from him and from no one else."[15] Royce's assertion of authority reflected the army tradition that the senior American headquarters supervised all American units in its area.

Mitchell arrived, showed them the order attaching the 1st Pursuit to his 1st Brigade, and made the same demand. Benjamin Foulois had created the 1st Brigade with Mitchell as its commander and given him charge of all the tactical aviation units at the front. When Foulois later learned that troops were needed to join the 1st Corps at Château-Thierry, he wanted to have a senior officer present "to supervise their service." Thus Mitchell claimed responsibility for supervising the 1st Pursuit Group and 1st Corps Observation Group in the Château-Thierry sector.[16]

"From the point of view of the First Pursuit Group," Philip Roosevelt later reflected, "a more unsatisfactory arrangement could not have been devised."[17] Atkinson and Roosevelt steered tactfully through the conundrum of serving three different masters, applying the lessons they had learned at Toul. As Roosevelt explained,

> I had to spend a lot of time seeming to obey their orders while really making my own dispositions. For the Group Commander let me pretty much alone though he backed me up to the limit whenever there was any question as to whether or not I had done right, and he was always standing by me and taking the responsibility for possible errors while giving me the credit for any successes. All our orders really came from the French—which [Mitchell] approved.[18]

Thus Atkinson shielded Roosevelt while wisely staying out of the fray. When Ralph Royce, an insider of even longer tenure than Atkinson, decided to go to the mat with Mitchell over who was in charge, he was relieved of command. "There is no question of Col. Mitchell's extraordinary personal magnetism and of his rather unusual ability," Roosevelt observed, "but . . . he blows in, puts everything in a stew, and then leaves the unfortunate Group Commander or Group Operations Officer to straighten it out and get things running again."[19] This confused arrangement added yet another complexity to effective command of the 1st Pursuit Group. Roosevelt added, "The *suggestions* of the Brigade Commander were often a source of extreme worry as it was impossible to obey both the orders of the 6th French Army" and Mitchell.[20]

To be fair, the U.S. Army was still working out the nuances of command relationships between the pursuit and observation groups and the corps and armies they supported. That these units were being committed to battle under a foreign army further complicated the matter. Mitchell had his orders from Foulois to supervise the American air units, and he was determined to do just that. He could exert considerable influence. In addition to the force of his personality, he was the senior American airman on the scene. Those who were junior to him owed him a degree of allegiance for this reason alone, and both Atkinson and Roosevelt also seemed to realize that his star was rising. Mitchell had authority but little real responsibility. His position enabled him to organize a tactical headquarters, gain the measure of his men, and observe firsthand army-level air operations during the most intensive air fighting of the war. The Château-Thierry campaign served as his postgraduate education in aerial warfare.

On 30 June the 1st Pursuit Group conducted familiarization flights of the new sector. Atkinson ordered his squadrons to engage in combat only "in cases where there is an extremely good chance of a successful result." He allowed no patrols of fewer than five planes to leave the immediate vicinity of Touquin. It was an opportunity for pilots to study the terrain, note landmarks on their maps, and reconnoiter routes to and from the front lines. In the 27th Squadron, Maj. Harold Hartney required pilots who had flown reconnaissance patrols to submit their maps, properly annotated, to him that night, for his personal inspection.[21]

Lt. Hamilton Coolidge joined the 1st Pursuit Group at the same time as Quentin Roosevelt, after the two were released from Issoudun. "My map is unquestionably the best friend I have," he wrote his mother, but he indicated that it needed to be memorized, as "it really is impractical to carry a map in your plane, because the minute you start to look at it some wily Boche is 'on your tail' in an instant out of nowhere." Coolidge explained that he had simultaneously and continuously to search the sky for enemy aircraft while keeping an eye on his patrol leader, the ground, enemy antiaircraft fire, and his instruments. No longer were there any lone voluntary patrols over the lines. "A lone man is practically certain to be nailed. . . . We must go at least six strong in formation."[22]

Lt. Hamilton Coolidge
Coolidge, a passenger with Meissner on the Orduna,
  joined the 94th Aero Squadron in June after serving as
  an instructor at Issoudun.
NATIONAL AIR AND SPACE MUSEUM,
  CD-ROM 2B-05671

Coolidge had been assigned to Meissner's flight in the 94th Squadron. Meissner confidently noted in his diary that day, "Took up my flight to look over the sector at 4 P.M. Looks good, lots of action and easy to locate."[23] Lt. Harold Buckley of the 95th Squadron remembered more forebodingly, "No longer would we hunt in pairs deep in the enemy lines, delighted if the patrol produced a single enemy to chase. Gone were the days when we could dive into the fray with only a careless glance at our rear. There was trouble ahead."[24]

The next day the 1st Pursuit Group supported an attack by the U.S. 2d Division on the fortified village of Vaux. This attack represented America's first air-land battle. The 2d Division was one of the first two divisions that Pershing sent to the French 6th Army in response to Pétain's request. Machine-gun units of the U.S. 3d Division arrived first and helped the French defend the bridges across the Marne at Château-Thierry. A few miles farther east the Marine Brigade of the U.S. 2d Division moved forward to replace French troops on the front line, resulting in the famous battle at Belleau Wood and the less well known but, from the standpoint of the development of American air power, more significant battle at Vaux.[25] The contrast between these two battles highlights the importance of air superiority at this stage of the war.

The Marine Brigade experienced 5,200 casualties at Belleau Wood—a 50 percent loss rate. The worst came on the first day of the attack, 6 June, as their well-aligned assault waves crossed wheat fields covered by German machine-gun fire, resulting in 1,087 losses—the costliest single day in Marine Corps history until the amphibious attack during World War II on Tarawa. The historian Edward M. Coffman has observed that Belleau Wood was more reminiscent of combat during the American Civil War than of modern warfare. He likens it to Cemetery Ridge, Pickett's Charge, and Little Round Top at Gettysburg. As Coffman notes, commanders at Belleau Wood depended "on the courage and spirit of their men rather than technique to win the battle."[26]

Although the wooded terrain was not ideal for aerial observation, the Germans made full use of it. A report by an observer from Pershing's headquarters on the first day of the battle stated that "the Boche have control of the air around the 2nd Div. Sector—a squadron of 7 planes goes where it wishes."[27] Over the next weeks the situation in the air continued to deteriorate. A 15 June intelligence report stated that the Germans maintained continuous aerial reconnaissance over the division's forward area. Observers counted fifty-seven airplanes flying over the sector, including several large patrols, and fifteen enemy observation balloons in the air at one time observing the American division's sector. The excellence of the enemy's observation capability indicated an increasing intensity of enemy artillery fire. The report also warned that it was difficult to predict what the enemy would do next because German air superiority kept friendly aircraft from observing movements behind the enemy's lines. Reports of as many as eighty enemy flights in a single day over the division's sector were not unusual.[28] Friendly pursuit units were obviously needed.

By mid-June, in response to this intolerable situation, Pershing's observer, Col. Walter S. Grant, sent a strongly worded recommendation to AEF headquarters in Chaumont: "I recommend that an observation and a pursuit squadron of aeroplanes be sent here to work with this division at [the] first opportunity. The Germans have control of the air and embarrass our movements and dispositions."[29] American aerial units did not arrive in time to assist at Belleau Wood, but as Atkinson and his men arrived at Touquin, the 2d Division was making final preparations for an attack on Vaux.

After securing Belleau Wood, the 2d Division shifted its effort to the right side of its sector to seize the fortified village of Vaux. The attack took place on 1 July, just a few days after Atkinson's unit landed at Touquin. Reconnaissance flights conducted during June helped develop an accurate picture of the enemy situation at Vaux. The division attack order included a detailed map of Vaux annotated with the location of enemy positions, barricades, and even the thickness of certain walls in the town. The attack was supported by a schedule of artillery fires designed to suppress enemy machine-gun fire and, in certain cases, destroy enemy observation points and strong points previously identified by aerial photographs. Fires were adjusted by observation airplanes and balloons as the attack progressed, while infantry contact planes helped commanders stay apprised of the location of the forward line of troops.[30]

The plan required command of the air. Orders directed the 1st Pursuit Group to protect friendly observation aircraft while preventing enemy observation aircraft from accomplishing their mission. On the day of the attack the 1st Pursuit Group flew eleven patrols over the 2d Division's sector. Initially, Atkinson and Roosevelt had planned to fly two patrols over the 6th Army front during the morning and then surge all of the group's aircraft over a much smaller sector between Château-Thierry and Belleau (the 2d Division sector) in three waves beginning at 5:00, 6:00, and 6:30 P.M. in conjunction with the 6:00 P.M. infantry assault. The group's leaders changed this plan early in the morning on 1 July, however, to ensure continuous coverage over the battle area throughout the day.[31]

The initial plan, though hastily conceived after the unit's arrival at Touquin, demonstrates that 1st Pursuit Group leaders understood the importance of concentrating their aircraft in large formations from the beginning to meet the enemy threat at Château-Thierry. Atkinson and Roosevelt changed the plan on the morning of the attack, after the dawn patrols had already been launched. This adjustment suggests that close coordination was taking place over the role of pursuit aviation in the battle. The group's initial plan of covering the battle zone only during the attack was probably determined to be unsatisfactory because ground commanders wanted to have air cover over the battle area throughout the day to protect the movement of a significant amount of short-range field artillery forward, out of concealed positions into the open, to support the attack. Friendly artillery planned to begin its program of preparatory fires twelve hours before the infantry assault, reaching a crescendo at H-minus-60-minutes. Friendly troops would be moving into attack positions during the day, and their movements needed to be screened from enemy aerial observation so that they would not be targeted by enemy artillery. The 2d Division G-2 reported twenty enemy airplane flights over the division sector during the afternoon on the day before the attack. The division also reported thirteen enemy flights on the morning of the attack. First Pursuit Group leaders scrambled to change their plan to stop these enemy incursions.[32] Philip Roosevelt described the aviation concept of operation for the attack on Vaux:

> A very strict barrage of the sector of the attack was maintained throughout the day, and in the evening when the infantry went forward they found themselves perfectly covered by the allied planes. Briefly, the steps in the ladder included infantry liaison planes, corps artillery adjustment planes, and three formations of pursuit [planes] of a squadron each at approximately 2,500, 3,500, and 4,500 meters altitude respectively, the whole ladder, leaning as it were into the German lines so that the planes at 4,500 meters altitude were working from twelve to seventeen kilometers over enemy territory.[33]

From Roosevelt's description it is clear that Atkinson intended to have squadron-size formations in the air, but according to 1st Pursuit Group operations reports, the size of his patrols actually ranged from four to ten aircraft and averaged about six. In some cases the accounting of these patrols is misleading. For example, the 95th Aero Squadron flew a four-plane patrol from 10:35 A.M. to 12:15 P.M., at an altitude of thirty-five hundred meters (about 11,500 feet), but it also flew a seven-plane patrol at about the same time, in the same sector, and at the same altitude. Consequently, most of the 95th Squadron was in the air over the battle zone at the same time or, at least, as much of it as was possible.

The 1st Pursuit Group's adjusted plan still surged aircraft over the battle zone around H-hour. Although the plan called for a total of five patrols at overlapping times during this period, only four appear to have been conducted. These patrols were indeed "laddered" at ascending altitudes during the crucial time period around H-hour: the 95th and 147th Squadrons each reported having eight-plane patrols at 2,500 meters (8,200 feet), the 95th reported having a second patrol of six planes at 3,500 meters (11,480 feet), and the 94th had a six-plane patrol at 5,000 meters (16,400 feet). The 94th Aero Squadron was responsible for the fifth patrol, which apparently was not flown—possibly because of damage sustained by this flight in an earlier combat that day.[34]

Lt. Elmer Haslett, operations officer in the 1st Corps Observation Group, flew in the back seat of an observation plane during the attack on Vaux. Haslett remembered, "There was only one time at Château-Thierry when the Boche did not have the complete supremacy of the air. This was on July first at the Battle of Vaux. . . . We had every American pursuit and observation plane we could get off of the ground." Apparently, most of the observation planes aloft were providing close-in protection to two key aircraft with special missions. Haslett continued,

> There were not less than ninety-six planes in that formation—their mission being to protect the infantry [contact] plane and to protect Brereton and me, who were doing the artillery work. There was such a swarm of planes above us that we practically never looked into the sky, but kept our attention entirely on the work before us.

The air cover was so good, Haslett remarked, that the attack on Vaux seemed like a training exercise.[35]

It did not seem like a training exercise to Lt. Harold Tittman, a pilot who had recently joined the 94th Aero Squadron. Tittman was flying in the upper-left position of a V formation of six airplanes, led by Jimmy Meissner, that had taken off from Touquin at three in the afternoon and penetrated deep into German airspace. As they flew south from Soissons their route took them close by the bases of JGs 1 and 3. A group of seven German fighters attacked Meissner's patrol from the sun-drenched western skies, achieving complete surprise. Meissner identified them as Fokker D-7s. "The first thing I knew about their presence," Tittman recalled, "were the tracer-bullets passing in front of me. I remember seeing one of the German planes headed directly toward me and it came so close that I could even distinguish the pilot's black moustache!"[36]

Anxious to get on the German's tail and shoot him down, Tittman left his patrol—the worst thing he could have done, he later realized. Finding himself suddenly alone, he tried to make his way back toward friendly territory, but five enemy fighters jumped him. Tittman was shot through the right lung, right arm, and right foot and crash-landed. Two hundred bullet holes were found in his airplane. His worst injuries, though, were caused by the crash itself, which he barely survived: he lost his left leg and spent the next twenty-two months in the hospital.[37]

Lt. Waldo Heinrichs of the 95th Aero Squadron was in the air for his second patrol that day as H-hour approached. His patrol of six airplanes had taken off at half past four that afternoon, but because of "wretched leading" by the flight leader, Lt. Sumner Sewall, the formation had broken up, and Heinrichs found himself in a patrol of only three airplanes. Even at this altitude, the artillery fire on Vaux, more than eleven thousand feet below him, was so intense it threw clouds of smoke and dust up to the altitude of his patrol. He noted in his diary that it was "desperately dangerous as Boche came over in droves of 12, 18, and 20. In fact 50, in 3 formations crossed our lines before 8 A.M. this day."[38]

Enemy aircraft were not encountered at the lowest altitudes of pursuit coverage during the attack. Quentin Roosevelt, also of the 95th Squadron, was airborne at the same time as Heinrichs but was flying three thousand feet closer to the ground. "We were scheduled to fly on the low level, at twenty-five hundred meters [8,200 feet]," he wrote home the next day, "to intercept any enemy photographers or reglage [artillery-adjusting] planes. There were two more patrols above us, one around four thousand and one up along the ceiling, keeping off their chasse planes. We didn't run into any of their planes." When Roosevelt returned to Touquin he found out that the top flight had been engaged in a fight with nine Fokkers.[39]

To those on the ground it seemed that the friendly pursuit planes had swept the Germans from the sky. The operations officer of the 23d Infantry Regiment, which formed the left wing of the attack, reported that "liaison with airplanes was excellent. Our airplanes overwhelmed those of the enemy. [The] attack seems to have been [a] complete surprise."[40] The 3d Brigade commander, who was in charge of the attack on Vaux, reported that by half past seven that evening his troops had secured the village. Complete reports of casualties were not yet in, but he believed the count to be about two hundred. More than six hundred Germans had been captured. "Before closing this brief report," he concluded, "the undersigned cannot refrain from expressing the appreciation of all concerned . . . [for] the excellence of the artillery work, both in preparation and during and after the attack."[41]

The 2d Division's attack on Vaux exemplified the combined-arms approach that Pershing wanted to see. He called the attack on Vaux "a brilliantly executed operation."[42] Gen. Hunter Liggett, the commander of the U.S. 1st Corps, called it "a very skillful piece of work."[43] The historian Edward M. Coffman refers to the attack as "a 'mechanically perfect' assault."[44] The contrast between the battles of Vaux and Belleau Wood illustrates the connection between aerial superiority and ground combat. Aerial photographs provided valuable intelligence that served as the basis for attack plans. Observation aircraft adjusted artillery fire during the battle, including devastatingly accurate fires that prevented German reinforcements from interfering with the attack. Infantry contact planes assisted ground commanders in keeping track of the progress of their troops, which helped ensure that friendly artillery did not kill the wrong troops. Because of the 1st Pursuit Group's control of the air, enemy aviation did not interfere with the 2d Division's attack. Enemy fighters did not shoot down friendly observation aircraft, nor did enemy battle planes strafe American ground troops. Finally, enemy observation aircraft were not able to adjust enemy artillery fire on friendly troops.

The chief of Air Service of the French 6th Army sent the 1st Pursuit Group written congratulations: "Yesterday's attack was a complete success. The protection given by the First Pursuit Group, USA, was very good."[45] Atkinson and Roosevelt must have felt proud to receive such praise from their new headquarters. In a matter of days, they had moved to a new base, integrated themselves into the command structure of the 6th Army, established a new line of logistical support, coordinated their efforts with the 1st Corps observation group, and fought America's first air-land battle. They had achieved command of the air against a numerically superior and more experienced opponent. In the greater scheme of things, the counterattack at Vaux was a minor action, but in the history of American air power it was an important milestone. Moreover, the Americans were advancing instead of retreating, and they were proving that they could conduct modern combined-arms warfare.

This is not to say that air superiority was a precondition for American victory at Vaux. The Marines achieved victory at Belleau Wood without air superiority, though at great cost. Aviation alone did not account for the difference in these two battles. The attack at Vaux occurred over more favorable terrain and was planned well in advance. Atkinson and Roosevelt also demonstrated that they understood the need to concentrate American pursuit aviation in the new sector. The group had practiced squadron-size formations back at Toul and did its best to conduct them at Château-Thierry, but there was difficulty in the execution of this intent because of late changes to the plan, the separation of pilots from their formations, and the limited number of available airplanes in each squadron. Nevertheless, they understood that the tactics used at Toul were no longer relevant in their new sector because they faced a different enemy situation.

The concentrated appearance of Nieuport 28s over the battle area at Vaux probably took the German air force by surprise. They countered by bombing the 1st Pursuit Group's airfield at midnight that same day. The twelve or so bombs that fell on and around the airfield did not cause any damage, but they did shake up the mechanics who lived in close proximity to the field.[46] On 2 July the 1st Pursuit Group began defending the entire 6th Army sector, using a combination of scheduled patrols and alerts. The daily plan called for two squadrons to alternate throughout the day on alert (one entire squadron on alert at a time) and two squadrons to fly two patrols each (later reduced to one patrol a day, to keep more aircraft available on the ground). Atkinson required the operations officer of the alert squadron to be on duty at group operations while his squadron was on alert. Atkinson's squadrons reported a total of fifteen combat incidents on 2 July, the most experienced in any single day at Touquin, compared with only two combats during the battle of Vaux. Most of these took place near Vaux, where heavy ground fighting continued. The 1st Pursuit Group's alert unit on this morning was the 27th Aero Squadron, and Major Hartney was on duty at group operations. At a quarter past six in the morning, Philip Roosevelt handed him an alert order that an enemy squadron had just taken off from near Fere-en-Tardenois.[47]

Hartney called his squadron, and within ninety seconds two flights of Nieuport 28s, a total of nine aircraft, were roaring into the sky. They approached Château-Thierry at different altitudes and encountered nine Fokker D-7s from JG 1. The Fokkers, seeing only the lower flight of Nieuports, thought they had a two-to-one advantage when they attacked, but the 27th Squadron's upper flight dived into the fray, evening the odds. The swirling dogfight that ensued lasted thirty minutes, during which time the 27th Squadron lost two of its pilots: Lt. Edward Elliot was shot down and killed. Lt. Walter Wanamaker was missing, though the squadron later learned that he had been wounded and taken as a prisoner of war; Ernst Udet, already back in the air and flying an all-red BMW-powered Fokker D-7, had brought him down. Despite the losses they had sustained, the 27th Aero Squadron thought they had done well. Hartney was sure that his unit had downed four of the enemy, though they received credit for only two. Disappointed with the award system, he wrote, "It is my honest belief that the 27th and, in fact, the whole 1st Pursuit Group, brought down fully twice as many German airplanes as were ever officially confirmed." Peter Kilduff's history of JG 1, however, indicates it recorded no losses that day.[48] If the German report can be trusted, the engagement was anything but a victory, but in the fog of war the men of the 27th Squadron believed they had won the day.

Hartney attributed much to the Nieuport 28 for helping the Americans claim their victories. He credited the swift reaction from alert to takeoff—only ninety seconds. "This could not be duplicated today starting with cold motors," he told his readers in 1940. He continued, "It was an even fight—nine against nine—fliers of about equal skill but with greater experience on the side of the Germans. To offset this we had the superior maneuverability of our faster and better climbing little Nieuports against the sluggishness of the Boche Fokker D VIIs." Hartney ensured that favorable comments about the Nieuport 28 made it into the 1st Pursuit Group operations report, as the squadron report noted that "the Nieuport 28 demonstrated superior climbing and manoeuvring [*sic*] ability." The only American technical disadvantage that concerned Hartney was the new Marlin machine gun, which proved to be inordinately prone to jamming. Pilots of the 147th Squadron experienced the same difficulty with these machine guns in their first combat, which took place later that day in the same area.[49]

Maj. Geoffrey Bonnell either led or accompanied the first patrols of the 147th Aero Squadron from Touquin, but he was not airborne for his squadron's first combat. Two flights, totaling nine Nieuports, took off from Touquin on a scheduled patrol at half past four that afternoon. Their mission was to patrol the right half of the 6th Army sector between Dormans and Château-Thierry. They flew in two formations—one flight high at eighteen thousand feet, the other low at thirteen thousand feet. Wilbert White led the five upper Nieuports, Ralph O'Neill the lower section. About an hour into the patrol they encountered twelve Pfalzes flying in two similar formations. A general melee ensued about five miles inside enemy lines and north of Château-Thierry. In fifteen minutes the combat was over. The 147th Squadron's pilots claimed they had downed at least four and possibly five of the Germans, but the squadron later received official credit for only one enemy aircraft, a victory shared among six of its pilots. The American patrol had not lost a single man. When the jubilant flyers returned they buzzed the Touquin airfield to announce their victories. O'Neill later received his first Distinguished Service Cross for this combat. He was developing into one the 147th Squadron's best leaders. During the next two days the 147th Aero Squadron managed to get patrols numbering ten and eleven aircraft into the air.[50]

At a quarter to eight on the morning of 5 July, eleven Nieuports of the 95th Aero Squadron took off to patrol the left side of the 6th Army sector, between Faverolles and Belleau. This patrol also flew with one flight high and another low, but the flights lost track of each other and became separated. Lieutenant Heinrichs flew as a part of John Mitchell's upper patrol. According to Heinrichs, two of the Nieuports in their flight dropped out along the way, reducing their number to four. About forty-five minutes into the patrol they encountered six enemy fighters at an altitude of fifteen thousand feet in the vicinity of Priez, three to four miles inside enemy lines. Heinrichs identified the enemy airplanes as Albatros D-5 aircraft of the famous Scarlet Scouts, with red noses, white tails, big black crosses on white background on the wings and tail, and scarlet diagonal stripes on the fuselage and upper wings.

"We engaged with slight advantage of altitude but numbers of 5 or 6 [enemy] to 4 [friendly]."[51] Mitchell, Heinrichs, and Sewall shared credit for one enemy aircraft, but the 95th Aero Squadron lost two men: Lts. Carlyle Rhodes and Sidney P. Thompson did not return from the patrol. In contrast to Hartney's glowing report about the Nieuport 28, the 95th Squadron reported that the enemy aircraft's climbing and maneuverability approximated that of the Nieuport 28. Heinrichs's diary entry stated that his opponent "out-climbed and outmaneuvered me."[52]

The 147th Squadron also fought the Germans on 5 July. Seven Nieuports of the unit responded to an alert between 8:38 and 9:50 A.M. At about sixteen thousand feet, the patrol, again led by O'Neill, encountered six enemy aircraft about two and three miles northwest of Château-Thierry, near the Vaux battle area. O'Neill recalled that his flight was down to four or five aircraft, several others having dropped out along the way, when they were "jumped by at least ten Germans, and they were of the Richthofen circus, all hideously painted." The enemy had the advantage of altitude, diving on the Americans,

Lts. Wilbert White, left, and Louis C. "Red" Simon, right

White and Simon pose by a Nieuport 28 with the Scotch terrier, the insignia of the 147th
Aero Squadron, on its fuselage.

NATIONAL AIR AND SPACE MUSEUM, CD-ROM 7B-01019

who were themselves climbing. After surviving the initial pass the Americans turned the tables on their attackers. O'Neill stated, "I shot down two Germans before my guns had jammed. . . . The Germans were only too glad to break off, because I saw them going back to Germany, so that was the end of that fight." Although he received his second award of the Distinguished Service Cross for this combat, he was credited only for one shared victory; the patrol received credit for two.[53]

The 94th Squadron scored its first victory on 7 July during an eleven-plane protection patrol led by Jimmy Meissner in support of a Salmson observation plane of the 1st Aero Squadron. Eddie Rickenbacker, flying the group's first SPAD 13, was part of this formation. At the end of the protection patrol, Meissner led four of the Nieuports in an attack on two Rumpler observation planes they had spotted near Bonnes at an altitude of sixteen thousand feet. All four initially peppered one of the Rumplers with machine-gun fire. Two of the Nieuports, experiencing jammed machine guns, broke off the attack, but Coolidge and Meissner pursued the Rumpler as it dived to get away. Coolidge wrote home, "We both shot at the Boche and a second later great hot, red flames burst out from beneath his fuselage." Coolidge's guns jammed, ending his attack. In the meantime a group of five Fokkers protecting the Rumpler had attacked the Americans. Meissner continued to pursue the Rumpler and gave it a final burst before breaking off to chase off a Fokker on Coolidge's tail. Lt. William Chalmers, who had been part of the flight, was shot down and taken prisoner.[54]

Victory credits were sometimes strange. In his letter home that day, Coolidge wrote, "I got a Boche today—or rather Jim Meissner and I got one together, but as we were too far inside their lines for our observation balloons to see it, we shall probably not receive official credit." Meissner's diary entry stated, "Boche confirmed to Coolidge alone." The final official confirmation in U.S. Air Service Victory Credits gave this one to Coolidge and Robert Cates.[55]

An eleven-plane patrol from the 95th Squadron, which was patrolling the left side of the 6th Army sector at about the same time, engaged in a dogfight with enemy fighters. The patrol flew in two echelons at about thirteen and fifteen thousand feet. Lt. John Hambleton, leader of the lower flight, spotted six enemy fighters three miles inside enemy lines and northwest of Château-Thierry. In a matter of moments, sixteen planes were "rushing around upside down and on their ear, some climbing and others diving." Sumner Sewall pursued one as it attempted to dive away and flee north, farther into German airspace. He finally caught up to it about six miles inside enemy lines, at an altitude of less than two hundred feet, and saw his tracers hit the enemy plane, which subsequently crashed into the middle of a town. The 95th Squadron lost Stewart McKeown, who was shot down and taken prisoner.[56]

The 147th Squadron also participated in a noteworthy operation that evening. Bonnell led a protection patrol that escorted three squadrons of French Air Service Breguet bombers. Although their flight path took them within a few miles of the bases of JGs 1 and 3, they encountered no enemy planes. The next day the 147th experienced its first casualty in the Château-Thierry sector. O'Neill was again leading a ten-plane patrol. Three of the Nieuports observed ten enemy aircraft six miles north of Dormans and gave chase. Low fuel caused two of them to break off and head home. Lt. Maxwell O. Parry continued alone and was never seen again. His loss marked the 1st

Pursuit Group's last day of operations at Touquin. During the early evening on 7 July, twenty British Sopwith Camels landed at Touquin. These were the first elements of the RAF's 9th Brigade, part of an aerial strike force that the Allied commander in chief, Gen. Ferdinand Foch, was assembling to counter the next German thrust. Consequently, the 1st Pursuit Group was ordered to move to Saints as friendly air units adjusted to make room for the air reserve.[57]

The 1st Pursuit Group sustained eight casualties and received official credit for ten victories during its short time at Touquin. The 94th and 27th Squadrons each lost two men, the 95th Squadron lost three, and the 147th Squadron lost one. One of these, Harold Tittman of the 94th Aero Squadron, was severely wounded; the other seven were listed as missing (it was later learned that three had been killed in action and four taken as prisoners of war). Three victories each were credited to the 95th and 147th Squadrons, and two each to the 94th and 27th Squadrons. The group's pilots claimed more than twice the number of victories, however; the 147th Squadron alone claimed ten.[58]

By this time both the 27th and 147th Squadrons had adopted unit insignia for their Nieuports. A recent Air Service policy restricted pursuit squadrons from painting insignia on their aircraft until the squadron had been credited with three enemy airplanes or upon being cited in orders for distinguished service. The 27th Squadron's Fighting Eagle design consisted of a bald eagle in flight with extended talons, superimposed over the sun. The 147th adopted a sad-eyed Scotch terrier.[59]

Since the arrival of the 1st Pursuit Group, the commander of JG 1 had faced a different situation. German fighters no longer held air superiority in the skies over Château-Thierry, though neither did the Americans. The airspace was contested, but the 1st Pursuit Group had shown that it could establish temporary local air superiority when necessary, as it had at Vaux. Atkinson's unit made it more difficult for enemy observation airplanes to accomplish their mission while also making life a bit easier for troops on the ground. "Since our group's arrival here the former Boche practice of machine-gunning the troops behind our lines from the air has ended," wrote Joseph Eastman.[60] The German air force was now clearly on the defensive; combats were regularly occurring about six miles in on the German side of the lines. As Coolidge reflected in a letter home,

> In my experience here I cannot recall a single instance when the Boche would come out and fight in our territory or even over the lines. Invariably we must

Pilots of the 27th Aero Squadron at Touquin, left to right: Alfred Grant, Robert
  Raymond, Robert Hill, Jerry Vasconcells, Jason Hunt, Ivan Roberts, William
  Hoover, Donald Hudson, and Lawrence Polk

First Pursuit Group legend has it that the 27th Aero Squadron's insignia, described by
  Walter Williams as "a bald eagle superimposed over the Worldly Sun," was copied from
  the illustration in an Anheuser-Busch beer advertisement.

NATIONAL AIR AND SPACE MUSEUM, CD-ROM 7B-39202

go to them. They are always to be found, often in large numbers, but they
seem to have the homing instinct to a high degree.[61]

The German air commander could not rate his enemy, as he had a month
before, as "very cautious" and claim that they were "completely on the defensive and only seldom [cross] the lines."[62]

Although it was the clear intent of the 1st Pursuit Group's leadership to fly
squadron-sized formations, logistical constraints prevented the squadrons from
getting more than two full flights airborne at one time on a regular basis. The 1st
Pursuit Group had only sixty-four of its seventy-two authorized aircraft on 1
July—and this was after receiving a special resupply of ten Nieuport 28s on 30
June. Because of the increased tempo of operations and the damage caused by
combat, the group's mechanics were able to keep only 70 to 80 percent of the
assigned aircraft operational. As a result, it was rarely possible to get more than
eleven aircraft from the same squadron in the air at one time. The typical patrol
was made up of nine to eleven aircraft. Reported aircraft status on the evening
of 8 July showed the 94th Squadron with twelve operational airplanes out of thir-

teen assigned; the 95th had fourteen ready out of sixteen assigned; the 27th had thirteen ready out of fourteen on hand; and 147th had eight operational of fourteen assigned.[63] Mitchell recognized this problem and took steps to increase the authorized number of aircraft per pursuit squadron from eighteen to twenty-four. He also wanted to increase the number of pilots in each pursuit squadron because he understood the stresses and strains of combat flying.[64]

Brig. Gen. Mason Patrick, the AEF chief of Air Service, signaled his esteem for the 147th Aero Squadron's recent achievements by dining with the officers of that squadron when he visited Touquin on 7 July.[65] Eastman may not have been the only member of the squadrons of the French tradition who resented the attention paid to the Canadian Circus.

> We are now being edified by the "147th Circus" by the most preposterous exploits of chasing and felling enemy planes thirty kilometers on the other side of the lines. This is rather galling to the 94th—in view of the hard earned manner in which it has made its name.

Eastman attributed their exaggerated victory count to their adherence to the more liberal British system in which fellow pilots could confirm victories.[66] Although the French system of confirmation by ground or balloon observers still ruled the official count, confirmations could take weeks to make their way through channels, and the 147th Squadron was making the most of its bragging rights.

The 1st Pursuit Group's spirit was in a precipitously balanced state as it moved to its new operating base at Saints. Its pilots thought they had been in intense combat, but what they had actually experienced was a lull. The Germans had been husbanding their resources and were preparing to launch yet another strike. The increasing strain of combat, with its daily reminder of death, also created a more existential outlook and a hardening of positions. Having the "right" airplane was a matter of survival. Whereas the squadrons of the French tradition valued speed and ruggedness, the squadrons of the British tradition valued the Nieuport 28's maneuverability. At the moment, the Canadian Circus was in its ascendancy, satisfied with its equipment and enjoying its newly won esteem. But its position was about to be challenged by the arrival of SPAD 13s to replace the Nieuport 28s. At the same time, an already shaky 1st Pursuit Group command team was about to be crippled by the transfer of its highly respected operations officer.

8

The Second Battle
of the Marne

Together for six months now, Atkinson and Roosevelt had melded into a cohesive command team. "We agree on all important subjects of tactics, organization, administration and discipline," wrote Roosevelt.[1] Atkinson's sense of determination and single-minded focus on accomplishing the mission were his greatest assets. But this aspect of his character was also his greatest weakness. To his men, he seemed humorless and severe. Roosevelt, who knew him better that anyone, described him about this time in a letter to his mother:

> I doubt if I have ever written you much about him. The reason is I know so very little, yet there are few men whom I know better than I know him. He never talks about himself. In fact, he does very little talking at all. . . . Atkinson seems very severe and dour [and] has a look which, in addition to his habitual state of silence, makes him appear very forbidding to most of his subordinate officers. In reality he has a very sly sense of humor which he uses continually, accompanied by quite a charming and very contagious smile which appears just when you least expect it. His limitation, or rather what would be his limitation in time of peace, is one of his strongest points now. He hasn't a thought outside the army and very

few outside the particular command in the army to which he is attached. He is about the last man whom I should choose as a companion if I were touring France, for he has thrown his whole mind and heart across the barbed wire and there is very little on this side of the German trenches that interests him.[2]

Atkinson and Roosevelt complemented each other. The witty Yankee helped reassure those who suffered the quiet southerner's occasional explosions of wrath when they deviated from his orders. As the operations officer, Roosevelt assigned squadrons their daily missions and served as a buffer between Atkinson and his commanders. Hartney regarded Roosevelt as "one of the most outstanding officers I ever met in any army."[3] Billy Mitchell paid Roosevelt the highest compliment by making him head of his own 1st Brigade operations section when the 1st Pursuit moved to Saints. Atkinson petitioned directly to Foulois for Roosevelt's return, but Mitchell protested that personnel assignments in his brigade must be left to his discretion.[4] Roosevelt's loss significantly weakened the 1st Pursuit Group command structure on the eve of the most intensive aerial fighting of the war.

His cousin, Quentin Roosevelt, accounted for the group's only victory during the first several days at Saints. Thirteen Nieuports of 95th Squadron took off to patrol the lines between Château-Thierry and Faverolles on the morning of 10 July. During the patrol some of the pilots dropped messages to the Germans requesting information about comrades who were still missing. Quentin became separated from the others and was starting to return to Saints when he saw a flight of three planes going northwest. Thinking they were part of his patrol, he caught up with them about six miles inside German lines and found, to his dismay, that he had joined up with an enemy flight. He shot down the trail airplane of the formation and managed to escape to friendly airspace. He sometimes exhibited the same abandonment on the ground, where he impressed his comrades by chugging bottles of champagne.[5]

At 8:20 A.M. on 14 July a patrol of thirteen airplanes from the 95th Squadron took off from Saints to protect an important aerial reconnaissance mission over the area where the Germans were suspected to be concentrating forces for an assault across the Marne River. Three airplanes, including the patrol leader's, dropped out because of mechanical difficulties. Lt. Edward Curtis took charge. After reaching Château-Thierry, the patrol turned east and followed the front lines along the Marne River. By 8:45 A.M. they had

Quentin Roosevelt

A passenger with Meissner on the Orduna, Roosevelt
joined the 95th Aero Squadron in June 1918 after
serving as an instructor at Issoudun.

NATIONAL AIR AND SPACE MUSEUM,
CD-ROM 2B-23336

reached an altitude of almost sixteen thousand feet over Dormans and were preparing to turn back when Curtis signaled by firing his machine guns in the direction of seven Fokkers over the Forêt de Riz, about four miles inside German lines. Curtis led the patrol to a higher altitude to gain a favorable attack position. By 9:05 A.M. they were at seventeen thousand feet, ready to swoop down on the Fokkers.

Seven Nieuports dived. James Knowles and Quentin Roosevelt made the mistake of diving after two of the enemy aircraft that had themselves descended to a lower altitude to act as decoys. The rest of the attacking Nieuports did not take the bait. Instead, they again climbed after their first attack to

Wreckage of Quentin Roosevelt's Nieuport 28
Roosevelt's body lies beside the plane.
NATIONAL AIR AND SPACE MUSEUM, CD-ROM 2B-23333

regain the superior position. Once they saw that Knowles and Roosevelt had come under attack, they dived to their aid. A general melee ensued for the next fifteen minutes; all the while, the American fighters were drifting deeper into German airspace because of the prevailing winds. When the dogfight ended they were so scattered that each individually flew home uncertain of how the rest had fared.[6]

Roosevelt did not return. As soon as Philip learned that his cousin was missing he began a frantic search. He first went to the French 6th Army's air commander "to try to get news and they asked all along the front but could learn nothing." The 1st Brigade operations officer next commandeered a flight up to the antiaircraft batteries but again nothing was learned. The next afternoon Philip returned to the front and found a French antiaircraft battery with an entry in its journal about an American fighter going down at 9:15 A.M. a few miles north of Dormans. Roosevelt wrote to his cousin, Theodore,

If Quentin has given his life we know that he gave it with a high heart in the performance of duty of prime importance,—for the photographs which were obtained played no small part in enabling one French army to know with some precision the nature of the attack which sixteen hours later was launched against it.

A radio intercept confirmed their fears. The former president's son was dead. A German newspaper account praised his courage and recounted an air battle between twelve Americans and seven Germans.[7]

In Eddie Rickenbacker's opinion, Roosevelt "was reckless.... We all knew he would either achieve some great spectacular success or be killed in the attempt."[8] Quentin's grief-stricken father died less than six months later. The last letter from his son, written a few days before he was shot down, ended with the following: "At the moment everyone is very much pleased in our squadron for we are getting new planes. We have been using Nieuports, which have the disadvantage of not being particularly reliable and being inclined to catch fire."[9]

Rickenbacker retrieved the 1st Pursuit Group's first SPAD 13 from Paris on 5 July. Louis Béchereau, the SPAD's designer, had distinguished himself by being among the first to abandon the rotary engine. Although it had several good qualities, designers found it increasingly difficult to increase its horsepower. Revolutions per minute (RPM) had to be kept low because of the centrifugal forces exerted by the whirling cylinders. Larger cylinders also increased centrifugal force. Wind resistance produced by the rotation of the cylinders and high fuel and oil consumption were additional limiting factors. The rotary design also made it more difficult to fill the cylinders with the most efficient fuel-air mixture.[10] It was increasingly apparent that the rotary engine was a technological dead end.

Béchereau designed the SPAD 7 for the Hispano-Suiza 150 horsepower water-cooled V-8 engine, a revolutionary new aircraft engine that emerged in 1915 and set the pattern for fighter engines well into World War II. The Swiss engineer Marc Birkigt's innovative design used a cast-aluminum block that incorporated fuel and water passages and thus eliminated the need for external pipes. Birkigt later increased the horsepower to 220 by changing the valve timing, which increased normal engine RPM to 2,200. A propeller turning at such high speeds, however, encountered serious problems. Consequently, Birkigt added a reduction gear, which turned a separate propeller shaft and lowered propeller RPM to 1,170. The gearing made it possible to transfer the increased energy of a high-RPM engine to a larger propeller with more torque.[11]

The SPAD design had a sturdy bulldog appearance, and the plane was as

Eddie Rickenbacker and the SPAD 13

Rickenbacker brought the first SPAD 13 to Touquin on 5 July 1918.

RICKENBACKER COLLECTION, AUBURN UNIVERSITY ARCHIVES

solid as it looked. The SPAD 13 preserved most of the SPAD 7's structural characteristics in a heavier airframe with larger dimensions. The wings were stronger and more heavily braced than those of the Nieuport 28. The SPAD was also less vulnerable to fire. Béchereau placed a contoured fuel tank on the bottom of the aircraft. A SPAD in the Lafayette Escadrille took hits in the tank that caused it to catch on fire. The fire blew the tank off the airplane, but the pilot managed to land it otherwise undamaged.[12]

The introduction of the SPAD 13 was slow by World War I standards. The first prototype appeared in April 1917, but problems with the 220-horsepower Hispano-Suiza engine delayed its delivery. The slow pace of delivery of the new SPAD was one of the few deficiencies in an otherwise mighty industrial effort under way in the French aircraft industry. The French Air Service alone was larger than the entire German air force, but owing to the SPAD 13 production problems most French fighters were still SPAD 7s when the spring offensive began. Maintenance of the complex engine proved to be a significant problem. A French report in May 1918 noted, "the shortcomings of the Hispano engine . . . , which, by virtue of the repairs thus necessitated in the escadrilles, immobilize two-thirds of 200 hp SPAD aircraft."[13] Because of these developmental problems, AEF procurement policy favored the SPAD 7 over the SPAD 13 as late as June 1918, when Foulois decided to get rid of the Nieuport 28. Large numbers of SPAD 13s finally began to arrive at the 1st Pursuit Group on 13 July. The 94th Squadron received them first, but conversion was exasperatingly slow, causing the squadron to miss the first phase of the Second Battle of the Marne.[14]

By early July intelligence reports convinced General Foch that the next German offensive would be a pincer-type attack by German armies on either side of Reims. As the Allied commander in chief repositioned forces to meet the threat, he assembled a large Allied air force as a strategic reserve. This aerial strike force consisted of the Division Aerienne (Air Division) and the RAF's 9th Brigade. The French Air Service's Air Division was the largest single aviation unit of the war. Its two brigades represented some 370 fighters (SPAD) and 230 bombers (Breguet), about 600 airplanes.[15] During the first week in July, Pétain moved the division to bases in the rear of the French army so that he could mount his aerial counterstrike where he expected the Germans to make their next offensive, between Château-Thierry and the Argonne Forest. The division's 2d Brigade occupied airfields about twelve miles west of Saints, near the towns of Sezanne and Villers-Saint-Georges, while the its 1st Brigade occupied airfields about sixty miles farther east to cover the Champagne region. The 2d Brigade consisted of Escadre 2 (three groups of fighters, four squadrons in each group) and Escadre 13 (two groups of bombers). Its mission was to attack enemy troop columns and crossings of the Marne between Dormans and Château-Thierry once the German offensive began.[16]

The arrival of the RAF's 9th Brigade at Touquin and adjacent fields provided an additional nine squadrons of offensive air power. The brigade's nine squadrons included four squadrons of Sopwith Camels, four squadrons of de Havilland DH-9 bombers, and one squadron of Royal Aircraft Factory SE-5a single-seat fighters.[17] In addition, the two French army corps covering the twelve miles of the Marne front between Dormans and Château-Thierry possessed their own five escadrilles of observation aircraft and four balloon companies. Because this sector of the Marne was the responsibility of the French 6th Army, the four pursuit squadrons of the 1st Pursuit Group would also be in the battle.[18]

The protection mission in which Quentin Roosevelt was shot down was only part of the intelligence-gathering effort that confirmed where and when the enemy would attack. Prisoners of war informed French intelligence officers of the exact moment of attack, enabling French artillery to fire a "counter-preparation" minutes before the German artillery bombardment began. Although an attack was clearly imminent, a foul-up in Army-level coordination left the 1st Pursuit without guidance for the first day of battle. Consequently, Atkinson developed a flexible plan that he issued on July 14.[19]

Atkinson's plan tasked Hartney, his most experienced squadron commander, to launch a squadron-sized low-level reconnaissance of the Marne River crossings at dawn. Immediately after returning, Hartney's unit was to remain on alert for the rest of the day. The entire 95th and 147th Squadrons would "stand by for a protection patrol at 6:00 [A.M.] to accomplish the mission sought for the last few days." Although Atkinson's order did not explain his overall concept, it appears that he intended to assess the situation with the dawn patrol and react as might be required with his other two available squadrons, based on the information he received from the dawn patrol.[20] The 1st Pursuit Group had a total of forty-three aircraft available for operations on 15 July. The 94th Squadron was converting to SPADs and so was unavailable. Atkinson needed to know how he was supposed to coordinate the operations of his aircraft with the French Air Division and the British 9th Air Brigade, but such information would not be received for another twenty-four hours.[21]

The reverberation of the guns at 12:10 A.M. on 15 July alerted Billy Mitchell that the battle had begun. He arrived at his headquarters a little before three in the morning and learned that the French air plan "had miscarried." He then went to Saints, borrowed a 1st Pursuit Group fighter, and conducted a nighttime low-level reconnaissance over the Marne that identified the location of German bridges. When he returned to Saints, "we immediately ordered the whole group to Dormans to attack the bridges and the German troops on the ground, and to clear the air over the combat between the Germans and our troops."[22] While Mitchell may have given these orders, he left readers of his memoirs with the impression that the entire 1st Pursuit launched at dawn and fought the Germans on Marne throughout the day—a story that became history but, in fact, did not happen.[23]

Hartney's patrol of seventeen Nieuports, the largest yet mounted by the 1st Pursuit Group, took off at 4:49 A.M. in accordance with the previous day's plan. It returned less than twenty minutes later because the ceiling was so low that the "mission was impossible to perform." One of Hartney's men crashed in the fog. For most of the day, the group was out of the battle. It launched a three-plane alert to the vicinity of Vaux at eight in the morning, with negative results, and three protection patrols for the 1st Corps Observation Group west of the Marne battle area. The information gleaned from these observation missions was important, though, in confirming that the German offensive remained east of Château-Thierry.[24]

The 1st Pursuit Group did launch two squadron-sized patrols into the battle area that evening. Bonnell led the first of these, a sixteen-plane patrol that took off at six o'clock. Bonnell and three of the patrol members had to return shortly after takeoff because of contaminated fuel—blamed in the squadron's report on "American gas." The patrol continued but apparently without formation integrity. Stragglers encountered hostile groups of planes, resulting in engagements in which two of the Nieuports were badly shot up and forced to land, though they claimed to have brought down two enemy planes. Both pilots returned to their squadron, but neither received a confirmation for his victory. The patrol report indicated that it had flown at an altitude of 3,500 meters (11,500 feet) and gave no account of strafing attacks on the Marne bridges or troops on the ground.[25] At 7:36 P.M. Hartney led the group's seventh and final patrol of the day, an eleven-plane escort for friendly bombers to Dormans, successfully accomplished without incident.[26]

The German attack gained them a bridgehead across the Marne between Château-Thierry and Reims. Hartney, mindful that earlier German advances had quickly overrun Allied airfields, ordered preparations for the evacuation of Saints. His troops packed up two trucks with spare parts and supplies and took them thirty miles to the rear. Cpl. Walter Williams noted in his diary, "Standby teams to destroy everything that can't be moved."[27] Closer to the front, the German advance had already necessitated the withdrawal of French artillery to new positions farther to the rear. Because the French artillery could not fire while it was withdrawing, it became the responsibility of aviation to interdict the enemy's movement across the river. Attacking the crossing points on the Marne River between Château-Thierry and Verneuil became the main effort of the French Air Division. The bombers of both brigades of the division, including those based in the Champagne area, attacked the Marne crossing.[28] Some four hundred fighters and bombers of the Air Division attacked into a twelve-mile-long area along the Marne, and many of these probably made multiple sorties. French officials were no doubt reluctant to commit additional Allied units into the same area without close coordination.

French planners had reason to be concerned about committing Allied aviation units into an intense battle without prior coordination. Fratricide had been a problem when the British 9th Air Brigade and the French Air Division cooperated against the German offensive thrust to the north in June. There had been instances of British pilots attacking French ground troops and French pilots and infantry firing upon RAF planes. Such occurrences impressed commanders with the necessity for close and continuous liaison during joint air operations. As a further precaution, the 9th Air Brigade also instituted the practice of conducting demonstrations at French airfields before combined operations to familiarize themselves with British aircraft.[29]

On 15 July the RAF conducted such a demonstration over Saints for about five minutes, and it appears to have taken the 1st Pursuit Group by surprise. The Americans gawked at the noisy but impressive display of low-altitude mock dogfighting above their field. Low-altitude aerobatics were strictly prohibited by Atkinson as unsafe. At such low altitudes, any miscalculation on the part of the pilot, or any malfunction of equipment, could easily result in loss of both pilot and airplane because there was no room in which to recover.[30]

Unaware of the purpose of this demonstration, Hartney thought his old comrades were simply showing off their superior skills and airplanes—a sort of challenge to the Americans. He lost his breath running to the hangars to get into his plane, but by the time he was airborne the Sopwith Camels were gone. Hartney decided to put on his own demonstration to prevent his "boys from gaining any impression that the British ships were better than ours." He wrote,

> I put on the damnedest one-man show I ever attempted, before or since. That Monosoupape was my pet engine and I had no fear of it stopping if I nursed it closely at every move. At very low altitude but very high speed I proceeded to do everything Maxwell and his crowd had done and then some.

Hartney's maneuvers in the Nieuport 28 surprised even himself. "Up to that time I had not fully realized what I could do and I did things I had never attempted before. Two loops were literally right off the ground."[31]

As soon as he landed Hartney received a message to report to the group commander. "'My God!' Atkinson exploded, fairly raging, 'Are you crazy?'"

Atkinson admonished Hartney for setting a poor example and for allowing the Englishmen to lead him "astray" and possibly kill himself. His former RAF colleagues, he told Hartney, were crazy to perform such stunts. Atkinson next warned, "If you pull that phony stuff again, you're through." Hartney accepted his reprimand and admitted to Atkinson that he had been foolish. But he was seething with anger on the inside. He wrote, "I could have smacked him in the eye. . . . But I was very docile."[32]

Atkinson was being consistent. He had scolded Alan Winslow of the 94th Squadron back at Toul for a similar infraction of the policy against aerobatics and then suspended him from flying for two days. While Hartney harbored hostility, Winslow was more circumspect. Immediately afterward, he noticed that his Nieuport 28 had sustained substantial damage from enemy machine-gun fire. "My foolish stunting," he later realized, "had almost finished the job for him. Quite rightly I was ordered to remain on the ground for the next two days."[33]

The contrast between Hartney's and Winslow's responses to Atkinson's strict enforcement of his policy against low-altitude aerobatics reflected the resentment growing toward Atkinson among the commanders of the Canadian Circus. Both Hartney and Bonnell were of the same rank as Atkinson. Though Atkinson retained some positional authority, his practice of commanding the group from the ground weakened his moral authority over the two majors, who regularly flew combat missions. Hartney considered Atkinson one of the "swivel chair ground officers behind the lines who knew nothing about flying."[34] Hartney's former training as a lawyer may have helped him muster the necessary self-control to keep his session with Atkinson from exploding into something worse.

While the British conducted the demonstration over Saints, plans to integrate all of the Allied aviation contingents into a counterattack against the German bridgehead were completed. French planners adopted the simplest control measures possible to coordinate the efforts of the three national contingents. They allocated specific times during which each would be responsible for aerial operations in the battle area and delineated the tasks that would be accomplished. The length of time allocated to each contingent depended on its relative size; the larger the national contingent, the more time was allocated for its operations. On 15 July Atkinson issued his operations order for the next day's battle.

The French Air Division's 2d Brigade was responsible for all aerial operations from daylight to nine in the morning and from half past noon until half past five in the evening. During the infantry attack, its task was to attack enemy ground troops. Orders for the 1st Pursuit Group and the 9th British Aviation Brigade were "TO BLIND THE ENEMY AIR SERVICE" and "TO ASSURE THE PROTECTION OF OUR ARMY CORP [sic] AVIATION, which during the period in mind will work at very low altitude." The plan called for establishing a "triple barrage" of low-, medium-, and high-altitude patrols "to create in the vicinity of our observation planes a zone of security." The density of this triple barrage was to attain its maximum at H-hour—the time at which a French Corps would begin its counterattack against the German bridgehead.[35]

The 1st Pursuit Group had responsibility for providing protection patrols during two periods, between 9:00 and 10:30 A.M. and between 5:30 and 7:15 P.M. The 9th Brigade was also responsible for two periods, 10:30 A.M. to 12:30 P.M. and 7:15 to 9:15 P.M. In addition, the Americans and British each had responsibility for providing an alert squadron during designated periods of the day. To meet these requirements, Atkinson planned to have all three of his available squadrons airborne at various altitudes during each of the patrol periods he was assigned—the densest air cover yet provided by the 1st Pursuit Group. He also assigned one of his squadrons to alert duty from 12:30 to 5:30 P.M.[36]

July 16 was the single most intensive day of combat of the month for the 1st Pursuit. Pilots engaged in a total of twenty-four combats with the enemy, resulting in the confirmed downing of six enemy planes and one balloon. The 27th Aero Squadron accounted for four of these victories, the 95th for two, and the 147th for one. The group lost three men. Daniel W. Cassard became the 147th Aero Squadron's second pilot to be killed in action; and the 27th Squadron lost two of its members: Malcom R. Gunn became that squadron's second pilot killed in action, and Robert F. Raymond was the third member of the squadron to be taken prisoner.[37] This information was not apparent at the time; all of these men were initially listed as missing, along with six other pilots who eventually managed to return after making forced landings. James Knowles of the 95th Aero Squadron, for example, was shot down and missing at the end of the day. He was uninjured, though, and back in his squadron two days later. "The stragglers were coming in all night," Hartney remembered.[38]

As often occurs in war, things did not go according to Atkinson's plan.

Although he had ordered three simultaneous squadron patrols over the battle area during the morning, the first patrols did not take off until the afternoon. The 95th, 27th, and 147th Squadrons took off at 12:45, 1:18, and 1:30 P.M. respectively. All three had returned by about three in the afternoon. The size of their patrols ranged from eleven to thirteen airplanes, and according to their reports, they were of sufficient size to outnumber the enemy formations they encountered. Occasionally, however, individuals or groups became separated from their squadrons. Most of the combats took place around the town of Dormans, where the Germans were making their main effort across the Marne.

Waldo Heinrichs was part of a thirteen-plane patrol from the 95th Squadron assigned the low-altitude mission. His unit encountered an enemy patrol of seven Fokkers in the region of Forêt de Riz and chased them deeper behind their lines. Later, part of the patrol attacked three Fokker triplanes, which were crossing the Marne and preparing to attack a bi-place SPAD observation plane but succeeded only in driving them off. Although the primary mission of the group was to engage in barrage patrolling, some of the patrols also strafed enemy troops. Such activities received scant mention in the official reports, however, suggesting that strafing was incidental to the air-superiority tasks specifically assigned by the operations order.[39]

American fighters were prohibited from engaging ground troops unless specifically ordered to do so. In this case, there was good reason for such restrictions, and the 1st Pursuit Group's general adherence to the orders it received from higher headquarters ensured that their efforts supported Foch's intent. In contrast, the 9th Brigade, which had extensive experience attacking ground troops, conducted attacks on the Marne bridges even though such targets were not included in their orders. "Within twelve hours the Commander of the 9th Brigade had received a letter of expostulation from General Foch's headquarters in which he referred to the bridges in question as 'mes ponts' (my bridges)," Roosevelt explained that by 16 July Foch had decided to launch his counteroffensive against the Germans from the left wing of the French army. He wished the bridges to remain intact so that the Germans would continue to build up in the bridgehead area as the left wing of the French army fell on them from behind. The 9th Brigade's attacks interfered with Foch's overall concept and thus engendered his rebuke. Atkinson's strict adherence to the tasks specified in the French operations order kept him from getting a similar reprimand.[40]

One of the 1st Pursuit Group's squadrons was specifically assigned a strafing mission on 16 July. An eleven-plane patrol from the 147th took off from Saints to strafe enemy troops on the roads leading north of Condé en Brie, a town located about four miles south of the Marne. No mention is made of strafing enemy troops, however, in the squadron's subsequent operations report. Later in the mission the squadron climbed to an altitude of about ten thousand feet and headed toward the Dormans area, where it encountered a formation of nine Fokkers near the Forêt de Riz. Lts. Charles Porter, Arthur Jones, and Francis Simonds each engaged in separate combats. Porter fired into one enemy aircraft and followed it down until he saw it crash into the ground. Jones dived on a Fokker and saw his tracers enter the enemy plane, causing it to topple out of control. Simonds attacked another Fokker, coming so close that his wing tip almost touched the enemy aircraft, and saw it turn over and drop out of control. Although each was sure of a victory in these separate engagements, the three pilots received shared credit for one victory. Porter also saw an enemy balloon go down in flames.[41] Zenos R. Miller of the 27th Aero Squadron had shot it down. Miller's patrol had taken off from Saints twelve minutes after the 147th Squadron to fly their patrol at five thousand feet. Miller also engaged in strafing enemy troops on this mission and received credit for downing a second balloon later that day—the beginning of a victory streak that would make him an ace by 20 July.[42]

The three squadrons began their second mission of the day at five o'clock that evening. An eight-plane patrol from the 147th Aero Squadron left first to cover the front of the U.S. 1st Corps sector in the Belleau Wood region. The near simultaneous activities of the three squadrons created such congestion on the small airfield at Saints that a collision occurred between Nieuports of the 147th and 27th Squadrons, resulting in a "washout" of one Nieuport.[43] The 27th and 95th Squadrons finally took off at 5:25 and 5:30 P.M. respectively, each squadron with twelve planes bound for the Marne Valley, the 27th Aero low and the 95th Squadron high at eighty-two hundred feet. Jerry Vasconcells and Kenneth Clapp in the 27th Squadron each destroyed a Rumpler observation plane. Vasconcells was initially reported missing, but he returned to the squadron late that night, a survivor of one of many forced landings that day. In the 95th Squadron Grover C. Vann received credit for bringing down one enemy aircraft when he forced it to land inside friendly lines, and Sumner Sewall and Edward P. Curtis brought down an enemy two-seater.[44]

German attacks against the U.S. 3d Division, which defended some seven and a half miles of the Marne from the eastern edge of Château-Thierry, ceased by noon on 16 July, as German leaders had called off the offensive.[45] Allied strafing and bombing attacks, together with artillery fire adjusted by Allied observation planes, contributed to the German defeat by making it difficult for the Germans to sustain the ten divisions that had initially succeeded in crossing the Marne.[46] The 1st Pursuit Group's operations contributed by helping the Allies establish air superiority over the battle area. Waldo Heinrichs of the 95th Aero Squadron noted in his diary that the air was so full of Allied planes that the "Boche didn't have a look in."[47] The Allies had established air superiority.

With the air war over the Marne well in hand, French planners decided that they would need only a small effort from the 1st Pursuit Group the next day. Poor weather also inhibited air activity. After two days of intensive operations, the 1st Pursuit Group planned and conducted only one patrol on 17 July. Fourteen planes of the 27th Squadron took off from Saints at half past five that evening to patrol the Château-Dormans sector above the Marne. They claimed two Rumplers but received confirmation for only one. Atkinson retained the 95th and 147th Squadrons in an alert status. It would have been difficult for the 95th Squadron to respond, though, because it was hastily converting to SPADs. Although the 95th Squadron's SPADs had arrived a few days earlier, Peterson wisely held off on making the switch until there was a lull in operations.[48]

Thus ended the 1st Pursuit Group's operations on the Marne. The French Air Division and the British 9th Brigade continued to support the counterattack against the Germans in the Marne Valley, but the 1st Pursuit Group received a change of mission to cover Foch's counteroffensive by the left wing of the French 6th Army beginning on 18 July. The initiative passed to the Allies. The Germans never regained it.

The 1st Pursuit Group's area of operations shifted to the western side of the 6th Army's sector, from Château-Thierry to Faverolles. Atkinson launched ten squadron-sized combat patrols, a total of 117 sorties—and the most patrols conducted by the group in a single day during July—to gain air superiority over the attacking divisions. Two squadrons flew the same sector simultaneously, one at five thousand feet, the other at eighty-two hundred feet. The Germans, whose attention was focused on the Marne, were taken completely by surprise. The 1st Pursuit easily established air superiority, reporting but one combat and no casualties.[49]

The 95th Squadron was already back in the air, having completed a remarkably swift conversion to the SPAD 13. The 94th Squadron was also finally flying missions. Its last patrol had been more than a week earlier, on 10

July, and its performance on its first day of patrolling was not impressive, in spite of the lengthy refit. Of the eleven SPADs that took off on the squadron's first patrol, three had to make forced landings. The unit launched only six airplanes on its second patrol, presumably owing to its maintenance difficulties. Atkinson decreased the number of planned patrols to a more sustainable pace for the remainder of the month, scheduling five patrols each day for the group so as to maintain an almost continual presence over their sector. Consequently, only one squadron had to fly more than one patrol each day. One squadron stood on alert at all times.

Aerial combat increased as the Germans reacted to the counteroffensive. The 27th Squadron shot down three enemy aircraft on 19 July. On the same day, Billy Mitchell ordered the group "to drive down balloons east and west of Chateau Thierry." Although none was destroyed, the attack by the 147th Squadron caused four balloons to be hauled down.[50] The next day would have been uneventful except for a breach of discipline that resulted in what Hartney termed "the most disastrous in the history of the 27th Squadron." The 27th and 147th Squadrons had been receiving Nieuport 28s from the 94th and 95th Squadrons, and five members of Hartney's squadron, led by Lt. John MacArthur, were conducting what was officially reported as a "trial flight." In reality this flight was a voluntary or "wildcat" patrol, another practice that was prohibited by Atkinson, for safety reasons, but winked at by Hartney as an overly cautious policy.

MacArthur, leading, sighted a formation of six French-made Breguet bombers and decided to tag along. The Nieuports subsequently became involved in a fight with seven German fighters about six miles inside German lines. According to the two survivors, the Germans finally broke off their attack to pursue the Breguets. The 27th lost MacArthur, Zenos Miller, and Fred Norton—Hartney's "three most trusted and substantial officers." Although he was taken prisoner, Miller became the 27th Squadron's second ace on this patrol by receiving credit for shooting down two Fokker D-7s. Norton, who sometimes led squadron-size patrols, managed to return. As he lay dying in the hospital, he left a last message to his squadron: "More power to you." Hartney made it the squadron's motto. MacArthur, who had become the squadron's first ace only a few days earlier, died of wounds in captivity.[51] Joseph Eastman, of the 94th Squadron, noted that "a number of new men have been sent to the group for replacements. The 27th lost seven men in two days—three as the result of MacArthur leading a patrol against orders over the lines with a stiff wind blowing to the Huns."[52]

By 21 July the 94th and 95th Squadrons were each equipped with twenty-six SPADs, reflecting Billy Mitchell's plan to increase the number of aircraft in pursuit squadrons to twenty-five aircraft, thereby enabling larger patrols. The 1st Pursuit Group had received more than sixty SPADs, and it was time to begin the conversion of a third squadron to the new fighter.[53] Both Hartney and Bonnell wanted to keep their Nieuport 28s instead of changing to the SPAD. They were still hopeful because new Nieuport 28s continued to arrive at Saints—four had arrived the previous day. The group had also recently received three Sopwith Camels to try out, which Atkinson gave to Hartney. These Camels, powered by 130-horsepower Clerget engines, were among forty-five such aircraft received by the Air Service during June and July.[54] A total of 266 Camels were supposed to be delivered from England that summer, but English factories were unable to complete the order. Hartney himself flew one of these Camels on at least two occasions during the fighting over the Marne.[55]

The concurrent delivery of Nieuports, SPADs, and Sopwith Camels to the 1st Pursuit Group during the Château-Thierry campaign created a degree of uncertainty that allowed the Canadian Circus to hope that the Nieuport 28 might be retained. While Atkinson was having significant difficulties with Hartney, his relationship with Bonnell had also deteriorated. Losing the Nieuport 28 was an even bigger bone of contention in the 147th Squadron. Coupled with Bonnell's bombastic personality and similar low regard for Atkinson, an explosive confrontation was bound to occur. All that was needed was an appropriate catalyst. The heightened tensions accompanying daily combat and questionable weather provided it.

"The fog was on the ground, it was not flying weather," recalled Lt. Ralph O'Neill of the 147th Squadron when they received an order for the entire squadron to fly to the front. Some of the members of the squadron thought they had been unfairly singled out for this hazardous mission in poor weather. O'Neill heard Bonnell tell the operations officer that "he could not obey the orders, he could not send his planes into the air in zero weather. He would not ask any of his pilots to do anything that he would not do himself." Bonnell next learned that the group commander was on his way to operations because of his refusal. He assembled his squadron in formation and counted his officers to make sure all were present. Atkinson arrived and repeated the order to carry out the mission. He added, "You know very well that you could be shot for disobeying an order in the face of the enemy."

> Bonnell said, "You can order the firing squad whenever you like. I am not sending a pilot off the ground in this weather, because I wouldn't fly in this weather and neither would you." Browe [Atkinson] said, "You'll hear from me," and he drove off in a huff with his eyes popping.[56]

The public refusal of orders orchestrated by Bonnell amounted to mutiny. Atkinson may have demanded more severe action from Mitchell than Bonnell and his adjutant's relief, but that was what he got. Both men were relieved of duty on 22 July. The next day the 147th Squadron received its first SPAD.[57]

Officers and men alike in the 147th Squadron were shocked by Bonnell's sudden dismissal. Even those who were not particularly fond of him thought he had been treated unfairly. The squadron history stated,

> It is true that he opposed the introduction of SPADs in place of the Nieuport 28 (admitted by the Germans to be the best pursuit machine the Allies ever had), and there may have been other faults unknown to outsiders, but the removal of Major Bonnell by the Commanding Officer of the First Pursuit Group will always be bitterly resented by those who served under him and who cherished his word of approval as an Army citation.[58]

Kenneth Porter, who considered Bonnell the heart and soul of the unit, remembered that as Bonnell bade his men farewell most of them openly shed tears.[59] "We all swore by Bonnell, wrote "Abe" Abernathy. "He had that 'devil-may-care' attitude which was supposed to be typical of the flyers of the day, and kept morale at a high level."[60]

Lt. John Hambleton, a flight commander in the 95th Squadron, assumed command of the unit upon Bonnell's relief. Hambleton had joined the Signal Officers Reserve Corps shortly before the United States declaration of war and had taken his initial flight training at the Newport News Curtiss School in early 1917. He had also commanded the 41st Aero Squadron at Selfridge Field for a short period of time. He joined the 95th Squadron in April and won two confirmed victories in the Toul sector. The 147th Squadron actually performed extremely well during his short tenure. On 24 July Hambleton helped his new unit shoot down four enemy airplanes. Only the 27th Squadron had received as many officially confirmed victories in a single day. But his tenure lasted only two days. The squadron endured yet another change of command. Meissner was shocked when he received orders to take charge of the troubled unit.[61]

Why another change? Atkinson probably chose Hambleton because he had already commanded a squadron and had performed well since arriving in the 1st Pursuit Group. The reason given for Meissner's assumption of command was that Hambleton had been selected to command one of the new pursuit squadrons being organized in the Toul sector, but Meissner could more easily have been sent to this unit without necessitating yet another disruption to the 147th Squadron. It seems more likely that Mitchell overruled Atkinson because he wanted a higher-scoring pilot to take over the unit. Rickenbacker, who was already an ace and the assistant squadron commander of the 94th Squadron, might well have been first choice had he been available. Because he was also five or six years older than most of the pilots, his maturity could have provided a stabilizing influence. But Rickenbacker was in the hospital again, having his eardrum lanced. Meissner had four victories, only one fewer than Rickenbacker at the time. He had proved himself as a flight commander and had been serving as assistant squadron commander in Rickenbacker's absence. In addition, Meissner's narrow escapes from the Nieuport 28's wing failures made him a perfect symbol of the Nieuport's weaknesses and the virtues of the SPAD. He had just made the transition to the SPAD, and he loved it.

Meissner thus became the first among the college men who joined the Air Service after the declaration of war to become a pursuit squadron commander. At the age of twenty-one he was the youngest squadron commander in the Air Service—six years younger than Bonnell and younger than many, if not most, of the pilots in the 147th Squadron.[62] He faced a daunting challenge in his first meeting with the squadron as its new commander. As O'Neill remembered,

> He came to the Squadron when were having breakfast one day. . . . He apologized for the appointment. He said he knew several pilots from the 147th that deserved the appointment more than he did, but he had to obey orders. He said he would not actually command the Squadron except nominally, that he would not lead the Squadron, and that he would follow us over the line until he had more experience and so forth. A nice fellow.[63]

As Meissner learned the ropes of squadron command he regularly flew his SPAD with the 147th Squadron's patrols. He delayed the conversion to

Nieuports while liberally approving leaves and lending out the squadron commander's Packard automobile. He even drove some of the pilots over to Touquin to meet with the RAF pilots.[64]

Shortly after Meissner took command the British 9th Air Brigade departed the sector. Previous observation missions by the 1st Corps had encountered little opposition from Germans in the air, but now their planes "were constantly interfered with by enemy aircraft." The decrease in Allied pursuit aviation caused American observation and pursuit casualties to mount, even though the 1st Pursuit Group was flying larger patrols because of the increased number of airplanes in each squadron.[65] William Muir Russel, who joined the 95th Aero Squadron at the end of July, described the spectacle of one of these large patrols taking off, forming into flights of V-shaped formations, and climbing toward the front:

> The eighteen machines stand in two columns with all motors going. When the signal is given, the first machine leaves the ground with the second not fifty yards behind, and then third, etc. On reaching an altitude of some thousand meters, they fall naturally into a circle, revolving about the field. When the last machine has reached altitude, the two flight leaders, or three it may be, break away from the circle, and the flights drop into position behind their leaders and start for the lines in a continual climb.[66]

Russel was killed in combat a little more than a week later.

By the end of July the 147th Aero was the only squadron that had not switched to the SPAD. The Hispano-Suiza engine was proving difficult to maintain in the other squadrons. First Pursuit Group patrol sizes ranged from thirteen to nineteen airplanes on 31 July, but at the end of the day 33 percent (nineteen of fifty-seven) of the SPADs were out of commission, whereas only 23 percent (seven of thirty-one) of the Nieuports were disabled. The SPAD maintenance problem was especially bad in the 94th Squadron, more than half (thirteen of twenty-five) of whose SPADs were not operational.[67]

July 31 was a difficult day for the 94th Aero Squadron, not only because of maintenance problems but also because it lost one of its best pilots. Alan Winslow was shot down while leading a fourteen-plane patrol. The counteroffensive by the left wing of the 6th Army had achieved great success, causing the salient to steadily shrink. Winslow's patrol flew to Soissons before turning back toward Reims. Flying at the lead of the lower flight of the patrol, he sighted a formation of six Fokkers protecting a German observation plane and fired a flare from his Very pistol to signal the attack. "I led our SPADs high above the German formation, until we were directly between them and the sun. They had seen us, however, and had begun the defensive maneuver of flying in a circle, following each other's tails."[68]

Just as Winslow came into firing range he spotted a lone Fokker hovering overhead. Worried that it might attack during the ensuing melee, he pulled back on his stick and zoomed up firing at the Fokker's belly but having no effect. Winslow had calculated that his fight was occurring at a higher altitude than the melee below him and that he did not have to worry about the other Fokkers. He was wrong. "I had not given sufficient credit to the remarkable climbing ability of the new Fokkers," he observed. While he was fixated on his opponent another enemy fighter shot him down. He became a prisoner of war and suffered the amputation of his left arm because of wounds.[69]

The next day the 27th Squadron experienced the largest number of casualties sustained by any of the 1st Pursuit Group's squadrons during the entire war. An eighteen-plane protection patrol was attacked by at least four different German fighter squadrons, including two from JG 1, near Fere-en-Tardenois. Six of the 27th Squadron's pilots were either killed or taken prisoner. These heavy losses underscored the danger of flying protection patrols, which could attract attacks from several different enemy fighter units while the fighter escort attempted to cover the friendly reconnaissance aircraft. Evidently, the unit lost its formation integrity even before the engagements began. Some of the Americans recalled being members of six or seven-plane patrols when the fighting began. One pilot remembered being part of a two-plane formation that degenerated further into a lone patrol. The survivors from the 27th Squadron requested six confirmations when they returned but received credit for only three.[70]

August 1 also marked the heaviest day of fighting for the 1st Pursuit Group since 16 July. Twenty-one combats were reported, though the 27th Squadron experienced the only casualties.[71] In one of the smaller engagements of the day, a two-plane alert from the 147th Squadron, consisting of Meissner and Brotherton, brought down an enemy observation plane. This was Meissner's first victory with the 147th Squadron, making him an ace and helping him establish credibility in his new command. There were now four aces on duty in the 1st Pursuit Group: Rickenbacker, Meissner, Peterson, and Hartney.[72]

Hermann Göring, wearing German pilot's badge,
Iron Cross, and Pour le Mérite (Blue Max)
*Göring commanded Jagdgeschwader 1, Richthofen's Flying
Circus, from 14 July 1918 until the end of the war.*
NATIONAL AIR AND SPACE MUSEUM, CD-ROM
2B-10708

The air battle in the Château-Thierry campaign culminated on 1 August
and tapered off afterward as poor weather curtailed operations for the next
week. Meanwhile, the counteroffensive under way by French and American
troops at times resembled a pursuit. Atkinson's operations section issued daily
memorandums describing the advance of the front line to enable the
squadrons to keep their maps current. By 24 July reports also included which
Germans airfields had been, or were in the process of being, abandoned. At

Mitchell's headquarters, Philip Roosevelt sensed that the steady advance of Allied troops "gave an added spur" to the energy of the 1st Pursuit Group's squadrons. As the Germans withdrew under steady Allied pressure from both sides of the Château-Thierry salient, the 1st Pursuit Group found itself farther and farther from the front lines. By 6 August, the Germans had retired to the high ground north of the Vesle River, where the lines finally stabilized, leaving Saints almost fifty miles from the front lines.[73]

The distance was so great that patrols were using up most of their fuel going to and from the lines. On 3 August Atkinson conducted a reconnaissance of a proposed advance-landing field at Coincy, the former base of JG 3, only six miles from the front lines. There was insufficient room for the entire group, however, because a French reconnaissance squadron had already taken it over. Consequently, Atkinson decided to use this airfield as a refueling stop to extend the time his patrols could spend over the sector. He selected Lt. Frederick Ordway of the 27th Squadron to command the advanced airfield. Ordway and his men left Saints on 5 August to establish the forward operating base. The next day Atkinson also sent the group's new mobile-park squadron to join Ordway.[74]

The mission of a mobile park, so named because it was expected to be capable of moving on twenty-four hours' notice, was to support the group by providing repair parts, maintenance, and salvage services. Previously, the 1st Pursuit Group had shared a park with the 1st Corps Observation Group, a system that proved unsatisfactory. The 4th Air Park was supposed to carry three days' worth of supplies for the squadrons and to perform more complicated maintenance than occurred at the squadron level, such as overhauling engines and salvaging damaged airplanes and motors for evacuation to the rear. Although initially based on the standard 150-man aero squadron, planners modified the air park to consist of 158 enlisted men, 7 officers, and 46 motor vehicles.[75]

The 1st Pursuit Group's last two victories of the Château-Thierry campaign occurred on 10 August, almost immediately after a sixteen-plane protection patrol from the 95th Squadron took off from Coincy. Enemy air activity opposing the 1st Pursuit Group continued to drop off because the British army launched the Amiens offensive on 8 August, so devastating that General Ludendorff referred to it as "the black day of the German army." Accordingly, the German air force concentrated against the British. The last day of real fighting in the 1st Pursuit Group's sector was 15 August.[76]

The 95th Squadron had six combats that day and claimed four enemy planes, though these were never confirmed. As the squadron history stated,

"Most of the fights were so far back in Germany that it was almost impossible to get confirmations from the French officials."[77] Harold Buckley remembered, "Once again we were looking hard to find the enemy as in the old days at Toul, and flying miles behind the enemy lines to do it."[78] By 24 August the 1st Pursuit Group operations section was informing its squadrons about the availability of the aerial gunnery range at Touquin. Squadrons also began to practice combat by conducting aerial maneuvers against one another.[79]

The 1st Pursuit Group received credit for thirty-nine enemy airplanes during the entire Château-Thierry campaign while sustaining thirty-one casualties: fifteen killed in action, twelve prisoners of war, two who died of wounds, and two severely wounded. Hartney's 27th Squadron led the group's victory count with sixteen confirmed victories, but his squadron lost fourteen pilots—74 percent of its authorized flying personnel and nearly half of the 1st Pursuit Group's total casualties. These losses, along with personnel transfers, caused almost a complete turnover in the squadron's pilots. When Ordway stopped by the squadron's lounge during a visit from Coincy, he noticed that it was difficult to find a familiar face. Of the original gang that had started out in Canada, only Alfred Grant, Vasconcells, and Hartney were left.[80]

The 95th Squadron downed eleven enemy aircraft while sustaining nine casualties. The 147th Squadron lost the fewest men for the number of aircraft downed, with ten victories at the cost of only three pilots. Bonnell's refusal to fly did indeed reflect a commitment to minimize losses. The 94th Squadron had the worst record, shooting down two enemy aircraft while sustaining five of the group's casualties, including two killed in a midair collision. The squadron had lost its spirit.

While the "exchange ratio" was important to the aviators, a more important indicator of the group's effectiveness is the assessment of its contributions by senior Army commanders. The commanding general of the 26th Division, which attacked in the counteroffensive as part of Liggett's 1st Corps, sent a letter of commendation to Atkinson at the end of July, praising the group for the protection it provided to the division's 12th Aero Squadron (Observation) and the "interest and gallantry" exhibited by the group in supporting the division.[81] Pershing also commended the group for its "praiseworthy record" in a 14 August letter to Chief of Air Service Mason Patrick. The letter emphasized the adversity the group had faced: "The handicaps under which this initial pursuit unit of [the] American Expeditionary Forces has been organized and begun the discharge of its duty are well known and recognized. With fine spirit and determination it has overcome obstacles and already achieved an enviable record."[82] "We had more than held our own," wrote Buckley, "fought it out with the crack squadrons of the German Air Force, and given more than we took."[83]

Hamilton Coolidge, in a letter home, commented on the near parity in friendly and enemy losses. "Curiously enough," he wrote, "a 'dogfight,' or general engagement, almost always splits even as far as losses are concerned."[84] Coolidge was describing attrition warfare. Even if the exchange ratios had tilted toward the Germans instead of the Americans, the Germans could not have afforded to continue such a tradeoff. American power was building at an accelerating rate on the ground and in the air. The German army had exhausted itself in a series of desperate offensives to win the war before the Americans could tip the balance. They had failed, and there was a now a feeling that Allied victory was inevitable. The strength of the AEF numbered a little more than a million troops at the beginning of August. By the end of August the Americans had twenty-five aero squadrons assigned to the front, twelve of which were pursuit squadrons organized into three pursuit groups.[85]

While the 1st Pursuit Group fought the Château-Thierry campaign, new pursuit squadrons continued to come on line in the Toul sector. The transfer of some of the group's best officers provided these new units with a cadre of experienced leaders, who brought with them the tactics and techniques they had learned in the 1st Pursuit Group. Most of these transfers were from the 95th Squadron. George Fisher left the 95th Squadron to become the commanding officer of the 49th Aero Squadron assigned to Davenport Johnson's 2d Pursuit Group. Edward Buford and Charles Woolley also left the 95th Squadron to become flight leaders in the 49th Squadron, as did John Wentworth from the 94th Squadron. John Hambleton took command of the 213th Aero Squadron in William Thaw's 3d Pursuit Group. William F. Loomis and S. E. Curtis of the 94th Aero Squadron also went to the 213th Squadron.[86]

Experience gained by the 1st Pursuit Group was also transmitted in a more formal way. Mitchell's 1st Brigade headquarters developed standard procedures for pursuit unit operations. These instructions explained the operations of patrols and alerts and their planning and coordination through a system of daily reports and operations orders. It also specified the duties and responsibilities of each commander and staff officer at the group and squadron headquarters, as well as those of patrol leaders and flight commanders.[87] John Wentworth later wrote that the Château-Thierry campaign had taught American airmen the importance of maintaining a formation once airborne. "The formation is the unit," he wrote. "All operations will be directed so as to maintain the unit. . . . Any separation means that the danger of attack by enemy planes is tremendously enhanced." Wentworth was convinced that discipline was the fundamental upon which a successful pursuit effort must build. It required discipline to keep the formation together and to follow the patrol leader.[88]

On 20 August Atkinson received a handwritten note from Mitchell, stating, "You will arrange to turn over command of the 1st Pursuit Group at once and upon completion of this, report to me for duty. Notify the Aeronautical Commander 6th French Army (Major [Paul] Gerard) of the action taken, keep the personal transportation you now own."[89] There was no doubt about Atkinson's replacement. Hartney was the only major left, and he commanded the highest-scoring squadron. Lt. Alfred A. Grant, who had been with the unit since Canada, replaced Hartney as commander of the 27th Squadron. The next day Atkinson bade the group farewell and left with his interpreter and another staff member to take command of the 1st Pursuit Wing.[90]

"It was unbelievable, I the Saskatoon lawyer was to direct the fortunes of such wonderful fliers as Eddie Rickenbacker, Jimmie Meissner, Reed Chambers, Ham Coolidge," wrote Harntey. "Through my dazed mind one thought kept whirling around—I must make this, by personal example and enthusiasm, the greatest unit of its kind in the world. What a responsibility!"[91] The most difficult work, however, had already been completed. Hartney did not have to concern himself with organizing America's first pursuit group, selecting its leaders, and guiding them through their first battles. Atkinson had already accomplished these tasks. The Château-Thierry campaign was the most difficult air operation the 1st Pursuit Group fought during the war. German aviation would never again be able to concentrate as it had because the Allies conducted simultaneous offensives across the German front during the remainder of the war. At the same time, new American units continued to come on line, adding to the overwhelming superiority of Allied numbers. Moreover, Hartney took over a group that had already established a winning tradition.

Atkinson's new command was accompanied by promotion to lieutenant colonel. The 1st Pursuit Wing was the largest assemblage of combat aircraft in the AEF during the war. Its organization was modeled after the brigades of the French Air Division: two fighter groups and a bombardment group. Mitchell returned Philip Roosevelt to Atkinson, thus reconstituting the command team for the AEF's first campaign. The lessons they learned at Château-Thierry were incorporated into the 1st Pursuit Wing's operating procedures, published on the eve of the St. Mihiel campaign.[92]

Emile Gauvreau, one of Billy Mitchell's earliest biographers, who knew Mitchell before he died in 1936, gave a highly complimentary account of Mitchell, portraying him as an unerring prophet and crusader of air power.[93] Gauvreau later wrote *The Wild Blue Yonder: The Sons of the Prophet Carry On*, a highly polemic history of American air power written at the height of World War II. He devoted a number of pages in this work to Atkinson, who took medical retirement after suffering a nervous breakdown shortly after returning from the war. Gauvreau considered Atkinson one of the unsung heroes of the development of American air power: "Such a history would not be complete without an account of the tragic experience of Colonel Bert M. Atkinson, now recognized in military aviation circles as the man largely responsible for the impetus which made Mitchell the crusader." Despite his high regard for Mitchell, Gauvreau gave much of the credit to Atkinson.

> Some of the most effective air strategy of the war was to come from Mitchell's conferences with Atkinson. . . . Atkinson contributed his ideas without the slightest desire for personal recognition. His face beamed and he cocked his cigarette holder at a more rakish angle when Mitchell hurried off to put them into effect. Some of the young Colonel's fiery adherents were less complacent when they saw Mitchell climb to the rank of Brigadier General. . . . But the Commander of the 1st Pursuit Wing remained in the background where he redoubled his energy.[94]

Gauvreau was not the only observer who ascribed to Atkinson a pivotal role in American combat aviation. While working on the official history after the war, Philip Roosevelt wrote his mother, "I believe [Atkinson] knows more about the Air Service than anyone else in the American Army."[95] To be sure, Mitchell, Atkinson, and Roosevelt learned about aerial warfare during the Château-Thierry campaign. As each of them assumed positions of greater authority in the hierarchy of the Air Service, each would in turn act as an agent in transferring the strategy, tactics, and techniques of aerial warfare to the rest of the AEF's Air Service.

For the western Allies the Second Battle of the Marne was the beginning of the end of the war. For American combat aviation, it was the end of the beginning.

9

St. Mihiel

Hartney used the lull in combat during the last part of August to gather the reins of leadership. "It gave me a chance for an intensive study of the squadrons, their history, their officers, men, and equipment," he stated. "I met every officer.... I visited other flying units, both French and American, talked with hundreds of the hard-working mechanics, cooks, office staff, and others." He also spent a lot of time studying the group's flying equipment and "digging into" such details as fuel and lubrication problems, wing repairs, and engine maintenance.[1]

Hartney's experience as a combat pilot and a fighting squadron commander distinguished him from his predecessor. He operated from a wider "comfort zone" that made it easy for him to check on the details that were important in combat. "Often I clambered up on a machine," he reflected, "and took a look at the manner in which the pilot had his ammunition placed in the belts leading to his guns." He was also cognizant of the need to lead as well as to command. "Iron discipline, even from childhood," he wrote in criticism of the German army, but perhaps also thinking of Atkinson, "is no substitute for real leadership." He realized that he could no longer fly to the extent that he had in the past, but he was determined to maintain a presence in the air, to personally test new equipment and experiment with new tactics. He did not expect his squadron commanders to lead every patrol, but he did expect them to lead some. He was especially firm in his conviction that the commander's leadership by example, especially his presence in the air, had a tremendous effect on "morale, enthusiasm, and the entire efficiency of the unit."

Hartney's style was more personable and engaging than Atkinson's had been. "By far the most important thing I did was to keep in constant personal touch with the officers and men of every squadron. I was among them all hours, learning their thoughts, their methods and their capabilities." Of his command of the 1st Pursuit Group, he stated, "I don't believe any commander ever kept in closer contact with his organization," perhaps inwardly comparing himself with Atkinson. In addition to getting out of the headquarters to see his units, he conducted frequent conferences with his officers to discuss tactics and operations. He reveled in the "free exchange of new ideas."[2]

Hartney instituted a training program to prevent his units from losing their edge. Squadron-sized patrols conducted maneuvers against one another while the 1st Pursuit Group waited for its new mission. During this two-day program, while two squadrons conducted maneuvers in the air, the pilots of the other two squadrons flew to Villacoublay (those with inoperable airplanes traveled by automobile) to inspect captured German airplanes and the latest French experimental aircraft. Afterward, the squadrons switched roles.[3] Additionally, he organized a flying competition among all the flight sections of the group, the objective being to practice formations, observation, and strict adherence to a flight plan.[4]

First Pursuit's pilots practiced their machine-gun and strafing skills by using the previous airfield at Touquin as a shooting range. Joseph Eastman and Ed Greene evaluated machine-gun training at the Touquin range from an observation position on the ground about two hundred yards from the target. They were close enough for Eastman to witness what it was like to be under fire from the air:

> When the planes came over and heeled up to dive for firing, the effect was paramount to their diving on us: which was an excellent thing as the fierce rain [of bullets] pouring near at hand produced somewhat the kind of a show our doughboys must have put up with when the Boches come across a straf-

ing. The morale blow must be tremendous. No wonder they want us to hover over them twelve hours a day![5]

Hartney also allowed his squadron commanders to grant leaves to those who had been through the heavy fighting of July and August. The 1st Pursuit Group resonated positively with his style of command. The 147th Squadron turned in its Nieuports on 13 August and spent the rest of the month preparing and testing their new SPAD 13s. Meissner detected a lessening of the squadron's disdain toward the SPAD by the latter part of August, noting in his dairy, "SPADs going fine, pilots enthusiastic."[6] Meissner also gave his veteran pilots opportunity for leaves. Ralph O'Neill had initially planned to accompany Kenneth Porter to Nice, on the Mediterranean, but changed his mind and hitched a ride on an RAF bomber to visit a buddy in England. On his return trip, he delivered a Sopwith Camel, equipped with the 150-horsepower Gnome Monosoupape rotary engine, to the AEF. Because of Hartney's preference for the rotary-engine fighter, these new versions of the Camel would eventually be sent to the 1st Pursuit Group.[7]

Rumors of imminent departure from Saints were accompanied by false starts. Units packed and unpacked equipment after being alerted for movement, only to learn that the orders had been countermanded. The 4th Air Park Squadron returned from the advanced field at Coincy on 24 August in anticipation of the group's imminent departure, and Capt. J. Gordon Rankin took command of the unit.[8] In addition to its supply and maintenance capabilities, the 4th Park had its own brass band. Cpl. Walter Williams, who in late August had earned himself yet another arrest by missing muster, was more impressed with the latter than the former. The 4th Park's band gave a concert at the recently christened Roosevelt Square in Saints the evening after it returned from Coincy. Hartney temporarily split up the 4th Park, assigning a section of it to each of his pursuit squadrons for training.[9]

On 28–29 August Hartney attended a planning conference at 1st Army headquarters at Ligny-en-Barrois to review plans for the attack on the St. Mihiel salient. Pershing had long planned on a major offensive in this area, which is why the U.S. 1st Army had been assembling in the Toul area. By early September, however, the St. Mihiel offensive had become a limited attack intended merely to reduce the salient, thereby gaining the use of an important railroad and securing the 1st Army's right flank for a coordinated Allied offensive later in the month. Success at St. Mihiel was also important because it represented the debut of army-level operations for the United States Army. As demonstrated here, the 1st Pursuit Group followed a methodical, step-by-step approach in its preparation for combat operations—organizational training, operations in a quiet sector, and operations under the supervision of an experienced French army. Pershing tried as much as possible to take this approach with all elements of the AEF. All aspects of the St. Mihiel operation were engineered for success.

Pershing ensured that the St. Mihiel offensive would succeed by concentrating overwhelming ground and air forces against the Germans who defended the salient. The salient was a German bulge in the French lines, measuring twenty-four miles across the base and fourteen miles deep, that had existed since 1915. The 1st Pursuit Group was familiar with its new area of operations because it had patrolled the southern portion of the salient while stationed at Toul. Pershing's plan called for a converging attack with mostly American troops on both sides of the salient to pinch off the enemy defenders. Two American corps formed one set of pincers and would make the main attack against the southern side. One American corps, consisting of both American and French troops, would form the other set of pincers and attack against the western side. The French 2d Colonial Corps would conduct a supporting attack against the nose of the salient.[10]

Billy Mitchell's performance at Château-Thierry had impressed Brig. Gen. Mason Patrick, and in late July Patrick replaced Benjamin Foulois with Mitchell as the chief of Air Service of the 1st Army. Foulois became Patrick's assistant and continued to focus on logistics and training. The appointment assured Mitchell's promotion to brigadier general and elevated him to first among equals with Foulois. Mitchell was Hartney's immediate superior for most of the remainder of the war.

The St. Mihiel campaign occupies a special place in air-power history because it was the largest single air operation of the war. The concentration of air power was nothing new, however, as the employment of the Allied air forces at the Second Battle of the Marne demonstrated. It is also worth noting that French advisers continued to have a strong influence on the Air Service. Mitchell shared his headquarters office with Paul Armengaud, the chief of the French aviation mission. Pershing's 1st Army was subordinated to the French army's commander in chief, Henri Pétain. Pétain and Foch reinforced Pershing with troops and combat multipliers, especially aviation units and artillery, because they wanted Pershing to expedite this attack, which they considered a prelude to the subsequent Franco-American offensive in the Champagne region and the Argonne Forest. In contrast to the Allied defensive battle on the Marne, Mitchell's plan supported an offensive and therefore took on an entirely different operational design.[11]

The French, British, and Italians provided air units to reinforce the American Air Service's twenty-eight squadrons. The greatest contribution came from the French Air Division, a total of fifty-eight squadrons, mostly pursuit and bombardment, which occupied airfields surrounding the salient by the end of the first week of September. Maj. Gen. Hugh Trenchard's Independent Force of the Royal Air Force provided eight night-bombardment squadrons in support of Mitchell but not under his direct command. The Italians provided three more night-bombardment squadrons. These contributions made for a total of 701 pursuit, 366 observation, 323 day bombers, and 91 night bombers—adding up to 1,481 airplanes, twelve balloons, and some 30,000 men. The Germans were outnumbered ten to one in pursuit aircraft.[12]

At the August planning conference, Pershing's generals reviewed the campaign plan with the aid of a large terrain model of the battlefield, which had been assembled by French balloon companies over several years. Each hill, forest, road, detached house, large building, railroad yard, ravine—practically every feature of the terrain—was depicted on it.[13] Mitchell illustrated its usefulness to Hartney: "I want you to go over to the map and look at that tiny field, then go back and prepare to slip in there overnight when I give the word, without fuss of any kind. The enemy mustn't know we're coming. Can you do it?" Hartney replied that he could.[14]

The 1st Pursuit Group moved from Saints to its new base at Rembercourt over a period of several days, from 29 August to 3 September, employing its now standard multiphased sequence of advance parties and main-body convoys, aircraft movement, and trail parties as before (see map on page 83).[15] Rembercourt served as the 1st Pursuit Group's base for the remainder of the war. Hartney described it as "unbelievably small and incredibly rough. . . . Every man who took off from or landed on that field had to do expert work with stick and rudder to avoid smashing himself and his plane to bits. And once again, mud, mud, mud."[16] Even experienced pilots were wary about landing on the bumpy, rocky field. Barracks were roughly constructed shacks hidden among the trees. Officers lived in tents, usually one flight section to a tent.

The new field had some important tactical advantages, though. It was located about twenty miles west of St. Mihiel and was thus relatively close to the front lines. Its small size and the surrounding forest provided for excellent concealment; even knowing its map location, Hartney had trouble finding it. Because of his difficulty, he was confident that the Germans would never bomb them, and they never did. The field's location on the western side of the 1st Army sector made it unnecessary to relocate for the subsequent Meuse-Argonne offensive. The headquarters of the French 2d Colonial Corps, one of the units the group would be supporting, was only a couple of miles away. The field was about fifteen miles from 1st Army headquarters, where Mitchell had established his own command post.[17]

Great efforts were being made to prevent the Germans from finding out exactly where and when the American offensive would begin, which probably explains why Mitchell did not allow Hartney to bring most of his airplanes to Rembercourt until 3 September. As soon as the airplanes landed they were placed in hangars to conceal their arrival from the enemy. Hartney enforced strict camouflage discipline at Rembercourt, often reminding his commanders to keep their airplanes under cover—a constant battle because maintenance activities were more difficult in the hangars. The group also maintained a continuous, single-plane patrol over the airfield to prevent observation by enemy aircraft.[18]

On 4 September the group began conducting continuous barrage patrols along the western side of the salient, from Watronville to St. Mihiel, a distance of about twenty miles. The new sector was on the side of the St. Mihiel salient, opposite the area that the group had patrolled while stationed at Gengoult during the previous spring. Consequently, old-timers were already familiar with the sector, having strayed into it either by accident or out of curiosity. The mission of these patrols was protection of friendly observation balloons and aircraft. Protection was essential: Meissner had seen a French balloon go down in flames the day after he arrived at Rembercourt. Hartney's orders directed the squadrons to fly their patrols in two echelons, one high (11,480 to 16,400 feet) and one low (8,200 to 11,500 feet). Each echelon was to consist of no more than five aircraft. Maintaining the continuous barrage required each squadron to fly about three patrols a day. He also maintained one flight on alert, referring to it as "a mobile reserve."[19]

As part of the security precautions, Hartney also ordered his patrols not to enter enemy territory, though this restriction was modified to allow aircraft to cross the lines if they were already involved in an engagement. In spite of these precautions, the Germans may already have known that the 1st Pursuit Group had arrived at Rembercourt. According to Corporal Williams, when the mechanics of the 27th Aero Squadron rolled into Rembercourt on 3 September, a German observation airplane flew overhead and dropped a message that said, "Welcome 27th Squadron, we are ready for you."[20]

Some of the eager flyers disobeyed Hartney's order not to cross into enemy territory. Among them was Lt. Norman Archibald of the 95th Aero Squadron, who was shot down by enemy antiaircraft fire on 9 September. Archibald was flying about one mile inside German lines and parallel to the front. He was at a lower altitude and had fallen behind the other two planes in his patrol because his engine RPMs had fallen off. Suddenly he was in the midst of a terrific antiaircraft artillery barrage. Shrapnel struck his motor as he attempted to climb away, causing his engine to quit, and he crash-landed behind German lines. According to Archibald, German officers threatened to execute him because one of his machine guns was loaded with incendiary ammunition. An informal convention among the opposing air forces forbade the use of incendiaries except for attacking balloons. Aviators on both sides, therefore, carried orders authorizing their use of incendiaries for that purpose. Archibald was not carrying such orders, and his German interrogators used this oversight to threaten him. At one point, when asked who should be notified in case of his death, Archibald quickly named his squadron commander and unit, giving away important intelligence information.[21]

Archibald knew that the St. Mihiel offensive was scheduled for 12 September, but he did not admit having disclosed this fact. The kicking mule on the side of his airplane identified his unit, and if we can believe Corporal Williams, the Germans may already have been aware of the 1st Pursuit Group's presence. Nevertheless, Archibald's capture and interrogation may have helped German intelligence officers conclude that the long-awaited attack against the St. Mihiel salient was imminent. A communiqué published at German Supreme Headquarters on 11 September, the day before the offensive, informed the German army defending the St. Mihiel salient of an impending attack: "The conversation of several American aviators captured the past few days, reveals that the American First Army with about 10 divisions is to attack between St. Mihiel and Pont-à-Mousson in the very near future."[22] In response to such warnings, the Germans began to evacuate the salient before Pershing launched his attack.

Mitchell issued his operations order for the St. Mihiel offensive at half past three on 11 September, the day before the offensive was to begin. The mission of aviation was to "take the offensive at all points with the object of destroying the enemy's air service, attacking his troops on the ground, and protecting our own air and ground troops." Atkinson's 1st Pursuit Wing, consisting of Davenport Johnson's 2d Pursuit Group at Toul, William Thaw's 3d Pursuit Group at Vacouleurs, and the 1st Day Bombardment Group at Amanty, operated from the southern side of the salient, where two corps would make the 1st Army's main attack. Mitchell ordered Atkinson's 1st Pursuit Wing to maintain "an absolute barrage" against enemy aviation and to attack enemy balloons. Additionally, Atkinson was to hold one pursuit group, loaded with bombs, in reserve to take off on fifteen minutes' notice for attacks on enemy troops or convoys.[23]

Hartney's 1st Pursuit Group covered the western side of the salient from Chatillon-sous-les-Côtes to St. Mihiel, where the U.S. 5th Corps formed the army's second set of pincers. This was practically the same sector the group had been patrolling since it had arrived at Rembercourt. Hartney's tasks included maintaining a barrage against hostile aviation, protecting observation aviation, and attacking hostile balloons opposite the 5th Corps. Attacking enemy ground troops when opportunities for strafing occurred was inherent to his mission.[24]

In addition to Mitchell's operation order Hartney probably also considered the 1st Army order issued on 7 September. Pursuit aviation tasks included defending the army front from hostile air attack, protecting observation aviation, and being prepared to attack troops on the ground in the immediate vicinity of the front. Mitchell's aviation annex elaborated further. It stated that at the beginning of the artillery preparation, army pursuit groups "will destroy all hostile aviation in front of our lines to a depth of five kilometers. Will insure absolute liberty of action of our observation aviation and balloons throughout this zone. Will attack those hostile balloons, which are considered especially dangerous." These tasks would continue during the attack along with the additional mission that low-flying patrols "should attack with bombs and machine guns, either enemy reinforcements marching to the attack or enemy elements retreating."[25]

While Atkinson's wing and Hartney's group were to operate within three miles of the front lines, Mitchell ordered the French Air Division to attack twelve to twenty miles behind the enemy's lines. Each brigade was to attack successively, from each side of the salient—like a boxer, striking first with his right and then with his left. The objective of these deep attacks was "to take the enemy aviation in reverse and force it towards our lines." The Air Division would also attack enemy ground troops when the opportunity offered itself.[26] Bombardment aviation would attack railheads, enemy command posts, airfields, and a bridge over the Meuse between Dun and Sedan.[27]

Hartney's operations section alerted the squadrons that he would issue the operations order at eleven o'clock that night.[28] The instructions included a patrol schedule that maintained a constant barrage patrol over the sector by scheduling ten patrols. Each patrol was to consist of two echelons of four planes each, the lower echelon flying at 2,500 to 3,500 meters and the upper echelon flying from 3,500 to 5,500 meters (18,040 feet). Hartney directed his pilots to "do their utmost" to observe and report on ground activity. He also required his squadrons to make liaison visits with the U.S. 5th Corps headquarters and the French 2d Colonial Corps to discuss the progress of troops, location of balloons, and missions being attempted.[29] A third liaison officer reported to Mitchell's headquarters at nine o'clock each night to receive battle orders for the next day.[30]

This planning cycle required the operations sections of the 1st Pursuit Group and its squadrons routinely to work late into the night to insure that group and squadron operations conformed to Mitchell's plan. Hartney's operations officer, Lt. Romer Shawhan, did not wait for the army order, however, to publish the daily group order. Instead, he anticipated Mitchell's orders as best he could and published his own order during the day. This procedure enabled squadrons to plan the next day's missions and to disseminate instructions to the pilots before they went to bed. Shawhan warned the squadrons that final orders, which they would receive around midnight, might change the next day's mission. Shawhan, who had been a pilot with the 147th Aero Squadron since Texas, had been serving as the 1st Pursuit Group's operations officer since the departure of Philip Roosevelt in early July.

The 1st Army's attack began at five the next morning as troops forming the right set of pincers went over the tops of their trenches. "Our men were on the job long before daylight," Hartney recalled, "but to the disgust of everybody, the weather was atrocious—pouring rain, with low hanging clouds. This, however, was perfect for one part of our plans—low flying."[31] The group launched sixteen patrols on the first day of the offensive, for a total of sixty-two sorties out of eighty-two planes reported available for combat. Because of the poor visibility and low ceilings, the size of these patrols ranged from one to eight aircraft, the most frequent size being a flight of two. Patrols rarely exceeded four of five airplanes. Most pilots reported flying at altitudes between a thousand and two thousand feet (300 and 600 meters); many flew just above the trees. Enemy opposition was negligible.[32]

Rickenbacker stated in *Fighting the Flying Circus* that the weather was so bad that none of the 94th Squadron's airplanes could take off until noon, when he and Chambers departed, but this is not so.[33] Between 7:20 and 10:00 A.M. all four squadrons in the pursuit group launched patrols. Rickenbacker was a cautious pilot. In his judgment the weather was too dangerous for flying, and while other pilots in the group probably agreed, they nevertheless dutifully flew to battle. The first to take off from Rembercourt were eight SPADs from the 27th Squadron. They flew in ones and twos because of poor visibility. Joseph F. Wehner flew alone toward Montsec, a fortified hilltop thick with antiaircraft defenses, where he attacked an enemy balloon at about 7:40. Although he fired one hundred rounds at it, the balloon did not catch on fire, but his attack did cause the crew to haul it down. Having survived heavy antiaircraft fire from enemy guns protecting the balloon, he subsequently strafed a train of seven wagons retreating through the woods northeast of St. Mihiel. He could not tell what, if any, damage this caused, except for the disruption created when the horses scattered, frightened by his attack.[34]

Lt. Frank Luke also took off with these first sorties from the 27th Squadron. Flying alone, Luke saw three enemy aircraft near Lavigneulle, a small town in the center of the 1st Pursuit Group's sector, and chased them toward Pont-à-Mousson, where they disappeared toward Metz. Subsequently, he saw an enemy balloon at Marieulles and attacked it. The Germans almost succeeded in hauling the balloon down, but on Luke's third pass the balloon burst into flames and collapsed on the winch. This victory was the first of many that earned Luke the nickname, "the balloon buster." He landed next to an American observation balloon on the friendly side of the lines, opposite the burning remnants of the enemy balloon, and secured written confirmation of his victory from Lt. Maurice Smith, one of the balloonists. Engine trouble, probably caused by battle damage, prevented his riddled and splintered airplane from flying back to Rembercourt. Luke spent the night with the balloonists and learned valuable information from Smith: Balloons were least covered by the overlapping fires of the carefully sited antiaircraft guns while being "walked" forward to their observation posts early in the morning and back to their nests in the evening and while in their beds at night. Luke returned to Rembercourt in a motorcycle sidecar.[35] His was the only confirmed victory by the 1st Pursuit Group during the first two days of the offensive.

The 94th Squadron was scheduled to fly the second patrol of the day. An orderly woke Joseph Eastman at six that morning. As Eastman's dull head cleared, he recalled having been advised in the middle of the night that assault troops from the 1st and 4th Corps would go "over-the-top" of their trenches at five. After a breakfast of coffee and eggs, he and the rest of his flight went out to the muddy airfield. The field was filled with puddles, and "a howling gale" caused the canvas on the hangars to flap. Eastman was thinking that no one in his right mind would ever fly in such weather when suddenly a half dozen orderlies came out of the headquarters "panting that the Major wants us to get off on the double-quick."

"One lucky thing about it," Eastman observed, "is that the water-soaked atmosphere will at least keep the motors cool for low flying—which is obviously the only way we can travel." The 94th Squadron also decided to fly in pairs. Eastman and Thorne Taylor piloted the first flight to take off from the unit at about a quarter to eight. They flew toward Verdun at about 650 feet altitude, with Taylor leading—and occasionally disappearing from Eastman's sight as the two planes passed through the undersides of the clouds. Five minutes short of Verdun, they turned southward to fly their assigned route along the lines. The violent agitation of the air intensified, making it even more difficult for Eastman to keep up with Taylor, as the gale-force winds blew them toward Germany. They were flying so low that they passed below a friendly observation balloon—it later broke free of its cable and was swept toward Germany. Another one of the 1st Army's balloons was blown into trees.[36]

As he and Taylor flew over the lines, Eastman could see the troops of the 5th Corps lined up in their trenches. In a few minutes it would be eight o'clock, and they would be "going over the top" as the 1st Army's left wing launched its attack against the salient. Eastman did not see any German infantry. "Except for the few groups of doughboys to be seen," he wrote, "the effect generally was of the greatest loneliness. . . . Now and then a few trucks, otherwise the roads stretched white and blank—not a soul." Most of the troop activity observed involved artillery crews busily firing their guns, adding to the convulsions of bursting shells that marked the battle area.[37]

U.S. observation balloon about to be "walked" from its nest to a forward location
 for an observation mission

Note the surrounding trees and camouflage net used for concealment.

The two-plane patrol spotted a single German airplane some distance into enemy territory. They wheeled after him, but the German promptly turned and fled. The change in direction, however, brought them into an area where the Allied artillery bombardment was particularly intense. Eastman described it as a "pyrotechnical extravagance." A semicircle of Allied guns outside the salient poured shells into a concentrated area, causing great pillars of fire and smoke to rise from four different towns. Just as they were about to enter this barrage, Taylor turned away from it, and they worked their way toward St. Mihiel. Taylor began a series of dives to within fifty feet of the ground. Eastman thought Taylor had spotted enemy troops and intended to strafe them, but because he saw no smoke from Taylor's guns, and he was not sure whether they were over friendly or enemy troops, he held his fire. As they approached St. Mihiel, Eastman "saw more fires, and everywhere steadily huge explosions sending up geysers of smoke and debris."

Because of their low altitude, Eastman perceived the battle differently than he had before: "Instead of the battle being a distant impersonal scene of flickers along a sweep of dull colored blotches—we were in it, surrounded by it at no more than good bellowing range." One enormous naval gun boomed so loudly from below that he both heard and felt its concussion over the noise of his airplane. Several times the rattle of machine guns sounded dimly in their path. In a curious juxtaposition of technologies, Eastman remarked that he could see the harnesses on the horses as he flew over army supply wagons.

Visibility improved in the afternoon as the ceiling rose to about a thousand feet, though the wind was even stronger. The group launched patrols consisting of four or five SPADs each. Eastman flew his second patrol around noon, as part of a four-plane flight led by Hamilton Coolidge. One of the airplanes from the patrol landed immediately after takeoff because of engine trouble, and ground fire caused another one to turn back, leaving only Eastman and Coolidge. Again, as they flew over the front lines on a fluid battlefield, their uncertainty as to whether they were passing over German or American troops kept them from strafing the soldiers below them.

The air was filled with Allied aircraft of all types; no German aircraft appeared. As they approached St. Mihiel the enemy's notorious antiaircraft batteries opened up on them. Eastman resisted his desire to maneuver out of the bursts and faithfully followed Coolidge. Unbeknownst to Eastman, Coolidge was slowly losing altitude because of a bad engine and doing his best to keep the plane airborne so that he could land within friendly lines. Eastman and Coolidge would be among the last targets of the St. Mihiel batteries. An hour later one of Eastman's fellow squadron members, passing over the city, saw no antiaircraft fire.

Rickenbacker and Reed Chambers also took off at about noon. They flew toward Verdun, as many did on the first leg of the patrol, and then turned east until they were over Vigneulles, in the center rear of the salient. The road network in the salient converged on Vigneulles, where a main highway led out of the salient, making it necessary for the retreating Germans troops to pass through this choke point. As Rickenbacker and Chambers passed over Vigneulles, the highway leading from it to Metz appeared "black with hurrying men and vehicles." They turned south toward St. Mihiel, flew low over the highway, and began a strafing attack. "All down the line we continued our fire—now tilting our aeroplanes down for a short burst, then zooming back up for a little altitude in which to repeat the performance," wrote Rickenbacker. "The whole column was thrown into the wildest confusion." Upon returning to Rembercourt they immediately reported that the Germans were retreating from St. Mihiel along the road to Vigneulles. Hartney relayed this important information to 1st Army headquarters.[38]

Fighters from the 1st Pursuit Group and Atkinson's 1st Pursuit Wing, along with fighters and bombers from the French Air Division, attacked German troops withdrawing through Vigneulles throughout the day.[39] One of the 1st Pursuit Group's last patrols of the day was a four-plane flight from the 95th Squadron that took off at half past five that evening. James Knowles dropped to about thirty feet altitude above the Vigneulles-Creue road. "It was jammed with stuff for about five or six kilometers. I flew up and down strafing until all my ammo was gone." Vigneulles was on fire. As soon as he landed at Rembercourt, Knowles reported the traffic jam and called for continued air and artillery attack.[40] Mitchell credited the 1st Pursuit Group's ground attacks with smashing German formations on some roads to such an extent that pursuing ground troops were able to capture several thousand prisoners.[41]

Reconnaissance reports like Rickenbacker's and Knowles's were valuable in helping American commanders stay abreast of the progress of their attacking columns. Because there were no intervening headquarters between the 1st Pursuit Group and Mitchell's headquarters, information from the 1st Pursuit Group arrived there and at 1st Army headquarters more rapidly than from other sources. Hartney's emphasis on keeping higher headquarters informed resulted in numerous reports. Because of the accuracy and importance of these reports, the 1st Pursuit Group earned the nickname, "Pursuit Observation."[42]

Pilots congregated throughout the day around the large-scale map posted in operations that displayed the stunningly rapid progress of the offensive. Later that evening, Eastman was amazed to learn that the enemy bastions at St. Mihiel and Montsec had already fallen. The attack was progressing more rapidly than expected. Eight thousand prisoners had been captured, and the Allies had undisputed air superiority. Eastman noted, "Our sky is congested with planes of all kinds, and groups of thirty Breguets have passed over to bomb—Conflans or Metz." Eastman's squadron commander, Capt. Kenneth Marr, had repeatedly predicted that the war would be over by Christmas. The optimists began to debate whether it would be best to go home by the Suez Canal or should they linger awhile in Europe? The pessimists groaned that a German counterattack was sure to come and "that the Hun 'Checker-boards' and 'Scarlet Scouts' will soon be flying against us."[43]

The American offensive at St. Mihiel succeeded so rapidly because the Germans had no intention of attempting to stop it. They had already withdrawn their heavy artillery and begun the execution of their demolition plan before the Americans attacked. The defenders were surprised, however, by the shortness of the artillery preparation and the swiftness of the American advance. These surprises disrupted their methodical withdrawal.[44]

Doughboys from each of the 1st Army's wings raced toward Vigneulles throughout the night of 12 September. The Germans succeeded in withdrawing most of their troops from the salient but still lost about sixteen thousand men, who were caught by the pincers that joined near Vigneulles early on the morning of 13 September.[45] As Mitchell put it, "The battle of St. Mihiel was really over on the first day."[46]

The 1st Pursuit Group continued its low-altitude ground strafing and reconnaissance on 13 September. The weather was "very cloudy all day but clearing occasionally," an improvement from the previous day.[47] The group launched seventy-six sorties in sixteen patrols—mostly consisting of five or six airplanes each, though seven of these were voluntary patrols consisting of only one or two airplanes. Some of these patrols flew just above the treetops, usually over the major roads at the rear of the fast-disappearing salient. Pilots reported seeing numerous small towns on fire. Just beyond the advancing infantry, they reported empty roads littered with abandoned equipment. Farther north, beyond the 1st Army limit of advance, the group's pilots observed thousands of German soldiers marching down the roads and railroad troop trains headed toward Metz, already safely behind a new defensive line, which had previously been prepared along the base of the salient. Pilots from the 1st Pursuit Group, along with those of Atkinson's 1st Pursuit Wing and the French Air Division, attacked the retreating columns throughout the day. The few enemy aircraft encountered by the 1st Pursuit Group immediately retreated at the appearance of the SPADs.[48]

As the weather improved during the afternoon, Hartney's operations section redirected priorities from low-altitude attack of enemy ground troops to protection of friendly observation aircraft. Hartney himself had returned from a mid-afternoon patrol over the sector with the commander of the 27th Squadron. The new order directed the squadrons to resume flying barrage patrols at altitudes between 2,500 and 5,500 meters (18,040 feet). Weather may have again worsened, though, for few patrols reported flying above 1,000 meters (3,280 feet) during the remainder of the day.[49]

By the evening of 13 September the St. Mihiel salient no longer existed. For the next several days, American and French troops continued mopping up bypassed points of resistance and consolidated their positions along the new defensive line. Army instructions for the Air Service directed it to continue its bombing and reconnaissance plan with special attention being given to enemy convoys and troops concentrations in the Moselle River Valley.[50] The

Army's daily intelligence summary reported that Allied aviation controlled the air "and contributed materially to the success of the operation."[51]

In contrast to the single balloon shot down by Frank Luke in the 1st Pursuit Group, Atkinson's 1st Pursuit Wing, together with the observation aircraft it was protecting, received credit for downing nine enemy aircraft on the first day of the offensive and another eleven the next day.[52] The greater activity in Atkinson's sector was probably attributable to a stronger enemy presence: the German air force concentrated what resistance it could muster against Pershing's main attack. Even Luke's victory had been in Atkinson's sector. Official confirmation was not received until 26 September, causing Hartney to carp, "I suppose it was because we had poached on Colonel [major at the time, Davenport] Johnson's preserves and this caused the delay."[53]

The 1st Pursuit Group received a new patrol sector on 14 September extending from Chatillon-sous-les-Côtes to Etang-de-Lachausee, known to American pilots as Three-Fingered Lake.[54] This new sector coincided with the front line of the U.S. 5th Corps, which was located along the base of the former salient. Atkinson's 1st Pursuit Wing continued to operate on the 1st Pursuit Group's right flank. The French Air Division, which remained under Mitchell's control until 20 September, also reverted to patrolling the 1st Army's new front lines. Consequently, patrols from the 1st Pursuit Group and the French Air Division operated in the same sector. After 17 September, Mitchell ordered the French Air Division's patrols to fly at 5,000 meters, to better coordinate the efforts of the French and American pursuit units.[55]

The weather cleared on 14 September, allowing the 1st Pursuit Group to launch 123 sorties—the largest number yet in a single day. At an early hour it became apparent that the Germans had significantly augmented their aerial forces. Hartney's patrols encountered formations of five to seven aircraft frequently throughout the day. The Germans continued to focus most of their attention, however, against Atkinson's 1st Pursuit Wing. Thus many of the 1st Pursuit Group's twenty-seven aerial combats that day occurred around Three-Fingered Lake.[56]

On one of these patrols Lt. Sumner Sewall of the 95th Aero Squadron survived almost certain death thanks to the ruggedness of his SPAD 13. This mission was one of the 95th Squadron's three assigned patrols of the group's eleven planned for that day. Group orders instructed these patrols to fly in two echelons of four planes each. The lower echelon was to operate at an altitude of 2,500 to 3,500 meters, while the upper echelon was to fly at 3,500 to 5,500 meters.[57]

Sewall's eight-plane patrol took off, as scheduled, at a quarter past eight in the morning. Once airborne, the patrol members lost sight of one another in the early morning mist. Sewall managed to link up with two other SPADs of his patrol. As they patrolled the lines, they spotted a formation of six enemy Fokkers at a higher altitude—about thirteen thousand feet. The SPADs retreated across the lines, climbed to sixteen thousand feet, and returned to attack. The maneuver seemed to work well. They found themselves a thousand feet above the enemy formation, just south of Three-Fingered Lake. As Sewall concentrated on the enemy formation below and prepared to dive on them, he made a final check behind him. He was shocked to find a Fokker on his tail, just opening fire.

Bursts of machine-gun fire began to strike Sewall's airplane, riddling it with holes, puncturing his windshield and water lines, cutting cables, and even slicing off a wheel. Sewall dived and then attempted a climbing turn but was unable to lose his attacker. Finally, he dived toward the ground, ten thousand feet below. The Fokker stayed with him, continuing to pour bursts of machine-gun fire into the SPAD. One of these bullets entered Sewall's fuel tank, causing it to explode and catch fire. Burning gasoline poured out of large hole in the fuel tank, but Sewall's SPAD did not catch fire, and he managed to level off just in time to land. His descent had been so rapid that he landed in time to see the wheel shot off earlier in the fight bounce across the field.[58] Sewall survived to serve as governor of Maine from 1941 to 1945.

At about the same time, Rickenbacker won his sixth victory while flying alone, also near Three-Fingered Lake. Hartney had relaxed Atkinson's prohibition against voluntary patrols, but only aces like Rickenbacker were allowed to cross the lines by themselves. In this engagement, Rickenbacker managed to maneuver undetected onto the rear of a formation of four scarlet-nosed Fokkers of the Richthofen Flying Circus. The appearance of Richthofen's JG 1 may have surprised Allied pilots. Previously, JG 1 had been operating near St. Quentin against the British. American Expeditionary Forces intelligence would not report the arrival of JG 1 in the American zone of operations until 28 September.[59] After downing his attacker, Rickenbacker narrowly escaped from the remainder of the enemy flight, who had turned against him.[60] The next day Rickenbacker won his seventh victory, again while flying alone. This time he met six Fokkers, which he paralleled for about twenty minutes. The German formation was stalking four SPADs of the 2d Pursuit Group, who were conducting a low-altitude bombing mission. Rickenbacker took advantage of their fixation on their quarry, overtook them from behind, and fired a long burst into one of them. His bullets hit the Fokker's fuel tank, and he watched it go down in flames.[61]

With this victory Rickenbacker achieved his long-sought title, "America's Ace of Aces." He was haunted, however, by the knowledge that the previous five pilots who had held this title had all been killed. They included Raoul Lufbery with sixteen official victories, Paul Baer of the 103d Aero Squadron with nine, Frank Baylies, who flew with the élite French Escadrille known as the Cigognes, with thirteen, and David Putnam of the 139th Aero Squadron with thirteen. Putnam had been shot down only a few days earlier, on the first day of the St. Mihiel offensive. Edgar Tobin of the 3d Pursuit Group had been the highest scorer among survivors, with six victories, but Rickenbacker now held the title with seven.[62] Rickenbacker reigned for only a single day, however, before Frank Luke surpassed him.

The number of encounters with enemy fighters dropped off sharply during the next two weeks. The 1st Pursuit Group's official history states that the Germans did not penetrate the group's aerial defense during this period. This may be the case, though it seems that high-flying Rumplers could have penetrated their sector if they had wanted to. Hamilton Coolidge wrote his mother a letter that described a flight commander's view of operations in the St. Mihiel sector:

> I am a "flight leader" now. A squadron contains three flights of six to eight planes and pilots each. These flights usually operate individually, following the daily operation schedule, and sometimes we even split up our flight, working in two groups of three, or one of four and one of two at different altitudes. Last week the only time we met Boches at all was when we outnumbered them so that they turned tail. You'd be surprised how hard it is to get Boches. Conditions are so very seldom right for a good combat at equal odds. I go out alone on voluntary patrols whenever I get a chance, but unless one is an "ace" he is not allowed to cross the lines alone.[63]

Foch's broad-front strategy made concentration by the German air force difficult, and Mitchell's initial aerial offensive kept German pursuit planes

arrayed against the 1st Army occupied with the defense against Allied bombing raids on important targets in the German rear. Bombers from the French
Air Division and Atkinson's own 1st Day Bombardment Group sustained
heavier casualties than the 1st Pursuit Group. A French bombing group, for
example, lost thirteen of its eighteen planes in an attack against Conflans.
Whenever possible, these raids were escorted by pursuit units, and the
bombers attracted enemy fighters, which were, in turn, attacked by the
American escorts. As an independent pursuit force, the 1st Pursuit Group did
not operate in conjunction with such bombing raids, which explains why out
of about fifty enemy airplanes brought down during the first four days of the
St. Mihiel operations, only four were credited to the 1st Pursuit Group. The
French Air Division remained under Mitchell's control until 20 September,
when it moved to support the French 4th Army for the upcoming Franco-
American offensive in the Champagne region and the Argonne Forest.[64]

After the St. Mihiel salient had been reduced, Mitchell placed American
pursuit aviation on the defensive. His orders restricted pilots to flying bar-
rages no deeper than three miles into enemy territory, unless they were protecting observation or bombing missions.[65] The intent of these orders, besides
protecting front-line American observation aircraft and balloons, was to prevent the German air force from observing the westward movement of
American units to new attack positions between the Meuse and the Argonne.
The German air force was also executing a defensive strategy on its side of the
lines. The negative aims of the opposing forces thus contributed to a general
decrease in aerial engagements. Because of the difficulty in bringing enemy
aircraft to combat, attacks against German observation balloons provided an
aggressive pilot with the best opportunity for scoring a kill. This was the strategy adopted by Frank Luke.

The rise of Frank Luke coincided with Mitchell's campaign to neutralize
enemy balloons. Although Mitchell's air armada had prevented enemy
airplanes from interfering with ground operations, American troops had
continually been brought under accurate enemy artillery fire because of the
presence of German observation balloons. Under pressure to neutralize the
balloon threat, Mitchell summoned Hartney to his headquarters and ordered
him to come up with a more effective method of attack. He reminded
Hartney that balloons were damp when they ascended in the morning and
would therefore not easily burn. He continued to elaborate, pointing out the

difficulty of achieving surprise by attacking from the rear because of the need to fly over enemy territory, a practice that alerted enemy fighters and balloon crews. All the while, Hartney listened intently, "cocking his head from one side to the other, saying, 'Precisely, precisely.'" Hartney hurried back to Rembercourt to find a solution.[66]

German observation balloons usually carried one observer equipped with binoculars of 6- and 18-power magnification, a long-range camera, and a parachute. From a typical altitude of three thousand feet they could see an expanse of about twenty miles. The balloon was tethered to the ground with a steel cable, which, by this time in the war, could be rapidly drawn down with a motorized winch.[67] The lowest-level organization was the balloon section, consisting of two balloons. One balloon section was allocated to each division. One balloon would be inflated while the other would be held in reserve. The unit's personnel consisted of three officers (observers) and about twenty men.[68]

In comparison with the airplane, the observation balloon provided a far superior platform for the adjustment of artillery. Balloon observers spoke directly to the artillery batteries by telephone, as opposed to the unreliable wireless telegraphy used by observers in airplanes. Moreover, the observer had precise knowledge of his own location, which made the adjustment of artillery a straightforward solution based on precise calculations and geometric principles. On the other hand, balloons could be seen for miles and were hardly capable of self-defense, though some observers mounted machine guns in their baskets. Because the balloons were so valuable as the eyes of the army, both sides went to great lengths to protect them. Therefore, any attack against a balloon was sure to involve flying through a gauntlet of machine-gun fire and exploding antiaircraft artillery shells set to explode at exactly the right altitude.

Recalling the advice of the American balloonist with whom he had spent the night, Lt. Frank Luke suggested attacking the balloons at dusk—just before it became too dark to see. Luke was different, in background and temperament, from the Ivy League fraternity types who comprised much of the 1st Pursuit Group's corps of pilots. Born and raised in Arizona, he was the classic self-reliant western individualist. He graduated from high school, where he played quarterback for the Phoenix Coyotes, at the age of twenty in 1917. He entered the army in September of the same year and joined the 27th Squadron in late July 1918. On one of his first patrols he left the formation and

German military observation balloon

This balloon was a copy of a French-designed Caquot-type observation balloon.

NATIONAL AIR AND SPACE MUSEUM, CD-ROM 2A-03849

claimed to have shot down an enemy aircraft. His victory was not confirmed, however, and his fellow pilots did not believe him, which made him bitter. Hartney, on the other hand, took him at his word. Sometime after downing his first balloon on 12 September, Luke decided to specialize in attacks on balloons. Enemy airplanes were scarce, but there were plenty of balloons, and Hartney had given orders to destroy them.[69]

Hartney equipped Luke and his frequent wingman, Joseph Wehner, with special 11-mm (.45-caliber) Vickers machine guns, also called balloon guns. The 1st Pursuit Group received a limited number of these large-caliber weapons at the beginning of September—enough that each squadron had a few. The Vickers fired a large incendiary bullet designed to ignite the hydrogen gas that filled the balloons. The bullet was filled through a hole with phosphorous. The hole was then sealed with an alloy that had a low melting point. The initial propellant explosion, and the passage of the bullet through the bore of the machine-gun barrel, melted the alloy seal, allowing the phosphorous to ignite.

Incendiary ammunition was also available for the smaller Vickers and

Marlin machine guns, standard fighter armament, but the probability of igniting a balloon's hydrogen gas was greater with the balloon gun because of the larger amount of phosphorous and the slower speed of the bullet. According to Hartney, the French had little or no confidence in this weapon. This was probably because the large, flat-nosed bullets were not very accurate and had a short range. Luke's success with this weapon made it the required armament for designated balloon strafers in the 1st Pursuit Group.[70]

Luke's score surpassed Rickenbacker's on 16 September. The next morning, Rickenbacker carefully noted in his diary that Luke had shot down two balloons for a total of eight victories in four days. Luke had left the field, he noted, about seven in the evening and shot down his first balloon at 7:20 and the second five minutes later. "Both were seen to fall in flames from our field," Rickenbacker continued. "He returned after dark and landed with flairs [*sic*] and was shot at all the way home by the French."[71]

Luke's wingman, Joseph Wehner, was also a loner. Because of his German ancestry he had been suspected of being a spy. The two outsiders shared a common sense of indignation and became fast comrades. Within a week, Luke had shot down ten balloons and three airplanes. Wehner shot down five enemy balloons before being shot down himself on 18 September. On that day, Luke and Wehner had set off just before dark to attack two balloons near Labeauville. Luke attacked and destroyed both balloons while Wehner flew cover above him and to the side. During the second attack, Wehner intercepted a group of Fokkers before being shot down and killed. Luke was climbing to join the fight when two Fokkers attacked him from the rear. Turning on them, Luke daringly headed straight for the leader. He reported, "We came head-on until within a few yards of each other, when my opponent turned to one side in a nose dive and I saw him crash on the ground. I then turned on the second, shot a short burst, and he turned and went into a dive."[72]

On the way home Luke saw four French SPADs, which had surrounded a Halberstadt observation plane and were firing at it at long range, trying to force it down in friendly territory. It was later learned that they were trying to force it to land, so they could capture it. Because a bullet had drained his main fuel tank, Luke had been hand-pumping fuel from his reserve tank. He banked sharply and abandoned his hand pump, causing his motor to die. As he dived between two of the French SPADs, he fired the last of his ammunition at the Halberstadt, sending it flaming to the ground. He then guided his shattered plane to a landing on an abandoned airfield at the rear of the French

Lt. Joseph Wehner, left, and Maj. Harold E. Hartney,
right
*Wehner paired with fellow loner Frank Luke, specializing
in attacks on enemy observation balloons.*
NATIONAL AIR AND SPACE MUSEUM,
CD-ROM 2B-11718

lines near Verdun. Thus Luke received official credit for five victories in the space of a few minutes—an astonishing feat.

Rickenbacker accompanied Hartney to fetch Luke the next day. Both leaders took note of the field, which was ideally located to serve the 1st Pursuit Group as an advance base during the next campaign. That night, the 94th Squadron hosted a group banquet at its mess in honor of Luke's record-setting accomplishment. Majors Hartney and Peterson (Peterson and Marr were both promoted that day), and Lieutenants Luke, Rickenbacker, and White gave speeches. Entertainment was provided by a group of theater favorites from the United States who were touring the AEF. In his diary Rickenbacker noted of Luke, "He certainly is a great boy." Eastman's diary comment was more revealing, "As the doctors say to the press, he is not expected to live."[73]

Luke had been lucky so far, but how long would his luck hold out? Veterans like Eastman doubted that the reckless young American ace would survive the war. To the veterans, Luke's arrogant sense of indestructibility was a fatal disease of the psyche that, if not brought under control, would ultimately result in his death.

The 1st Pursuit Group continued its patrols of the St. Mihiel sector until 23 September.[74] Friendly casualties at St. Mihiel were light. The 1st Pursuit Group lost five men while achieving twenty-two confirmed victories. Luke and Wehner accounted for most of them—fifteen between them. The audacity of these two pilots blossomed in the squadron that most reflected the British tradition of aggressiveness. Because of their achievements, the 27th Squadron again led the group in victories at St. Mihiel, as it had at Château-Thierry. Yet unlike its performance at Château-Thierry under Hartney, the 27th Squadron no longer led in group casualties. Its single loss at St. Mihiel was Luke's wingman, Joseph Wehner.

Meissner's 147th Squadron followed at a distant second with four victories, two of which were won by Wilbur White, one of Meissner's flight commanders. Meissner lost one man, who had joined the squadron toward the end of July; Hartney must have noticed the strain on his youngest commander, as he sent Meissner to Paris for a long weekend.[75] The 94th Squadron, no longer on the bottom, followed, with Rickenbacker's two victories and no friendly losses.

The 95th Aero Squadron scored one victory but lost three men. As noted earlier, Norman S. Archibald was taken prisoner after being shot down by antiaircraft fire just before the offensive began. Waldo Heinrichs, who left an excellent diary of his experiences in France, was shot down and taken prisoner on 17 September. Heinrichs had been part of an eight-plane patrol ordered to destroy an enemy balloon. The patrol flew with three SPADs in the lower echelon at an altitude of about eight thousand feet, while the upper echelon followed about sixteen hundred feet higher. John Mitchell was the flight leader of the lower formation that included Heinrichs. As the patrol approached Three-Fingered Lake, Mitchell and Heinrichs spotted a formation of nine Fokkers, flying in a step formation. Mitchell decided to attack the last enemy airplane, which was trailing below and far behind the rest, but it was only bait.

Heinrichs followed Mitchell in the attack. Heinrichs later wrote, "No one

Lt. Frank Luke, the "Balloon Buster," leaning against his SPAD 13
Luke's arrogance made him unpopular with most of the other pilots.
NATIONAL AIR AND SPACE MUSEUM, CD-ROM 2B-17760

followed me, and the upper echelon at 3000 meters left us entirely." Mitchell's and Heinrichs's machine guns jammed after a few bursts. It was later learned that the links had been placed in the belt upside down. Meanwhile, at least six of the Fokkers reversed direction to intercept the Americans, and Heinrichs suddenly found himself under attack from enemy aircraft diving at him from a higher altitude. He attempted to evade with a vertical bank but fell into a spin, which brought him lower than his attackers. He headed for friendly lines but was cut off. He later described what happened next:

> The other Fokkers were on me by now and one of them joined the attack on me. . . . I escaped one terrible burst of my first opponent and ran directly through the spider web of the tracers & explosives of the second. I shall never forget the rat-tat-tat of those two guns never jamming and firing in very rapid synchronization. Felt a bullet tear thru my mouth and it felt as tho my whole lower jaw were gone and my mouth became a gaping cavern. Remember spitting out teeth and blood and then turned again for our lines. Again ran into

their fire and felt a terrible blow on my left arm. Tried to yank throttle wide open but got no more speed out of it—seemed it wouldn't work. Looked down to see my arm hanging useless by my side—broke. Spat again as the blood was choking me and blood blew back in my face blinding me and covering my face and goggles. Felt another bullet get me in the left thigh between hip and knee underneath. Let go my stick for I saw the game was up, and threw up my goggles up on my forehead and saw [a] bullet-hole thru my windshield, perhaps, the same one that went through my mouth.[76]

Heinrichs's SPAD dived toward the woods below. He managed to grab the stick, pulled back to level off, and flew under a telegraph wire. His right wing hit the telephone pole and broke off. Heinrichs crashed into the field beyond and was taken prisoner. One of the pilots in the upper echelon of this patrol reported that he had not pressed the attack because "the wind was quite sharp from the west," and the fight was taking place deep behind the lines.[77] William Taylor, one of the old-timers of the squadron who had recently rejoined it after recovering from injuries incurred on an abortive takeoff in June, took off the next day on a voluntary patrol to avenge Heinrichs's loss. Taylor was never seen again; his plane was reported to have gone down in flames.[78]

Clearly, there were problems in the 95th Aero Squadron. Its low score, the failure to aid Heinrichs, and Taylor's reckless revenge mission were but symptoms of a deeper malaise.

10

Meuse-Argonne

"A Gimper is a bird who would stick by you through anything," explained Rickenbacker. The ace continued. "If you were up in the air and ran into a dozen enemies and were getting the worst of it, perhaps, and the fellow with you stuck with you and gave it to them until they fled, you'd know he was a Gimper." Gimpers did not offer any one of a dozen excuses, he added, such as motor trouble or jammed guns, to return home during a dangerous patrol. "A Gimper is a scout who does everything just a little better than he has to."[1]

The 94th Aero Squadron was widely known as the Hat-in-the-Ring Squadron. But among ourselves," Rickenbacker noted, "it's [the] Gimpers. . . . All Gimpers have to live up to the idea of the squadron emblem. Every man has a picture of a hat in a ring on his machine. That means that he is ready to fight at any time, whether he wants to or not." Every man had "to prove himself a Gimper by actions. When a new chap arrives he's an Egg. All good Eggs soon become Vultures, and then they're promoted to the Gopher class. Then is when they have to prove themselves Gimpers." According to Rickenbacker, a pilot who did not become a Gimper was not allowed to stay in the squadron.[2]

Newspapers throughout the United States followed the wartime career of Eddie Rickenbacker. Already a famous race-car driver when he entered the war, his celebrity advanced another magnitude when he became an ace. An August 1918 article stated, "In his Escadrille they call him the 'Head Gimper' because he is naturally a leader and the life of that unit." The American public learned about the Gimpers during the summer of 1918 in a series of syndicated newspaper interviews with Rickenbacker. Many of these occurred while Rickenbacker was in the hospital during July and August. Throughout the summer he was plagued by an ear infection, probably caused by the rapid changes in altitude and temperature during operations in the Toul sector. Eventually he required double mastoid surgery.

As Walter Boyne observes in *Aces in Command,* Rickenbacker's hospital stay played an important role in his transformation, dividing his combat tour into three parts—a period of learning, a period of introspection, and a period of excelling. Rickenbacker used the hospital stay to analyze each of his fights, reexamine tactics, and modify his personal habits. He resolved not to drink alcohol for at least twenty-four hours before flying.[3]

Since Huffer's departure the 94th Squadron had been performing poorly. The loss of Hall, Campbell, and Winslow and the transfer of Peterson and Meissner affected the squadron, but more than anything else the unit's poor performance was the result of the ineffectiveness of Huffer's replacement. According to Reed Chambers, who filled in as second in command after Meissner left, Capt. Kenneth Marr was never around and commanded the squadron in name only. "He was disliked. He never made a flight over the lines with us, and he didn't even work at being commanding officer," recalled Chambers. The work of actually running the squadron often fell on the shoulders of whoever happened to be second in command, a situation certain to cause confusion and misunderstanding in the best of times but a severe loss of confidence in the strain of combat.[4]

With a successful campaign behind him, Hartney was in a position to begin ridding his unit of weak commanders, and Marr was first in his sights. The 94th Squadron was "badly slipping," as Hartney put it, and Marr obviously failed to lead by example. He was quietly eased out because of injuries and sent back to the United States without farewell. "When it became necessary to appoint a new commander for the 94th," Hartney remembered, "there were several excellent men in line, but it seemed the best results would be obtained by jumping Rickenbacker over their heads and giving him the job." Flight commanders Hamilton Coolidge and Reed Chambers were both senior to Rickenbacker and highly respected. Mitchell was surprised and dubious about the plan to put Rickenbacker in command, wrote Hartney, "but he backed me up and the appointment was made."[5] On the night of 24 September Rickenbacker was informed that he would take charge of the Gimper Squadron the next day.

Rickenbacker immediately went to group operations to get the latest tally of kills awarded to each squadron. He learned that the 27th Squadron led his unit by six victories. He called a meeting of the squadron's officers. For the next thirty minutes he lectured them, expressing his displeasure at their performance and the changes he expected to see. He demanded that they do their jobs and shoot down Germans. He assured them that he would not ask any of them to undertake a mission that he himself would not fly. He was determined to see his unit regain its lost supremacy. The rest of the squadron shared Eastman's opinion, expressed in his diary: "It is no small good fortune that Rick has been given command over the 94th."[6]

He then conducted a similar session with his mechanics, for whom he had a special affinity, having been a mechanic himself. He told them how much the squadron depended on their efforts. He probably discussed some of the mechanical problems they were having with the Hispano-Suiza. He offered more than platitudes and exhortations. During his convalescence in Paris, he had become acquainted with the chief engineer of Hispano-Suiza. Using this connection, and that with his roommate during basic flight training at Tours, Cedric E. Fauntleroy, he established an unofficial repair-parts supply system for his squadron. One of Fauntleroy's officers remembered that "Rickenbacker's outfit would make up a list of whatever supplies they needed and would give it to Faunt who, in turn, would procure and ship it." Fauntleroy's room was so packed with spare parts that "there was literally an aisle-way from the door to the bed, with no other available empty space. Rick's outfit would come in with sedans, trucks, or whatever wheeled vehicles they could find and load up the spare parts at night."[7]

The next day Rickenbacker shot down two enemy planes, a feat for which he later received the Medal of Honor. Morale improved tremendously in the 94th Squadron. Hartney observed that "Rick, with his experience and natural executive ability, straightened things out immediately."[8]

In the Meuse-Argonne campaign the U.S. 1st Army acted as the right wing of a general Allied offensive to penetrate the Hindenburg line and eject the German army from northern France. The Hindenburg line was actually a

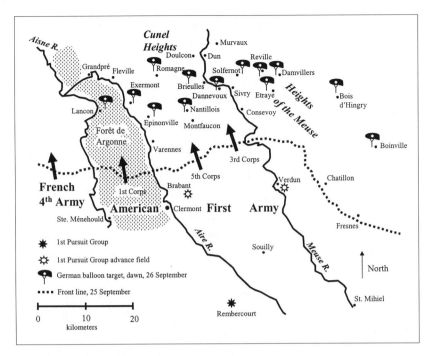

Meuse-Argonne

The 1st Pursuit Group established two advance fields with an alert flight at each to provide frontline units immediate response against German observation balloons and airplanes attacking American troops.

Created by the author, based on data from "Plan of Attack of First Army, Meuse-Argonne Operation, 26 September 1918," Map 115 in *The United States Army in the World War, 1917–1919*, vol. 9, *Military Operations of the American Expeditionary Forces* (Washington, D.C.: Center of Military History, U.S. Army, 1990), 128; German balloon locations from 1st Pursuit Group, Operations Order 148, 25 September 1918, Gorrell's *History of the American Expeditionary Forces Air Service* (Microfilm Publication M990), 1917–19, series C, vol. 9, RG120, National Archives at College Park.

series of defensive lines that had been prepared in depth since the stalemate of 1914. The American attack zone lay between the Argonne Forest and the Meuse River. The 1st Army had to attack about nine miles through a fortified zone, prepared in ideal defensive terrain, to reach the main defenses of the Hindenburg line. A railroad line that was vital to the German position, about thirty miles from the jumping-off point, was the ultimate objective. The American attack was coordinated with the French 4th Army on its immediate left. Pershing expected that, because his sector was opposite the most sensitive part of the German front being attacked, his unit would meet stiff resistance.[9]

Mitchell initially planned to place Hartney's pursuit group under Atkinson's 1st Pursuit Wing, but he decided to retain it as a separate unit after French army officials urged him to develop a plan to combat low-flying German battle planes that strafed friendly troops. Such German air units had given the French considerable difficulty earlier in September. By now the 1st Pursuit Group was Mitchell's old guard and Hartney his favorite fighter commander. Mitchell gave Hartney responsibility for low-altitude operations across the entire 1st Army front; his mission: the destruction of German observation balloons and low-flying airplanes. Mitchell also directed Hartney to establish advanced airfields close to the front lines, where detachments of fighters would be ready for immediate takeoff. Close liaison was to be maintained with ground observation posts, the antiaircraft artillery, the corps observation units, and Atkinson's 1st Pursuit Wing, which was responsible for maintaining a heavy barrage at medium and high altitudes to a depth of six miles into enemy territory and keeping one pursuit group in reserve armed with bombs for ground attack.[10]

Rembercourt's location, on the left side of the old St. Mihiel salient, placed it generally in the center of the sector for the offensive, with the front lines about twenty-five miles distant. The 1st Pursuit Group remained at Rembercourt for the remainder of the war. By 23 September Hartney's squadrons were maintaining a constant presence in the air in three different patrol areas, to prevent enemy observation aircraft from crossing the line while American troops moved into their attack positions: the old St. Mihiel sector, the new sector between the Meuse River and the Argonne Forest (Charny to Neuvilly), and a single-airplane, high-altitude patrol well behind lines, from Souilly to Clermont-en-Argonne. Rickenbacker's double victory on 25 September was against an escorted reconnaissance mission attempting to penetrate the new sector. First Army headquarters, with Mitchell's Air Service command post, was moved to Souilly, about nine miles north of Rembercourt.[11]

The practice of patrolling multiple areas ceased when Hartney issued new orders on 23 September announcing that the group's sector would extend from Chatillon-sous-les-Côtes to the Aisne River. He directed his pilots to study the new sector and to learn the exact location of the advanced landing fields. Lt. Jerry Vasconcells, the commander of B Flight of the 27th Squadron, prepared to move his flight to the advance field that had been selected near Verdun, where he would operate "as a self-sustaining unit" and with his "own initiative on alert work." Hartney further directed him to establish "perfect liaison with all neighboring units." Two aircraft were to be on alert at all times during the day, "with motors warmed up according to the exigencies of the operations." Hartney gave similar orders to Lt. Alexander McLanahan, who commanded A Flight of the 95th Squadron. Orders for a third advanced field, established by Lt. Arthur Jones of the 147th Aero Squadron at Brebant-en-Argonne, were issued later.[12]

On 25 September, the day before the offensive, Hartney ordered reconnaissance patrols to scout the enemy's balloons in the 1st Army sector. He divided the sector into three parts and assigned all squadrons, except the 95th Squadron, responsibility for determining "the exact locations and peculiarities of enemy balloons on their portion of the front." As a starting point, the operations section provided each squadron with reported locations of enemy balloons. Pilots were cautioned to remain in their sectors and not to attack the enemy balloons. Upon completion of their reconnaissance, they were to provide detailed reports to the operations section, which would be used to develop the group's attack plan for the next day.[13]

Hartney was so busy the night before the offensive that he had no time to sleep. All of the pilots assembled on the airfield at half past seven that evening for a demonstration of the newly installed airfield lighting system. Hartney briefed them on their mission, though the operations section did not publish the written operations order until the early morning hours of 26 September. It read, "Tomorrow morning at 5 h 45 this group will attack all the balloons on the sector [from] Chatillon-sous-les-Cotes to the Aisne, followed by low flying patrols for the purpose of destroying enemy low flying machines and protecting Infantry liaison machines." Hartney's order called for a simultaneous attack on thirteen enemy balloons at precisely 5:45 A.M. He divided the front among his four squadrons. Each unit had specific balloons to attack and sectors to patrol afterward.

Starting in the west and moving across the 1st Army front, the 95th Squadron would attack three balloons on the army's left front at Lancon, Exermont, and Epinonville. The 94th Squadron would attack two balloons opposite the left center at Romagne and Nantillois. The 147th Squadron would attack four balloons opposite right center at Dannevoux, Bois de Brieulles, Reville, and Damvillers; and the 27th Squadron would attack four balloons in the east at Solfernot Ferme, Etraye, Bois d'Hingry, and Boinville.

That the 27th and 147th Aero Squadrons were assigned more balloons than the 94th Squadron suggests that Hartney had greater confidence in their abilities. All of the balloons assigned to the 27th Squadron, and two assigned to the 147th Squadron, were located on the high ground east of the Meuse River known to the airmen as the Heights of the Meuse. Although American troops would not be attacking through the Heights of the Meuse, it was important that these balloons be neutralized, because German batteries in this area could direct enfilading fire along the American line.

The squadron attack groups were to consist of up to six SPADs, depending on the number of balloons assigned. The enemy balloons were between four and nine miles behind enemy lines, with a lateral distance between them of about two and a half or three miles. The object in attacking at dawn was to catch the balloons in their nests and burn them on or near the ground. If the 1st Pursuit Group was successful, enemy observation and artillery fire against Pershing's doughboys would be significantly disrupted.[14]

The balloon strafers were to be seated in their planes at five in the morning with motors warmed up and ready to take off. Squadron commanders would time takeoffs to insure a simultaneous attack of all the balloons across the front at 5:45 A.M. Subsequently, all squadrons would patrol their assigned sectors between six and eight o'clock to a depth of one kilometer (.62 mile) at an altitude of 800 meters (2,624 feet). An alert force consisting of half of a squadron would be ready for immediate takeoff throughout the day. This duty would be rotated between the 95th, 94th, and 147th Aero Squadrons. Finally, the order directed the squadrons to attack any other balloons they might encounter in their designated sector. It also suggested that balloons should be attacked head on, because the nose of the balloon contained more hydrogen gas and thus a front-end hit would produce the most damage.[15]

That night the members of the 1st Pursuit Group heard the heaviest artillery barrage they could remember, and many did not sleep because of the noise and anticipation. The 95th Squadron assigned six of its most experienced pilots for balloon attack. The SPADs of this attack group were to begin taking off at 5:10 A.M., about thirty-five minutes before daylight, at thirty-second intervals. This first wave would be followed by two more at 5:44 and 6:30. About half the pilots of the squadron would land at the 95th Squadron's advance field; the others would return to Rembercourt and remain there on alert. At the advance field, two airplanes were to be kept on alert at all times, "with pilots in the seats ready to take [to] the air for quick shock attack." Other squadrons issued similar orders for the attack of their designated balloons and subsequent operations.[16]

Each squadron flew its best pilots in the first wave. The 95th Squadron's balloons opposite the 1st Army left flank were the most distant, so the Kicking Mules were among the first to take off. Six SPADs took off at 5:10 the next morning with the aid of searchlights and electric lights strung down the center of the field. This was the first time most of them had ever flown in the dark. Harold Buckley, one of the members of this patrol, recounted the moments after takeoff: "Overhead the stars shone coldly. Beneath us the dusty roads were dimly visible, crisscrossing the fearsome blackness with strips of gray. The canals and rivers were ribbons of silver. Here and there the fiery exhaust of some other ship glowed for a minute, then faded away." As they approached the front lines the artillery barrage appeared as "a broad belt of living fire." To Buckley it was "a terrifying inferno which thrilled us with its magnitude and beauty, but sickened us with its ghastly portent."[17]

The pilots of this flight flew north to their rendezvous point over the town of Clermont. The rendezvous accomplished, the patrol crossed the lines just as dawn was beginning to break. A heavy layer of low-lying fog concealed the balloon nests, making an attack on them impossible. Alexander McLanahan, the patrol leader, spotted an enemy two-seater west of Montfaucon and chased him farther back into enemy territory. McLanahan was unable to close on it because he was himself attacked from above by a Fokker. In the combat that followed, McLanahan shot it down.[18]

The plan was to land at the advanced field. Although McLanahan and Buckley had selected the field earlier, they were unable to locate it, though the rest of the pilots who had been designated to land there found it. Unfortunately, all but one of the airplanes were damaged while landing on the rough field. Hartney himself flew up at mid-morning to see how his advanced field project was working out. He glided in for a landing, bounced about thirty feet in the air after hitting an obstruction, nosed in, and snapped off his propeller. He commandeered the only operational SPAD and flew back it back to Rembercourt, determined to vent his rage at McLanahan and Buckley for their poor choice of fields.

Hartney immediately issued orders terminating the operations at the 95th Squadron's advance field, recalling its personnel and equipment, but not in sufficient time to prevent yet another crash-landing by a hapless pilot who had recently taken off from Rembercourt. Buckley later confessed in his memoir that their commander, Capt. David McK. Peterson, advised him and McLanahan to disappear to avoid Hartney's wrath. The guilty parties "spent the better part of the day hiding in a little café, patting each other on the back and bolstering up their lost dignity with a bottle or two of wine."[19]

The second and third waves from the 95th Squadron consisted of a two-plane flight that took off at 5:50 A.M. and a three-plane flight that took off at 6:30 A.M. They found neither balloons nor enemy planes in their six-mile-wide squadron zone.[20]

Rickenbacker led the Gimpers' attack, on the 95th Squadron's right, with better results. Coolidge, flying one of six planes in the first wave, wrote home about it a few days later.

> At 5:05 we were sitting in our SPADs, all groomed up for the occasion, with our motors warming up lazily. It was pitch dark save for the row of searchlights, which illuminated the takeoff. One by one we taxied down the path of light and took off into the blackness beyond.

Coolidge narrowly missed a collision with another aircraft, probably from the 95th Aero Squadron, just as he left the ground. From his cockpit in the SPAD, Coolidge saw a heavy mist below him that was especially dense in the valleys. Unused to night flying and having difficulty seeing, he had second thoughts about continuing with the mission but pushed these out of his mind and continued.[21]

As he approached the front lines, Coolidge was also astonished at the spectacle before him: "As far as I could see to the west and southeast thousands of flashes glared out of the mist below in alternate glows and twinkles. It seemed almost a colossal band of flame about a kilometer wide." He circled to get his bearings and was able to make out the Meuse River because the fog above it was whiter than the rest. Because of the barrage, the location of front lines was unmistakable. With this information digested, he took a deep breath and plunged in. As he passed above friendly artillery, he could hear the boom of the guns above his airplane's engine, and his SPAD rocked and shivered from their concussions. At times he thought he saw shells fly by his airplane, appearing as a sudden streak, or a thread of pink, against the darkness. He marveled that none hit him.

Coolidge passed over the dark swath of no-man's-land and into German airspace. As he penetrated beyond the impacting artillery the sky became peaceful. Several green flaming balls would ascend in one place while red or blue signal rockets glowed at another. As the dawn broke he saw a patch of woods where he thought his balloon was supposed to be. He circled and came down low for a look but saw nothing in the shape of a balloon. Suddenly, lines of green tracers whizzed up in front of him, then another line, and still more. Most of the machine-gun fire seemed to issue from one spot in the woods. Coolidge circled and pointed the nose of his SPAD at the spot. A stream of incendiaries from his balloon gun silenced the enemy machine fire.

Coolidge could not find any of the squadron's designated balloons. He could just begin to distinguish the towns, roads, and forest in the dawning light. He again dropped to a low altitude and spotted a supply convoy moving along the road. He was low enough that he could positively identify them as German by their helmets. He circled, gained a little height, and returned to make the first of four strafing attacks on the enemy column. When he departed he saw "horses rearing on fallen men; wagons crosswise in the road; [and] men again dashing for the gutter."

After breaking off his strafing attack, it was light enough for Coolidge to see many of the Allied airplanes and bursts of enemy antiaircraft artillery in the air. As he reentered friendly lines, he saw doughboys packed in solid ranks and others dotting the trenches. He circled close and waved but had no cigarettes or newspapers to throw to them, as was becoming customary. As Coolidge continued toward Rembercourt, Allied balloons loomed up like great gawky sausages, with the first gleams of the sun reflected on their wet sides. They were so close together that he dared not pass beneath them for fear of hitting an unseen cable. He stated, "It did my heart good to realize that in each of those uncouth craft sat one or two observers regulating our barrage fire and watching movement of the troops." All the way back to Rembercourt, formations of Allied planes kept passing Coolidge on the way out. It was plain to him that the

Allies had supremacy in the air. He was elated—as if he were back at Harvard playing football and beating the Crimson's archrival, Yale.

Rickenbacker was the last member of his patrol to leave Rembercourt, taking off at 5:20 A.M. He too witnessed the "terrific barrage of artillery fire" that illuminated the horizon "from Lunéville on the east to Reims on the west." The sight reminded him of a giant switchboard emitting thousands of electric flashes as invisible hands manipulated the plugs.[22] His route took him north along the Meuse River, then left and over the lines. Enemy tracer bullets from the ground pierced the sky as he approached his objective. A gigantic fireball in the mist signaled him that one of the balloons had been destroyed. Even before the glare of the first explosion had died, he saw a second balloon go up in flames. Reed Chambers and Harvey Cook received credit for the two hits. Both of his squadron's assigned balloons having been destroyed, Rickenbacker flew toward Damvillers, where a cluster of four balloons had been assigned to the 27th and 147th Aero Squadrons.

As Rickenbacker approached, another gush of flame announced the destruction of his intended target. Suddenly, a Fokker surprised him, but in the engagement that followed he managed to shoot it down. Unfortunately, the enemy's bullets had damaged his propeller. He guided his stricken SPAD to an emergency landing at the Verdun advance field operated by the 27th Squadron. Jerry Vasconcells, who had destroyed a balloon near Damvillers, greeted him. Vasconcells's mechanics put a new propeller on the SPAD, and by half past eight Rickenbacker was back at Rembercourt, where the initial inflated reports indicated that the group's first wave had brought down ten balloons.[23]

On the Gimpers' right, the 147th Squadron's seven-plane patrol took off and followed the Bar-le-Duc–Verdun road, a broad white pathway in darkness that was easy to follow. They reached the Meuse River at Verdun and followed it northward. As they approached the lines they saw the American balloons already up and silhouetted against the breaking dawn. The balloon strafers circled as they waited for the precise moment to attack. Meissner later wrote, "Seconds seemed hours as we waited for the 'zero hour' of our show to approach. At five forty-two we started over, each directly opposite his balloon, came down low over the supposed location and searched in the dusk for the big gas bag."[24]

They found and attacked two of their four balloons but did not destroy them. Meissner attacked the balloon in the Bois de Brieulles and managed to fire four bursts of incendiaries into it at close range. Although he observed smoke on the surface of the balloon, there was no explosion. Another member of the squadron attacked a balloon at Reville at the same time, but it too refused to burst into flames. A six-plane patrol from the squadron followed again to scour the sector at six o'clock. They found and attacked two balloons near Damvillers, also failing to destroy them but causing them to be winched down. A third patrol of five SPADs, led by Kenneth Porter, departed at 6:40 A.M. to sweep the sector again. Porter and another member of this patrol attacked a balloon at Bois de Septsarges, slightly north of Montfaucon. Before his balloon gun jammed Porter saw his tracers striking, but again to no avail. The balloon's crew hastily winched it down. Though these attacks failed to destroy the balloons, they were nonetheless successful: A balloon that had been taken down was at least temporarily unable to perform its mission. As Meissner observed, "When daylight came we saw the effectiveness of our work, not an enemy sausage was in the air." Meanwhile, Allied balloons were packed so close together they looked to Meissner like a picket fence.[25]

Lt. Russel Pruden, the Fighting Eagles' supply officer, was temporarily in charge of the squadron's advanced field near Verdun until Vasconcells arrived. The night before the attack Pruden lay on his cot smoking cigarettes, unable to sleep because of the tremendously loud artillery preparation, punctuated by the concussions from two thirteen-inch naval guns mounted on railroad cars adjacent to their landing field. He had first set his eyes on the squadron's outpost a few days earlier, when he and Vasconcells had conducted a reconnaissance of several possible sites. They chose an abandoned French airfield located only a few hundred yards from the edge of Verdun—the same field where Luke had made his forced landing.

A number of old stone stables, a large barracks, and two big hangars, all in various states of ruin, dotted the field. The artillerymen who serviced the heavy artillery already occupied the best buildings. They cheerfully warned the airmen that the fire of their big guns would probably draw immediate return fire from the Germans and that they expected to be bombed every night. Undaunted—because there was no better alternative—the pursuit officers returned to Rembercourt to make final arrangements. Pruden led a detachment of mechanics with their parts and equipment back to Verdun the following day and prepared for operations, which he knew would begin early the next day.[26]

At about six o'clock the next morning, Pruden heard a startling noise and looked out to see that a SPAD had crash-landed. The other members of the patrol, led by Jerry Vasconcells, soon landed. Pruden learned that Vasconcells had brought down an enemy balloon. Another member of Vasconcells six-plane patrol had attacked two of the squadron's other balloons, but these had been pulled down without bursting into flames. The squadron's second patrol to sweep the sector took off at a quarter to six and shot down another balloon. The squadron's third patrol took off five minutes later and had nothing to report. Two alert flights were launched from the advanced field during the day. The 27th Squadron commander, Lt. Alfred Grant, landed late in the afternoon and stayed for supper. "We take great delight in watching the faces of our visitors when the big guns go off," Pruden noted in his diary. "Alfred would have jumped eight feet, but the wall of the building was in his way."[27]

Hartney ordered a group-level attack against a particularly troublesome balloon at Reville during the afternoon. His plan for the attack established a pattern that would be repeated throughout the Meuse-Argonne campaign: a group-level operation in the afternoon, based on reports received during the morning, that concentrated the efforts of several of the group's squadrons on a single objective. In this balloon attack, the 95th Squadron provided two balloon strafers, the delinquent McLanahan and Buckley, equipped with balloon guns and a five-plane escort. Hartney tasked the 27th and 94th Squadrons to provide five-plane protection patrols. Each of the flights from the different squadrons was to take a different route, to deceive the enemy, with all arriving over the balloons just as the strafers were making their first pass. McLanahan and Buckley partially redeemed themselves for their earlier airfield fiasco by shooting down this balloon.[28]

Hartney ordered another coordinated attack against balloons at Dun-sur-Meuse and Milly-devant-Dun at six that evening. Wilbur White of the 147th Aero Squadron and Ivan Roberts of the 27th Aero Squadron were the designated balloon strafers. The 94th and 147th Aero Squadrons were each tasked to provide a six-plane protection patrol. Again, separate routes would be used so that the patrol planes would converge above the balloons just as the strafers made their first pass.[29]

By this time Frank Luke, who had been on leave in Paris as a reward for his victories, was back at Rembercourt. Instead of going on the six o'clock balloon mission, Roberts accompanied Luke on an attack against balloons near Consenvoye and Sivry. During the attack they ran into a flight of five Fokkers; Roberts was shot down and killed. Luke claimed one of the Fokkers, but his victory was never confirmed. Roberts was the second of Luke's wingmen to die and one of the group's two losses that day.[30]

Consequently, the coordinated group attack was launched without Roberts. The escort encountered five Fokkers as they approached the balloons. White dived on one and fired seventy-five incendiary rounds into it before his balloon gun jammed. He saw smoke coming from the balloon, but it did not burst into flames, and the Germans hauled it to the ground.

On the first day of the offensive the 1st Pursuit Group launched 143 sorties—its record, in one day, for the entire war. The group received official credit for downing five balloons and five enemy aircraft—its record for a single day in the war—and was praised in the Army Air Service report of operations. The balloon attacks disrupted the enemy's observation and artillery fire and also seem to have prevented German battle planes from impeding the progress of American ground troops. The general impression at 1st Army headquarters was that the first day's attack had been completely successful. It had met with little infantry and artillery resistance and had sustained few losses.[31]

Army objectives for the day were not, however, reached. The overly ambitious plan had called for an impossible advance of ten miles on the first day so that its troops could penetrate the Hindenburg line on the morning of the second day. Such a deep penetration was double the rate of advance on the first day of the St. Mihiel operation. Instead of advancing ten miles, the line had advanced about seven, still a remarkable feat. The first day's advance had been rapid because the forward elements of the German defensive zone were lightly defended. By the second day, however, enemy reserves had arrived, and resistance stiffened. For the remainder of the month the doughboys slowly pushed the Germans back while taking heavy casualties.[32]

During the next four days of heavy ground fighting, the group shot down eleven enemy airplanes and eight balloons. Frank Luke received credit for four balloons and one enemy aircraft during this period, about one-fourth of the group's victories. Luke continued to have a rocky relationship with his squadron commander. Grant was angry with Luke for his actions on the opening day of the offensive. By taking Roberts with him, Luke had upset the group-level balloon attack because Roberts had been one of the designated balloon strafers. Moreover, if Roberts had been on the group attack in accordance with the operation order, he might still be alive because of the protection of the fighter escort.

Grant grounded Luke on 27 September for his disobedience, but Luke was, as Rickenbacker put it, "as blandly indifferent to reprimands as to orders." Luke shot down a balloon and an enemy airplane the next day, but instead of returning to his squadron, he landed at the field of the élite French squadron, the Cigognes. He failed to notify his unit of his whereabouts, however, and was therefore listed as missing in action. When he returned to his squadron the next morning, Grant again ordered him grounded, but Luke promptly took off for the squadron's advanced field. When Grant found out, he phoned Vasconcells at the advance field and told him to arrest Luke. Grant planned to recommend Luke for a Distinguished Service Cross for valor, but he also intended to court-martial him for his disobedience.[33]

By this time Grant knew that he was no longer capable of controlling Luke. He was especially concerned because he had heard that Luke had decided that he would no longer go on patrol with the squadron. He intended to attack balloons on his own. By this time pursuit squadron and flight commanders firmly believed in the importance of formation flying. As Hartney observed, they "knew from experience that the time of formation and chain formation engagements had come; that the pilot who dropped out of formation jeopardized not only his own chances, but also those of the team he had deserted." Luke's rebellion threatened this closely held value of teamwork. It also set a bad example for other budding prima donnas—and many had earned their way into ranks of pursuit aviation. Perhaps even more important to Grant, Luke's flagrant disregard for Grant's orders challenged his authority over the squadron.[34]

Realizing he had lost control of the situation, Grant sought Hartney's help and explained that Luke had flown to the advance field against orders. Hartney covered for Luke, telling Grant that he had given Luke permission to fly to the advance field and for a subsequent attack on the enemy balloons. Hartney admitted in his memoir that he had lied. He needed the balloons on the Heights of the Meuse, opposite the Verdun advance field, destroyed. Later that day, Hartney flew his Sopwith Camel up to the advanced field. He stated that he wanted to make sure that Luke did not take off until just before dark, but he did not remain there to ensure that Luke waited.[35]

Capt. Alfred A. Grant, commanding officer of the 27th Aero Squadron
Grant's stern expression reflects his reputation as a strict disciplinarian.
NATIONAL AIR AND SPACE MUSEUM, CD-ROM 2B-10972

Luke took off near sundown, flew to an American observation balloon, and dropped a message instructing them to watch three German balloons on the Meuse River near the town of Dun-sur-Meuse. He then headed straight for the balloon hovering over the town of Dun. After setting it aflame he next tackled the one on the bank of the Meuse River over the Brier farm, destroying it also. His third victim was located on the edge of the town of Milly. By this time Luke was so badly wounded by antiaircraft fire that he was forced to land near the village of Murvaux. According to testimony by some villagers who witnessed the event, the wounded pilot got out of his SPAD to quench his thirst at a small stream. After he had gone about fifty yards a group of German soldiers approached to take him prisoner. Luke drew his revolver—and fell dead a moment later with a bullet in his chest. Grant subsequently changed the recommendation for a Distinguished Service Cross to the Medal of Honor. Luke received it posthumously.[36] However, it should be noted that historians continue to argue about whether or not a shoot-out occurred.

Hartney analyzed his handling of Luke in his memoir: "Did I treat him right? I think so. Did I give him too much leeway? I think not." Hartney admits, however, that Luke's judgment, toward the end, no longer corresponded with reality: "At this time Luke got the idea that he could take on the entire German airplane and balloon services single handed, without support of any kind. He was certainly the most reckless, unafraid, and self-confident flier in the United States Army." Hartney correctly framed the problem in his concluding remarks about Luke, when he stated that "in wartime flying service there must be discipline but it must be adjusted to the individual and tempered with reason."[37] If there was ever a case in which a leader needed to intervene to restrain the self-destructive behavior of a subordinate, it was the case of Frank Luke.

Rickenbacker empathized with his fellow squadron commander's predicament: "Luke's very mischievousness and irresponsibility made every one of us feel that he must be cared for and nursed back into a more disciplined way of fighting—and flying—and living. His escapades were the talk of the camp and the despair of his superior officers." Rickenbacker thought men and planes were too valuable to be put at risk in reckless acts like Luke's. Luke consistently violated Rickenbacker's emphasis on teamwork and his rule of thumb that one should never take more than a fifty-fifty chance unless absolutely necessary. Luke was not a Gimper; but Rickenbacker wanted to make him one. Rickenbacker thought he could control Luke, and he had already arranged for Luke's transfer to the 94th Squadron. If Luke had survived another day, he would have become a member of the Hat-in-the-Ring Squadron and, perhaps, lived to fight another day.[38] Rickenbacker was the only squadron commander in the 1st Pursuit Group capable of controlling Frank Luke.

Hartney's treatment of Luke was consistent with his British-influenced high-risk–high-casualty command style. Above all, he wanted to get those balloons for Mitchell. The squadron commanders, Rickenbacker and Grant, were not willing to allow Luke to plunge recklessly toward his death. To what extent is it the combat leader's responsibility to control such reckless acts on the part of subordinates? Were Luke's victories worth his death? Rickenbacker and Grant did not think so. Hartney equivocated. The doughboys rejoiced.

Hartney thought that his group had brought down seventeen enemy balloons that day, though the official credits would later record five. On the night Luke died, the 1st Army paused to replace several of its front-line divisions and prepared to resume the offensive on 4 October.[39]

In addition to its low-flying patrols, the 1st Pursuit Group also conducted several special reconnaissance flights in keeping with its nickname, Pursuit

Observation. On 27 September Edward P. Curtis of the 95th Squadron conducted a low-level reconnaissance up the Meuse River for about twelve miles behind the lines and reported on enemy movements along the roads and railroads. Mitchell arrived at the group on 30 September at half past six on the evening in need of an urgent reconnaissance to determine whether eleven trains carrying the Prussian Guard had left Metz to reinforce the enemy. Rickenbacker volunteered and flew about thirty-seven miles into Germany to locate the trains. He returned at eight that night, having survived friendly antiaircraft fire, and reported that there were no such trains—to which Mitchell responded, "Thank God."[40]

German air force reinforcements were also a concern. According to intelligence reports, during the last week in September and the first week in October the enemy increased the number of squadrons opposing the 1st Army in all categories. Pursuit squadrons against the 1st Army increased from five to twelve, battle-plane units from six to seven, and reconnaissance squadrons from twelve to thirteen. According to operations reports, enemy aircraft bombed and machine-gunned front areas of the 1st Army during the afternoon on 3 October. In subsequent days there was a noticeable increase in enemy aircraft on the right side of the sector along the Meuse River. Enemy pursuit planes also made several attacks on 1st Army balloons and were observed flying in larger formations. One report indicated that twenty-one hostile planes had penetrated about six miles behind American lines.[41]

The battle for air superiority was primarily the responsibility of Atkinson's 1st Pursuit Wing. Intense air battles were taking place between large formations of opposing aircraft high in the skies over the battlefield. The 1st Pursuit Group's low-flying, relatively small patrols of camouflage-painted SPADs enjoyed some security in that they were difficult to acquire. Nevertheless, the group's patrols also began encountering formations of enemy aircraft in groups of ten, eleven, and sixteen airplanes during the first week of October.[42] Low-level operations were becoming increasingly dangerous.

Hartney's daily program began with a predawn takeoff of a small flight, usually two or three planes with balloon guns, which swept the 1st Army front of balloons at dawn. These were followed by sector patrols, which began at dawn. On 2 October the 94th Squadron was ordered to patrol the army front at dawn with two patrols of six planes each. Each patrol was given a sector corresponding to half of the Army front and was to fly no higher than 600 meters (about two thousand feet). The 95th Squadron followed, taking off at eight o'clock with six planes flying in two echelons, covering the entire Army front until ten o'clock. The 147th, the Scotch Terrier Squadron, followed with a similar mission from ten until noon. The 27th and 94th Squadrons patrolled the front for two hours each between noon and four o'clock.

The last major operation of the day was a group-level sweep of the lines involving all available planes, usually from three squadrons, between four and six in the afternoon. This "concentration patrol" required each squadron to fly a separate route to a designated group-rendezvous point over the lines. Once the group had conducted the rendezvous, one squadron served as the "pivot squadron," which guided the others as the group "scoured" the lines of low-flying planes and balloons. The concentration patrol was followed by the usual evening balloon-strafing mission, consisting of two or three planes that usually landed after dark. Meissner's squadron opened the group's second advance field on 28 September with one alert flight stationed at Brebant, near the Argonne Forest, covering the left side of the army sector.[43]

When the weather was good the group launched between seventy and eighty sorties a day, and sometimes more. The largest number of sorties was 111 on 2 October. Daily flight operations typically consisted of between ten and fifteen patrols. The group flew about half as many sorties during poor weather, which occurred frequently. Occasionally the weather was so bad that the group was unable to launch any combat missions.

The 1st Pursuit Group conducted a special attack on the afternoon of 3 October. This balloon strike illustrates the increasing sophistication of the effort to destroy enemy balloons. The objective was three enemy balloons located in the vicinity of the towns of Aincreville, Bantheville, and Cunel. They covered the Cunel Heights, one of the key fortified areas of the third defensive line of the Hindenburg line, called the Kriemhilde Stellung. Penetration of this line and seizure of the Cunel Heights was one of the major objectives of the 1st Army offensive set to resume at dawn the next day.[44]

Unlike the group's standard afternoon concentration patrol, which attacked targets of opportunity, this operation was a carefully planned attack against a specific objective. The strafers were to strike the balloons at exactly 4:40 P.M. Each of the group's four squadrons supported the balloon strafers with a protection formation of eight planes. Each squadron had an assigned rendezvous point, or attack position, just inside friendly lines. These rendezvous points traced the arc of a semicircle, about twelve miles wide, with its edge on the 1st Army's front. The plan called for them to loiter over these points and time their departure so as to arrive over the balloons at 4:41 P.M., exactly one minute after the strafers made their attack.

In the west, the 27th Aero Squadron would rendezvous over Fleville on the edge of the Argonne Forest. The 147th and the 94th Squadrons would do so in the center at Epinonville and Cuisy, and the 95th Squadron on the right at Dannevoux near the Meuse. Each squadron flew at a different designated altitude between 500 and 1,000 meters (1,640 and 3,280 feet) so that they would converge simultaneously in the objective area, from different directions and altitudes, to provide a layered cover for the balloon strafers.

Immediately after the attack on the balloon, the entire group was to withdraw to friendly airspace and rendezvous over Montfaucon. From there the group would sweep the sector from the Meuse to the Argonne, at the discretion of the patrol leaders, but at an altitude not to exceed 600 meters.[45]

Factors such as unforeseen alerts and aircraft availability made it necessary to adjust the plan before takeoff. The 27th and 147th Aero Squadrons, both maintaining a flight at the group's two advance bases, supplied only four and two planes, respectively, for the mission. To make up for the shortage, the 94th and 95th Aero Squadrons provided thirteen and eleven aircraft, respectively. Rickenbacker had as many machines as possible from his squadron on this mission. He knew an attack on these important balloons guaranteed that there would be a fight.[46]

At four o'clock on the afternoon of 3 October, the thirty-SPAD strike force took off from Rembercourt. The three balloon strafers flew in their own formation. Walter Avery, a respected pilot from the 95th Aero, led this group. Avery had the distinction of having shot down Carl Menckoff, one of Germany's top aces with thirty-nine victories, in early August on the Château-Thierry front. Rickenbacker placed his senior flight commander, Hamilton Coolidge, with the strafers. Coolidge had two victories to his credit by this time. The third strafer was Charles I. Crocker, who had recently joined the 94th Squadron. The strafers were supposed to fly low, below the 94th Aero Squadron's protective formation, leading the attack.

Rickenbacker was the only squadron commander flying on this mission. He placed one of his flight commanders, Thorne Taylor, in charge of the 94th Aero Squadron's protective formation so that he himself could fly independently. Rickenbacker took off last and maneuvered to a higher altitude than the rest. As he arrived in the vicinity of the rendezvous area, he could see the large protective patrol from the 94th Squadron near the rendezvous point near Cuisy, about three miles behind friendly lines. The balloon strafers circled closer to the lines on the other side of Montfaucon. As Rickenbacker approached, the strafers suddenly streaked toward their targets. They had begun the attack several minutes early, though they were supposed to have synchronized their watches to ensure a coordinated attack.[47]

In the strafing group, Coolidge followed Avery across the lines and dived on an enemy balloon. He saw that it was without a basket and considered it a likely trap—the Germans had reportedly been enticing Allied aviators to attack decoy balloons, leaving the airmen vulnerable. He flew toward the next balloon. "I hardly had time to think of the Archie fire and streams of machine gun bullets that flew by as I dove on my balloon," he wrote. "I could see my incendiaries pour into the old gas bag, and the observer jump out in his parachute." A few seconds later, the balloon burst into flames. As Coolidge pulled up he saw a formation of seven Fokkers nearby with a SPAD climbing straight at them.[48]

Avery was piloting this SPAD and may have mistaken the Fokkers for one of the 1st Pursuit Group's protection patrols, for he climbed right into their midst. In a second they were upon him, and the melee went circling to the ground. Coolidge shrieked, "Look out, Walter!," but the words never got beyond his mouth because of the roaring exhaust. "I was so mad I saw red," Coolidge wrote, "and dove upon the nearest of them . . . and riddled him with bullets." As the Fokker went down Coolidge looked around to see

> the most god-awful mess of Huns you ever saw, with two right on my tail, and I knew it was "fini." Lord, it was like a melodramatic movie. Here, just in the nick of time, comes the galloping cowboys over the hill—and ol' Thorne's for-mation pounces on the birds that have me cold-cocked.

Thorne Taylor's protective formation arrived just in time for Coolidge, as one SPAD after another flashed down into the engagement, but too late for Avery. Fokkers and SPADs merged into a confused, whirling mass of airplanes that battled with one another for the next fifteen minutes. "The air was streaked in every direction with the smoke of the tracer bullets."[49]

Rickenbacker had immediately begun to follow the strafers; his early movement toward the balloons may have helped signal the rest to follow. As he penetrated enemy airspace, however, he diverted his course to attack two enemy aircraft that threatened the attack. One of them turned back, but Rickenbacker was able to surprise the other and shoot it down. He then flew toward the Cunel Heights. Rickenbacker later recalled the scene that met him:

> The SPADs were scattered all over the sky and our formation was hopelessly destroyed. I determined to call them together and take them back to our lines. Our balloon was in flames, our mission ended, and we were taking unwise risks fighting ten miles within the German lines where a mishap would drop some luckless pilots prisoners in their territory.[50]

It seems doubtful that Rickenbacker was actually able to "call them together and take them back" to friendly airspace. Coolidge wrote, "Things happened too fast and changed too often to enable any of us to retain anything but a confused impression of that awful combat. Gradually we edged toward our lines and finally crossed them with the Fokkers in hot pursuit." Once the American planes were in friendly territory the Fokkers broke off the attack. Subsequently, most of SPADs returned to Rembercourt. Gimpers Rickenbacker and Coolidge, and Edward P. Curtis of the 95th Squadron, however, cooperated in shooting down a LVG (Luftverkehrsgesellschaft) reconnaissance plane that attempted to penetrate their airspace before calling it a day.[51]

Eastman called it the biggest "rat-fight" yet.[52] The 94th Squadron received credit for six official victories, including the balloon that Coolidge brought down. The group lost two pilots: Avery and one of the new men in the 94th Squadron became prisoners of war. Coolidge's SPAD was so shot up that it had to be replaced. He cut the hat-in the-ring insignia off the fuselage of his airplane and sent it home. His three victories that day made him an ace.

The 94th Squadron had the most airplanes aloft—thirteen out of thirty. It was the only formation that was heavily engaged in the fifteen-minute air battle. What happened to the rest of the protection patrols? Pilots in the 94th Aero Squadron knew they were performing under Rickenbacker's watchful eye, and they followed the example of their talented flight commanders. Moreover, Rickenbacker's personal involvement and decisions had shaped events. He placed his flight commanders in key positions and positioned himself to coordinate their efforts. In the days before fighters had radios, coordination of separate elements was an almost impossible task, but Rickenbacker managed a commendable degree of coordination.

In his memoir, Rickenbacker also pointedly tells his readers whether or not his subordinates acted in accordance with his orders. Concerning the early departure of the strafers, he wrote, "They disobeyed orders." In describing Taylor's protective formation approaching the attack position, he remarked that they did so with "implicit obedience to [his] orders." Eastman noted,

> Rick has established the custom of collecting all pilots before these affairs—which have become regular balloon straffing [*sic*] expeditions—and carefully outlining all details possible of the operation. It really is an excellent practice, this discussion, yet for one I confess it would be more to my liking were it done in a more off-hand manner.

Rickenbacker was intensely serious and did not hesitate to discuss the worst-case scenario. As Eastman witnessed, "I am sure that I can see the nerves of the others responding to the [in]tensity of these get-togethers."[53]

On 10 October, after a period of bad weather, the group launched another carefully planned balloon strike that incorporated lessons learned in the command and control of multisquadron operations from the attack on 3 October. The target was an observation balloon at Doulcon. The plan called for two balloon strafers to attack the balloon while six formations, of four planes each, provided cover.

Instead of a converging attack from widely dispersed attack positions, the three squadrons would fly parallel routes spread over a three-mile front. The 94th Squadron would be in the center; the 147th Squadron on the left, and the 27th Squadron on the right. Time was still used as a control measure—the squadrons were required to pass over designated towns at 3:40 P.M. and arrive at the balloon at 3:46, but by staying within visual range of one another they would be better able to coordinate their approach, so as to arrive in the target area at the same time. Being part of such a large formation would also help stiffen the courage of those who might otherwise not continue. The second major difference was that the strafers would not form their own group, as before. Instead, they would station themselves fifty meters (about fifty-five yards) ahead and fifty meters below the lead flight of their respective squadron.[54]

According to Rickenbacker, "I was placed in command of the expedition and was to arrange all minor details."[55] Hartney and his staff may have done the overall planning, but by this time it was obvious that multisquadron operations needed a single airborne commander, and Rickenbacker was picked for the job. Rickenbacker designated his best flight commander, Reed Chambers, as the strafer who would lead the squadron. He made the attack a maximum effort in his squadron, using fourteen airplanes rather than six.

Meissner also chose his best pilots for the key attack positions. His designated balloon strafer was William Brotherton, an experienced pilot with credit for two enemy aircraft and one balloon. One of these was a Rumpler he had shot down earlier that day. Wilbert White, one of the 147th Aero Squadron's flight commanders, led the squadron's protection. At this time, White and Meissner were the only aces in the squadron.

The plan did not work. From Rickenbacker's vantage point several thousand feet above the rest, he saw the balloon being winched down as his huge formation approached it. Moreover, two formations of defending Fokkers were approaching from opposite directions, in such a way as to catch the group in an aerial pincers movement. By the time Coolidge and Chambers arrived in the target area there was not a balloon in sight. The Fokkers came piling down on them a few minutes later. Meanwhile, Meissner and White's flight had pulled away from the rest of the group: Brotherton, seeing no balloon at Doulcon, flew across the Meuse River to attack one he saw on the ground at Dun. His comrades followed his headlong plunge into danger. Because a number of Fokkers also dived on them, a low-level melee developed over the banks of the Meuse River.

As Brotherton dived on the balloon he was hit by antiaircraft fire. His SPAD was last seen spiraling slowly to the earth, bursting into flames a few yards above the ground. Meanwhile, White had reversed direction and raced back to help one of the squadron's new pilots, who was under attack by the Fokkers. Meissner wrote,

> They kept diving on [Charles] Cox as White raced back, head on at it, firing without effect. He must have realized that Cox would be shot down unless he put the Boche out of the fight, so he never swerved. I watched them come together, thought for a moment they would just pass side by side, but the next instant off came a wing of each plane amid a cloud of splinters and shreds of fabric, and down they went spinning like tops.[56]

Because of White's sacrifice, Cox survived the fight.

Meanwhile, Meissner was under attack by four Fokkers.

[They] were coming my way so I opened my motor wide and went back to our lines with one Boche not a hundred meters behind shooting all around me. As we got back to our lines Rickenbacker and some others saw the chase and dove on the Fokkers, getting three of them, so I was a pretty good decoy as I've been before.

After this harrowing experience, Meissner joined up with two other members of his squadron and returned to sweep the lines as the group operations order directed. They brought down an enemy Rumpler.[57]

On this day the 1st Pursuit Group received nine confirmed credits, the second-largest number ever achieved by the group in a single day during the war. Six of the victories occurred on this mission—four for the 94th Squadron and two for the 147th Squadron, including White's collision victim. In addition, the 147th Squadron had downed three other enemy airplanes during the day, including one by Brotherton; perhaps the strain of the earlier mission affected him on his final flight. White had also been busy that day. He shot down a Hannover with the help of fellow flight commander Kenneth Porter, at about the same time as Brotherton's victory. Porter also brought down an enemy Fokker that had been strafing American troops.

Such repetitive combats reflected the intensity of operations. It required an extra amount of determination and effort for squadrons to place a large number of aircraft in the air on the late-afternoon mission. Rickenbacker earned his nineteenth and twentieth victories on this balloon raid; Coolidge won his seventh. The failure of this mission convinced Rickenbacker of the inadvisability of similar daylight attacks against balloons. He had destroyed a balloon himself on a dusk attack the night before.[58]

These carefully planned daylight balloon attacks show how the 1st Pursuit Group continued to experiment with the development of new tactics. These attacks were particularly dangerous because they required relatively deep penetrations at low altitude. Besides the ever-present antiaircraft defenses, the German fighters always had the twin advantage of altitude and time to react. In both cases the raiders had to fight their way back to friendly lines. There seems to have been a common understanding that once the balloon strafing was over, it was time to return. The airmen did not remain in the objective area to fight it out with the Germans.

Rickenbacker considered it unwise to take unnecessary risks so deep in enemy territory. The tactical plan was optimized for a balloon raid, not an air battle to sweep German fighters from the sky. Indeed, the changes in the plan for the second attack clearly demonstrate a concerted effort among 1st Pursuit Group planners and Rickenbacker to minimize the risks of such a difficult mission by having the entire attack group fly together. Two factors that greatly influenced the development of American fighter tactics were risk and technology.

In a thoughtful article written shortly after the war, Rickenbacker compared the attitude toward risk of the Americans, the British, and the French. As he saw it, the American aviators' attitude fell in between that of the two Allies. "The French were inclined to be cautious," he wrote,

> as a settled military policy of getting the best results with the least expenditure of valuable lives and costly planes. The British were foolhardy as a matter of principle and morale, because they found that they got the best results with their people in that way. Compared with the French, playing their own game in the way they had settled down to it toward the end of the war, our men seemed reckless. Compared with the British they seemed cautious.

Rickenbacker appreciated and respected each of the different approaches. "Each had worked out a method of scientific murder that did the job. We were working out ours with the experience of both to help us, and the methods of both to choose from. The result was, generally, a sort of compromise."[59]

That the American approach to aerial warfare represented a sort of compromise, or synthesis of the British and French systems, should not be surprising. The 1st Pursuit Group developed through a transfer of technology from the British and French air forces. This transfer included the traditional hardware, such as airplanes, and the less tangible skills, tactics, and organizational structures, along with associated values. These technologies and values merged with the influences of American progressivism and the engineering mentality in which so many of the pilots had been indoctrinated. The balloon attacks were carefully planned, pragmatic, and experimental as pursuit leaders sought to uncover the optimal solution.

The SPAD 13 was ideal for the tactics the group adopted for these attacks. Although the Fokker D-7 could outclimb it, the SPAD could dive away from the D-7 and was also faster in level flight. A pilot who wanted to withdraw from combat could do so much more easily with the SPAD 13 than with the Nieuport 28. Although it seems doubtful that Rickenbacker was actually able to communicate his decision to withdraw during the balloon attacks, the concurrent maneuvers by the members of the squadron—the edging toward the lines, as Coolidge put it—shows that the squadron reacted in combat as if its members were of one mind.

Included among the values that were taking shape in the cauldron that was the 1st Pursuit Group was the expectation of leadership by example and the fighting squadron commander. Rickenbacker embraced the value of leadership by example. He spent more time in the air than anyone in his squadron. He later wrote,

> I am convinced after my six weeks' experience as squadron commander that my obedience to this principle did much to account for the wholehearted and enthusiastic support the pilots of my squadron gave me. And only by their loyalty and enthusiasm was their squadron to lead all the others at the front in number of victories and number of hours over enemy lines.[60]

The moral influence of Rickenbacker's behaviors should not be discounted. Most of these aviators were not fearless beings cut in the mold of Frank Luke. Rickenbacker's protégé, Jimmy Meissner, also adopted this style of air leadership. Although the 27th Squadron's commander, Alfred Grant, did not take part in the balloon attack, he had led a sector patrol earlier that morning.[61] By October David McK. Peterson was the only squadron commander in the 1st Pursuit Group who was not regularly flying missions.

Peterson had credit for one victory with the Lafayette Escadrille and three more with the 1st Pursuit Group, which had been won over a two-day period in May, before Hartney joined the group. Since assuming command of the 95th Squadron, Peterson, like Marr, had been noticeably absent in the air. They seemed to share a belief, perhaps reinforced by Atkinson while he commanded the group, that once a pilot had earned the prestige of command, he no longer needed to fly combat missions.

The tally kept in group operations showed Hartney that the 95th Squadron had the least number of victories during the St. Mihiel campaign. Additionally, in total victories since the beginning of the Meuse-Argonne offensive, it shared the bottom rung with the Scotties, but most of its successes had been won during the first days of the campaign. In terms of victories accumulated since October, the 95th shared the bottom rung with the Fighting Eagles, whose victory count had plummeted since the loss of Frank Luke. Thus performance as measured by victories was trending downward. By mid-October the 95th Squadron definitely held last place.

There also appears to have been an alcohol problem in the 95th Squadron. Drinking occurred in all of the squadrons. Hartney had a liberal attitude toward the consumption of alcohol and claimed that it was not a problem in the 1st Pursuit Group:

> In our particular niche of the air service [alcohol consumption] was never a problem. . . . A flier could indulge or not, according to his choice, but if, on any job, there was the slightest indication of his drinking habits prejudicing his work his ticket to the rear was as good as written.[62]

The bottle or two of wine that McLanahan and Buckley had enjoyed while hiding from Hartney after the advance-field debacle may have fortified their courage for an attack on a stationary balloon, but it dulled their reflexes for air-to-air combat with opposing fighters. During the 95th Squadron's earliest days, Davenport Johnson had gained favor by allowing consumption of alcoholic beverages, which had previously been prohibited, in the unit mess. This policy was probably not unusual, but it became an issue of enough concern that Buckley dwelt upon it at some length in his memoir—an indication that alcohol occupied a prominent place in the daily life of the Kicking Mules.[63]

More indicative of a serious drinking problem is James Knowles's remembrance of drinking immediately before and during combat missions during the Château-Thierry campaign. "We'd go into Paris," he later recalled, "and sit around the Café de la Paix for a couple of hours, return to Orly, and fly back to the front a little bit fried and go out for a two-hour patrol. Most of the boys usually had a jug with them in their airplane."[64]

Although alcohol seems to have been consumed in all the officer's messes of the group, the 95th was the only squadron that established its own bar, constructed shortly after moving to Rembercourt and "stocked with a truck load of liquor," complete with boot rail, white-coated bartender, and "unlimited credit for the customers." Later additions included a piano looted from the conquered St. Mihiel salient during September.[65]

Most of the squadron's officers, including key leaders, were drunk the night before the St. Mihiel offensive began. Knowles remembered, "Russ Hall and I were up at the 95th hangar in a crap game and also drinking fairly heavy. Ed Butts, our operations officer, had lost the battle orders for the next morning as far as the 95th was concerned." Walter Avery also remembered heavy drinking that day: "Everyone has been drunk all day. Capt. Pete [Peterson] is clear under. . . . Ed Butts, the operations officer, came into the tent about 10 P.M. drunk as the devil and made a long sentimental speech that the drive starts at 5 A.M."[66]

Officers in the 95th Squadron were not the only ones with drinking problems. In August, while Marr was commanding the 94th Squadron, he was found "rotten drunk" in a Parisian bar. Interestingly, it was 95th Squadron officers who had found him and brought him back to the camp.[67] Marr's drinking problem probably figured in his relief.

In addition to their low victory tally and alcohol problems, Hartney had been in a rage over the 95th Squadron's advance-field fiasco. The 95th Squadron's poor sites resulted not only in several crash-landings, including Hartney's, but also in Hartney's failure to fully accomplish his mission, which included establishing two advance fields.[68] Nor was this the first major faux pas by the 95th Squadron that was significant enough to be noticed at 1st Army's Air Service headquarters. Lt. Norman Archibald of the 95th Squadron had been shot down behind enemy lines before the St. Mihiel offensive, in violation of a general order restricting flying over the lines, to maintain secrecy over the concentration of air units in the region.

Poor performance and weak discipline finally reached levels that Hartney could not ignore. When he received a request to send two aviators back to the United States to serve as trainers,[69] Hartney used the opportunity to remove Peterson from command and placed Lt. John Mitchell in charge of the squadron on 13 October.

Lansing Holden, who had joined the 95th Squadron at the end of July, wrote home expressing, "We are delighted with John Mitchell as C. O." because he "flies with us although he doesn't have to." With Peterson gone, Hartney had completed his purge of the Lafayette Flyers from the 1st Pursuit Group. All of his squadrons were commanded by fighting commanders. During the last month of combat, the 95th Squadron received more victory credits than any other squadron in the 1st Pursuit Group.[70]

A fifth fighter squadron joined the 1st Pursuit Group in October to become America's first night-fighter squadron. "For a long time we had [night flying] in mind," Hartney noted, "but the French tried to tell us it was a crazy idea." In fact, the French had been experimenting with night pursuit for more than a year, but it was the British who had the most experience in this new category of aviation, experience gained in their defense of London against German strategic bombing attacks, first by Zeppelins and later by Gotha twin-engine bombers. It was not until June 1918, however, that the British began tactical night pursuit on the front lines. In that month Squadron 151, which was equipped with Sopwith Camels, arrived in France to support the British army. A second squadron followed in October. The United States had high hopes for night pursuit in the closing days of the war. Plans called for the training of three hundred night-pursuit pilots, but only one squadron was organized before the war ended.[71]

The 185th Aero Squadron was organized on 11 November 1917 at Kelly Field and left the United States on 31 January 1918. The squadron did not arrive in France until August, however, because it remained in England to support RFC training activities as part of the arrangement that Bolling had negotiated, whereby the Americans promised to provide fifteen thousand mechanics to augment the RFC training bases in England. In return, the American mechanics received training and experience.[72]

The 185th Squadron finally departed from England and arrived at St. Maxient in France, where Seth Low took command on 16 August. A few days later, Low led the squadron to the 1st Air Depot at Colombey-les-Belles, where the unit took charge of the depot's airfield operations. By this time, the squadron had a complement of pilots and SPADs, but they were being used as replacements. Seventeen of them were transferred to various pursuit groups on the third day of the Meuse-Argonne offensive, leaving Low with only two pilots and two flight commanders.

Meanwhile, Hartney had been accumulating Sopwith Camels in the 147th Aero Squadron. These Camels were powered by 165-horsepower Gnome Monosoupape engines. By 3 October the 147th Squadron was reporting six Sopwith Camels on hand, in addition to 24 SPADs. By 8 October, all had been transferred out of Meissner's squadron to the 185th Squadron.[73]

The presence of these Sopwith Camels in the 1st Pursuit Group probably stemmed from Hartney's desire to find a rotary-engine replacement for his beloved Nieuport 28. One of his first acts upon taking command of the 1st Pursuit Group had been to speak with Air Service Supply chief Halsey Dunwoody, in Paris, about the possibility of getting Sopwith Camels with Monosoupape motors. This request from the army's premiere pursuit commander could not have been better timed. During August the Air Service began receiving the new Camels powered by the same rotary engine as the Nieuport 28. Hartney joyfully called them "the finest little all-around pursuit ships on the entire front, friendly or enemy."[74]

Hartney thought the rotary-engine fighter was ideal for cooperation with searchlight crews because the pilot could shut off the engine and glide quietly for minutes at a time, providing searchlight crews an opportunity to listen for approaching bombers. Searchlight beams were rarely successful in illuminating the bombers, but the direction of the beam could give the pursuit pilot a good indication of where to investigate.[75]

The 185th Aero Squadron arrived at Rembercourt on 7 October, under the command of Lieutenant Low, one of the original members of the first team aboard the *Orduna* and also one of the first officers to arrive at Villeneuve. He was one of the officers Atkinson had traded to the 103d Squadron in return for experienced flight commanders needed in the 94th Squadron (Hall, Marr, and Peterson). The 185th did not learn that it would become a night-fighter unit until after arriving at Rembercourt, and Low immediately confronted numerous challenges. His pilots were not trained for night flying; many of them had never flown in the dark. They also had to become acquainted with the use of unfamiliar gear on their airplanes, including wing flares, parachutes flares, and instrument lights. Experience had to be gained in coordinating operations with searchlights and antiaircraft batteries. Moreover, the pilots had to learn to fly the Sopwith Camel, notorious for its sensitive handling characteristics and now equipped with a motor that, if not properly operated, could catch fire. Finally, organization and training of the night-fighter squadron was undertaken during combat. It was another pioneering effort for the 1st Pursuit Group.[76]

By 12 October trial flights had begun with a complement of fourteen Camels. Hartney steadily filled the squadron using a combination of new pilots and pilots transferred from the other squadrons of the 1st Pursuit Group, so that by the end of the war there were nineteen pilots in the squadron. The group issued the squadron orders for its first official mission on 19 October, placing several Camels on nighttime alert. The squadron dis-

Capt. Jerry Vasconcells, commanding officer of the 185th Aero Squadron

According to legend, the squadron's bat insignia (barely visible on the fuselage of his
SPAD 13) inspired the Batman logo.

NATIONAL ARCHIVES

patched two patrols, which flew the sector from Verdun to St. Mihiel but did
not encounter enemy bombers.[77]

On the night of 21 October one of the squadron's aircraft answered an alert
call. It was airborne in one minute and arrived at its destination at Troyon six
minutes after the alert had been sounded.[78] There were seven night flights on
21 October. Hartney himself flew a patrol that night. He experienced a series
of close calls that demonstrated the dangers associated with this new mission
and new equipment.

During the patrol he shut off his engine. He had been gliding for ten minutes, when he saw about ten searchlight beams converge in the air near
Verdun. Switching on his engine he climbed to the point of the beams' con-
vergence and saw the telltale blue exhaust flames of a Gotha bomber. He
approached the bomber unseen, fired both guns, and observed his tracers
enter the aircraft. As he was thinking how easy it had been to make this attack,
his engine suddenly quit—he had made the unforgivable mistake of running

out of fuel. Although Hartney's personal aircraft was a Sopwith Camel, he had misjudged the available flying time in a Camel equipped with a larger engine and faster rate of fuel consumption.

Hartney quickly turned on his reserve fuel tank and went into a dive to restart the engine. Such a midair restart was not possible with the Hispano-Suiza. It had been months, however, since he had operated an aircraft with the Monosoupape engine. Hartney had inadvertently switched off his engine, and fuel from the reserve tank began to accumulate in the crankcase. Finally, he realized his error. But when he switched on the engine, it caught fire. Hartney coolly continued to dive, and the fire went out after about a minute. His next problem was making it back to the airfield on his limited fuel supply. Daytime forced landings were almost routine in the pursuit group, but a nighttime forced landing could easily by disastrous.

Hartney had established a dummy airfield to deceive the enemy; it also served as a reference point for night flights. Having oriented himself by the dummy airfield's searchlight, he turned toward Rembercout. As he approached, he "pulled a parachute flare," to signal his arrival, and flashed the recognition signal. He received "an instant response from the flimsy control tower on the headquarters roof." The crew on the ground commenced the rudimentary landing procedure. Men lined up on the airfield with flashlights and flat pieces of wallboard, on which they shone the lights to give Hartney perspective. Meanwhile the dummy airport turned on its boundary lights three miles away. Hartney made yet another mistake as he made his landing approach: "For no good reason, I turned on my right wing magnesium flare. Why I did it I don't know, because I was scared to death of those things. But I did many foolish things that night." Nevertheless, Hartney landed safely. Feeling foolish because of his mistakes, he did not claim the Gotha that he had attacked. He was certain that he had shot it down, however, and claimed later to have found its wreckage.[79]

The next night the 185th Squadron conducted eight night flights, including two experimental bombing missions in which each Camel dropped two twenty-pound bombs. While returning from his bombing attack, Lt. Elihu H. Kelton strafed a railroad train but was unable to provide a damage report because of the poor visibility.[80] The next night interception took place in the vicinity of St. Mihiel against five enemy bombers, but without success. On the night of 27 October the 185th Aero Squadron launched three night patrols. Lt. George Ewing, who was returning from one of these patrols, crashed on the airfield and burned to death.

Cpl. Walter Williams was just returning to Rembercourt when this incident occurred and observed the accident. According to him, Ewing had made a mistake similar to Hartney's. As Williams looked up into the dark night, Ewing was gliding in for a landing. Williams heard Ewing "cut [on] the motor selector switch" and saw the engine burst into flames. The flames flashed back toward the pilot's face, causing him to lose control. The Camel nosed down at a steep angle and crashed just off the airfield. Men from the group quickly arrived at the scene of the accident but could do nothing because of the flames and exploding ammunition. Ewing's screams could be heard a mile away. Williams wrote, "A most horrible sight . . . but that's the way of them DAM [*sic*] SOPWITHS."[81]

Seth Low was relieved of command on 6 November 1918 and ordered to proceed to Colombey-les-Belles for duty with the assistant chief of Air Service, Zone of Advance—the usual assignment for relieved commanders. Hartney's memoir states, "On October 25, Low was peremptorily snatched from me for other staff duties, and I placed Jerry Vasconcells of the 27th in command. . . . I have never seen a finer, more enthusiastic and intelligent officer."[82] Vasconcells had proved himself capable of independent command at the Verdun field. It seems likely that Hartney, unhappy with Low, had him removed.

There is no record that Low himself conducted patrols with his squadron. He also lacked the technical expertise in rotary-engine fighter operations needed for this assignment. Moreover, he had gained his combat experience in the 103d Aero Squadron, which was still largely manned with Lafayette flyers—a connection that probably rubbed Hartney the wrong way.

By this time Hartney was at the height of his power. His powerful ally, Billy Mitchell, had been promoted to brigadier general to assume command as chief of Air Service of the Group of Armies. Moreover, Hartney was the only pursuit-group commander whose mission directly supported the troops on the front line. Because Mitchell had been criticized for focusing too much of his effort on the enemy rear, he could point to Hartney's efforts and successes when defending his air strategy.

By 27 October the 1st Army had begun concentrating all of its combat aviation in bombing and strafing attacks against the enemy's troops. On this occasion, the 1st Pursuit Group's mission required it to provide low-level protection for a strafing and bombing attack by Atkinson's 1st Pursuit Wing. Hartney's part of this mission called for the 27th, 94th, and 95th Squadrons to rendezvous at Grandpré at a quarter to three, at an altitude of 600 meters, and proceed north, "clearing the way of all low-flying machines" for two of the 1st Pursuit Wing's pursuit squadrons to strafe and bomb at Morthomme. The group was then to remain in the vicinity to protect the bombardment group's attack on Briquenay from low-flying enemy fighters. Hamilton Coolidge, who had recently been promoted to captain, was shot down by enemy antiaircraft fire on this mission. The next day Rickenbacker flew to where Coolidge had fallen and saw "poor Ham on top [of the wreckage] all burnt to a crisp."[83] Coolidge thus joined his best friend, Quentin Roosevelt, in death. Only one more pilot from the group was killed in action before war's end.

Total confirmed victories during the Meuse-Argonne campaign (26 September to 11 November) were almost three times as great as they had been at Château-Thierry. During the Meuse-Argonne offensive, the 1st Pursuit Group received credit for 111 official victories, including 35 of the 39 balloons destroyed by the American Air Service. In comparison, the group had thirty-nine confirmed victories during the Château-Thierry campaign. The 94th Squadron led the group with forty-four victories during the Meuse-Argonne campaign. The 95th and 27th Squadrons followed with twenty-nine and twenty-three, respectively. The 147th Aero Squadron had seventeen, the fewest victories of any squadron involved in the campaign.[84]

During the Meuse-Argonne campaign, the 1st Pursuit Group counted eighteen casualties, pilots who were either killed in action, killed by accident, severely wounded, or taken prisoner. This number was about half of the thirty-one casualties sustained during Château-Thierry. The 27th and 94th Aero Squadrons led, with five casualties each; the 95th and 147th Aero Squadrons experienced a remarkably low number of three casualties each; and the 185th Aero Squadron sustained two casualties.[85]

Capt. J. Gordon Rankin, commander of the 1st Pursuit Group's 4th Air Park Squadron, remembered, "In the last analysis, it all got down to a question of supply. I attribute the wonderful record of the 1st Pursuit Group largely to the fact that we were able to work out a system of supply." According to Rankin, both Atkinson and Hartney made a concerted effort to develop a group-level logistics organization that insured a fair and equitable distribution of supplies among the units. Rankin continued,

> I visited both the 2nd and 3rd Pursuit Groups, and found one of them was
> using their park to do the fatigue and police work of the group, and the other

was using their park to build a road in the airdrome while supplies were still being obtained by the squadron supply officers.[86]

Rankin was obviously proud of the 4th Air Park.

By the end of October, pursuit-aircraft availability had reached a crisis. On 30 October, Mitchell's chief of staff sent him a memorandum entitled, "SPAD XIII Airplanes and Hispano 220 Motors." It stated, "The Pursuit Groups find themselves at a critical time far short of their allowance in airplanes and motors." Compiled statistics revealed that of the 300 pursuit aircraft authorized in the groups, only 281 were on hand, and of these, only 165 were capable of flying in combat. "The Enemy has concentrated his Air Forces in far greater strength than ever before against us. At the same time, our Pursuit Groups can only put into the air 53% of their authorized strength." The memo continued with an alarming statement: "Unless this condition is remedied at once, the Allies may be driven from the air in this sector." The memo called for increased issue of replacement airplanes, motors, and spare parts for the Hispano 220 motors to alleviate the situation.[87]

Although its maintenance organization had received high praise at Mitchell's headquarters, the 1st Pursuit Group was also struggling to cope with the airplane problem. With its five squadrons, the 1st Pursuit Group was authorized to have 125 aircraft. During the last five days of October the group reported between 97 and 101 airplanes on hand. The number of airplanes available for combat operations ranged between fifty-three and sixty-three.[88]

Contrary to the alarming memorandum sent to Mitchell, from the perspective of 1st Pursuit Group the enemy situation seemed well in hand. "Enemy still indifferent about attacking," stated the group's operations report for 31 October. On 5 November the group reported having launched eighty-seven sorties organized into sixteen patrols. At the end of the day the 1st Pursuit Group operations officer noted that "north and west of the Meuse there was absolutely no enemy activity." East of the Meuse, several formations consisting of seven to ten Fokkers were encountered, but "they were not aggressive, as usual." Nevertheless, the group counted four confirmed victories, including two balloons by the 95th Aero Squadron.[89]

Maj. Maxwell Kirby, who was slated to command the 5th Pursuit Group, had been assigned to that squadron to gain experience at the front. Kirby had left Rembercourt on a trial flight on 9 November. Owing to bad weather he was unable to return to the airfield, and so he landed elsewhere. He failed to report this fact, though, and was reported missing. On his way back to Rembercourt the next day, he emerged from a fogbank about 10:50 A.M., encountered a Fokker, and shot it down.[90] Kirby's was the group's last victory of the war.

By the beginning of November, 1st Pursuit Group pilots were aware that peace was at hand. Austria signed an armistice with Italy on 2 November, and American troops were rapidly gaining ground after breaking through the Hindenburg line. Many probably felt like Lt. Joseph C. Raible of the 147th Aero Squadron, who wrote on 5 November, "Anticipating end of war any moment. Can't see taking a chance unnecessarily when doing work. Reluctant to go up on patrol." Rickenbacker, Meissner, and others managed to get three-day leaves in Paris during the first week of November. Meissner hoped the Armistice would be signed while he was in Paris.[91]

To be sure, if the November victory tallies can be taken as a reflection of each squadron's aggressiveness, it seems obvious that the messmates of the 94th and 147th Squadrons had decided to avoid taking risks. Meissner's squadron had no victories. Rickenbacker's received credit for two victories. One of these was by an American pilot who had recently transferred from the RAF, the other was Kirby's. Rickenbacker himself achieved his last victories, numbers twenty-five and twenty-six, on 30 October. He finished the war as America's leading ace and was later awarded the Medal of Honor. The war continued with increased vigor, however, in Mitchell's 95th Aero Squadron, which won thirteen victories between the first and tenth of November.[92]

November 8 was the last day the 1st Pursuit Group launched a large number of sorties. In spite of bad weather, eighty-seven sorties took to the air, forming twenty-four patrols that scoured the lines and enemy rear areas. The group destroyed three planes and four balloons. Mitchell's 95th Squadron accounted for the lion's share of the victories, including two balloons and two airplanes. It rained on 9 November, and a Fokker landed at the advance field at Verdun. The pilot had become lost in the bad weather and inadvertently landed at the American field. The plane became a trophy of the 95th Squadron because Mitchell's unit had taken over operations of the field on 7 November. This Fokker was later put on display at the Smithsonian Institution. The group now had two enemy aircraft in its possession. The other was a Hannover that Rickenbacker had forced down in early October. Other than the landing of the disoriented Fokker, November 9 was an uneventful day. In the absence of combat activity, the airmen were becoming restless: The antics involving Rickenbacker, Meissner, Chambers, and an official AEF movie photographer in producing "An Aeroplane Movie Show" are the subject of one of the closing chapters in *Fighting the Flying Circus.*[93]

The 1st Pursuit Group had more success using wireless radio communications during the Meuse-Argonne campaign than it had at Château-Thierry. Wireless messages from observers on the front lines were especially effective in keeping the group operations section informed of enemy balloon locations and ascensions. The group's radio operators were also eavesdropping on German communications concerning armistice negotiations. On 7 November they informed Hartney and Rickenbacker that the German delegation had crossed the lines to negotiate terms. At about eight o'clock on the evening of 10 November, the radio operators again provided Hartney with important news:

> We intercepted on our radio the instructions to the German envoys at Foch's train, telling them to sign up on his terms at 11 A.M. the following day. The war was over. We knew it. We had won. I leaped to the telephone and notified every squadron. And then all hell broke loose.[94]

Most of the pilots in the 1st Pursuit Group had already retired to their tents for the evening when Hartney made the call to his men. Eight pilots, including the squadron commander, occupied the 95th Aero Squadron's "First Tent." The lamps were still on when the phone rang, but the various conversations ceased as John Mitchell threaded his way through trunks, tables, and chairs to the corner of the tent and picked up the receiver. One of the tent's occupants remembered Mitchell's phone conversation:

> "What's that?" [Mitchell] cried, his voice pitched high in amazement. Then he turned and, with a puzzled look in his eyes and a voice which struggled for calm, he said, "The War is over. The Armistice will be signed at eleven o'clock in the morning. Hartney just got the news from Headquarters."[95]

In the 94th Squadron Joseph Eastman heard the cheering outside and went to the door of his tent. He saw "a parade of enlisted men—drumming a tin pan, tooting a bugle, mob cheers." Before he could make out the cause of excitement Meissner ran over "from the 147th barracks across the way, very much in a twitter. 'They've signed an Armistice, official wire up at the Operations from C. A. S. All hostilities to cease tomorrow at 11:00,' he tells us—and, 'Everybody come on over to the 95th's bar.'"[96]

Colored landing rockets and red and green flares lit up the sky as the Gimpers made their way across the dark, muddy field to the Kicking Mule mess. The sounds of cowboy yells and revolver shots also filled the night, and machine-gun fire occasionally rattled dangerously over their heads. Cpl. Walter Williams and his comrades in the 27th Squadron did not believe it when an officer told them that the war was over, but they too scrambled out of their barracks when they heard the commotion. "Holy smokes," he wrote, "Over at headquarters, they are going crazy,— shooting off flares, machine guns, setting off small bombs."[97]

Most of the officers assembled in the 95th Squadron mess and bar. Laurence Driggs, already with the 94th Squadron to ghostwrite Rickenbacker's famous memoir, insisted that the group commander give a speech. Hartney was hoisted up on the bar, but before he could begin he was interrupted by a terrific racket outside caused by the 4th Air Park brass band. Everyone immediately poured outdoors.[98]

Officers and enlisted men formed a circle around the band. Meanwhile, someone turned on the searchlights and passed the beams back and forth over the field. Rickenbacker began to lead a swaying serpentine "shirt tail parade" in time with the band's jazz tune. Someone slipped and fell, tripping the persons behind him into a small pile. The entire line soon disintegrated into a series of groups of playful wrestlers, smearing one another's faces in the mud. As Hartney made his way across the field he had to lie down to avoid the whizzing bullets. Hartney's thoughts seem to have been the same as most everyone who recorded them on this wild, unforgettable night. "A great weight was lifted from us. We had lived through it. We had lived through the war."[99]

Corporal Williams and his friends had rolled a couple of planes onto the field and were firing their machine guns to add to the commotion. Although he was participating in the celebration, Williams remained skeptical. Then he looked toward the front lines and saw similar fireworks in the night sky and realized, "It surely must be true, even up at the combat areas, the sky is lighted up with flares and such. . . . At last it's over."[100]

11

Conclusion

The case of the 1st Pursuit Group is a success story in American military history. The group received credit for 201 victories, including 151 enemy airplanes and 50 enemy balloons, during World War I. These totals represented 24 percent of the total number of airplanes brought down by the Air Service and 83 percent of the total number of observation balloons destroyed. Because of the importance of enemy observation balloons in World War I combat, the 1st Pursuit Group contributed more directly to the success of Gen. John J. Pershing's Meuse-Argonne offensive than any other combat aviation unit. These results were obtained at the cost of seventy-three casualties, including thirty-three who were killed in action and five who were severely wounded. Twenty-one of the group's casualties were prisoners of war. One of them successfully escaped.

Rickenbacker's own 26 victories and his effective leadership of the 94th Aero Squadron helped propel his unit to top place in the 1st Pursuit Group and in the American Air Service with 67 total victories. The 27th Squadron followed, with 56 total victories. Because of Frank Luke's 14 balloon credits, the 27th led the group in total number of balloons destroyed, with 22. It was followed by the 95th Squadron, with 47 victories, and the 147th Squadron, with 31. The 27th and 95th Squadrons led the group in total casualties with 22 each. The 94th Squadron followed, with 17 casualties, and the 147th Squadron, with 9, had the fewest. In terms of exchange ratios, the 94th Aero Squadron was also the most efficient, achieving the most victories at the least cost, downing 3.9 enemy aircraft for each friendly casualty. The 147th followed with 3.4, the 27th with 2.5, and the 95th with 2.1.[1]

American air power in the Great War represents a successful case in technology transfer. These achievements would not have been possible without the assistance of the French and British allies, who provided aircraft, key personnel, training, equipment, and ideas that helped establish the AEF's Air Service. A successful transfer of technology, however, depends as much on the recipient as on the transmitters of that technology. The architects of American air power realized that the United States trailed far behind the Europeans. They approached this problem in a systematic fashion by structuring a process of technology transfer that operated at several levels and involved many activities. In the case of the 1st Pursuit Group, it consisted of the training of pilots and mechanics by the French and British, the procurement of Allied fighter aircraft, the importation of technically competent leaders who had gained experience in air combat in the French and British air forces, the final preparation of units in organization and training centers, and their introduction to combat under the command of the French army. It also represented the adaptation of ideas and values that accompanied the transfer.

Pershing's role in this process should not be overlooked. The AEF commander in chief was familiar with the poor state of American aviation because of his experience in the Mexican punitive expedition. His decision to conduct the final organization and training of the Air Service in France set the stage for the transfer of skills, equipment, and ideas while the Air Service and its units were in their most receptive, formative stages of organization. Those concerned with the organization and training of the 1st Pursuit Group and its squadrons were conscious of the progenitor role it would serve in the AEF. Pershing insisted upon "a system based on correct principles" and "approved and systematic methods" in completing the organization and training of the AEF.[2]

The aviation planners within the AEF followed Pershing's guidance and developed what was arguably the finest training and organization program in the world by borrowing from the best elements of the British and French systems of training and adapting them to their own requirements. The people who entered this training system represented the cream of America's youth from its best universities. The allure and romance of becoming a fighter pilot, together with America's huge and previously untapped manpower, provided an enormous resource pool from which the best candidates were culled for ground schools. Further quality cuts occurred at each phase of training. Those who graduated to become *chasse* pilots had passed through a number of screenings in an intensely competitive process.

The 1st Pursuit Group was not the only AEF unit that functioned as a progenitor or model for others to follow. Many organizations performed similar roles as the American Army transformed itself from a constabulary force to one capable of fighting in the European war. Gen. Hunter Liggett formed the U.S. 1st Corps as a model unit that would set the pattern for subsequent corps and instructed his staff to approach their tasks with this intent in mind. Although the 1st Pursuit Group always operated tactically at the level of the Army, when it was in the Toul sector it came under the administrative jurisdiction of Liggett and his air chief, Billy Mitchell, who approached the newly organized Air Service units, including the 1st Pursuit Group, with Liggett's guidance in mind. In this sense the 1st Pursuit Group differed significantly from its German counterpart, Baron Richthofen's Flying Circus. Rather than a collection of élite fighter squadrons, the American unit was a problem-solving organization tasked with leading the way for the development of American combat aviation.

One of the most difficult problems the Air Service faced was finding capable leaders to command the pursuit units. The AEF solved this problem by importing leaders who had served with the French and British air forces. At some point, however, Regular Army officers had to be in charge to ensure that technologies, tactics, and techniques being imported from the European allies were adapted to the needs of the AEF. Brig. Gen. Benjamin Foulois selected Bert Atkinson, one of the small group of aviation officers who had served with him on the Mexican punitive expedition, to perform this role in the creation of American pursuit aviation. The insiders occupied key positions throughout the Air Service, and their network of relationships served as an informal organization that allowed them to expedite the process of building the Air Service. Atkinson used this network to help solve the problems he encountered in building, equipping, and staffing the 1st Pursuit Organization and Training Center and its first squadrons.

As career professionals the insiders held certain values especially dear, including efficiency, order, and discipline. These core values were partly derived from an American society under the influence of progressivism and its technological companion, the efficiency movement, which produced Henry Ford's system of mass production. Atkinson's earlier experience at the Air Service's mobilization base at Kelly Field provided him a unique insight on the scope of his mission. He had personally observed the mass of humanity daily arriving at the base in central Texas and its conversion into standard-service aero squadrons. He understood that this activity was but the first step in a larger mobilization system that would transform these squadrons into units trained and equipped for the specialized missions of observation, bombardment, and pursuit.

The process that began at Kelly Field was an organization and training system that spanned two continents. Atkinson's familiarity with it helped him understand the dynamics of the Air Service problem in France—to rapidly transform standard-service aero squadrons into specialized pursuit units. He reasoned that superior numbers would win the war in the air and that bottlenecks must be avoided. Because he was consumed with the necessity of efficiently accomplishing his mission, he saw it largely in terms of logistics—the final assembly of pilots, mechanics, airplanes, vehicles, and other unit equipment into pursuit squadrons. He may have been an aviator, but his mission, as he saw it, was as a manager, not a combat leader.

Atkinson's progressive, managerial orientation brought him into conflict with the agents of technology transfer, the veterans of the French and British air forces. Raoul Lufbery was the most competent aerial fighter assigned to the 1st Pursuit Organization and Training Center, but Atkinson had him relieved from squadron command because he did not measure up in terms of the Army's progressive agenda. A good officer must be an efficient officer, so the reasoning went, and Lufbery hardly fit the image of administrative efficiency. Davenport Johnson's unusual pressing of court-martial charges against Jean Huffer was another example of this clash of cultures. For the most part, however, the representatives of the two cultures adapted to one another, and a working consensus of values developed. A distinctive organizational culture began to emerge in the early days of the 1st Pursuit Group while it was based in the Toul sector. This consensus was upset by the identification of technical problems with the Nieuport 28 and the concurrent arrival of the Canadian Circus.

The RFC-trained squadrons arrived with a degree of confidence and cohesiveness that challenged the rest of the 1st Pursuit Group. Their outstanding esprit de corps resulted from several factors. The officers and men of these new squadrons had been together for some months longer than the squadrons of the French tradition. Both RFC-trained squadrons were led by their original squadron commanders, who had personally trained many of the pilots to fly, while the squadrons of the French tradition were on their second and third commanders. It is likely that Geoffrey Bonnell felt the same cultural superiority to the French that Harold Hartney articulated in his memoir. The pilots also probably felt that they were better trained, as they had completed two training systems, the British Gosport system in Canada and Texas, and the French system at Issoudun.

Differences in values between these two sets of squadrons became apparent in the conflicting attitudes toward the Nieuport 28. It is evident from Hartney's memoir, written more than two decades after the war, that he always considered the Nieuport 28 superior to the SPAD 13. He took command of the 1st Pursuit Group too late to save the French rotary-engine fighter, but he succeeded in collecting Sopwith Camels, powered by the same 160-horsepower Monosoupape engine, for the night-fighter squadron that he organized and trained late in the war. It seems strange that many World War I aviation historians have summarily dismissed the Nieuport 28 as obsolescent, while the most experienced and successful pursuit commander in the AEF insisted otherwise. Similarly, there has been a mistaken assumption that the Air Service's first pursuit squadrons received the Nieuport 28 because the SPAD 13 was not available. As this study has shown, the Nieuport 28 was America's first fighter because of the agreement negotiated by Raynal Bolling at the end of August 1917. More to the point, the SPAD 13 had so many developmental problems that Air Service officials did not aggressively pursue procurement of this airplane until June 1918—after Foulois had taken steps to withdraw the Nieuport 28.

The conflict within the group over what constituted the best fighter plane reflected the high degree of subjectivity about which airplane represented the best technology. In the final analysis, choices over competing technologies are often subjective because it is not apparent which one will be most successful. In this case, preference depended upon the values reflected in competing lines of aircraft engines. Preference for the rotary-engine Nieuport 28 design reflected a high value on maneuverability, while preference for the SPAD 13 reflected a high value on ruggedness and diving speed. Attitudes toward these choices were largely influenced by fighting styles. The more aggressive squadrons of the British tradition favored a dog-fighting aircraft. The squadrons of the French tradition preferred the surprise slashing attack followed by a dash away from danger. In spite of the best efforts of Hartney and Bonnell, the Americans opted for the latter.

The decision to withdraw the Nieuport 28 was not made within the 1st Pursuit Group. Indeed, there appears to have been an attempt by some of the officers, perhaps orchestrated by Mitchell, to cover up its defective upper wing. Perhaps this was to save the airplane by organizing an emergency modification. The Nieuport was already doomed, however, because it had taken on a symbolic significance in the conflict between the AEF and the Department of War when a confused and overwhelmed Foulois characterized it to Pershing as an inferior airplane. Mitchell's strong endorsement of the airplane challenged Foulois's stated position. The airplane thus became an issue in the struggle between Foulois and Mitchell. After Foulois relieved Mitchell of command in early June, he completed his victory against his rival by taking the Nieuport 28 out of service and replacing it with the SPAD 13.

Pilots in the Canadian Circus, who disagreed with this decision, had the audacity to go over Foulois's head and appeal directly to the chief of Air Service Supply. Emotions ran high in the Canadian Circus over the prospect of giving up their Nieuport 28s in the heat of battle for SPAD 13s. These emotions contributed to a leadership crisis in which the squadron commanders of the British tradition repeatedly challenged Atkinson's authority.

Atkinson's policy against low-altitude aerobatics reflected the value of efficiency. His policies against voluntary patrols and small patrols flying across the front lines were similarly motivated. He was carefully managing his resources for combat operations. Hartney's low-altitude aerobatics represented a flagrant breach of discipline within the command structure. A few days later, Hartney also disregarded the policy against voluntary patrols, which resulted in the loss of five pilots on a single mission. He never openly challenged Atkinson, but he had no respect for the man as a pursuit-group commander because Atkinson never flew. Perhaps it was Hartney's legal training that provided him the skill to manage this conflict. The more bombastic Bonnell openly rebelled and was relieved of duty.

One of the items of consensus in organizational values that had developed in the 1st Pursuit Group before the arrival of the Canadian Circus involved expectations regarding what sorts of behaviors were important for pursuit-squadron commanders. The RFC-trained commanders were appalled by the paucity of fighting commanders. Atkinson himself may have contributed to the development of an organizational culture that made it acceptable for pursuit-squadron commanders not to fly regularly in combat: How could he demand that his squadron commanders fly in combat when his own airplane remained always in the hangar? It is hard to understand why Atkinson failed in this aspect of his leadership. If he had lacked courage, he would never have learned to fly on more uncertain and dangerous aircraft at North Island and in Mexico. He sent the pilots of the 95th Aero Squadron back to school because he knew they had no business flying over the front without having first finished gunnery school. Did he apply the same rule to himself, or was he so engrossed in the efficient running of his organization that he failed to realize the importance of allocating enough time out of his busy schedule to master the new technology?

It is in this respect that Atkinson and Mitchell differed so markedly. One of Mitchell's strengths was his awareness that his success depended on his ability to personally master the new technologies inherent in aerial warfare. He was not a qualified aviator when he arrived in Europe, nor was he a member of the close-knit group of veterans from the Mexican punitive expedition. He was an outsider, and as an outsider he was especially cognizant of the necessity to learn. That is what he did. He toured the war zone, met with the experts, observed, and often stayed up late into the night reviewing and recording his observations on his portable typewriter. No one in the AEF received a better education in aerial warfare. He was fortunate that he did not assume significant responsibilities for direct command until after Château-Thierry. Yet one gets the impression that if he had assumed such large responsibilities earlier, he would still have found time to master the new technologies.

Hartney and Bonnell brought the idea of a fighting squadron commander into the 1st Pursuit Group, and it was Hartney who made it a core value in its organizational culture. In terms of the relative British and French influences, it is true that veterans of the Lafayette Escadrille were important conduits of tactics, techniques, and procedures that helped the 1st Pursuit Group establish a winning tradition in its early days. On close inspection, however, their sustained effectiveness as combat leaders and ultimate contributions to the 1st Pursuit Group's identity may not have been as great as one might suppose. Lufbery and James Norman Hall were casualties during the group's earliest days at Toul. Huffer, Peterson, and Marr were all relieved of squadron command for various ignominious behaviors. There is no evidence that any of the Lafayette squadron commanders provided energetic leadership in the air. Hartney established leadership by example as a core value in the unit through the dismissal of Marr, Peterson, and Low and their replacement with fighting commanders during the final offensives.

The 1st Pursuit Group was fortunate to have had two excellent group commanders whose styles matched those required at different stages in the group's development. Hartney was the one who became famous. As an ace himself, he symbolized the fighting commander, as did Eddie Rickenbacker and Jimmy Meissner, that would serve as the role models of leadership for the future. But the group and the Air Service were also well served by the cautious and efficiency-minded Atkinson. Atkinson's safety restrictions prevented unnecessary loss of life. He anticipated the intense fighting that would take place at Château-Thierry and prepared the group by ordering practice in squadron-size formations. He demonstrated in planning for the battle of Vaux that he understood the importance of placing large numbers of aircraft over the front at the same time.

It is fortunate that the entire 1st Pursuit Group did not sustain the same casualty rate as Hartney's 27th Aero Squadron at Château-Thierry. The Air Service needed experienced veterans to lead its new pursuit units. No experienced veterans were transferred from the 27th Squadron to other newly formed squadrons at the end of Château-Thierry because there were hardly any veterans left in Hartney's squadron. In retrospect, Atkinson was a man of sound judgment. Perhaps his decision, which Mitchell apparently overruled, to place John Hambleton in command of the 147th Aero Squadron would have had better results than giving such a difficult task to the young Meissner.

The aggressive, high-risk culture in the 27th Aero Squadron was an ideal environment for the emergence of a pilot like Frank Luke. The new generation of fighting commanders who replaced the veterans of the British and French air forces sought a middle ground between the two national traditions. This attitude toward risk was reflected in their tactics. They stressed the importance of disciplined formation flying and teamwork. These officers may have been recruited with romantic allusions to "knights of the sky," but in their careers as fighter pilots they related to one another as team members. Their daily life was most guided by the sports analogy. To them, combat was the great game. This was natural because most of them had been student-athletes. The most accomplished of them, Rickenbacker, was a professional sportsman.

Academic engineers were also well represented because the ground schools had been established at the nation's premier engineering schools. Meissner is a good example of one of these student-athlete-engineers. Rickenbacker was also an engineer, but of the shop tradition. The attacks by the 1st Pursuit Group against enemy balloons during the final offensive reflected an attempt to engineer victory through carefully planned and synchronized group-level tactics. The pragmatic, calculated, problem-solving approach of the engineer, wedded to the value of teamwork acquired from sports, was far more influential in the 1st Pursuit Group than any romantic notion of modern-day knighthood. Rickenbacker's description of aerial combat as scientific murder is the best example of the fallacy of the knightly analogy. The close relationship that developed between the 94th and 147th Squadrons, messmates during the final offensives, symbolized the end of French-British conflict and the emergence of a new consensus—a distinctly American synthesis that resulted from the adaptation of the French and British traditions.

Pursuit aviation contributed to American success on the ground by securing aerial superiority, which allowed observation airplanes and balloons to direct friendly artillery fire. The first American air-land battle at Vaux demonstrated the significant contribution air superiority could make in World War I combat at an early stage of American involvement in actual fighting. Those who argue that observation was the most important function that aviation provided during this war must admit that what holds true for the American side also held true for the enemy. The 1st Pursuit Group's low-altitude operations against enemy balloons contributed directly to the success of operations on the ground by denying the enemy observation of friendly movements and disrupting its fire-control system for long-range artillery fire. Strafing attacks and bombing (by other pursuit units) also contributed directly to battlefield success. The advantage of this duality of contributions provided by pursuit aviation is the reason that air superiority continues to be the first priority for American combat aviation.

This study has examined the history of the 1st Pursuit Group in the Great War and the development of its organizational culture. Culture is an elusive organizational phenomenon that is difficult to define and measure. Yet it is significant because its influence is pervasive, and like an individual's personality, organizational culture tends to endure. To what extent did the 1st Pursuit Group's organizational culture, forged in the crucible of the Great War, persist? From the end of the war and demobilization until the 1930s, the 1st Pursuit was the only pursuit group in the recently organized Air Corps. As the Air Corps again expanded, the 1st Pursuit Group would again serve as the springboard for expansion and the progenitor of American pursuit aviation in yet another war.

Notes

INTRODUCTION

1. Diary of Joseph Houston Eastman, 10 October 1918, Joseph Houston Eastman Collection, Hoover Institution Archives, Stanford, California.

2. First Pursuit Group, Headquarters, "Low Pursuit Work and Balloon Straffing in an Offensive," 28 October 1918, Gorrell's History of the American Expeditionary Forces Air Service, 1917–19, series C, vol. 9, Microfilm Publication M990, RG120, National Archives at College Park (NACP). Gorrell's History is a collection of Air Service organizational records, including correspondence, journals, reports, and narrative histories composed immediately after war's end.

3. Edward V. Rickenbacker, *Fighting the Flying Circus,* ed. W. David Lewis (1919; reprint, Chicago: R. R. Donnelley and Sons, 1997), 354; "My Seventeenth and Eighteenth Victories," transcribed 10 December 1918, Edward V. Rickenbacker Papers, box 91, Library of Congress; 1st Pursuit Group, Operations Order 23, 10 October 1918, Gorrell's History, series C, vol. 9.

4. First Army Air Service, Headquarters, Battle Order 7, 25 September 1918, series 314.7, RG18, NACP.

5. Peter Kilduff, *The Red Baron Combat Wing: Jagdgeschwader Richthofen in Battle* (London: Arms and Armour Press, 1997), 224.

6. "147th Aero Squadron, Argonne-Meuse Sector," p. D.3.5, Gorrell's History, series N, vol. 6.

7. Hamilton Coolidge to Mother, 13 October 1918, in Hamilton Coolidge, *Letters of an American Airman* (Boston, 1919), 214.

8. Rickenbacker, *Fighting the Flying Circus,* 357.

9. C. G. Sweeting, *Combat Flying Equipment: U.S. Army Aviators' Personal Equipment, 1917–1945* (Washington, D.C.: Smithsonian Institution Press, 1989), 79.

10. Rickenbacker, *Fighting the Flying Circus,* 358.

11. "History of the 17th Pursuit Squadron (Formerly 147th Aero Squadron)," pp. 23–24, file SQ-FI-17-HI, U.S. Air Force Historical Research Agency, Maxwell Air Force Base, Montgomery, Alabama.

12. Ibid., 24.

13. James A. Meissner to Mama, 17 October 1918, Meissner file, Lafayette Collection, Wings Over the Rockies Air and Space Museum, Denver, Colorado.

14. 1st Pursuit Group Operations Office, News Bulletin 1, 11 October 1918, Gorrell's History, series C, vol. 9.

15. Meissner to Mama, 17 October 1918.

16. Aerospace Studies Institute, *U.S. Air Service Victory Credits, World War I*, U.S. Air Force Historical Study 133 (Montgomery, Alabama: Maxwell Air Force Base, Air University, Historical Research Division, June 1969), 98–99.

17. First Army, Headquarters, Operations Report 41, 10 October 1918, Gorrell's History, series N, vol. 1.

18. Bernard C. Nalty, *Winged Shield, Winged Sword: A History of the United States Air Force,* vol. 1, *1907–1950* (Washington, D.C.: Air Force History and Museums Program, 1997), 38.

1. THE INSIDERS

1. First Pursuit Group diary, 16 January 1918, Bert M. Atkinson Papers, Auburn University Library; "History of the First Pursuit Group," p. 49, Gorrell's History of the American Expeditionary Forces Air Service, 1917–19, series C, vol. 9, Microfilm Publication M990, RG120, National Archives at College Park.

2. Stephen L. McFarland, *A Concise History of the U.S. Air Force* (Washington, D.C.: Air Force History and Museums Program, 1997), 4. Sam H. Frank, "Organizing the U.S. Air Service," pt. 3, "Training Activities in the United States," *Cross and Cockade* 6 (Winter 1965): 362–72, 363; Benjamin D. Foulois with C. V. Glines, *From the Wright Brothers to the Astronauts: The Memoirs of Major General Benjamin D. Foulois* (New York: McGraw-Hill, 1960), 150.

3. Bert M. Atkinson diary, 1911 to 1915, Atkinson Papers; Emile Gauvreau, "Bert M. Atkinson, Lt. Col. Aviation, U.S. Army," 5 December 1942, four-page biographical sketch, Atkinson Papers.

4. Charles de Forest Chandler and Frank P. Lahm, *How Our Army Grew Wings: Airmen and Aircraft before 1914* (New York: Ronald Press, 1943), 194n, 231n, 245–50.

5. Bernard C. Nalty, *Winged Shield, Winged Sword: A History of the United States Air Force,* vol. 1, *1907–1950* (Washington, D.C.: Air Force History and Museums Program, 1997), 30–31; Juliette A. Hennessey, *The United States Army Air Arm, April 1861 to April 1917* (Washington, D.C.: Office of Air Force History, 1985), 169–70; Foulois, *From the Wright Brothers to the Astronauts,* 118–37; Herbert Malloy Mason Jr., *The Great Pursuit: Pershing's Expedition to Destroy Pancho Villa* (New York: Smithmark, 1995), 103–09; John S. D. Eisenhower, *Intervention: The United States and the Mexican Revolution, 1913–1917* (New York: W. W. Norton, 1993), 239, 254–57, 262–63, 276.

6. Flight log for weeks ending 25 March and 8 April 1917, 3d Aero Squadron, Fort Sam Houston, Texas, in Michael Lobb, *A Brief History of Kelly Field, 1916–1918* (San Antonio, Texas: Kelly Air Force Base, Office of History, n.d.), 22, 24; Ann Krueger Hussey, Robert S. Browning III, Michael J. Obert, and Elizabeth A. Manning, *A Heritage of Service: Seventy-five Years of Military Aviation at Kelly Air Force Base, 1916–1991* (San Antonio, Texas: Kelly Air Force Base, Office of History, ca. 1991), 11; Henry David Kroll, *Kelly Field in the Great World War* (San Antonio, Texas: Press of San Antonio Printing, 1919), 24.

7. Edward V. Rickenbacker, *Fighting the Flying Circus,* ed. W. David Lewis (1919; reprint, Chicago: R. R. Donnelly and Sons, 1997), 30.

8. Philip J. Roosevelt to Capt. [Arthur R.] Brooks, 14 February 1921, Records of the 1st Pursuit

Group, file GP-HI (FTR), U.S. Air Force Historical Research Center, Maxwell Air Force Base, Montgomery, Alabama; Ministère de la Guerre, *Les Armées françaises dans la Grande Guerre,* vol. 6 (Paris, France: Imprimerie Nationale, 1931), 166; John H. Morrow Jr., *The Great War in the Air: Military Aviation from 1909 to 1921* (Washington, D.C.: Smithsonian Institution Press, 1993), 281.

9. Harold Buckley, *Squadron 95* (Paris, France: Obelisk Press, 1933), 28.

10. Philip J. Roosevelt to Walter Tufts Jr., for Harvard 1920 *Classbook,* Philip J. Roosevelt Papers, family collection of Philip J. Roosevelt II, Chappaqua, New York.

11. Ibid.

12. Philip Roosevelt obituary, *New York Times,* 9 November 1941, file CR-608000-01, National Air and Space Museum Archives; Ernest La Rue Jones, "Chronology of Military Aeronautics (1793–1948)," 1 August 1916, 28 August 1916, 3 May 1917, 19 July 1917, file 168.6501, U.S. Air Force Historical Research Agency (AFHRA), Maxwell Air Force Base, Montgomery, Alabama.

13. Roosevelt to Mother and Father, 11 January 1918, Roosevelt Papers.

14. Ibid.

15. "Training Section and Annexes," p. 41, Gorrell's History, series J, vol. 1; Lucien H. Thayer, *America's First Eagles: The Official History of the U.S. Air Service, A.E.F., 1917–1918,* ed. Donald Joseph McGhee and Roger James Bender (San Jose, California: R. James Bender Publishing, 1983), 115.

16. J. Gordon Rankin to Capt. Arthur R. Brooks, 13 February 1921, Records of the 1st Pursuit Group, file GP-HI (FTR), AFHRA.

17. Roosevelt to Brooks, 14 February 1921. The SPAD took its name from the French company that manufactured it, the Société Provisoire des Aéroplanes Deperdussin.

18. Ibid.

19. Roosevelt to Mother, 21 January 1918, Roosevelt Papers.

20. J. Gordon Rankin to Col. B. M. Atkinson, 15 January 1928, Atkinson Papers.

21. Philip F. Roosevelt to Mother, 31 January 1918, Roosevelt Papers.

22. First Pursuit Group diary, 16 February 1918; Roosevelt to Brooks, 14 February 1921, p. 3.

23. First Pursuit Group diary, 11 February 1918.

24. Buckley, *Squadron 95,* 22–25.

25. "History of the 95th Aero Squadron," Gorrell's History, series E, vol. 13, p. I-1.

26. Jones, "Chronology of Military Aeronautics," 19 July 1917.

27. Hennessey, *United States Army Air Arm,* 146.

28. Maj. William M. Mitchell, memorandum, Subject: Air Policy in France, 13 June 1917, Gorrell's History, series A, vol. 23; H. A. Jones, *The War in the Air: Being the Story of the Part Played in the Great War by the Royal Air Force,* vol. 4 (Oxford, England: Clarendon Press, 1934), 111n, 286–87; Tables of Organization for Units of the AEF Air Service, 15 January 1918, Gorrell's History, series A, vol. 12; Charles Christienne and Pierre Lissarague, *A History of French Military Aviation,* trans. Frances Kianka (Washington, D.C.: Smithsonian Institution Press, 1986), 123; Ministère de la Guerre, *Les Armées françaises,* 167.

29. I. B. Holley Jr., *Ideas and Weapons: Exploitation of the Aerial Weapon by the United States during World War I* (Washington, D.C.: Office of Air Force History, 1983), 47–48.

30. Jones, "Chronology of Military Aeronautics," 20 August 1917.

31. Bert M. Atkinson to Aunt Minnie, 15 October 1917, Atkinson Papers; Foulois, *From the Wright Brothers to the Astronauts,* 158.

32. "History of the 94th Aero Squadron," p. 2, Gorrell's History, series E, vol. 12; "History of the 95th Aero Squadron," p. 1; "History of the 96th Aero Squadron," p. 1, Gorrell's History, series E, vol. 14.

33. Buckley, *Squadron 95,* 25–26.

34. Frank W. Bailey, "The 103rd Aero USAS (Formerly Lafayette Escadrille)," *Cross and Cockade* 19 (Winter 1978): 289–343, 291; 1st Pursuit Group diary, 17 February 1918.

35. First Pursuit Group diary, 18–19 February 1918; "Daily Diary of First Fighter Group" (a compilation of the daily journals of the units assigned to the 1st Pursuit Group), 17 February 1918, file GP-I-HI (FTR), AFHRA.

36. Buckley, *Squadron 95*, 26.

37. James J. Sloan, *Wings of Honor: American Airmen in World War I* (Atglen, Pennsylvania: Schiffer Military History, 1994), 101–05; 1st Pursuit Group diary, 20 February 1918; Roosevelt to Mother, 19 February 1918, Roosevelt Papers.

38. Philip M. Flammer, *The Vivid Air: The Lafayette Escadrille* (Athens: University of Georgia Press, 1981), 22–23, 26–27.

39. James Norman Hall and Charles B. Nordhoff, *The Lafayette Flying Corps,* vol. 1 (Boston: Houghton Mifflin, 1920), 49.

40. Ibid., 334.

41. Herbert Molloy Mason Jr., *The Lafayette Escadrille* (New York: Random House, 1964), 295–96; Flammer, *Vivid Air,* 172.

42. First Pursuit Group diary, 22–23 January 1918; "History of the 95th Aero Squadron"; Mason, *Lafayette Escadrille,* 272–73.

43. First Pursuit Group diary, 24 January 1918; B. M. Atkinson, Maj., U.S.A., to Maj. Lufbery, 24 January [1918], Atkinson Papers.

44. Commanding Officer, 1st Pursuit Organization and Training Center, Zone of Advance, to Chief of Operations, Air Service, Zone of Advance, memorandum, Subject: Maj. R. Lufbery, 25 January 1918, Atkinson Papers. Foulois designated Col. Robert O. Van Horn as operations officer of the Air Service, with his office at Colombey-les-Belles (the concentration point for all the equipment to be issued to aero squadrons), but Pershing's chief of staff disapproved of this title, so it was changed to chief of the Advance Section, Zone of Advance. See Jones, "Chronology of Military Aeronautics," December 1917.

45. "Daily Diary of First Fighter Group," 10 February 1918.

46. Hall and Nordhoff, *Lafayette Flying Corps,* 335.

47. Hall and Nordhoff, *Lafayette Flying Corps,* 330; Arch Whitehouse, *Legion of the Lafayette* (New York: Doubleday, 1962), 261.

48. Hall and Nordhoff, *Lafayette Flying Corps,* 332; Flammer, *Vivid Air,* 16. *Chasse* is a French word meaning "hunt." It was often Anglicized by Americans and spelled "chase," as in pursuit.

49. Mason, *Lafayette Escadrille,* 275.

50. William Mitchell, *Memoirs of World War I* (New York: Random House, 1960), 135–36; Nalty, *Winged Shield,* 51.

51. Louis Galambos, "Technology, Political Economy, and Professionalization: Central Themes of the Organizational Synthesis," *Business History Review* 57 (Winter 1983): 487–92.

52. Allan R. Millett and Peter Maslowski, *For the Common Defense: A Military History of the United States of America* (New York: Free Press, 1984), 253; Peter Karsten, "Armed Progressives: The Military Reorganizes for the American Century," in *The Military in America: From the Colonial Era to the Present* (New York: Free Press, 1980), 251.

53. Roosevelt to Brooks, 14 February 1921, p. 3.

54. "History of the 95th Aero Squadron," p. I-2; Buckley, *Squadron 95,* 27.

55. "James Ely Miller: Miller Field," biographical file, National Air and Space Museum Archives; Henry Greenleaf Pearson, *A Business Man in Uniform: Raynal Cawthorne Bolling* (New

York: Duffield, 1923), 58, 66–70; Sloan, *Wings of Honor,* 106; Jones, "Chronology of Military Aeronautics," 22 June 1916.

56. Jones, "Chronology of Military Aeronautics," 2 June 1916; Hennessey, *United States Army Air Arm,* 167.

57. Jones, "Chronology of Military Aeronautics," 5 April 1916.

58. "Training Section and Annexes," p. 55; Lobb, *A Brief History of Kelly Field,* 22–24.

59. Hennessey, *United States Army Air Arm,* 177; Gen. Tooey Spaatz, interview by Brig. Gen. George W. Goddard, Interview 1925, 1 December 1967, file K239.0512-1925, U.S. Air Force Oral History Program, AFHRA; "Training Section and Annexes," pp. 7, 55.

60. Philip J. Roosevelt, speech at dedication of Miller Field, Staten Island, Roosevelt Papers.

61. First Pursuit Group diary, 20 February–8 March 1918; "Daily Diary of First Fighter Group," 8 March 1918.

62. Roosevelt, speech at dedication of Miller Field.

63. Ibid.

64. Frank P. Lahm, *The World War I Diary of Col. Frank P. Lahm, Air Service, A.E.F.,* ed. Albert F. Simpson (Montgomery, Alabama: Maxwell Air Force Base, Air University, Historical Research Division, 1970), 50; Thayer, *America's First Eagles,* 118; Rickenbacker, *Fighting the Flying Circus,* 28–29.

65. Philip Roosevelt to Mrs. Miller, 10 March 1918, Roosevelt Papers.

66. Bert M. Atkinson to Aunt Minnie, 6 February 1918, Atkinson Papers.

67. Bert M. Atkinson to Mrs. Gladys K. Miller, 12 March 1918, Atkinson Papers.

68. "Biographical Notes Pertaining to Major General Davenport Johnson," file K110.7004-85, AFHRA.

69. "Training Section and Annexes," pp. 7, 58; 1st Pursuit Group diary, 24 January 1918.

70. Diary of Joseph Houston Eastman, 19 December 1918, Joseph Houston Eastman Collection, Hoover Institution Archives, Stanford, California.

2. JIMMY MEISSNER AND THE FIRST TEAM

1. David Wright, *The Harley-Davidson Motor Company: An Official Eighty-Year History* (Osceola, Wisconsin: Motorbooks International, 1987), 52–55; James A. Meissner diary, 20 May 1917, in "[World War I] Diaries," Lafayette Collection, Wings Over the Rockies Air and Space Museum, Denver, Colorado; *Encyclopedia of American Business History and Biography,* vol. 4, *Iron and Steel in the Twentieth Century,* ed. Bruce E. Seely (New York: Facts on File Publications, ca. 1994), s.v. "Meissner, Carl."

2. Meissner diary, 26 April, 12 May 1917; Ernest La Rue Jones, "Chronology of Military Aeronautics (1793–1948)," 3 May 1917, file 168.6501, U.S. Air Force Historical Research Agency (AFHRA), Maxwell Air Force Base, Montgomery, Alabama; Henry Greenleaf Pearson, *A Business Man in Uniform: Raynal Cawthorne Bolling* (New York: Duffield, 1923), 109.

3. *Quentin Roosevelt: A Sketch with Letters,* ed. Kermit Roosevelt (New York: Charles Scribner's Sons, 1921), 31–33.

4. Hiram Bingham, *Explorer in the Air Service* (New Haven: Yale University Press, 1920), 18.

5. Ibid., 20–21, 27; Sam H. Frank, "Organizing the U.S. Air Service," pt. 3, "Training Activities in the United States," *Cross and Cockade* 6 (Winter 1965): 362–72, 364.

6. Meissner diary, 24–27 May 1917.

7. Bingham, *Explorer,* 47–51.

8. Meissner diary, 18 June–16 July 1917.

9. Juliette A. Hennessey, *The United States Army Air Arm, April 1861 to April 1917*

(Washington, D.C.: Office of Air Force History, 1985), 181; Pearson, *Business Man in Uniform*, 136; Lucien H. Thayer, *America's First Eagles: The Official History of the U.S. Air Service, A.E.F., 1917–1918*, ed. Donald Joseph McGhee and Roger James Bender (San Jose, California: R. James Bender Publishing, 1983), 41.

10. Bingham, *Explorer*, 78–79.

11. Ibid., 52–53; Waldo Heinrichs diary, 20 July 1917, in *First to the Front: The Aerial Adventures of 1st Lt. Waldo Heinrichs and the 95th Aero Squadron, 1917–1918*, ed. Charles Woolley (Atglen, Pennsylvania: Schiffer Military History, 1999).

12. Douglas A. Campbell, Interview 531, 8 July 1964, p. 3, file K239.0512-531, U.S. Air Force Oral History Program, AFHRA; Thayer, *America's First Eagles*, 41.

13. Roosevelt, *Quentin Roosevelt*, 1–3, 27, 30–34.

14. *New England Aviators* (Boston: Houghton Mifflin, 1919), 1:62; Hamilton Coolidge to Mother, 22 July 1917, in Hamilton Coolidge, *Letters of an American Airman* (Boston, 1919), 1–2; Bingham, *Explorer*, 10; Heinrichs diary, 24 July 1917, in Woolley, *First to the Front*.

15. John Davies, *The Legend of Hobey Baker* (Boston: Little, Brown, 1966), 67–91; Hennessey, *United States Army Air Arm*, 183–84; Jones, "Chronology of Military Aeronautics," 3 May 1917.

16. Heinrichs diary, 18–24 July 1917, in Woolley, *First to the Front*; Douglas Campbell, letter, 22 July 1917, in *Let's Go Where the Action Is! The Wartime Experiences of Douglas Campbell*, ed. Jack R. Eder (Knightstown, Indiana: JaaRE Publishing, 1984), 3.

17. Douglas Campbell, "Captain Douglas Campbell, 94th Aero Squadron," interview by A. J. Lynch, *Cross and Cockade* 6 (Spring 1965): 30.

18. Campbell, letter, 15 August 1917, in *Let's Go Where the Action Is!*, p. 8; Campbell, Interview 531, pp. 3–4; Meissner diary, 11–14 August 1917.

19. Meissner diary, 15 August 1917.

20. James J. Davilla and Arthur M. Soltan, *French Aircraft of the First World War* (Stratford, Connecticut: Flying Machine Press, 1997), 142.

21. Bingham, *Explorer*, 84; Heinrichs diary, 16 August 1917, in Woolley, *First to the Front*.

22. Davilla and Soltan, *French Aircraft of the First World War*, 144.

23. George Clark Moseley, *Extracts from the Letters of George Clark Moseley during the Period of the Great War* (Chicago, ca. 1923), 64–66, 73.

24. Meissner diary, 23 September 1917; Moseley, *Extracts*, 80–81; Heinrichs diary, 24 September 1917, in Woolley, *First to the Front*. Altitudes are converted from meters to feet and rounded to the nearest fifty feet.

25. James J. Hudson, *Hostile Skies: A Combat History of the American Air Service in World War I* (Syracuse: Syracuse University Press, 1968), 29.

26. Meissner diary, 23 September, 1917; Heinrichs diary, 24 September 1917, in Woolley, *First to the Front*.

27. Heinrichs diary, 3 October 1917, in Woolley, *First to the Front*; Meissner diary, 1–2 October 1917.

28. Douglas Campbell, *Let's Go Where the Action Is!*, 23.

29. Percival T. Gates, diary entry, 30 June 1918, in *An American Pilot in the Skies of France: The Diaries and Letters of Lt. Percival T. Gates, 1917–1918*, ed. David K. Vaughan (Dayton, Ohio: Wright State University Press, 1992), 63.

30. Heinrichs diary, 12 October 1917, in Woolley, *First to the Front*.

31. Meissner diary, 15 October 1917; Bingham, *Explorer*, 141; Davilla and Soltan, *French Aircraft of the First World War*, 355–56, 416.

32. Heinrichs diary, 26 October 1917, in Woolley, *First to the Front*.

33. Meissner diary, 15 to 26 October 1917, 25 October 1917.

34. Bingham, *Explorer,* 117; "Training Section and Annexes," p. 53, Gorrell's History of the American Expeditionary Forces Air Service, 1917–19, series J, vol. 1, Microfilm Publication M990, RG120, National Archives at College Park.

35. James J. Cooke, *The U.S. Air Service in the Great War, 1917–1919* (Westport, Connecticut: Praeger, 1996), 19–20; Maj. Douglas A. Galipeau, "Issoudun: The Making of America's First Eagles," p. 29, Research Paper, Air Command and Staff College, March 1997, Maxwell Air Force Base, Montgomery, Alabama.

36. Campbell, Interview 531, pp. 4–5; Bingham, *Explorer,* 127–28; John E. Tynan, "U.S. Air Service: Emerging from Its Cradle," *Airpower Historian* 10 (July 1963): 87.

37. Meissner diary, 27 October 1917; "Training Section and Annexes," pp. 53, 64.

38. Reed M. Chambers, interview by Kenneth Leish, October 1960, pp. 18–19, file K146.34-26, Oral History Research Office, Butler Library, Columbia University.

39. Q. Roosevelt, letter, 7 September 1917, in Roosevelt, *Quentin Roosevelt,* 58; Meissner diary, 4 November 1917.

40. Campbell, letter, 10 October 1917, in *Let's Go Where the Action Is!,* 21.

41. Meissner diary, 4–6 November 1917.

42. Gates, *An American Pilot in the Skies of France,* 61.

43. Meissner diary, 6–12 November 1917.

44. Bingham, *Explorer,* 143–44.

45. Meissner diary, 13–19 November 1917.

46. E. V. Rickenbacker, interview by Donald Shaughnessy, 20 February 1960, p. 4, file K146.34-88, AFHRA.

47. W. David Lewis, Historical Introduction to Edward V. Rickenbacker, *Fighting the Flying Circus,* ed. W. David Lewis (1919; reprint, Chicago: R. R. Donnelley and Sons, 1997), xxiii–xxx, xl–xli.

48. Rickenbacker, interview, pp. 1–2.

49. Meissner diary, 4 December 1917.

50. Chambers, interview, pp. 21–23.

51. Meissner diary, 1–6 December 1917.

52. Bingham, *Explorer,* 145–50; Meissner diary, 11 December 1917.

53. Leroy Prinz, interview by Kenneth Leish, July 1960, p. 10, file K146.34-82, AFHRA.

54. Edwin C. Parsons, *I Flew with the Lafayette Escadrille* (Indianapolis: E. C. Seale, 1963), 67.

55. Meissner diary, 11–12 December 1917.

56. Q. Roosevelt, 27 January, letter, in Roosevelt, *Quentin Roosevelt,* 108.

57. Meissner diary, 15 December 1917–8 January 1918.

58. "Training Section and Annexes," p. 57.

59. Ibid., 33; Meissner diary, 1–31 January 1917.

60. Campbell, letter, 15 August 1917, in *Let's Go Where the Action Is!,* 9.

61. Galipeau, "Issoudun: The Making of America's First Eagles," p. 29.

62. Meissner diary, 1–18 February 1917.

63. Ibid., 19–20 February 1917.

3. ORGANIZATIONAL TRAINING

1. James A. Meissner diary, 20–27 February 1918, in "[World War I] Diaries," Lafayette Collection, Wings Over the Rockies Air and Space Museum, Denver, Colorado; Eddie Rickenbacker diary, 2

March 1918, Lafayette Collection; 1st Pursuit Group diary, 26–27 February, 1918, Bert M. Atkinson Papers, Auburn University Library.

2. Charles Christienne and Pierre Lissarague, *A History of French Military Aviation,* trans. Frances Kianka (Washington, D.C.: Smithsonian Institution Press, 1986), 40–41.

3. Bert L. Frandsen and W. David Lewis, "Nieuports and Spads: French Pursuit Planes and American Airpower in World War I," *History of Technology* 21 (1999): 189–202; James J. Davilla and Arthur M. Soltan, *French Aircraft of the First World War* (Stratford, Connecticut: Flying Machine Press, 1997), 349–420.

4. Lionel S. Marks, *The Airplane Engine* (New York: McGraw-Hill, 1922), 176–79; Robert F. Zilinsky, "Rotaries," *Cross and Cockade* 14 (Winter 1973): 348–53; Lee Kennett, *The First Air War, 1914–1918* (New York: Macmillan, 1991), 103–04.

5. Gene DeMarco, "Flying the Nieuport 11," *World War I Aero* 171 (February 2001): 44.

6. R. C. Bolling to Chief Signal Officer of the Army, Washington, D.C., memorandum, Subject: Report of Aeronautical Commission, 15 August, 1917, p. 5, Gorrell's History of the American Expeditionary Forces Air Service, Microfilm Publication M990, 1917–19, series A, vol. 16, RG120, National Archives at College Park (NACP).

7. R. C. Bolling, Headquarters, A.E.F., Paris, France, to Chief Signal Officer, Cable 96-S, Washington, D.C., 12 August 1917, Gorrell's History, series A, vol. 17, p. 174.

8. "Agreement of French Government dated Aug. 30, 1917," p. 5, Gorrell's History, series I, vol. 28; Lucien H. Thayer, *America's First Eagles: The Official History of the U.S. Air Service, A.E.F., 1917–1918,* ed. Donald Joseph McGhee and Roger James Bender (San Jose, California: R. James Bender Publishing, 1983), 18–20.

9. General Ragueneau to Chief of Air Service, A.E.F., 30 November 1917, ID 657, box 34, RG120, NACP; The Under-Secretary of State for Military Aeronautics to Col. R. C. Bolling, Paris, 16 December 1917, series E 633, box 576E, RG120, NACP.

10. First Pursuit Group diary, 13 February 1918, Bert M. Atkinson Papers, Auburn University Library.

11. Benjamin Foulois, Chief of Air Service, to Commander-in-Chief, 14 February 1918, file 452.1, RG120, NACP.

12. "History of the Airplane Division," p. 14, Technical Section, AEF Air Service, 29 November 1918, Gorrell's History, series A, vol. 16.

13. H. A. Toulmin, *Air Service American Expeditionary Force 1918* (New York: D. Van Nostrand, 1927), 75–76.

14. First Pursuit Group diary, 21–25 February 1918.

15. Assistant Chief of Air Service (Operations Dept.) to Chief of Supply, 28 February 1918, file 452.1, RG120, NACP.

16. J. Gordon Rankin to Capt. Arthur R. Brooks, 13 February 1921, Records of the 1st Pursuit Group, file GP-HI (FTR), U.S. Air Force Historical Research Agency (AFHRA), Maxwell Air Force Base, Montgomery, Alabama.

17. Philip J. Roosevelt to Capt. [Arthur R.] Brooks, 14 February 1921, p. 3, Records of the 1st Pursuit Group, file GP-HI (FTR), AFHRA.

18. First Pursuit Group diary, 6 March 1918; Rickenbacker diary, 6 March 1918.

19. Meissner diary, 7 March 1918.

20. Roosevelt to Brooks, 14 February 1921, p. 4.

21. First Pursuit Group diary, 14 March 1918; Waldo Heinrichs diary, 14 March 1918, in *First to the Front: The Aerial Adventures of 1st Lt. Waldo Heinrichs and the 95th Aero Squadron, 1917–1918,* ed. Charles Woolley (Atglen, Pennsylvania: Schiffer Military History, 1999).

22. Richard A. Blodgett to Mrs. Mabel F. Blodgett, 18 March 1918, in Woolley, *First to the Front,* 74.

23. First Pursuit Group diary, 15 March 1918.

24. Rickenbacker diary, 18 March 1918.

25. Rankin to Brooks, 13 February 1921.

26. Harold Buckley, *Squadron 95* (Paris, France: Obelisk Press, 1933), 33–34; Roosevelt to Brooks, 14 February 1921, p. 4.

27. Q. Roosevelt, letter, 29 March 1918, in *Quentin Roosevelt: A Sketch with Letters,* ed. Kermit Roosevelt (New York: Charles Scribner's Sons, 1921), 131–32.

28. Heinrichs diary, 15 March 1918, in Woolley, *First to the Front.*

29. Ibid.

30. Blodgett to Blodgett, 18 March 1918.

31. Meissner diary, 13–17 March 1918; Heinrichs diary, 18 March 1918, in Woolley, *First to the Front;* Rickenbacker diary, 20 March 1918.

32. Roosevelt to Brooks, 14 February 1921, p. 4.

33. Ibid.

34. [B. M. Atkinson], 1st Pursuit Organization Center, to Col. J. E. Carberry, 16 March 1918, Atkinson Papers, Auburn University Library. The account and quotations given in the three paragraphs that follow are also from this letter.

35. *The U.S. Air Service in World War I,* ed. Mauer Mauer (Washington, D.C.: Office of Air Force History, 1978), 1:283.

36. Heinrichs diary, 20 March 1918, in Woolley, *First to the Front.*

37. "History of the 95th Aero Squadron," Gorrell's History, series E, vol. 13, p. I-3; Heinrichs diary, 19 March 1918, in Woolley, *First to the Front.*

38. Buckley, *Squadron 95, 36.*

39. Henry Lyster, memorandum, 6 March 1918, Atkinson Papers; "Daily Diary of First Fighter Group," 7 March 1918, file GP-I-HI (FTR), AFHRA; James Norman Hall and Charles B. Nordhoff, *The Lafayette Flying Corps,* vol. 1 (Boston: Houghton Mifflin, 1920), 320, 449.

40. Hall and Nordhoff, *Lafayette Flying Corps,* 281.

41. Reed M. Chambers, interview by Kenneth Leish, October 1960, p. 33, file K146.34-26, Oral History Research Office, Butler Library, Columbia University; James J. Sloan, *Wings of Honor: American Airmen in World War I* (Atglen, Pennsylvania: Schiffer Military History, 1994), 114.

42. "History of the 94th Aero Squadron," p. 2, Gorrell's History, series E, vol. 12.

43. Ibid.; "Daily Diary of First Fighter Group," 7 March 1918; 1st Pursuit Group diary, 27 March 1918; Rickenbacker diary, 27 March 1918.

44. Rickenbacker diary, 18–28 March 1918.

45. Campbell, letter, 28 March 1918, in *Let's Go Where the Action Is! The Wartime Experiences of Douglas Campbell,* ed. Jack R. Eder (Knightstown, Indiana: JaaRE Publishing, 1984), 50.

46. Thayer, *America's First Eagles,* 90–99.

47. Sloan, *Wings of Honor,* 146–47; William Mitchell, *Memoirs of World War I* (New York: Random House, 1960), 184.

48. Office of Advance Section, Zone of Advance, unsigned typed memorandum, 21 March 1918, Frank Purdy Lahm Papers, file 167.601-3, AFHRA.

49. "History of Personnel Section. Assistant Chief of Air Services, Zone of Advance. Headquarters, First Air Depot," Gorrell's History, series A, vol. 8, p. 1; Dennis Gordon, *The Lafayette Flying Corps: The American Volunteers in the French Air Service in World War One* (Atglen, Pennsylvania: Schiffer Military History, 2000), 285–88; Hall and Nordhoff, *Lafayette Flying Corps,* 325–27.

50. First Pursuit Group diary, 26 March 1918.

51. B. M. Atkinson to Assistant Chief of Air Service, Zone of Advance, memorandum, Subject: Organizational Training for Pursuit Units, 6 April 1918, Lahm Papers, file 167.601-3. The material in the following four paragraphs is from this source.

52. Juliette A. Hennessey, *The United States Army Air Arm, April 1861 to April 1917* (Washington, D.C.: Office of Air Force History, 1985), 167; Frank P. Lahm, *The World War I Diary of Col. Frank P. Lahm, Air Service, A.E.F.,* ed. Albert F. Simpson (Montgomery, Alabama: Maxwell Air Force Base, Air University, Historical Research Division, 1970), 228.

53. Frank W. Bailey and Richard Duiven, "L'Escadrille de Chasse, SPA 95," *Cross and Cockade* 19 (Spring 1978): 75.

54. Atkinson to Assistant Chief of Air Service, Zone of Advance, memorandum, Subject: Organizational Training for Pursuit Units, 6 April 1918. The material in the following three paragraphs is from this source.

55. Roosevelt to Brooks, 14 February 1921, p. 3.

56. Q. Roosevelt, letter, 16 February 1918, in Roosevelt, *Quentin Roosevelt,* 113–14.

57. Carl von Clausewitz, *On War,* ed. and trans. Michael Howard and Peter Paret (Princeton: Princeton University Press, 1976), 89.

4. FIRST VICTORIES

1. B. H. Liddell Hart, *The Real War, 1914–1918* (Boston: Little, Brown, 1930), 387.

2. Henry Greenleaf Pearson, *A Business Man in Uniform: Raynal Cawthorne Bolling* (New York: Duffield, 1923), 198–201.

3. P. Roosevelt to Father, 4 April 1918, Philip J. Roosevelt Papers, family collection of Philip J. Roosevelt II, Chappaqua, New York; Charles Christienne and Pierre Lissarague, *A History of French Military Aviation,* trans. Frances Kianka (Washington, D.C.: Smithsonian Institution Press, 1986), 125; John H. Morrow Jr., *The Great War in the Air: Military Aviation from 1909 to 1921* (Washington, D.C.: Smithsonian Institution Press, 1993), 283, 297, 311.

4. First Pursuit Group diary, 27–31 March 1918, Bert M. Atkinson Papers, Auburn University Library; James A. Meissner diary, 30 March 1918, in "[World War I] Diaries," Lafayette Collection, Wings Over the Rockies Air and Space Museum, Denver, Colorado.

5. P. Roosevelt to Mother, 3 April 1918, Roosevelt Papers; Campbell, letter, 6 April 1918, in *Let's Go Where the Action Is! The Wartime Experiences of Douglas Campbell,* ed. Jack R. Eder (Knightstown, Indiana: JaaRE Publishing, 1984), 52; 1st Pursuit Group diary, 31 March 1918; B. M. Atkinson to Assistant Chief of Air Service, Zone of Advance, 6 April 1918, series E 633, box 569, RG120, National Archives at College Park (NACP).

6. Reed M. Chambers, interview by Kenneth Leish, October 1960, p. 26, file K146.34-26, Oral History Research Office, Butler Library, Columbia University; "Daily Diary of First Fighter Group," 1 April 1918, file GP-I-HI (FTR), U.S. Air Force Historical Research Agency (AFHRA), Maxwell Air Force Base, Montgomery, Alabama.

7. Edward V. Rickenbacker, *Fighting the Flying Circus,* ed. W. David Lewis (1919; reprint, Chicago: R. R. Donnelley and Sons, 1997), 31–32; 1st Pursuit Group diary, 2 April 1918.

8. First Pursuit Group diary, 31 March 1918.

9. "Daily Diary of First Fighter Group," 27 March 1918.

10. Dennis Gordon, *The Lafayette Flying Corps: The American Volunteers in the French Air Service in World War One* (Atglen, Pennsylvania: Schiffer Military History, 2000), 193–97; James Norman Hall and Charles B. Nordhoff, *The Lafayette Flying Corps,* vol. 1 (Boston: Houghton Mifflin, 1920), 258. Also see Hall's autobiography, *My Island Home* (Boston: Little, Brown, 1952).

11. Gordon, *Lafayette Flying Corps,* 355–57; Hall and Nordhoff, *Lafayette Flying Corps,* 383–84.

12. Gordon, *Lafayette Flying Corps,* 316–18; Hall and Nordhoff, *Lafayette Flying Corps,* 353–54.

13. Rickenbacker, *Fighting the Flying Circus,* 31.

14. Ibid., 32–33; Eddie Rickenbacker diary, 2–11 April 1918, Lafayette Collection.

15. Rickenbacker diary, 11 April 1918.

16. James J. Sloan, *Wings of Honor: American Airmen in World War I* (Atglen, Pennsylvania: Schiffer Military History, 1994), 89; Rickenbacker diary, 4 April 1918.

17. Lee Kennett, *The First Air War, 1914–1918* (New York: Macmillan, 1991), 140–42.

18. Chambers, interview, 29.

19. Ibid., 1–17.

20. Leroy Prinz, interview by Kenneth Leish, July 1960, pp. 1–3, 28–29, file K146.34-82, AFHRA.

21. "Daily Diary of First Fighter Group," 20 March, 10 April 1918; "History of the 94th Aero Squadron," p. 3, Gorrell's History of the American Expeditionary Forces Air Service, 1917–19, series E, vol. 12, Microfilm Publication M990, RG120, NACP; "History of the Squadron Insignia," 1st Pursuit Group History, series 767D, NACP; Rickenbacker, *Fighting the Flying Circus,* 36; Jon Guttman, Allan D. Toelle, Howard Fisher, and Greg Van Wyngarden, "94th Aero Squadron 'Hats in the Ring,'" pt. 1, "Nieuports at Toul," *Over the Front* 6 (Summer 1991): 157.

22. The National Air and Space Museum restored a Nieuport 28 with Meissner's markings, to be displayed at the new museum at Dulles International Airport.

23. Guttman and others, "94th Aero Squadron 'Hats in the Ring,'" 158–63; information on Rickenbacker's medallion from W. David Lewis, personal correspondence, ca. 1 March 2001.

24. Diary of Joseph Houston Eastman [ca. 13 May 1918], Joseph Houston Eastman Collection, Hoover Institution Archives, Stanford, California.

25. Alan Winslow, "No Parachutes," *Liberty* 10 (4 March 1933): 22.

26. Meissner diary, 5 April 1918.

27. Philip J. Roosevelt to Capt. [Arthur R.] Brooks, 14 February 1921, p. 5, Records of the 1st Pursuit Group, file GP-HI (FTR), U.S. Air Force Historical Research Center, Maxwell Air Force Base, Montgomery, Alabama.

28. P. Roosevelt to Father, 13 April 1918, Roosevelt Papers; William E. Roosevelt to P. J. Roosevelt, 30 April 1918, Roosevelt Papers.

29. Campbell, letter, 6 April 1918, in *Let's Go Where the Action Is!,* 53.

30. Rickenbacker diary, 5 April 1918.

31. James S. Alford, "History of the 1st Pursuit Group," vol. 1, "The 1st Pursuit Group in World War I," unpublished manuscript, 1959, file GP-1-HI, AFHRA.

32. John J. Pershing, *Final Report of Gen. John J. Pershing, Commander-in-Chief, American Expeditionary Forces* (Washington, D.C.: Government Printing Office, 1920), 9–10; James G. Harbord, *The American Army in France, 1917–1919* (Boston: Little, Brown, 1936), 309.

33. Hunter Liggett, *Commanding an American Army: Recollections of the World War* (Boston: Houghton Mifflin, 1925), 21–24; Frank P. Lahm, *The World War I Diary of Col. Frank P. Lahm, Air Service, A.E.F.,* ed. Albert F. Simpson (Montgomery, Alabama: Maxwell Air Force Base, Air University, Historical Research Division, 1970), 56; Edward M. Coffman, *The War to End All Wars* (Madison: University of Wisconsin Press, 1986), 155.

34. Lahm, *World War I Diary,* x, xiv, 56–57.

35. First Pursuit Group diary, 7 April 1918.

36. First Pursuit Group diary, 8 April 1918; Campbell, letter, 13 April 1918, in *Let's Go Where the Action Is!,* 54; Van Horn to Chief Air Service, telegram, 21 April 1918, series E 633, box 569, RG120, NACP.

37. Liggett, *Commanding an American Army,* 21–24.

38. James J. Cooke, *Billy Mitchell* (Boulder, Colorado: Lynne Rienner Publishers, 2002), 51–65.

39. William Mitchell, *Memoirs of World War I* (New York: Random House, 1960), 165–66.

40. Benjamin D. Foulois with C. V. Glines, *From the Wright Brothers to the Astronauts: The Memoirs of Major General Benjamin D. Foulois* (New York: McGraw-Hill, 1960), 160–62.

41. Mitchell, *Memoirs,* 179.

42. Lahm, *World War I Diary,* 46.

43. "Tactical Distribution of Air Service Units," chart, Gorrell's History, series A, vol. 23.

44. Mitchell, *Memoirs,* 190–91.

45. Rickenbacker and Meissner diaries, 12 April 1918.

46. Ninety-fourth Aero Squadron, Operations Report, 12 April 1918, Gorrell's History, series E, vol. 12, p. 174.

47. Lahm, *World War I Diary,* 59.

48. *The U.S. Air Service in World War I,* ed. Mauer Mauer (Washington, D.C.: Office of Air Force History, 1978), 1:284–86.

49. Campbell, letter, 15 April 1918, in *Let's Go Where the Action Is!,* 55.

50. Rickenbacker, *Fighting the Flying Circus,* 37.

51. Rickenbacker, untitled transcription of the events of 14 April 1918, Edward V. Rickenbacker Papers, box 91, Library of Congress.

52. Ibid.

53. Chambers, interview, p. 27.

54. Ibid., 28; Rickenbacker, *Fighting the Flying Circus,* 38–44.

55. Winslow, "No Parachutes" (4 March 1933): 18.

56. Alan Winslow, "No Parachutes," *Liberty* 10 (25 February 1933): 11.

57. Winslow, "No Parachutes" (4 March 1933): 18, 22–25.

58. Campbell, letter, 15 April 1918, in *Let's Go Where the Action Is!,* 55–58; Rickenbacker, *Fighting the Flying Circus,* 444–45; Mitchell, *Memoirs,* 190–92; Theodore Hamady, "The First Victory," *Air Force* 71 (April 1988): 68–73.

59. Advance Section, Zone of Advance, Headquarters, General Order 17, 24 April 1918, series E 633, box 569, RG120, NACP.

60. Winslow, "No Parachutes" (4 March 1933): 25.

61. Mitchell, *Memoirs,* 190–91.

62. Rickenbacker, *Fighting the Flying Circus,* 48–59; Rickenbacker diary, 23–29 April 1918.

63. Waldo Heinrichs diary, 2 May 1918, in *First to the Front: The Aerial Adventures of 1st Lt. Waldo Heinrichs and the 95th Aero Squadron, 1917–1918,* ed. Charles Woolley (Atglen, Pennsylvania: Schiffer Military History, 1999); Richard A. Blodgett to Mrs. Mabel F. Blodgett, 18 March 1918, in Woolley, *First to the Front,* 87.

64. Lucien H. Thayer, *America's First Eagles: The Official History of the U.S. Air Service, A.E.F., 1917–1918,* ed. Donald Joseph McGhee and Roger James Bender (San Jose, California: R. James Bender Publishing, 1983), 100.

65. Roosevelt to Brooks, 14 February 1921, pp. 5–6.

66. First Pursuit Group diary, 3–4 May 1918.

5. WINGS

1. James A. Meissner diary, 1 March and 14 March 1918, in "[World War I] Diaries," Lafayette Collection, Wings Over the Rockies Air and Space Museum, Denver, Colorado.

2. Waldo Heinrichs diary, 14 March 1918, in *First to the Front: The Aerial Adventures of 1st Lt.*

Waldo Heinrichs and the 95th Aero Squadron, 1917–1918, ed. Charles Woolley (Atglen, Pennsylvania: Schiffer Military History, 1999); Edward V. Rickenbacker, *Fighting the Flying Circus,* ed. W. David Lewis (1919; reprint, Chicago: R. R. Donnelley and Sons, 1997), 51.

3. Winslow to Mother and Father, n.d., letter in 94th Aero Squadron World War I file, file 8097, Military History Institute, Carlisle Barracks, Pennsylvania.

4. Mitchell to Chief of Air Service, telegram, 1 May 1918, RG120, National Archives at College Park (NACP).

5. Richard Hallion, *Rise of the Fighter Aircraft, 1914–1918* (Baltimore: Nautical and Aviation Publishing, 1984), iii–iv, 115.

6. Mason Patrick, memorandum for Chief of Staff, 12 July 1918, series D 657, box 34, RG120, NACP.

7. William Mitchell, *Memoirs of World War I* (New York: Random House, 1960), 173.

8. Ibid., 181.

9. Ninety-fourth Aero Squadron Alert Log, National Air and Space Museum Archives, file 1247, p. 216.

10. Mitchell, *Memoirs,* 197.

11. J. Gordon Rankin to Capt. Arthur R. Brooks, 13 February 1921, Records of the 1st Pursuit Group, file GP-HI (FTR), U.S. Air Force Historical Research Agency (AFHRA), Maxwell Air Force Base, Montgomery, Alabama.

12. Lucien H. Thayer, *America's First Eagles: The Official History of the U.S. Air Service, A.E.F., 1917–1918,* ed. Donald Joseph McGhee and Roger James Bender (San Jose, California: R. James Bender Publishing, 1983), 77.

13. The account that follows is taken from James Meissner, "Some New Experiences," pp. 1–3, n.d., Meissner file, Lafayette Collection.

14. Meissner diary, 2 May 1918.

15. Gustav Bock, "Air Fights and Air Battles between the Meuse and the Moselle," trans. Paul Nami, *Cross and Cockade* 24 (Spring 1983): 116–17.

16. Rickenbacker, *Fighting the Flying Circus,* 38–40; R. L. Cavanagh, "The 94th and Its Nieuports: 15 April–11 June 1918," *Cross and Cockade* 21 (Autumn 1980): 203–04.

17. Meissner diary, 2 May 1918.

18. Meissner, "Some New Experiences," pp. 2–3.

19. James Norman Hall, *High Adventure: A Narrative of Air Fighting in France* (New York: Houghton Mifflin, 1929), 234–35; Paul L. Briand Jr., "A Fateful Tuesday, 1918: The Last Combat Flight of James Norman Hall," *Airpower Historian* 11 (April 1964): 34–38.

20. Eddie Rickenbacker diary, 17 May 1918, Lafayette Collection.

21. Rickenbacker, *Fighting the Flying Circus,* 62–63.

22. Bert M. Atkinson, "Time: May 19, 1918; Place: Gengoult Airdrome, Toul, France," p. 1, undated essay, Bert M. Atkinson Papers, Auburn University Library.

23. Ibid., 2; 94th Aero Squadron, Operations Report, 19 May 1918, Gorrell's History of the American Expeditionary Forces Air Service, Microfilm Publication M990, 1917–19, series E, vol. 12, RG120, NACP; Combat Report of Lt. Gude, 19 May 1918, "94th Aero Squadron Combat Reports," Gorrell's History, series E, vol. 12; Mitchell, *Memoirs,* 199.

24. Rickenbacker, *Fighting the Flying Circus,* 117–18.

25. Atkinson, "Time: May 19, 1918," p. 2.

26. Mitchell, *Memoirs,* 200–01.

27. Ibid.

28. Rickenbacker, *Fighting the Flying Circus,* 119.

29. Royal D. Frey, "A.E.F. Combat Airfields and Monuments in France, WWI," *American Aviation Historical Society* 17 (3d quarter 1972): 196.

30. Rickenbacker, *Fighting the Flying Circus*, 119.

31. "History of the 94th Aero Squadron," Gorrell's History, series E, vol. 12.

32. Atkinson, "Time: May 19, 1918," p. 3; B. M. Atkinson, "Casualties of 1st Pursuit Group," 10 June 1918, series 657, RG120, NACP.

33. Alan Winslow, "No Parachutes," *Liberty* 10 (11 March 1933): 27, and *Liberty* 11 (18 March 1933): 39.

34. Meissner diary, 19 May 1918.

35. Heinrichs diary, 19 May 1918, in Woolley, *First to the Front*.

36. Harold Buckley, *Squadron 95* (Paris, France: Obelisk Press, 1933), 62.

37. Meissner diary, 3 June 1918.

38. Philip J. Roosevelt, "Thing Called Courage," *Colliers* (29 January 1921): 20.

39. Meissner diary, 30 May 1918.

40. Combat Report of Lt. Rickenbacker, 30 May 1918, "94th Aero Squadron Combat Reports," Gorrell's History, series E, vol. 12; Rickenbacker, *Fighting the Flying Circus*, 136.

41. [Royal Frey], "The Nieuport Described," *Cross and Cockade* 12 (Summer 1971), 117; Rickenbacker, *Fighting the Flying Circus*, 142.

42. Capitaine Du Doré, de la Section Aéronautique de la Mission Français, prés l'Armée Américaine, "Rapport," 965/00, le 8 Juin 1918, file 1559, RG120, NACP.

43. Theodore Hamady, "Destined to Fail: The Nieuport 28 Wing," *Air Power History* 46 (Winter 1999): 14.

44. Atkinson, "Casualties of 1st Pursuit Group," 10 June 1918.

45. Thayer, *America's First Eagles*, 130.

46. Du Doré, "Rapport."

47. B. M. Atkinson to C.A.S. [Foulois], 1st Army, 9 June 1918, file 1559, RG120, NACP. The account given in the following three paragraphs is from this source.

48. Rickenbacker frequently flew Huffer's airplane. See Cavanagh, "The 94th and Its Nieuports," 207.

49. J. W. F. M. Huffer to Chief Air Service, 1st Army, American E.F., memorandum, Subject: Report of Nieuport "28" Planes, 10 June 1918, file 1559, RG120, National Archives at College Park.

50. Buckley, *Squadron 95*, 71.

51. Diary of Joseph Houston Eastman, 17 May 1918, Joseph Houston Eastman Collection, Hoover Institution Archives, Stanford, California.

52. H. A. Toulmin, *Air Service American Expeditionary Force, 1918* (New York: D. Van Nostrand, 1927), 79.

53. Philip Roosevelt to Father, 8 July 1918, Philip J. Roosevelt Papers, family collection of Philip J. Roosevelt II, Chappaqua, New York; Frank P. Lahm, *The World War I Diary of Col. Frank P. Lahm, Air Service, A.E.F.*, ed. Albert F. Simpson (Montgomery, Alabama: Maxwell Air Force Base, Air University, Historical Research Division, 1970), 79–80.

54. Benjamin D. Foulois with C. V. Glines, *From the Wright Brothers to the Astronauts: The Memoirs of Major General Benjamin D. Foulois* (New York: McGraw-Hill, 1960), 172.

55. Lahm, *World War I Diary*, 83.

56. Foulois, *From the Wright Brothers to the Astronauts*, 173; B. D. Foulois, "The Air Service American Expeditionary Forces, 1917–1918," Enclosure D, pp. 14–17, Benjamin D. Foulois Papers, U.S. Air Force Academy Library Special Collections.

57. Heinrichs diary, 3 June 1918, in Woolley, *First to the Front*.

58. B. D. Foulois to C.A.S., AEF, 12 June 1918, memorandum, Subj: Report and Recommendations on Nieuport, Type 28 Aeroplanes, file 1559, entry 657, RG120, NACP.

59. Chief of Air Service, 1st Army, to Commander-in-Chief, American Expeditionary Forces, 4 June 1918, in Foulois, "The Air Service American Expeditionary Forces, 1917–1918," Enclosure D, p. 14.

60. Rickenbacker diary, 4 June 1918; 1st Pursuit Group diary, 4 June 1918, Atkinson Papers.

61. "History of the 94th Aero Squadron," p. 4; 1st Pursuit Group diary, 4 June 1918.

62. Mitchell, *Memoirs,* 192–93.

63. Eastman diary, 22 May 1918.

64. James J. Parks, "David Lewis' Wartime Experiences," pt. 4, "Escadrille SPA 79," *Cross and Cockade* 25 (Winter 1984): 342–43.

65. John Shy, "First Battles in Retrospect," in *America's First Battles, 1776–1965,* ed. Charles E. Heller and William A. Stofft (Lawrence: University of Kansas Press, 1986), 327–53.

66. Buckley, *Squadron 95,* 78.

67. James Norman Hall and Charles B. Nordhoff, *The Lafayette Flying Corps,* vol. 1 (Boston: Houghton Mifflin, 1920), 280–81.

68. John Satterfield to Maj. [Bert] Atkinson, 1 June 1918, Atkinson Papers.

69. Col. Cedric E. Fauntleroy, Interview 540, conducted at the request of *Cross and Cockade,* 3 June 1962, file K239.0512-40, U.S. Air Force Oral History Program, AFHRA.

70. Satterfield to Atkinson, 1 June 1918.

6. THE CLASH OF CULTURES

1. William E. Chajkowsky, *Royal Flying Corps: Borden to Texas to Beamsville* (Ontario, Canada: Boston Mills Press, 1979), 52; H. A. Jones, *The War in the Air: Being the Story of the Part Played in the Great War by the Royal Air Force,* vol. 5 (Oxford, England: Clarendon Press, 1935), 461–66.

2. "History of the 27th Aero Squadron," p. 1, Records of the 1st Pursuit Group, file 314.7, RG18, National Archives at College Park (NACP); Walter S. Williams diary, May–June 1917, Walter S. William Papers, U.S. Air Force Academy Library Special Collections.

3. Williams diary, 24 June–3 July 1917; Walter S. Williams, "Biography," pp. 2–3, Williams Papers.

4. Chajkowsky, *Royal Flying Corps,* 45; Williams diary, "Incidents of Canada."

5. Williams diary, "Incidents of Canada."

6. Frederick I. Ordway, "A New Hampshire Pursuit Pilot," interview by John H. Tegler, *Cross and Cockade* 4 (Autumn 1963): 217–19.

7. Richard Hallion, *Rise of the Fighter Aircraft, 1914–1918* (Baltimore: Nautical and Aviation Publishing, 1984), 33, 46.

8. Harold Hartney, *Up and At 'Em* (Garden City, New York: Doubleday, 1971), 2, 41, 59, 71, 79, 87; Norman Franks, *Who Downed the Aces in WW1?* (London: Grub Street, 1996), 18–19.

9. The five American squadrons that actually trained in Canada were the 17th, the 22d, the 28th, the 139th, and the 147th. See Chajkowsky, *Royal Flying Corps,* 54.

10. Ordway, "A New Hampshire Pursuit Pilot," 219–20; Chajkowsky, *Royal Flying Corps,* 56–57; Hartney, *Up and At 'Em,* 95–99.

11. "History of the 17th Pursuit Squadron (Formerly 147th Aero Squadron)," pp. 2–3, file SQ-FI-17-HI, U.S. Air Force Historical Research Agency (AFHRA), Maxwell Air Force Base, Montgomery, Alabama. The lineage and honors of the 147th Aero Squadron were later merged into the 17th Pursuit Squadron history, as well as this unit history.

12. Geoffrey H. Bonnell file, in 147th Aero Squadron file, Lafayette Collection, Wings Over the Rockies Air and Space Museum, Denver, Colorado; Hallion, *Rise of the Fighter,* 33–35; Franks,

Who Downed the Aces in WW1?, 8–9. For Boelcke's enduring significance see Mike Spick, *The Ace Factor: Air Combat and the Role of Situational Awareness* (Annapolis, Maryland: Naval Institute Press, 1988), 49–54.

13. Chajkowsky, *Royal Flying Corps*, 23.

14. Geoffrey H. Bonnell, Record of Service, National Personnel Records Center, Military Personnel Records, St. Louis, Missouri; Bonnell file, Lafayette Collection.

15. "History of the 17th Pursuit Squadron (Formerly 147th Aero Squadron)," p. 3.

16. "Daily Diary of First Fighter Group," 22 January–20 March1918, file GP-I-HI (FTR), AFHRA; Williams, "Biography," p. 8; "History of the 27th Aero Squadron," p. 2; Hartney, 102–03, 106–07.

17. Kenneth Lee Porter and Clarence Richard Glasebrook, "Combat Flight Commander," chap. 3, Lafayette Collection.

18. Hartney, *Up and At 'Em*, 118; "History of the 17th Pursuit Squadron (Formerly 147th Aero Squadron)," p. 8.

19. Hartney, *Up and At 'Em*, 118–21.

20. Ibid.; Kenneth Porter diary, April 1918, Lafayette Collection; "Daily Diary of First Fighter Group," 22 April 1918.

21. Williams diary, 24–25 April 1918; Williams, "Biography," p. 13.

22. Hartney, *Up and At 'Em*, 126; Porter diary, 9 May to 1 June 1918.

23. Hartney, *Up and At 'Em*, 121, 129, 131–32.

24. Ibid., 111.

25. H. F. King, *Sopwith Aircraft, 1912–1920* (London: Putnam, 1980), 146–53; John H. Morrow Jr., *The Great War in the Air: Military Aviation from 1909 to 1921* (Washington, D.C.: Smithsonian Institution Press, 1993), 243.

26. Hallion, *Rise of the Fighter Aircraft*, 59, 115, 166–67, 117, 122.

27. Hartney, *Up and At 'Em*, 110–12, 121, 131.

28. Ibid.

29. Ibid., 124.

30. Heinz Gollwitzer, *Europe in the Age of Imperialism, 1880–1914* (New York: W. W. Norton, 1969), 51–52; Felix Gilbert with David Clay Large, *The End of the European Era: 1890 to the Present* (New York: W. W. Norton, 1991), 32, 56; *Crime, Madness, and Politics in Modern France: The Medical Concept of National Decline* (Princeton: Princeton University Press, 1984).

31. Hartney, *Up and At 'Em*, 127.

32. Porter diary, 9 May to 1 June 1918.

33. Hunter Liggett, *Ten Years Ago in France* (New York: Dodd, Mead, 1928), 74; B. H. Liddell Hart, *The Real War, 1914–1918* (Boston: Little, Brown, 1930), 411–14; John J. Pershing, *My Experiences in the World War* (1931; reprint, Blue Ridge Summit, Pennsylvania: Tab Books, 1989), 2:62.

34. "Daily Diary of First Fighter Group," 2–4 June 1918; "History of the 27th Aero Squadron," p. 3; "History of the 17th Pursuit Squadron (Formerly 147th Aero Squadron)," p. 14.

35. James A. Meissner diary, 31 May 1918, in "[World War I] Diaries," Lafayette Collection.

36. Leroy Prinz, interview by Kenneth Leish, July 1960, p. 10, file K146.34-82, AFHRA.

37. Diary of Joseph Houston Eastman, 1 June 1918, Joseph Houston Eastman Collection, Hoover Institution Archives, Stanford, California.

38. First Pursuit Group, Operations Order 11, 1 June 1918, Gorrell's History of the American Expeditionary Forces Air Service, 1917–19, series C, vol. 9, Microfilm Publication M990, RG120, NACP; 1st Pursuit Group, Operations Order 16, 8 June 1918.

39. Waldo Heinrichs diary, 31 May and 5 June 1918, in *First to the Front: The Aerial Adventures*

of *1st Lt. Waldo Heinrichs and the 95th Aero Squadron, 1917–1918,* ed. Charles Woolley (Atglen, Pennsylvania: Schiffer Military History, 1999).

40. Hartney, *Up and At 'Em,* 182.

41. Dunwoody to B. D. Foulois, telegram, 18 June 1918, file 1559, RG120, NACP.

42. Foulois to Dunwoody, telegram, 19 June 1918, file 1559, RG120, NACP.

43. Dunwoody to B. D. Foulois, telegram, 20 June 1918, file 1559, RG120, NACP.

44. Eastman diary, 15 June 1918.

45. Edward V. Rickenbacker, *Fighting the Flying Circus,* ed. W. David Lewis (1919; reprint, Chicago: R. R. Donnelley and Sons, 1997), 185–88. Rickenbacker, who had recently scored his fifth victory, was hospitalized at the end of June because of a fever and did not fly in this battle.

46. *Order of Battle of the United States Land Forces in the World War,* vol. 1, *American Expeditionary Forces: General Headquarters, Armies, Army Corps, Services of Supply, Separate Forces* (Washington, D.C.: Center of Military History, U.S. Army, 1988), 18, 89.

47. Frank P. Lahm, *The World War I Diary of Col. Frank P. Lahm, Air Service, A.E.F.,* ed. Albert F. Simpson (Montgomery, Alabama: Maxwell Air Force Base, Air University, Historical Research Division, 1970), 90.

48. "Daily Diary of First Fighter Group," 16 June 1918; Eddie Rickenbacker diary, 16 June 1918, Lafayette Collection.

49. Harold Buckley, *Squadron 95* (Paris, France: Obelisk Press, 1933), 78–79.

50. Heinrichs diary, 11 June and 21 June 1918, in Woolley, *First to the Front.*

51. Hartney, *Up and At 'Em,* 140.

52. First Pursuit Group diary, 22 June 1918, Bert M. Atkinson Papers, Auburn University Library; Rickenbacker diary, 22 June 1918; Harold Tittman, "Memories," p. 24, file 167.60011, AFHRA.

53. Court Martial 127115, RG153, NACP.

54. W. David Lewis, Historical Introduction to Rickenbacker, *Fighting the Flying Circus,* lxiv–lxviiii.

55. Edward M. Coffman, *The War to End All Wars* (Madison: University of Wisconsin Press, 1986), 80.

56. Nancy K. Bristow, *Making Men Moral: Social Engineering during the Great War* (New York: New York University Press, 1966), xvii–xviii, 92, 135.

57. Pershing, *My Experiences in the World War,* 1:177.

58. John J. Pershing, *Final Report of Gen. John J. Pershing, Commander-in-Chief, American Expeditionary Forces* (Washington, D.C.: Government Printing Office, 1920), 15.

59. Eastman diary, ca. 14 May 1918.

60. Elmer Haslett, *Luck on the Wing: Thirteen Stories of a Sky Spy* (New York: E. P. Dutton, 1920), 50.

61. P. Roosevelt to Mother, 6 June 1918, Philip J. Roosevelt Papers, family collection of Philip J. Roosevelt II, Chappaqua, New York.

62. Norman L. R. Franks and Frank W. Bailey, *Over the Front: A Complete Record of the Fighter Aces and Units of the United States and French Air Services, 1914–1918* (London: Grub Street, 1992), 63–64; Douglas Campbell, *Let's Go Where the Action Is! The Wartime Experiences of Douglas Campbell,* ed. Jack R. Eder (Knightstown, Indiana: JaaRE Publishing, 1984), 77.

63. Rickenbacker diary, 12 June 1918.

64. Map locations from H. Hugh Wynne, "Project Aerodromes," *Over the Front* 6 (Spring 1990): 33–73.

65. Gustav Bock, "Air Fights and Air Battles between the Meuse and the Moselle," trans. Paul Nami, *Cross and Cockade* 24 (Summer 1983): 112, 119, 135.

66. First Pursuit Group, Operations Order 8, 30 May 1918.

67. Bock, "Air Fights and Air Battles," 123.

68. Rickenbacker, *Fighting the Flying Circus,* 133–35.

69. Morrow, *Great War in the Air,* 298–99.

70. William Mitchell, *Memoirs of World War I* (New York: Random House, 1960), 202.

71. Douglas A. Campbell, Interview 531, 8 July 1964, p. 17, file K239.0512-531, U.S. Air Force Oral History Program, AFHRA.

72. Hartney, *Up and At 'Em,* 128, 137.

73. Alan Winslow, "No Parachutes," *Liberty* 10 (11 March 1933): 28–29.

74. Ibid.

75. First Pursuit Group, Operations Order 15, 6 June 1918; Campbell, Interview 531, 16.

76. Aerospace Studies Institute, *U.S. Air Service Victory Credits, World War I,* U.S. Air Force Historical Study 133 (Montgomery, Alabama: Maxwell Air Force Base, Air University, Historical Research Division, June 1969), 131, 143–44, 146–47, 160.

77. P. Roosevelt to Mother, 24 May 1918, Roosevelt Papers.

78. Philip J. Roosevelt, 1st Pursuit Group, Operations Memorandum, 26 May 1918, Gorrell's History, series C, vol. 19.

79. Ibid.

80. Norman L. R. Franks and Frank W. Bailey, *Over the Front: A Complete Record of the Fighter Aces and Units of the United States and French Air Services, 1914-1918* (London: Grub Street, 1992), 64.

81. P. J. Roosevelt to mother, 24 May 1918.

82. Christopher Shores, Norman Franks, and Russell Guest, *Above the Trenches: A Complete Record of the Fighter Aces and Units of the British Empire Air Forces, 1915-1920* (London: Grub Street, 1990), 7.

83. P. Roosevelt to Mother, 8 May 1918, Roosevelt Papers.

84. Hartney, *Up and At 'Em,* 145–50.

85. Ibid.

86. Lt. Edgar H. Lawrence file, in 147th Aero Squadron file, Lafayette Collection.

87. "History of the 17th Pursuit Squadron (Formerly 147th Aero Squadron)," p. 14; 1st Pursuit Group Casualties, 12 December 1918, in "History of the 1st Pursuit Group," file 314.7, RG18, NACP; Kenneth Lee Porter and Clarence Richard Glasebrook, "Combat Flight Commander," chap. 6, Lafayette Collection.

88. "Daily Diary of First Fighter Group," 25 June 1918.

89. Thayer, *America's First Eagles,* 130.

90. Buckley, *Squadron 95,* 58; 1st Pursuit Group Casualties, 12 December 1918; "History of the 95th Aero Squadron," Gorrell's History, series E, vol. 13, p. 7; James J. Sloan, *Wings of Honor: American Airmen in World War I* (Atglen, Pennsylvania: Schiffer Military History, 1994), 130–31.

91. Rickenbacker, *Fighting the Flying Circus,* 105–12; B. M. Atkinson, "Casualties of 1st Pursuit Group," 10 June 1918, series 657, RG120, NACP.

92. Eastman diary, 17 May 1918.

93. Bock, "Air Fights and Air Battles," 135.

94. R. L. Cavanagh, "The 94th and Its Nieuports: 15 April–11 June 1918," *Cross and Cockade* 21 (Autumn 1980): 214–15.

95. First Pursuit Group diary, 26–28 June 1918.

96. Eastman diary, 30 June 1918.

97. Williams diary, 27 June 1918.

7. AMERICA'S FIRST AIR-LAND BATTLE

1. Edward M. Coffman, *The War to End All Wars* (Madison, Wisconsin: University of Wisconsin Press, 1986), 212–14; William Mitchell, *Memoirs of World War I* (New York: Random House, 1960), 208.

2. Lucien H. Thayer, *America's First Eagles: The Official History of the U.S. Air Service, A.E.F. (1917–1918)*, ed. Donald Joseph McGee and Roger James Bender (San Jose, California: R. James Bender Publishing, 1983), 158.

3. P. Roosevelt, "The Air Service in the Château Thierry Campaign," pt. 1, "First Pursuit Group Tactics," pp. 1–2, Gorrell's History of the American Expeditionary Forces Air Service, 1917–19, series C, vol. 1, Microfilm Publication M990, RG120, National Archives at College Park (NACP); Harold Buckley, *Squadron 95* (Paris, France: Obelisk Press, 1933), 82; Diary of Joseph Houston Eastman, 30 June 1918, Joseph Houston Eastman Collection, Hoover Institution Archives, Stanford, California; Walter S. Williams diary, 30 June 1918, Walter S. William Papers, U.S. Air Force Academy Library Special Collections.

4. Edward V. Rickenbacker, *Fighting the Flying Circus*, ed. W. David Lewis (1919; reprint, Chicago: R. R. Donnelley and Sons, 1997), 216.

5. "Daily Diary of First Fighter Group," 28 June 1918, file GP-I-HI (FTR), U.S. Air Force Historical Research Agency (AFHRA), Maxwell Air Force Base, Montgomery, Alabama; 1st Pursuit Group, Operations Memorandum 4, 3 July 1918, Gorrell's History, series C, vol. 9.

6. Mitchell, *Memoirs,* 219.

7. Eastman diary, 3 July 1918.

8. Peter Kilduff, *The Red Baron Combat Wing: Jagdgeschwader Richthofen in Battle* (London: Arms and Armour Press, 1997), 44–45, 60–61, 157.

9. Ibid., 69, 107–10, 194–216.

10. Ibid., 211; General Headquarters of the Armies of the North and the Northeast, Bulletin of Aerial Information 20, 15 July 1918, series E633, RG120, NACP.

11. Kilduff, *Red Baron Combat Wing,* 220–22; John H. Morrow Jr., *The Great War in the Air: Military Aviation from 1909 to 1921* (Washington, D.C.: Smithsonian Institution Press, 1993), 300–01; Buckley, *Squadron 95,* 92.

12. Roosevelt, "First Pursuit Group Tactics," p. 2.

13. Mitchell, *Memoirs,* 216.

14. Juliette A. Hennessey, *The United States Army Air Arm, April 1861 to April 1917* (Washington, D.C.: Office of Air Force History, 1985), 86–87; Ernest La Rue Jones, "Chronology of Military Aeronautics (1793–1948)," 19 July 1917, file 168.6501, AFHRA; *The U.S. Air Service in World War I,* ed. Mauer Mauer (Washington, D.C.: Office of Air Force History, 1978), 2:196–202; Elmer Haslett, *Luck on the Wing: Thirteen Stories of a Sky Spy* (New York: E. P. Dutton, 1920), 73.

15. P. Roosevelt to Father, 8 July 1918, Philip J. Roosevelt Papers, family collection of Philip J. Roosevelt II, Chappaqua, New York.

16. "Development of Air Service Command at Front," Gorrell's History, series C, vol. 1, pp. 2–3; Benjamin D. Foulois with C. V. Glines, *From the Wright Brothers to the Astronauts: The Memoirs of Major General Benjamin D. Foulois* (New York: McGraw-Hill, 1960), 174.

17. Roosevelt, "The Air Service in the Château Thierry Campaign," pt. 3, "First Pursuit Group Administration," p. 1.

18. P. Roosevelt to Father, 8 July 1918, Roosevelt Papers.

19. Ibid.

20. Roosevelt, "First Pursuit Group Administration," pp. 1–2 (emphasis added).

21. First Pursuit Group, Operations Order 20, 1 July 1918, Gorrell's History, series C, vol. 9;

27th Aero Squadron, Operations Order 44, 30 June 1918, Gorrell's History, series E, vol. 6.

22. Hamilton Coolidge to Lu, 30 June 1918, in Hamilton Coolidge, *Letters of an American Airman* (Boston, 1919), 151–52.

23. James A. Meissner diary, 30 June 1918, in "[World War I] Diaries," Lafayette Collection, Wings Over the Rockies Air and Space Museum, Denver, Colorado.

24. Buckley, *Squadron 95,* 81.

25. Coffman, *War to End All Wars,* 212–21.

26. James G. Harbord, *The American Army in France, 1917–1919* (Boston: Little, Brown, 1936), 285–93; Coffman, *War to End All Wars,* 215.

27. "Report on Conditions in 2d Division, A.E.F., by an Observer from G.H.Q., A.E.F., 6 June 1918," in *The United States Army in the World War, 1917–1919,* vol. 4, *Military Operations of the American Expeditionary Forces* (Washington, D.C.: Center of Military History, U.S. Army, 1989), 359.

28. "Intelligence Report, G2 2d Division, 16 June 1918," in *United States Army in the World War,* 4:493; "Intelligence Report, G2 2d Division, 23 June 1918," in *United States Army in the World War,* 4:533.

29. Col. Walter S. Grant to [Col. Fox] Connor, 15 June 1918, in *United States Army in the World War,* 4:490.

30. Second Division, Field Order 9, 30 June 1918, in *United States Army in the World War,* 4:639–48.

31. First Pursuit Group, Operations Orders 21 and 22, 1 July 1918.

32. Second Division, Field Order 9, 30 June 1918; 2d Division Intelligence Report, 1 July 1918, in *United States Army in the World War,* 4:661–62.

33. Roosevelt, "First Pursuit Group Administration," p. 3.

34. First Pursuit Group, Operations Report, 1 July 1918, Gorrell's History, series C, vol. 9.

35. Haslett, *Luck on the Wing,* 77–78.

36. Meissner diary, 1 July 1918; Harold H. Tittman, "Memories," file 167.60011, pp. 25–26, AFHRA.

37. Jim Streckfuss, "Wounded in Action: The Story of Harold H. Tittman," *Over the Front* 3 (Autumn 1988): 241–42; Douglas Robinson, "The Ordeal of Harold Tittman, *Over the Front* 5 (Winter 1990): 324–25.

38. Waldo Heinrichs diary, 1 July 1918, in *First to the Front: The Aerial Adventures of 1st Lt. Waldo Heinrichs and the 95th Aero Squadron, 1917–1918,* ed. Charles Woolley (Atglen, Pennsylvania: Schiffer Military History, 1999).

39. Roosevelt, letter, 2 July 1918, in *Quentin Roosevelt: A Sketch with Letters,* ed. Kermit Roosevelt (New York: Charles Scribner's Sons, 1921), 155–56.

40. Plans and Training Officer, 23d U.S. Infantry, to B-1 C.O., 23d U.S. Infantry, in *United States Army in the World War,* 4:665–66.

41. Commanding General, 3d Brigade, to Commanding General, 2d Division, 2 July 1918, in *United States Army in the World War,* 4:675.

42. John J. Pershing, *My Experiences in the World War* (1931; reprint, Blue Ridge Summit, Pennsylvania: Tab Books, 1989), 2:90.

43. Hunter Liggett, *Ten Years Ago in France* (New York: Dodd, Mead, 1928), 84.

44. Coffman, *War to End All Wars,* 222.

45. "Daily Diary of First Fighter Group," 2 July 1918.

46. Williams diary, 2 July 1918.

47. First Pursuit Group, Operations Order 23, 1 July 1918; Harold Hartney, *Up and At 'Em* (Garden City, New York: Doubleday, 1971), 157.

48. Hartney, *Up and At 'Em*, 159–60; Kilduff, *Red Baron Combat Wing*, 222–23, n. 239; Aerospace Studies Institute, *U.S. Air Service Victory Credits, World War I*, U.S. Air Force Historical Study 133 (Montgomery, Alabama: Maxwell Air Force Base, Air University, Historical Research Division, June 1969), 68.

49. Hartney, *Up and At 'Em*, 158.

50. First Pursuit Group, Operations Reports, 2–4 July 1918; Kenneth Clendenin, "147th Aero Squadron Excerpts," p. 6, unpublished manuscript, 1964, AFHRA; Aerospace Studies Institute, *U.S. Air Service Victory Credits*, 68.

51. Heinrichs diary, 5 July 1918, in Woolley, *First to the Front*.

52. First Pursuit Group, Operations Report, 5 July 1918.

53. Ibid.; 147th Aero Squadron, Daily Report 30, 5 July 1918, Gorrell's History, series N, vol. 6; "An Interview with Ralph O'Neill," ed. Noel Shirley, *Over the Front* 2 (Summer 1987): 116-38, 130; Aerospace Studies Institute, *U.S. Air Service Victory Credits*, 68.

54. First Pursuit Group, Operations Report, 7 July 1918; Combat Report of Lt. Sherry, 7 July 1918, "94th Aero Squadron Combat Reports," Gorrell's History, series E, vol. 12.

55. Coolidge to Mother, 7 July 1918, in Coolidge, *Letters of an American Airman*, 153–54; Meissner diary, 7 July 1918; Aerospace Studies Institute, *U.S. Air Service Victory Credits*, 69.

56. Heinrichs diary, 7 July 1918, in Woolley, *First to the Front*; Sumner Sewall to Mother, n.d., in Woolley, *First to the Front*, 123.

57. First Pursuit Group, Operations Report, 7–8 July 1918; Clendenin, "147th Aero Squadron Excerpts," p. 6; Hartney, *Up and At 'Em*, 160–61.

58. First Pursuit Group Casualties, 12 December 1918, "History of the 1st Pursuit Group," file 314.7, RG18, NACP; Aerospace Studies Institute, *U.S. Air Service Victory Credits*, 68–69; claims from "Daily Diary of First Fighter Group," 1–8 July 1918.

59. Col. O. S. Eskridge, Services of Supply, memorandum, Subject: Numbers and Insignia to be painted on Aeroplanes, 6 May 1918, series 767D, Records of the 1st First Pursuit Group, RG120, NACP.

60. Eastman diary, 12 July 1918.

61. Coolidge to Mammy, 10 July 1918, in Coolidge, *Letters of an American Airman*, 156.

62. Kilduff, *Red Baron Combat Wing*, 216.

63. First Pursuit Group, Report for the Month of July 1918, series E808, RG120, NACP; 1st Pursuit Group, Operations Report, 8 July 1918.

64. James J. Cooke, *The U.S. Air Service in the Great War, 1917–1919* (Westport, Connecticut: Praeger, 1996), 94.

65. First Pursuit Group diary, 7 July 1918, Bert M. Atkinson Papers, Auburn University Library.

66. Eastman diary, 12 July 1918.

8. THE SECOND BATTLE OF THE MARNE

1. Philip J. Roosevelt to Mother, 19 December 1918, Philip J. Roosevelt Papers, family collection of Philip J. Roosevelt II, Chappaqua, New York.

2. Roosevelt to Mother, 26 August 1918, Roosevelt Papers.

3. Harold Hartney, *Up and At 'Em* (Garden City, New York: Doubleday, 1971), 138, 163.

4. William Mitchell, *Memoirs of World War I* (New York: Random House, 1960), 231.

5. First Pursuit Group, Operations Report, 10 July 1918, Gorrell's History of the American Expeditionary Forces Air Service, 1917–19, series C, vol. 9, Microfilm Publication M990, RG120, National Archives at College Park; Waldo Heinrichs diary, 10 July 1918, in *First to the Front: The Aerial Adventures of 1st Lt. Waldo Heinrichs and the 95th Aero Squadron, 1917–1918*, ed. Charles Woolley (Atglen, Pennsylvania: Schiffer Military History, 1999); Q. Roosevelt, 11 July 1918, in

Quentin Roosevelt: A Sketch with Letters, ed. Kermit Roosevelt (New York: Charles Scribner's Sons, 1921), 163–64; Reed M. Chambers, interview by Kenneth Leish, October 1960, p. 44, file K146.34-26, Oral History Research Office, Butler Library, Columbia University.

6. First Pursuit Group, Operations Report, 14 July 1918; Edward V. Rickenbacker, *Fighting the Flying Circus,* ed. W. David Lewis (1919; reprint, Chicago: R. R. Donnelley and Sons, 1997), 231; James Knowles's account in Woolley, *First to the Front,* 132–37.

7. P. Roosevelt to Theodore Roosevelt, 16 July 1918, Roosevelt Papers.

8. Rickenbacker, *Fighting the Flying Circus,* 229.

9. Q. Roosevelt, 11 July 1918, in Roosevelt, *Quentin Roosevelt,* 164.

10. Andrew Nahum, *The Rotary Aero Engine* (London: Her Majesty's Stationery Office, 1987), 40, 47.

11. J. M. Bruce, "The SPAD Story," pt. 1, *Air International* 10 (May 1976): 239–41; Lionel S. Marks, *The Airplane Engine* (New York: McGraw-Hill, 1922), 122, 127; Bill Gunston, *The Development of Piston Aero Engines: From the Wrights to Microlights* (Somerset, Great Britain: Patrick Stephens Limited, 1993), 82–83; "Propellers Approved for Use on Airplanes of Types in Use by the American Expeditionary Forces," compiled by Technical Data Division, Technical Section, U.S. Air Service, AEF, November 1918, National Air and Space Museum Archives.

12. J. M. Bruce, "The SPAD Story," pt. 2, *Air International* 10 (June 1976): 289; Roland Richardson, "Spad XIII," *Aerospace Historian* 17 (Winter 1980): 257–59; B. S. Kelsey, "The Real SPAD," *Over the Front* 8 (Summer 1993): 114–22, 117; James J. Davilla and Arthur M. Soltan, *French Aircraft of the First World War* (Stratford, Connecticut: Flying Machine Press, 1997), 502.

13. Bruce, "SPAD Story," pt. 2, 291.

14. H. C. Whitehead to Chief of Supply Section, AEF, memorandum, Subject: European Deliveries of Planes Ordered by Air Service, 12 June 1918, series 657, RG120, National Archives at College Park (NACP); H. Dunwoody to Monsieur le Sous-Secretaire d'Etat de l'Aeronatique Militaire, 17 June 1918, series 657, RG120, NACP.

15. "Opérations de la première Division aérienne," *Revue de l'Aéronautique Militaire* (July–August 1921): 4; H. A. Jones, *The War in the Air: Being the Story of the Part Played in the Great War by the Royal Air Force,* vol. 6 (Oxford, England: Clarendon Press, 1937), 402.

16. Ministère de la Guerre, *Les Armées françaises dans la Grande Guerre,* vol. 6 (Paris, France: Imprimerie Nationale, 1931), 418, 429, 454; "Opérations de la première Division aérienne," 75.

17. Jones, *War in the Air,* 6:401–01, 6:412–13; "Order of Battle of the RAF on 8 August 1918," in Jones, *War in the Air,* Appendix 24, 116–17.

18. Ministère de la Guerre, *Les Armées françaises,* 481.

19. Philip Roosevelt, "The Air Service in the Château Thierry Campaign," pt. 1, "First Pursuit Group Tactics," Gorrell's History, series C, vol. 1; Edward M. Coffman, *The War to End All Wars* (Madison: University of Wisconsin Press, 1986), 223; Mitchell, *Memoirs,* 220.

20. First Pursuit Group, Operations Order 36, 14 July 1918, Gorrell's History, series C, vol. 9.

21. First Pursuit Group, Report for the Month of July 1918, series E 808, RG120, NACP.

22. Mitchell, *Memoirs,* 219–21.

23. James J. Hudson, *Hostile Skies: A Combat History of the American Air Service in World War I* (Syracuse: Syracuse University Press, 1968), 101–02.

24. First Pursuit Group, Operations Report, 15 July 1918.

25. 147th Aero Squadron, Operations Report, 15 July 1918, Gorrell's History, series N, vol. 5.

26. Twenty-seventh Aero Squadron, Operations Report, 15 July 1918, Gorrell's History, series E, vol. 6; 1st Pursuit Group, Operations Order 36, 14 July 1918.

27. Hartney, *Up and At 'Em,* 170; Walter S. Williams diary, 15 July 1918, Walter S. William Papers, U.S. Air Force Academy Library Special Collections.

28. "L'Aéronautique militaire française pendant la Guerre en 1914–1918," vol. 2, "1917–1918," *Icare: Revue de l'aviation française* 88 (1979): 64; "Opérations de la première Division aérienne," 76.

29. Jones, *War in the Air*, 6:404.

30. Hartney, *Up and At 'Em*, 162–63 (although Hartney states that this incident occurred on 10 July, the correct date appears to be either 14 or 15 July—see Jones, *War in the Air*, 6:412–13); James A. Meissner diary, 14–15 July 1918, in "[World War I] Diaries," Lafayette Collection, Wings Over the Rockies Air and Space Museum, Denver, Colorado; Heinrichs diary, 15 July 1918, in Woolley, *First to the Front*.

31. Hartney, *Up and At 'Em*, 162–63.

32. Ibid.

33. Alan Winslow, "No Parachutes," *Liberty* 10 (18 March 1933): 37.

34. Hartney, *Up and At 'Em*, 162–63.

35. First Pursuit Group, Operations Order 37, 15 July 1918.

36. Ibid.

37. First Pursuit Group, Report for the Month of July 1918; Aerospace Studies Institute, *U.S. Air Service Victory Credits, World War I*, U.S. Air Force Historical Study 133 (Montgomery, Alabama: Maxwell Air Force Base, Air University, Historical Research Division, June 1969); 1st Pursuit Group Casualties, 12 December 1918, "History of the 1st Pursuit Group," file 314.7, RG18, NACP.

38. Hartney, *Up and At 'Em*, 168–69.

39. Heinrichs diary, 16 July 1918, in Woolley, *First to the Front*.

40. Roosevelt, "First Pursuit Group Tactics," pp. 4–5.

41. 147th Aero Squadron, Operations Report, 16 July 1918.

42. First Pursuit Group, Operations Report, 16 July 1918; Aerospace Studies Institute, *U.S. Air Service Victory Credits*, 70.

43. 147th Aero Squadron, Operations Report, 16 July 1918.

44. First Pursuit Group, Operations Report, 16 July 1918; "History of the 95th Aero Squadron," Gorrell's History, series E, vol. 13, p. I-9.

45. Coffman, *War to End All Wars*, 224; John J. Pershing, *My Experiences in the World War* (1931; reprint, Blue Ridge Summit, Pennsylvania: Tab Books, 1989), 2:153.

46. B. H. Liddell Hart, *The Real War, 1914–1918* (Boston: Little, Brown, 1930), 422.

47. Heinrichs diary, 16 July 1918, in Woolley, *First to the Front*.

48. "Daily Diary of First Fighter Group," 17 July 1918, file GP-I-HI (FTR), U.S. Air Force Historical Research Agency (AFHRA), Maxwell Air Force Base, Montgomery, Alabama.

49. First Pursuit Group, Operations Order 41, 17 July 1918; 1st Pursuit Group, Operations Report, 18 July 1918; 1st Pursuit Group, Report for the Month of July 1918.

50. First Pursuit Group, Operations Report, 19 July 1918.

51. First Pursuit Group, Operations Report, 21 July 1918; 1st Pursuit Group Casualties, 12 December 1918; Hartney, *Up and At 'Em*, 174.

52. Diary of Joseph Houston Eastman, 20–24 July 1918, Joseph Houston Eastman Collection, Hoover Institution Archives, Stanford, California.

53. First Pursuit Group, Operations Report, 21 July 1918; 1st Pursuit Group diary, 12–21 July 1918, Bert M. Atkinson Papers, Auburn University Library.

54. "Airplanes Delivered by U.S. Air Service from All Sources," Gorrell's History, series A, vol. 16.

55. Hartney, *Up and At 'Em*, 169; John H. Tegler, "A New Hampshire Pursuit Pilot," *Cross and Cockade* 4 (Autumn 1963): 217, 225–26.

56. "An Interview with Ralph O'Neill," ed. Noel Shirley, *Over the Front* 2 (Summer 1987): 133.

57. Mitchell, *Memoirs*, 230; William E. Brotherton diary, 24–25 July 1918, in "[World War I] Diaries," Lafayette Collection.

58. Kenneth Clendenin, "147th Aero Squadron Excerpts," p. 7, unpublished manuscript, 1964, AFHRA.

59. Kenneth Lee Porter and Clarence Richard Glasebrook, "Combat Flight Commander," pp. 28–30, Lafayette Collection.

60. Thomas Abernathy to Bill, 20 November 1971, 147th Aero Squadron file, Lafayette Collection.

61. James J. Sloan, *Wings of Honor: American Airmen in World War I* (Atglen, Pennsylvania: Schiffer Military History, 1994), 290; Aerospace Studies Institute, *U.S. Air Service Victory Credits,* 25; Meissner diary, 24 July 1918.

62. Officer biographies, 147th Aero Squadron file, Lafayette Collection.

63. Shirley, "An Interview with Ralph O'Neill," 134.

64. Meissner diary, 25 July to 1 August 1918.

65. "Notes on Observation at Château-Thierry Campaign," Gorrell's History, series C, vol. 1, p. 4.

66. William Muir Russel, *A Happy Warrior: Letters of William Muir Russel, An American Aviator in the Great War, 1917–1918* (Detroit, Michigan: Saturday Night Press, 1919), 209.

67. First Pursuit Group, Operations Report, 31 July 1918.

68. Winslow, "No Parachutes," *Liberty* 10 (18 March 1933): 38–41.

69. Ibid.

70. "Daily Diary of First Fighter Group, 1 August 1918"; Hartney, *Up and At Em,* 177–78; William R. Puglisi, "27th Aero Black Day," *Cross and Cockade* 3 (Autumn 1962): 229–38; Peter Kilduff, *The Red Baron Combat Wing: Jagdgeschwader Richthofen in Battle* (London: Arms and Armour Press, 1997), 227.

71. First Pursuit Group, Operations Report, 1 August 1918.

72. Aerospace Studies Institute, *U.S. Air Service Victory Credits,* 72–73.

73. Hartney, *Up and At Em,* 181–82; 1st Pursuit Group, Operations Memorandums 9–13, 24–30 July 1918, Gorrell's History, series C, vol. 9; Philip Roosevelt, "First Pursuit Group Tactics," p. 5.

74. First Pursuit Group diary, 3–6 August 1918.

75. Office of Chief of Air Service, Memorandum 37, Subject: Air Service Plane of Supply, Salvage, and Repair, 9 August 1918, p. 2, series E 633, box 576 E, NACP; Air Park, table 630, Tables of Organization for Units of the AEF Air Service, 8 September 1918, Gorrell's History, series A, vol. 12.

76. Harold Buckley, *Squadron 95* (Paris, France: Obelisk Press, 1933), 112–14; Aerospace Studies Institute, *U.S. Air Service Victory Credits,* 74; Hart, *The Real War,* 430.

77. "History of the 95th Aero Squadron," p. I-12.

78. Buckley, *Squadron 95,* 114.

79. First Pursuit Group, Operations Memorandum 22 [24 August 1918]; 1st Pursuit Group, Operations Reports, 22–23 August 1918.

80. Aerospace Studies Institute, *U.S. Air Service Victory Credits,* 68–76; 1st Pursuit Group Casualties, 12 December 1918; Tegler, "A New Hampshire Pursuit Pilot," 227.

81. Maj. Gen. C. R. Edwards to Commanding Officer, 1st Pursuit Group, 31 July 1918, "Daily Diary of First Fighter Group," 1 August 1918.

82. Commander-in-Chief, AEF, to Chief of Air Service, AEF, 14 August 1918, "Daily Diary of First Fighter Group," 15 August 1918.

83. Buckley, *Squadron 95,* 119.

84. Hamilton Coolidge to Lu, 5 August 1918, in Hamilton Coolidge, *Letters of an American Airman* (Boston, 1919), 170–71.

85. Pershing, *My Experiences in the War,* 2:192; Edgar S. Gorrell, *The Measure of America's World War Aeronautical Effort: A Lecture Delivered by Colonel Edgar S. Gorrell* (Burlington, Vermont: Lane Press, 1940), 29.

86. Sloan, *Wings of Honor,* 129–35; 1st Pursuit Group diary, 6 August and 13 August 1918.

87. Untitled memorandum, Headquarters, 1st Brigade, 13 July 1918, file 248.282-40, AFHRA; Circular 1, Headquarters, Chief of Air Service, 1st Army, 19 August 1918, in *The U.S. Air Service in World War I,* ed. Mauer Mauer (Washington, D.C.: Office of Air Force History, 1978), 3:41–43.

88. John Wentworth, "Pursuit Aviation and Perfection Training for Aviation," pp. 1–2, file 248.282-45, AFHRA.

89. Mitchell to Atkinson, 20 August 1918, Atkinson Papers.

90. First Pursuit Group diary, 20–22 August 1918.

91. Hartney, *Up and At 'Em,* 188–89.

92. "Plan of Employment of Air Service Units, First Pursuit Wing," 11 September 1918, Atkinson Papers.

93. Emile Gauvreau and Lester Cohen, *Billy Mitchell, Founder of Our Air Force and Prophet without Honor* (New York: E. P. Dutton, 1942).

94. Emile Gauvreau, *The Wild Blue Yonder: Sons of the Prophet Carry On* (New York: E. P. Dutton, 1944), 113, 117.

95. P. Roosevelt to Mother, 19 December 1918.

9. ST. MIHIEL

1. Harold Hartney, *Up and At 'Em* (Garden City, New York: Doubleday, 1971), 198.

2. Ibid., 193–94.

3. First Pursuit Group, Operations Reports, 22–23 August 1918, Gorrell's History of the American Expeditionary Forces Air Service, 1917–19, series C, vol. 9, Microfilm Publication M990, RG120, National Archives at College Park (NACP).

4. First Pursuit Group, Operations Order 88, 23 August 1918, Gorrell's History, series C, vol. 9.

5. Diary of Joseph Houston Eastman, 29 August 1918, Joseph Houston Eastman Collection, Hoover Institution Archives, Stanford, California.

6. James A. Meissner diary, 13–18 August 1918, in "[World War I] Diaries," Lafayette Collection, Wings Over the Rockies Air and Space Museum, Denver, Colorado.

7. "An Interview with Ralph O'Neill," ed. Noel Shirley, *Over the Front* 2 (Summer 1987): 135.

8. "Daily Diary of First Fighter Group," 24 August 1918, file GP-I-HI (FTR), U.S. Air Force Historical Research Agency, Maxwell Air Force Base, Montgomery, Alabama.

9. Walter S. Williams diary, 24 August 1918, Walter S. William Papers, U.S. Air Force Academy Library Special Collections; Walter S. Williams, "Biography," p. 16, Williams Papers.

10. First Pursuit Group diary, 28 August 1918, Bert M. Atkinson Papers, Auburn University Library; Edward M. Coffman, *The War to End All Wars* (Madison: University of Wisconsin Press, 1986), 275.

11. William Mitchell, *Memoirs of World War I* (New York: Random House, 1960), 237; Coffman, *War to End All Wars,* 269–75.

12. "Opérations de la première Division aérienne," *Revue de l'Aéronautique Militaire* (July–August 1921): 77; James J. Cooke, *The U.S. Air Service in the Great War, 1917–1919* (Westport, Connecticut: Praeger, 1996), 177; James J. Hudson, *Hostile Skies: A Combat History of the American Air Service in World War I* (Syracuse: Syracuse University Press, 1968), 139.

13. Mitchell, *Memoirs,* 237.

14. Hartney, *Up and At 'Em,* 201.

15. First Pursuit Group diary, 29 August–3 September 1918.

16. Hartney, *Up and At Em,* 202.

17. "History of the 27th Aero Squadron," Gorrell's History, series E, vol. 6, p. 4.

18. Eastman diary, 7 September 1918; Meissner diary, 3 September 1918; 1st Pursuit Group, Operations Order 104, 3 September 1918.

19. First Pursuit Group, Operations Order 105, 5 September 1918; 1st Pursuit Group, Operations Order 114, 7 September 1918.

20. Williams, "Biography," p. 17.

21. Norman Archibald, *Heaven High, Hell Deep* (New York: Albert and Charles Bone, 1935), 199–201.

22. "Indications Point to French-American Attack at St. Mihiel," German Supreme Headquarters, 11 September 1918, in *The United States Army in the World War, 1917–1919*, vol. 8, *Military Operations of the American Expeditionary Forces* (Washington, D.C.: Center of Military History, U.S. Army, 1990), 299.

23. First Army Air Service, Operations Order 1, 11 September 1918, file 314.7, box 23, RG18, NACP.

24. Ibid.

25. First Army, Field Order 9, 7 September 1918, in *United States Army in the World War*, 8:206; [Aviation] Annex 3, Field Order 9, 7 September 1918, in *United States Army in the World War*, 8:215–16.

26. First Army Air Service, Operations Order 1, 11 September 1918.

27. *United States Army in the World War*, 8:216.

28. First Pursuit Group, Operations Memorandum 27, 11 September 1918, Gorrell's History, series C, vol. 9.

29. First Pursuit Group, Operations Order 121, 11 September 1918.

30. First Pursuit Group, Operations Memorandum 28, 12 September 1918.

31. Hartney, *Up and At 'Em*, 202–04.

32. First Pursuit Group, Operations Reports, 11–13 September 1918.

33. Edward V. Rickenbacker, *Fighting the Flying Circus*, ed. W. David Lewis (1919; reprint, Chicago: R. R. Donnelley and Sons, 1997), 259.

34. Combat Report of Lt. J. F. Wehner, 12 September 1918, "History of the 27th Aero Squadron," Gorrell's History, series E, vol. 6.

35. Combat Report of Lt. Frank Luke, 12 September 1918, "History of the 27th Aero Squadron," Gorrell's History, series E, vol. 6; William Paul Haiber and Robert Eugene Haiber, *Frank Luke: The September Rampage* (La Grangeville, New York: Info Devel Press, 1999), 109 n. 69; Norman S. Hall, *The Balloon Buster: Frank Luke of Arizona* (New York: Doubleday, Doran, 1928), 83–91.

36. Eastman diary, 12 September 1918; Mitchell, *Memoirs*, 252.

37. Eastman diary, 12 September 1918; the account in the next four paragraphs is from this source.

38. Rickenbacker, *Fighting the Flying Circus*, 262.

39. First Army Air Service, Operations Report, 12 September 1918, file 314.7, box 23, RG18, NACP.

40. James Knowles, "Recollections of France: James Knowles, 95th Aero Squadron," interview by H. Huge Wynne, *Cross and Cockade* 10 (Winter 1969): 359; "History of the 95th Aero Squadron," Gorrell's History, series E, vol. 13, p. I-15.

41. Mitchell, *Memoirs*, 252.

42. "Daily Diary of First Fighter Group," 12 September 1918.

43. Eastman diary, 12 September 1918.

44. Holger H. Herwig, *The First World War: Germany and Austria-Hungary, 1914–1918* (London: Arnold, 1997), 423.

45. "Final Report of G-2," in *The United States Army in the World War, 1917–1919*, vol. 14, *Reports of the Commander-in-Chief, Staff Sections and Services* (Washington, D.C.: Center of Military History, U.S. Army, 1991), 321; James H. Hallas, *Squandered Victory: The American First Army at St. Mihiel* (Westport, Connecticut: Praeger, 1995), 171–79.

46. Mitchell, *Memoirs*, 249–50.

47. "History of the 95th Aero Squadron," p. I-16.

48. First Pursuit Group, Operations Report, 13 September 1918.

49. First Pursuit Group, Operations Orders 126–27, 13 September 1918.

50. First Army, Field Order 11, 13 September 1918, in *United States Army in the World War*, 8:261.

51. *The United States Army in the World War*, vol. 13, *Reports of the Commander-in-Chief, Staff Sections and Services* (Washington, D.C.: Center of Military History, U.S. Army, 1991), 321.

52. Aerospace Studies Institute, *U.S. Air Service Victory Credits, World War I*, U.S. Air Force Historical Study 133 (Montgomery, Alabama: Maxwell Air Force Base, Air University, Historical Research Division, June 1969), 82–83.

53. Hartney, *Up and At 'Em*, 249.

54. First Pursuit Group, Operations Order 125, 13 September 1918.

55. First Army Air Service, Battle Orders 4—6, 14–16 September 1918, file 314.7, box 23, RG18, NACP.

56. First Pursuit Group, Operations Report, 14 September 1918.

57. First Pursuit Group, Operations Order 126, 13 September 1918.

58. Ninety-fifth Aero Squadron, Operations Report, 14 September 1918; Sumner Sewall's essay in Woolley, *First to the Front*, 179–82.

59. Summary of Air Information, 28 September 1918, in General Headquarters, AEF, *Summary of Air Information*, Bulletin 58, 940.4473Un3s, Maxwell Air Force Base, Montgomery, Alabama.

60. Rickenbacker, *Fighting the Flying Circus*, 277–78.

61. Ibid., 279–81; "Daily Diary of First Fighter Group," 15 September 1918.

62. Rickenbacker, *Fighting the Flying Circus*, 275, 282.

63. Hamilton Coolidge to Mother, 25 September 1918, in Hamilton Coolidge, *Letters of an American Airman* (Boston, 1919), 197.

64. Lucien H. Thayer, *America's First Eagles: The Official History of the U.S. Air Service, A.E.F., 1917–1918*, ed. Donald Joseph McGhee and Roger James Bender (San Jose, California: R. James Bender Publishing, 1983), 202; "Opérations de la première Division aérienne," 77; Aerospace Studies Institute, *U.S. Air Service Victory Credits*, 82–86.

65. First Army Air Service, Battle Order 4, 14 September 1918.

66. Mitchell, *Memoirs*, 253; Hartney, *Up and At 'Em*, 249, 255.

67. Paul Vittali, "Balloon Commander: Reminiscences of Paul Vittali," trans. Peter Kilduff, *Over the Front* 6 (Fall 1991): 241.

68. Supplement to the Air Service Intelligence Bulletin 12, German Aviation, 1 September 1918, series E 633, box 575, RG120, NACP.

69. Haiber and Haiber, *Frank Luke: The September Rampage*, 45, 48; Hall, *Balloon Buster*, 3–16, 63.

70. Harold Hartney, "The Story of Frank Luke," *U.S. Air Service* 1 (April 1919): 13; Harry Woodman, *Early Aircraft Armament: The Aeroplane and the Gun Up to 1918* (Washington: Smithsonian Institution Press, 1989), 78, 165.

71. Eddie Rickenbacker diary, 16 June 1918, Lafayette Collection; Joseph Christopher Reifsneider diary, 9 September 1918, in "[World War I] Diaries," Lafayette Collection.

72. Rickenbacker, *Fighting the Flying Circus*, 291; Combat Report of Lt. Frank Luke, 18 September 1918, "History of the 27th Aero Aquadron," Gorrell's History, series E, vol. 6.

73. John Kosek, "The Search for Frank Luke," *Over the Front* 13 (Winter 1998): 337–38; Hartney, *Up and At 'Em*, 239–67; Eastman diary, 18 May 1918.

74. First Pursuit Group, Operations Order 142, 23 September 1918.

75. Meissner diary, 19 September 1918.

76. Waldo Heinrichs diary, 17 September 1918, in *First to the Front: The Aerial Adventures of 1st Lt. Waldo Heinrichs and the 95th Aero Squadron, 1917–1918*, ed. Charles Woolley (Atglen, Pennsylvania: Schiffer Military History, 1999).

77. Report of Lt. Thomas Butz, in Woolley, *First to the Front*, 187.

78. Harold Buckley, *Squadron 95* (Paris, France: Obelisk Press, 1933), 132–35.

10. MEUSE-ARGONNE

1. "'Gimper,' Flier Stopping at Nothing, Definition Given by Eddie Rickenbacker," *Detroit News*, 21 July 1918, Rickenbacker Scrapbook 1, Auburn University Archives.

2. "Hat in the Ring Is the Gimpers' Emblem," *Cincinnati Ohio Post*, 7 August 1918, Rickenbacker Scrapbook 1, Auburn University Archives; "'Gimper,' Flier Stopping at Nothing, Definition Given by Eddie Rickenbacker."

3. Walter Boyne, *Aces in Command: Fighter Pilots as Combat Leaders* (Washington, D.C.: Brassey's, 2001), 42–43.

4. Reed M. Chambers, interview by Kenneth Leish, October 1960, p. 45, file K146.34-26, Oral History Research Office, Butler Library, Columbia University.

5. Harold Hartney, *Up and At 'Em* (Garden City, New York: Doubleday, 1971), 214.

6. Edward V. Rickenbacker, *Fighting the Flying Circus*, ed. W. David Lewis (1919; reprint, Chicago: R. R. Donnelley and Sons, 1997), 298; Diary of Joseph Houston Eastman, 24 September 1918, Joseph Houston Eastman Collection, Hoover Institution Archives, Stanford, California.

7. Eddie Rickenbacker diary, 23–24 July 1918, Lafayette Collection, Wings Over the Rockies Air and Space Museum, Denver, Colorado; "Leigh Wade: Test Pilot," ed. Noel C. Shirley, *Cross and Cockade* 21 (Autumn 1980): 240–43.

8. Hartney, *Up and At 'Em*, 214–15.

9. "Final Report of G-3," in *The United States Army in the World War, 1917–1919*, vol. 14, *Reports of the Commander-in-Chief, Staff Sections and Services* (Washington, D.C.: Center of Military History, U.S. Army, 1991), 40–41; John Keegan, *The First World War* (New York: A Knopf, 1999), 412; B. H. Liddell Hart, *The Real War, 1914–1918* (Boston: Little, Brown, 1930), 461–62; John J. Pershing, *My Experiences in the World War* (1931; reprint, Blue Ridge Summit, Pennsylvania: Tab Books, 1989), 2:281.

10. Col. F. F. Hunter, British Army observer with the American Expeditionary Forces, "Report of Air Service, 1st Army, AEF," 16 November 1918, p. 2, file 167-401-21, U.S. Air Force Historical Research Agency (AFHRA), Maxwell Air Force Base, Montgomery, Alabama; "Plan of Employment of Air Service Units, 17 September 1918," in *The United States Army in the World War, 1917–1919*, vol. 9, *Military Operations of the American Expeditionary Forces* (Washington, D.C.: Center of Military History, U.S. Army, 1990), 99–100; First Army Air Service, Battle Order 7, 25 September 1918, file 314.7, box 23, RG18, National Archives at College Park (NACP).

11. First Pursuit Group, Operations Order 140, 21 September 1918, Gorrell's History of the American Expeditionary Forces Air Service, 1917–19, series C, vol. 9, Microfilm Publication M990, RG120, NACP.

12. First Pursuit Group, Operations Order 143, 23 September 1918; 1st Pursuit Group, Operations Order 144, 24 September 1918; Hartney, *Up and At 'Em*, 215.

13. First Pursuit Group, Operations Memorandum 43, 25 September 1918, Gorrell's History, series C, vol. 9; 1st Pursuit Group, Operations Order 147, 25 September 1918.

14. First Pursuit Group, Operations Order 148, 25 September 1918; Harold Buckley, *Squadron 95* (Paris, France: Obelisk Press, 1933), 139.

15. First Pursuit Group, Operations Order 148, 25 September 1918.

16. Ninety-fifth Aero Squadron, Operations Order 116, 26 September 1918, Gorrell's History, series E, vol. 13.

17. Buckley, *Squadron 95,* 139.

18. Ninety-fifth Aero Squadron, Operations Report, 26 September 1918; "History of the 95th Aero Squadron," Gorrell's History, series E, vol. 13, p. 22.

19. Buckley, *Squadron 95,* 156–57; 1st Pursuit Group, Operations Order 152, 26 September 1918.

20. Ninety-fifth Aero Squadron, Operations Report, 26 September 1918.

21. Hamilton Coolidge to Lu, 29 September 1918, in Hamilton Coolidge, *Letters of an American Airman* (Boston, 1919), 199–204. The account given in the following four paragraphs is from this source.

22. Rickenbacker, *Fighting the Flying Circus,* 310.

23. Aerospace Studies Institute, *U.S. Air Service Victory Credits, World War I,* U.S. Air Force Historical Study 133 (Montgomery, Alabama: Maxwell Air Force Base, Air University, Historical Research Division, June 1969), 89; Rickenbacker, *Fighting the Flying Circus,* 309–14.

24. James Meissner, "Low Flying," *U.S. Air Service* 1 (April 1919): 27–28.

25. Operations Report, 26 September 1918, "History of the 147th Aero Squadron," Gorrell's History, series N, vol. 6; Meissner, "Low Flying," 28.

26. Diary of Russel Pruden, 24–25 September 1918, Jerry Vasconcells Papers, U.S. Air Force Academy Library Special Collections; Hartney, *Up and At 'Em,* 266.

27. Pruden diary, 26–27 September 1918; "History of the 27th Aero Squadron," Records of the 1st Pursuit Group, file 314.7, p. 25, RG18, NACP; 27th Aero Squadron, Operations Report, 26 September 1918, Gorrell's History, series E, vol. 6.

28. First Pursuit Group, Operations Order 151, 26 September 1918; "History of the 95th Aero Squadron," p. I-22.

29. First Pursuit Group, Operations Order 153, 26 September 1918.

30. Hartney, *Up and At 'Em,* 268–69.

31. First Pursuit Group, Operations Report, 26 September 1918, Gorrell's History, series C, vol. 9; Aerospace Studies Institute, *U.S. Air Service Victory Credits,* pp. 89–90; 1st Army, Operations Report, 25 September 1918, Gorrell's History, series N, vol. 1; *United States Army in the World War,* 9:137.

32. Edward M. Coffman, *The War to End All Wars* (Madison: University of Wisconsin Press, 1986), 311; Pershing, *My Experiences in the World War,* 2:297.

33. Rickenbacker, *Fighting the Flying Circus,* 320; 27th Aero Squadron, Operations Report, 29 September 1918; Walter S. Williams diary, 28 September 1918, Walter S. William Papers, U.S. Air Force Academy Library Special Collections; Norman S. Hall, *The Balloon Buster: Frank Luke of Arizona* (New York: Doubleday, Doran, 1928), 162.

34. Harold Hartney, "The Story of Frank Luke," *U.S. Air Service* 1 (April 1919): 13.

35. Hartney, *Up and At 'Em,* 270–71.

36. Fred W. Erdman to J. J. Smith, April 1972, in 27th Aero Squadron file, Lafayette Collection; Hartney, *Up and At 'Em,* 275; Hall, *Balloon Buster,* 183.

37. Hartney, *Up and At 'Em,* 269.

38. Rickenbacker, *Fighting the Flying Circus,* 320; Chambers interview, p. 51.

39. Hartney, *Up and At 'Em,* 211; Aerospace Studies Institute, *U.S. Air Service Victory Credits,* 93.

40. "History of the 95th Aero Squadron," p. I-23; Rickenbacker diary, 30 September 1918; Rickenbacker, *Fighting the Flying Circus,* 323–34.

41. Summary of Air Information, 29 September, in General Headquarters, AEF, *Summary of Air Information,* Bulletin 59, 940.4473Un3s, Maxwell Air Force Base, Montgomery, Alabama; Summary of Air Information, 6 October 1918, in *Summary of Air Information,* Bulletin 66; First Army, Intelligence Report, 3 October 1918, in *United States Army in the World War,* 9:201; Summary of Air Information, 8 October 1918, in *Summary of Air Information,* Bulletin 68.

42. First Pursuit Group, Operations Report, 5 October 1918.

43. First Pursuit Group, Operations Orders 3–4, 2 October 1918; "Daily Diary of First Fighter Group," 26 September 1918, file GP-I-HI (FTR), AFHRA; James A. Meissner diary, 27 September 1918, in "[World War I] Diaries," Lafayette Collection.

44. Pershing, *My Experiences in the War,* 2:321–22.

45. First Pursuit Group, Operations Order 5, 3 October 1918.

46. First Pursuit Group, Operations Report, 3 October 1918.

47. Rickenbacker, *Fighting the Flying Circus,* 338–40; Charles I. Crocker diary, 6 October 1918, Lafayette Collection.

48. Eastman diary, 4 October 1918; Coolidge to Mother, 5 October 1918, in Coolidge, *Letters of an American Airman,* 208.

49. Coolidge to Mother, 5 October 1918, 208–09.

50. Rickenbacker, *Fighting the Flying Circus,* 341.

51. Ibid., 342.

52. Eastman diary, 4 October 1918.

53. Rickenbacker, *Fighting the Flying Circus,* 339–40; Eastman diary, 10 October 1918.

54. First Pursuit Group, Operations Order 23, 10 October 1918.

55. Rickenbacker, *Fighting the Flying Circus,* 353.

56. Coolidge to Mother, 13 October 1918, in Coolidge, *Letters of an American Airman,* 213–15; Rickenbacker, *Fighting the Flying Circus,* 353–61; 1st Pursuit Group Operations Office, News Bulletin 1, 11 October 1918, Gorrell's History, series C, vol. 9; Meissner to Mother, quoted from James Parks, "No Greater Love: The Story of Lt. Wilbert W. White," *Over the Front* 1 (Spring 1986): 46–58, 53.

57. Meissner to Mother, in Parks, "No Greater Love," p. 53.

58. Aerospace Studies Institute, *U.S. Air Service Victory Credits,* 97–99; Rickenbacker, *Fighting the Flying Circus,* 361.

59. Edward Rickenbacker, "Aces' Luck," *U.S. Air Service* 1 (March 1919): 15.

60. Ibid.

61. Twenty-seventh Aero Squadron, Operations Report, 10 October 1918.

62. Hartney, *Up and At 'Em,* 140.

63. Buckley, *Squadron 95,* 33.

64. James Knowles, "Recollections of France and the 95th," *Cross and Cockade* 10 (Winter 1999): 361.

65. Buckley, *Squadron 95,* 124, 145.

66. Knowles, "Recollections of France and the 95th," 358; Walter Avery diary, 11 September 1918, "The War Diary and Letters of Walter L. Avery," *Over the Front* 1 (Fall 1986): 226.

67. Walter Avery diary, 22–23 August 1918.

68. Harold Hartney, "Low Flying in the Offensive," 24 September 1918, Frank Purdy Lahm Papers, file 167.601-3, AFHRA.

69. Eastman diary, 1 October 1918

70. Aerospace Studies Institute, *U.S. Air Service Victory Credits,* 100–14; "The War Diary and Letters of Lansing Holden, Jr., 95th Aero Squadron Ace," ed. Thomas E. Kullgren, *Over the Front* 1 (Fall 1986): 256.

71. Hartney, *Up and At 'Em,* 221; William Edward Fischer Jr., *The Development of Military Night Aviation to 1919* (Montgomery, Alabama: Maxwell Air Force Base, Air University Press, 1998), 92–95.

72. "History of the 185th Aero Squadron," Gorrell's History, series E, vol. 20, pp. 1–7; Lucien H. Thayer, *America's First Eagles: The Official History of the U.S. Air Service, A.E.F., 1917–1918,* ed. Donald Joseph McGhee and Roger James Bender (San Jose, California: R. James Bender Publishing, 1983), 250.

73. 147th Aero Squadron, Operations Reports, 28 September–8 October 1918.

74. First Pursuit Group diary, 25 August 1918, Bert M. Atkinson Papers, Auburn University Library; "Airplanes Received by U.S. Air Service," Gorrell's History, series A, vol. 16; Hartney, *Up and At 'Em,* 221–22.

75. Hartney, *Up and At 'Em,* 221–22.

76. "History of the 185th Aero Squadron," p. 7.

77. First Pursuit Group, Operations Report, 19 October 1918.

78. "History of the 185th Aero Squadron," p. 8.

79. Hartney, *Up and At 'Em,* 224–26; 1st Pursuit Group, Operations Report, 21 October 1918.

80. First Pursuit Group, Operations Report, 23 October 1918.

81. "History of the 185th Aero Squadron," p. 8; Walter S. Williams, "Biography," p. 22, Williams Papers.

82. AEF Air Service, Headquarters, Special Orders 103, 6 November 1918; Hartney, *Up and At 'Em,* 232.

83. First Pursuit Group, Operations Order 46, 27 October 1918; 1st Pursuit Group, Operations Report, 27 October 1918; Philip Roosevelt, "The Argonne-Meuse Offensive," pp. 3–5, in "History of the 1st Pursuit Wing," Gorrell's History, series N, vol. 7; Rickenbacker diary, 28 October 1918.

84. Aerospace Studies Institute, *U.S. Air Service Victory Credits,* 88–114.

85. First Pursuit Group Casualties, 12 December 1918, "History of the 1st Pursuit Group," file 314.7, RG18, NACP.

86. J. Gordon Rankin to Capt. Arthur R. Brooks, 13 February 1921, Records of the 1st Pursuit Group, file GP-HI (FTR), AFHRA.

87. W. C. Sherman to CAS [Foulois], Group of Armies, 30 October 1918, series E 633, NACP.

88. First Pursuit Group, Operations Reports, 27–31 October 1918.

89. First Pursuit Group, Operations Report, 5 November 1918.

90. "Daily Diary of First Fighter Group," 9–10 November 1918; Rickenbacker, *Fighting the Flying Circus,* 402–05.

91. Joseph C. Raible diary, 5 November 1918, in "[World War I] Diaries," Lafayette Collection; Rickenbacker, *Fighting the Flying Circus,* 400; Meissner diary, 5–9 November 1918.

92. Aerospace Studies Institute, *U.S. Air Service Victory Credits,* 46, 107–14.

93. First Pursuit Group, Operations Report, 8 November 1918; Brian Flanagan, "The History of Fokker D VII 'U.10,'" *Cross and Cockade* 5 (Summer 1964): 128–42; Rickenbacker, *Fighting the Flying Circus,* 365–78.

94. Rickenbacker diary, 7 November 1918; Hartney, *Up and At 'Em,* 234, 236.

95. Buckley, *Squadron 95,* 163.

96. Eastman diary, 9 November 1918.

97. Ibid.; Williams, "Biography," p. 23.

98. Ibid.; Hartney, *Up and At 'Em,* 236.

99. Eastman diary, 9 November 1918; Rickenbacker, *Fighting the Flying Circus,* 409; Hartney, *Up and At 'Em,* 236.

100. Williams, "Biography," p. 23.

11. CONCLUSION

1. Aerospace Studies Institute, *U.S. Air Service Victory Credits, World War I,* U.S. Air Force Historical Study 133 (Montgomery, Alabama: Maxwell Air Force Base, Air University, Historical Research Division, June 1969), 177–78; 1st Pursuit Group Casualties, 12 December 1918, "History of the 1st Pursuit Group," file 314.7, pp. 1–4, RG18, National Archives at College Park.

2. John J. Pershing, *Final Report of Gen. John J. Pershing, Commander-in-Chief, American Expeditionary Forces* (Washington, D.C.: Government Printing Office, 1920), 15.

Index